DOR

A History of English Field-Names

Approaches to Local History

General Editor: David Hey

Local history has been a spectacularly successful growth area in recent years, amongst professional historians and enthusiastic amateurs alike. In this new series, Longman will be publishing books on particular themes and aspects of the subject, written by experts for a student and lay readership. It will include practical volumes that explore the methodology of local research, and volumes that themselves illuminate the hidden lives of ordinary people in times past.

Already published:
A History of British Surnames   Richard McKinley
A History of English Field-Names   John Field

A History of
English Field-Names

John Field

Longman
London and New York

Longman Group UK Limited,
Longman House, Burnt Mill,
Harlow, Essex CM20 2JE, England
and Associated Companies throughout the world.

*Published in the United States of America
by Longman Publishing, New York*

First published 1993

ISBN 0582 08157 2 CSD
ISBN 0582 08158 0 PPR

British Library Cataloguing-in-Publication Data

A catalogue record for this book is
available from the British Library

Library of Congress Cataloging-in-Publication Data

Field, John, 1921–
    A history of English field names / John Field.
        p.   cm. – (Approaches to local history)
    Includes bibliographical references and index.
    ISBN 0–582–08157–2. – ISBN 0–582–08158–0 (ppr)
    1. Field names – England – History.   2. Names, Geographical –
England.   3. England – History, Local.   4. Names, English.
I. Title.   II. Series.
DA645.F525   1993
914.2′0014 – dc20
                                                            92–32747
                                                                CIP

set in 10/12pt Times
Produced by Longman Singapore Publishers (Pte) Ltd.
Printed in Singapore

Contents

Contents

Contents

List of plates

Editorial preface

In recent years a quiet revolution has taken place in the study of British place-names. Yet it was not until the publication of Margaret Gelling's book *Signposts to the Past* (1978) that the general public became aware of the substantial shift in scholarly opinion on how place-names should be interpreted. Many of the older works that were once thought of as standard now have to be treated with care. Interpreting place-names is a minefield for the unwary. There is little that the amateur historian can do to contribute to the debate that is conducted by the members of the English Place-Name Society and landscape historians, for the interpretation of settlement names requires a deep knowledge of old languages. All that he or she can do is to try to keep up with modern findings, exemplified by Margaret Gelling's next book, *Place-Names in the Landscape* (1984).

But with field-names it is different. Here the amateur comes into his own. Few documents record field-names so far back in time that only a trained linguist can be trusted to interpret the evidence. With field-names that were coined in much later periods the historian who knows a locality intimately is in a far better position than the linguist to offer a convincing explanation. Every parish has a large collection of field-names recorded on old maps, surveys, deeds and numerous other documents. Even places which no longer have any fields, such as our great Victorian cities, have records of field-names from earlier times and often have street-names which commemorate the names of former fields.

It is a happy coincidence that the member of the English Place-Name Society who has established his reputation by the study of field-names should bear such an appropriate surname. John Field is already well known to local historians for his *English Field-Names, a*

Dictionary, first published in 1972. Field on Field-Names has become one of the local historian's best-known reference books. The present work takes the subject much further. It shows us how field-names are not only fascinating in their own right but are a form of evidence that can be tapped to illustrate many of the concerns of the local historian. Whereas the dictionary is a quick and effective guide to individual names, in this book John Field draws on his unrivalled experience to demonstrate how field-names can be used collectively to help to explain topics as diverse as clearing woods, tanning leather, flavouring food or perambulating boundaries.

Collecting all the field-names of a single parish has proved an attractive labour of love for individual local historians and for groups of like-minded people. Much good work has been done, but as yet only a small proportion of the thousands of parishes throughout the land has been covered in this way. The county volumes of the English Place-Name Society did not originally include field-names, but the ones published in the last three decades have been increasingly concerned to record this material, even if little space is devoted to its interpretation. The counties that have not been tackled by the EPNS, and those which were covered by the Society's early volumes, have often not even reached the collecting stage as far as field-names are concerned.

In this book John Field raises our sights from the collection and the interpretation of individual names, while making clear the importance of these preliminary tasks. His approach is to lead us on from an initial curiosity and delight in the more extravagant field-names to a sense of their importance to the local historian in so many endeavours. His numerous examples, drawn from each quarter of the land, suggest that every parish will turn up much of interest. Field-names are clearly an important source of evidence for us all.

DAVID HEY

Preface

The growth of interest in local history and other studies during the past half-century has generated a much wider acquaintance with field-names. However, although it is no longer necessary to explain that every field has a name, there is still a tendency to regard the meaning of all but the most obviously self-explanatory names as 'anybody's guess'. Systematic investigation has been going on for many years and the published results obviate the need for conjecture about large numbers of names. The present work arose from the author's conviction that there is a greater continuity between the older nomenclature and the more recent names than is often asserted. The book also aims to indicate how further research on the contexts of the occurrence of many names can contribute to a greater understanding of their significance. Methods of interpretation are also discussed, partly to show that this is not a mysterious process, but chiefly to enable readers to apply similar techniques, however tentatively, to other field-names they may encounter during the course of their own research.

Typographical and other conventions observed in the book may be briefly explained. Counties (their names abbreviated as in the list on page xvii) are those existing before the local government boundary changes of 1965–74. The county abbreviation, within parentheses, follows the parish or township name locating a field-name, or the last of a series if there are several examples from the same county. Obsolete names, early forms of current names, and field-name elements are printed in italics. To avoid ambiguity, initial capitals have been employed for early names, whether or not they are used in the source. Apart from dates, no documentary details have been given for early forms, which, like some of the quoted comments, can be traced in the appropriate English Place-Name Society volumes. Single quotation marks are used for definitions. The sources of verbatim extracts (within double quotation marks), other than those from EPNS county volumes, are given in the end-notes for the relevant chapter.

Acknowledgements

Many of the examples in this book are from the county volumes and the *Journal* of the English Place-Name Society. Unpublished lists made by schools on behalf of the Society have also been drawn on, utilizing those in the Brynmor Jones Library, University of Hull, and in Northamptonshire Record office. Some of the unpublished Lincolnshire material has been kindly provided by Professor Kenneth Cameron, for whose continuing friendship, help and encouragement sincere thanks are due. Dr Margaret Gelling kindly offered constructive comments on some early chapters. Her advice, and the friendly criticism given at a later stage by David Hey, the General Editor, have helped the author to make various improvements in presentation and to avoid a number of pitfalls, but they, and the persons named below, are in no way responsible for such defects as remain in the work.

Grateful acknowledgement is made for help and information on particular topics, and for transcribed lists of names, provided by numerous individuals. Among these must be mentioned Mrs Mary Atkin, Miss Constance Burton, Mrs Ann Cole, Mrs C. Daniel, Mrs Anne Farnworth, Mrs Mary Higham, Mrs Pamela Lemmey, Miss Jennifer Scherr, Mrs Jean Tsushima, Mrs Linda Worrall, Dr Mark Bateson, Messrs Michael Beacham, Anthony Brown and Anthony M. Carr, Professor Richard Coates, Mr Michael Costen, Professor Barrie Cox, Messrs Paul Cullen, the late George Foxall, Paul Hartley, Kenneth Heselton, Ralph Ison, Peter Keate, Charles Keene, Peter Liddell, David Mills, P.A.S. Pool, Dr Karl Inge Sandred, Messrs Maurice de Soissons, David Tew, Victor Watts and Roy Workman. Thanks are due for help provided (in some instances over many years) by staff at the Bedfordshire, Devon, Dorset,

Hereford & Worcester, Hertfordshire, Leicestershire, Northampton-shire and Shropshire County Record Offices. Help and advice with illustrations have kindly been provided by some of those already mentioned, and also by staff at the Museum of English Rural Life (University of Reading) and the Museum of Somerset Rural Life (Glastonbury).

A formal expression of gratitude is a quite inadequate acknowl-edgement of the help provided by my wife with many practical details. Without her interest and encouragement the book could not have been completed.

We are grateful to the following for permission to reproduce illustra-tive material:

The Board of Trustees of the Victoria and Albert Museum (Plate 1.1); Leicestershire Museums, Art Galleries and Records Service (Plates 2.1 and 2.2); *from* Richard and Nina Muir, *Fields*, Macmillan, 1979, p. 114 (Plate 2.3); Bedfordshire Record Office (Plate 2.4); Mrs Heather Lovett (Plate 3.1); the Chatsworth Settlement Trustees, from the Devonshire Collection, Chatsworth (Plate 3.2); Shropshire Records and Research Unit, photographs by Anthony M. Carr (Plates 3.3 and 5.4); Somerset Rural Life Museum Photographic Archive (Plate 4.2); Institute of Agricultural History and Museum of English Rural Life, University of Reading (Plates 5.1, 5.2, 5.3 and 8.2); Dr Michael Wintle (Plates 5.5 and 5.6) Times Newspapers Ltd (Plate 5.7); Rothamsted Experimental Station, Harpenden (Plates 5.8 and 6.1); Henley Photo-Graphics (Plate 5.9); Dorset County Record Office (Plate 8.1); Hereford and Worcestershire Record Office (Plate 9.1); Peter Keate (Plate 9.2); J. Bricklebank (Plate 10.1).

List of abbreviations

Beds	Bedfordshire
Berks	Berkshire
Bucks	Buckinghamshire
c.	*circa* ('about'), e.g. *c.* 1333, 'about 1333'
c.	century, e.g. 17c. 'seventeenth century'
Cambs	Cambridgeshire
Ches	Cheshire
Corn	Cornwall
Corn.	Cornish (language)
Cumb	Cumberland
Derbys	Derbyshire
Dev	Devon
dial.	dialect(al)
Dor	Dorset
Dur	Durham
EPNS	English Place-Name Society
Ess	Essex
Glos	Gloucestershire
Hants	Hampshire
Herefs	Herefordshire
Herts	Hertfordshire
Hunts	Huntingdonshire
Lancs	Lancashire
Leics	Leicestershire
Lincs	Lincolnshire
ME	Middle English (the language between *c.* AD 1100 and 1500)
Middx	Middlesex

Norf	Norfolk
Notts	Nottinghamshire
Nthants	Northamptonshire
Nthumb	Northumberland
OE	Old English (the language of the Anglo-Saxons, between *c.* AD 500 and 1100)
ON	Old Norse
Oxon	Oxfordshire
Rut	Rutland
Shrops	Shropshire
Som	Somerset
Staffs	Staffordshire
Suf	Suffolk
Sur	Surrey
Sus	Sussex
t.	*tempore* ('in the time of'), e.g. *t.* Jas 1, 'in the time or reign of James I'
Warks	Warwickshire
Westm	Westmorland
Wilts	Wiltshire
Worcs	Worcestershire
YE	Yorkshire, East Riding
YN	Yorkshire, North Riding
YW	Yorkshire, West Riding

CHAPTER ONE

Place-names and field-names

Local historians investigating the development of their own towns and villages will have met, and probably recorded, such strange field-names as *Sufferlong, Scotch Groats, Shoe Bread Close, Cock'd Hat, Dunkirk* and *Treacle Nook*. Indeed, some studies restrict their selection to those that can be looked upon as 'quaint', and ignore or treat as self-explanatory many others, such as *Wheat Close, Mill Field, Ten Acres* or *Red Lands*. In this book will be discussed a wide range of English field-names, both strange and commonplace. The meanings of the former may occasionally be disappointing, but both they and many of the 'ordinary' ones may prove to be more significant than at first glance they seem. A comparison of early and later forms is intended to show the continuity of the naming system in much of the country, across the divide (both historical and spatial) created by the enclosure of common fields, and a similar develop-ment in parts of England in which open fields have not been traced.

The limitation of this work to the field-names of England is for reasons which include the interrelated complexities of language, history, and national cultures, as well as the limitations of the experience of the author. Welsh and Scottish field-names have an interest of their own, but their interpretation will obviously make demands quite different from what is required in the analysis and explanation of their English counterparts. Almost any Welsh survey will include both Welsh and English names. In Llancarfan (Glamor-gan) in 1622, for instance, there were fields called *Beane Meadowe, Chapple Close, Buttlandes, Calves Close* and *The Harpeacre*, but in 1840 Welsh names were recorded, including *Caerceffil* 'horse enclo-sure' and *Caerbrwynog* 'rushy enclosure', as well as others containing terms borrowed from English, e.g. *Caer Styill* 'stile close' and *Twyn-y-slade* 'hillock by or with a depression'.

Scottish field-names may be in Gaelic, in Scots or in Southern English. *Schuilbraidis* is mentioned among the *Shovelbroad* names in Chapter Six, below, and in the same place (Eyemouth, Berwickshire) there are also *Heidland Acre* and *Blackcroft,* and in Gatehouse of Fleet (Kirkudbrightshire) the modern names Dam Field, Ash Tree Field, Three Corner Field and Cow Park, which have parallels in England. In Wales *Hill Park Close, Stubby Land, Castlecroft, Lynacre* and *Shortlands,* in Robeston (Pembrokeshire) in 1607, and *The Beane Acre* and *Higher Middleclose,* occurring in Porthkerry (Glamorgan) in 1622, could also have been found in England at the same time or later. To extend the scope of this book to the entire stock of names in the Celtic countries, however, would entail an exploration of the diversity of social customs, field-systems, cultivation practices, land-tenure conventions, law and administration reflected in the terminology, in addition to the details of religious history and personal nomenclature underlying the minor place-names and field-names of Wales and Scotland.

The study of field-names requires an appreciation of the substantial part played by agriculture in the lives of our medieval forebears and its development in subsequent periods. In open-field areas the holdings of tenants would be in separate strips, sometimes widely scattered in the furlongs of three or more fields. After the enclosure of the common fields, the newly created closes also received names, many of which throw considerable light on the social and agricultural history of the township. As well as in parishes with well-documented open fields, for those with no evidence of common-field agriculture, medieval grants and deeds, together with the later records of estates and individual farms, will provide a sequence of field-names often going back several centuries.

So long as the historical layering of the various examples can be observed, and there is evidence to identify the location, it is justifiable to trace the origin of the name of a modern enclosed field back to a form recorded in the thirteenth century or earlier. The modern name may refer to a smaller area than its predecessor, but the users of a name must have given some thought to its appropriateness; otherwise, it has been suggested, they would not have gone on using it, in its developing forms, for several hundred years. This raises the questions, of course, applicable to all names: to what extent do users of a name either understand its literal meaning or pay conscious attention to its significance?

The names themselves are essentially words. Inevitably, therefore, the discussion of their individual development will be primarily in terms of language, although all place-names (including field-names) must be viewed in their historical and geographical contexts. Many names found in the early records still exist, changed only by normal linguistic developments, or even, like many surnames, surviving in a form long obsolete in corresponding words of the current language. The emphasis in this book will be on the generation and development of field-names; their meanings will be explored in the light of the history of the English language and the progress of agriculture, technology and society itself.

Field-names of all periods differ in structure from major place-names. Most major names (i.e. the names of settlements, including cities, towns and villages) are single words, e.g. Brighton, Tring, Sunderland or Carlisle. Field-names usually consist of two recognizably separate words, e.g. *North Field, Wood Furlong, Mill Close,* even though occasionally in both earlier and modern forms the parts are combined, e.g. *Eastmedowe* or *Millfield.* The terms *specific element* or *specifier,* for the first word of the phrase, and *generic* or *denominative,* for the second, describe their respective functions and enable the significance of each to be established. The definite article, rarely found in major place-names, is used in a good many field-names, but often no particular importance seems to have been placed on its inclusion or omission. In a minority of field-names, the number of components may be increased by qualifiers or modifying phrases, so that forms such as *Hill Close* may develop into *Nether Hill Close* and then become *First (Second, Third,* etc.*) Nether Hill Close,* or even produce such wordy paradoxes as *Far Part of Near Nether Hill Close.* Usually there is no difficulty in distinguishing the parts into which a single large close has been divided and determining the underlying name.

The techniques of interpreting field-names follow the normal practices of place-name study. Precise spellings are collected from all accessible archive material. The languages of the elements in the earliest forms of the names must be discovered and the possible reasons for any subsequent changes explored. Then a meaning may be suggested by exploring the significance of the elements when the name was first used.[1] It is also necessary to examine the agricultural background and factors in the history and topography of the locality. These include, where appropriate, the size, location and conformation of the land, soil and natural life, crops and livestock, buildings, ownership and matters connected with religion, folklore, recreation, social conditions and public administration.

Terms from the languages of pre-Saxon Britain which had some influence in name formation are much rarer in the field-names of most English counties than in river-names and the names of major settlements. The substantial body of Celtic field-names in Cornwall is now being revealed, and the Celtic origin of some elements in field-names in other parts of the country is also duly recognized. Useful comparisons can also be made between the English field-names and their counterparts in Wales and Scotland. Welsh field-names in Cumbria and in the English border counties are not ignored, but there is no evidence that more than a small minority of these date from the centuries of the Roman occupation or earlier periods.

The elements composing field-names of English origin are customarily given in the Old English (Anglo-Saxon) form, sometimes in a dialectal variant. A number of these elements can be identified in the names of features recorded as landmarks in Anglo-Saxon charter bounds. Relatively few field-names, however, can be traced in an unbroken sequence all the way back to the Saxon period, and the earliest forms of many names would be more accurately described as Middle English.

In the area of England known as the Danelaw, names of Scandinavian origin are encountered, as well as many terms of mixed parentage. If large numbers of Scandinavian words occur in the field-names of an area, even where the village-names are mostly English, it is safe to infer that there was a considerable Danish or Norse presence there when the names were first recorded,[2] but it is hazardous to draw chronological conclusions about Scandinavian settlement on the basis of field-names. Difficulties arise from the similarity between Old English and Scandinavian terms for the same thing, e.g. Old English *æcer* and Old Norse *akr* both meaning 'a plot of arable land', but occasionally similar words mean different things, e.g. Old English *geat* 'a gate' and Old Norse *gata* 'a way, a road', either of which may lie at the root of later names ending in -*gate*.

Such generics as *Close* and *Piece* entered Middle English from French. *Malpas,* which occurs as a major name in Cheshire, appears as a field-name in several counties; other names of French origin are *Boverie* 1296 'an ox-farm', in Culworth (Nthants) and *The Vatcherie* 1546 'the dairy-farm', in Maresfield (Sus). In early records the article *Le* (or, apparently indiscriminately, *La*) often gives the misleading impression that a name is French, e.g. *La Vente* 1355, in Boarstall

(Bucks), which is the dialectal form *vent* from Old English *fent* 'a split or rift'. In some documents otherwise written throughout in Latin, names will often be found in their English form, but they are sometimes Latinized or are converted into terms derived from post-Classical Vulgar Latin.

The names devised for closes created in the eighteenth and early nineteenth centuries, and many of those listed in Tithe Apportionments, embody terms from current modern English. Obviously some field-names with a long history contain Middle English or Old English elements, and rural dialect words enter into the composition of others. Acreage names are quite frequent, and the family names of owners or occupiers of all periods are often brought into service. Unfamiliar terms will be found in names such as *Catsbrain, Piletts* and *Neat,* used respectively for certain types of soil, crops and farm animals, as well as the numerous popular names for wild plants and the creatures of the countryside. Unprofitable land is picturesquely castigated, fertile fields receive complimentary names, and to closes at some distance from the village the names of remote places are occasionally given. In addition to these, and a few other main categories, there are exotic names bestowed upon the fields seemingly quite capriciously and yet surviving for many generations.

A further distinction between field-names and major place-names is to be found in the difference between the records which are for the student the principal sources of information. Early forms of major names are discoverable in large numbers in charters and similar documents issued by the Crown, and in the records of departments of central government, or of the London-based courts of law. The principal (but not the sole) sources of early field-names will be records originating and still preserved in or near the localities concerned. Important cartularies (medieval collections of transcribed charters), rentals, registers and similar manorial and monastic documents may be in national archives (the Public Record Office or the British Library) but are often available in printed editions, or may be seen in photocopy or microfilm form in local studies libraries or county record offices. For the early modern period, Glebe Terriers are a very fruitful source, especially as there is often a sequence of these documents extending over two or more centuries.[3] Terriers and estate maps, often to be found among manorial documents, also date from this time.

During the past century, annotated listings and studies of field-names have been published, usually in the reports or transactions of

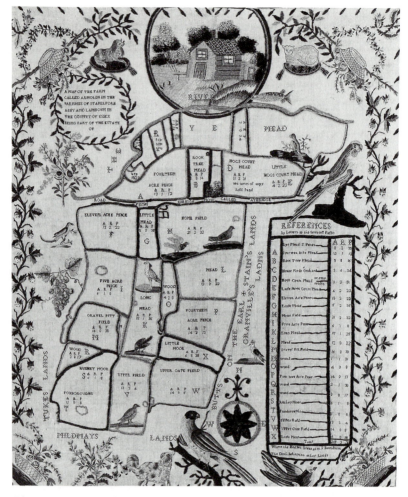

Plate 1.1 A late eighteenth-century embroidered field-map of *The Farm called Arnolds*, Lambourne, Essex

county archaeological societies. Candler's paper 'On the significance of some East Anglian field-names', published in 1892, has remained the only comprehensive study of these names in Norfolk and Suffolk. Canon Thornley's account of Kirkoswald (Cumberland) field-names appeared in 1897. A few years earlier, W.C. Waller, refusing to be daunted by the size of his task, began transcribing Essex Tithe

Apportionments and published his collections over a period of about ten years. These transcripts, extensive but not quite complete, have provided many of the Essex examples used in this work. In 1918 Miss Hoare's *History of an East Anglian Soke* listed the Tithe-Apportionment names of a small area of Norfolk, together with excerpts from earlier records and a few annotations.[4] In the following decades, listing began to be supplemented with discussion, and some writers looked beyond single localities.

A more general approach was shown in Mawer's paper 'The study of field-names in relation to place-names' (1933) and in F.T. Wainwright's short article in *Antiquity* (1943). The latter was followed in 1945 by a paper on the field-names in the Tithe Awards of Amounderness Hundred of Lancashire, illustrating their value to local historians and the possible archaeological significance of some of the names. Fraser's *Field-names in South Derbyshire* (1947) broke further new ground by drawing general applications from his local study.[5]

In the mainstream of place-name research, the publications of the English Place-Name Society offered only fragmentary information about field-names until the early 1930s, when modern names began to be collected from Tithe documents and from oral evidence obtained by school-pupils in counties then being surveyed. Until that time, coverage in the volumes had been limited to the names of natural features, and occasionally remnants of open fields, marked on the 6-inch Ordnance Survey maps. In subsequent volumes, the examples became more numerous and their discussion more detailed. This improvement coincided with the general increase in awareness of field names which came with the growth of local historical studies after 1945.

In subsequent chapters of this work field-names are discussed both as a set of signals encoding the history of agriculture and rural life in this country and as factors in our knowledge of the development of the English language. Many terms which were regarded as problematic fifty years ago can now be explained as a result of research findings during the intervening period. However, some explanations now offered with a moderate degree of confidence may well have to be revised within the next few years. Definitions need to be amended, or at least refined, especially those involving conditions better known to local people than to those outside the area. Individual historians and groups of local students in various parts of the country have made important contributions to field-name studies.

This book is designed to help and encourage others to follow the same path.

NOTES AND REFERENCES

1. The standard reference works for place-name elements are A.H. Smith (ed.), *English Place-Name Elements* (EPNS Vols XXV–XXVI) (with additions and corrections in the *Journal of the English Place-Name Society* **1** (1968–69), pp. 9–52) and O.J. Padel (ed.), *Cornish Place-Name Elements* (EPNS Vol.LVI/ LVII).
2. As Ekwall observed many years ago, noting the occurrence of such terms as *wong, afnám, flat* and *intake,* discussed in later chapters of the present work. See E. Ekwall, 'The Scandinavian element' in A. Mawer and F.M. Stenton, *Introduction to the Survey of English Place-Names* (EPNS Vol. I) (CUP 1924), pp. 55–92, especially p. 89, Wainwright makes similar comments in 'Field-names of Amounderness Hundred', pp. 202–3, and (with Leicestershire field-name examples) in his *Archaeology and Place-Names and History* (Routledge & Kegan Paul, 1962), pp. 86–7.
3. M.W. Beresford, 'Glebe Terriers and open field Leicestershire', *Trans. Leicestershire Arch. and Historical Society* **24** (1948), pp. 77–126, provides open-field and furlong names from the Terriers and useful supplementary material about the documents themselves. See also the same author's 'Glebe Terriers and open field Buckinghamshire', *Records of Buckinghamshire* **15** (1947–52), pp. 283–98 and *ibid.* **16** (1953–60), pp. 5–28, and his 'Glebe Terriers and open-field Yorkshire', *Yorkshire Archaeological Journal* **37** (1948–51), pp. 325–68.
4. C. Candler, 'On the significance of some East Anglian field-names', *Norfolk Archaeology* **11** (1892), pp. 143–78. Canon [J.J.] Thornley, 'The field-names of the parish of Kirkoswald', *Trans. Cumberland & Westmorland Antiq. & Arch. Soc. 15* (1897, pp. 44–81. W.C. Waller, regular contributions to *Trans. Essex Arch. Soc.* in consecutive volumes from **5** (1894–9) to **9** (1903–05). C.M. Hoare. *The History of an East Anglian Soke* (Bedford, Bedfordshire Times Publishing Co., 1918).
5. A. Mawer, 'The Study of field-names in relation to place-names', *Historical Essays in Honour of James Tait* (priv. pub., 1933). F.T. Wainwright, 'Field names', *Antiquity* **17** (1943), pp. 57–66; 'The

field-names of Amounderness Hundred (modern, *c.* 1840)', *Trans. of the Historic Soc. of Lancashire and Cheshire* **97** (1945), pp. 181–222. W. Fraser, *Field-Names in South Derbyshire* (Ipswich, Adlard, 1947).

CHAPTER TWO

Common fields and the process of enclosure

OLD AND NEW FIELD SYSTEMS

In a large part of England, the transition from the communal cultivation of open fields to the present system of separate enclosed farms can be traced both by a close observation of the landscape and by the study of written records. Field-name evidence of the open system often remains long after enclosure, and can play its part in establishing the location of particular furlongs in the former open fields.

The primary purpose of the names was not of course to supply material for future research, but to identify holdings of individual tenants within recognizable areas of cultivation. Seen in historical sequence, many of the names provide valuable insights into the agricultural activities under the earlier system, and into changes in the techniques of husbandry caused by the enclosure process or helping to bring it about.

Field was the usual name for one of the main units of cultivation into which the arable land of a settlement was divided. However, the term had a more general application, to include grassland etc., even in the Middle Ages. Langland, writing in the fourteenth century of "a faire felde ful of folke", seems to have understood the word in a broader sense, for the multitude seen in Piers Plowman's vision would hardly have assembled on arable land. When *Field* is used of modern enclosed land, it does not normally signify anything larger than *Close, Leasow, Park,* etc. in counties where those terms are appropriate. Most of the names in the Tithe Apportionment for Clowne (Derbys) have *Close* as a generic element, but there are also

Old Field (*The Oldfield* 1658), and Pale Field, replacing the earlier *Pail Close* (probably 'an enclosure surrounded by a paling').

What is often regarded as the standard (the so-called 'Midland') pattern of two or three open fields was not found all over the country, or indeed with uniform regularity even throughout the area covered by the term.[1] In 1279–80, Wakefield (YW) had nine open fields. In the same century, King's Walden (Herts) had at least twenty-five and Berkhamsted more than thirty. Wymondham (Norf) had eight fields in the fourteenth century, and the number varied from time to time. Lists of the names of common fields may seem to a casual reader, as the vocabulary of *Bradshaw's Railway Guide* did to Sherlock Holmes, "nervous and terse, but limited". There was little reason why it should be otherwise. If there were two fields, to call one *North Field* and the other *South Field* was adequate for the purposes of the local husbandmen. When the community broke new ground, or marked out a third field, to name it *Middle Field, West Field* or *East Field* was both logical and useful. Compass directions and reference to landmarks would be habitual to outdoor workers.

The names of two open fields, North Field and West Field, survived as enclosure-names in Hillam (YW), but their eastern counterpart is remembered only in a road name, Austfield Lane. A document of 1620 refers to *terra in campo orientali vocat' sup' Austfeilde,* i.e. 'land in the east field called *on Austfeilde*', illustrating an unusual instance of a Scandinavian form of one of the open-field names, from Old Norse *austr* 'east'. In Long Crichel (Dor), North East Field and Great South West Field exemplify compass directions used less frequently in field-names. The great fields later came to bear descriptive, rather than compass-directional, names, sometimes after passing through a referential stage, when they received the names of adjoining parishes. In Shawbury (Shrops), the three thirteenth-century fields were *Versus Hadenhale, Versus Parvam Withiford* and *Versus Foret super Crokes* 'Towards Hadnall, Towards Little Wytheford' and 'Towards Moreton Corbet' (taking *Foret* as an error for *Moret'*, the contracted form of Moreton).[2] Great and Little Wytheford are on the southern edge of Shawbury; Moreton Corbet parish adjoins Shawbury to the north. A prepositional phrase may be used. *Beneath the Town Field* 1768, in Olney (Bucks), i.e. 'the field below the village', is the counterpart of the not uncommon *Bovetown* or *Bufton Field*.[3]

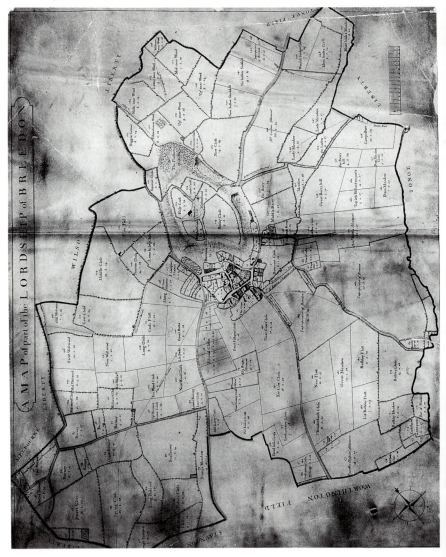

Plate 2.1 Breedon (Leics) before enclosure

Plate 2.2   Breedon (Leics) after enclosure in 1758
   The early closes have retained their boundaries. The furlongs of the open fields have been enclosed and renamed.

FURLONGS, SHOTS, AND QUARTERS

Literally 'the length of a furrow', *furlong* developed separate senses – one, the more precise, a linear measurement, and the other, 'a division of a common field, in which the furrows lie in the same direction', is that occurring in field-names. There is no question of equality of area being found in furlongs either within the same parish or from one place to another. In the West Field of Laxton (Notts), the areas of the furlongs varied between two and twenty-three acres, and there was an even greater range of sizes among those in the other common fields.

Occasionally, the term is used alone, e.g. Furlong, in Winterbourne Houghton (Dor), and in Chelford (Ches), or *ij closes called the Furlonges* 1567, in Pulham (Dor). *Sufferlong* 1652, in Kibworth Beauchamp (Leics), may be derogatory but is more likely to be 'south furlong'. Another term relating to land measurement, *ferling,* is sufficiently similar to *furlong* to cause occasional confusion. Postan refers to "villages of the small-holding group whom the documents might describe as 'ferlingers', i.e. holders of quarter virgates of customary land".[4]

Shot represents Old English *scēat,* 'a projecting piece of land', and was possibly first used to describe particular blocks of land rather than to be a general synonym for *furlong.* It is common in southeastern England. The open fields of Streatley with Sharpenhoe (Beds) contained Hitch Way Shot, Birchmore Bottom Shot, Fox Hill Shot and a number of other similarly named furlongs. In Hertfordshire the term is sometimes replaced in modern names, or omitted from them. *Homeshot* 1561, in Walkern, later becomes Home Field: *Lakerssete* 1283, *Lakershote* 1427, in Watford, is later reduced to The Lagger. Some early forms, like *Lakerssete* just mentioned, are derived from the related *scīete,* which often develops into *Shoot.* On an eighteenth-century map of the Bridgewater estate, *Hemstead Road Shoot, Three Acre Shoot, Lott Shoot* and *Apple Pie Piece Shoot* are some of the divisions of *Dagnal Field* in Edlesborough (Bucks).

Surrey field-names include ten in Battersea ending with *-shot,* and among the names in sixteenth-century documents relating to Merstham were *Crooked Land Shott, the Middle Shott* and *The North Shott.*[5] The field-system of Kent was organized in a different way from the arrangements in neighbouring counties, but both *Furlong* and, less frequently, *Shot* are found in use for the main divisions of the fields. The Glebe Terrier, dated 1616, of St Margaret at Cliffe states that the glebe 'lyeth in severall Shotts or furlongs of land'.

Drove Shott, Second Shott, Cholk-Pitt-Shot and *Teen-End-Shott* are found on a 1709 estate map of Ringwould, and Hitherlong Shot and Farther Shot occur in Littlebourne.

Other terms for the principal divisions of fields appear locally, e.g. *Quarter,* applied to a number of furlongs grouped for cropping purposes. In Oxfordshire, Chadlington has Broadslade Quarter and Lockland Quarter but also Peas Furlong and Castle Furlong. Milcombe has Brier Furlong Quarter and Brook Furlong Quarter, as well as Tithes Furlong and Town Furlong. *Quarters,* not always in precisely the same sense, were found also in other counties. In Appleby (Westm), *The Oke Quarter* 1539 is explained as "doubtless a subdivision of the township". The 1601 Glebe Terrier for Goxhill (Lincs) states that the parish is divided into "foure feildes or quarters as they are called" and enumerates them as *Horsegate Quarter, Chappell Quarter, Swallowmyln Quarter* and *Hallands Quarter.* A similar arrangement is found in other Lincolnshire parishes.

In upland areas particularly, the more level ground would be preferred for ploughing, while the slopes remained rough pasture. Old Norse *flat* meant primarily 'a level piece of land', and later developed to 'a unit of cultivation'. Examples are to be found in areas of Scandinavian settlement, e.g. in the West Riding of Yorkshire, where Cross Flatt in Gluxburn survived into the Tithe Apportionment, as did Simon Flat, in Skipton, and Hall Flatt, in Hetton. Early names in Everingham (YE) include *le Northflat* 1310, *le Southflat* 1310, *Squierflat in the West Field c.* 1335, and *The Flattes* 1582. In the former North Riding, *Wreckeflatte* 1236 is said to commemorate the throwing up of wreckage from the sea at Fylingdales. *The Elline Tree Flatt, Byflatt, Grasing Flatt* and *Barn Flatt* 1527, in Hope Woodlands (Derbys), survived with little change to modern times.

Nottinghamshire examples include Pearson Flat, in Treswell, Elder Tree Flatt and Short Flatt, in Blyth, Swan Flatt, in Stokeham, and White Flat, in Clayworth. The original sense may survive in the Lancashire names Orchard Flat, in Great Eccleston, Bank Flat, in Out Rawcliffe, Thistly Flat, in Carleton, Sandy Flat, in Lytham, and North Flat, in Little Marton. Oxen Flatt, in Tickhill (YW), was *Oxehouseflatt* in 1540, and Gorsty Flatt, in Sandbach (Ches), was so called from 1673. In Bradley (Staffs) earlier names include *Henshawe Flat, Burnt Oake Flatt* and *The Hursthead Flatt* 1614.

LANDS AND HEADLANDS IN THE OPEN FIELDS

The term *land* is ambiguous. In many documents it has the sense 'arable land' (as opposed to grassland), and then, more precisely, 'a selion, a strip'. Common formulae in the Leicestershire Glebe Terriers are "Lands in the North Field (&c.)", contrasting with "Leys in the Brook Meadow (&c.)". Land Close, in Brooksby (Leics), is more than fifty-nine acres in area, and may be a consolidation of an unspecified number of *lands*. The adjoining close, Middle Field, sixty-nine acres in extent, is a considerable part of one of the common fields. *Land* may be specified by terms alluding to shape, crops, soil and occupiers, animals and endowment. In Essex are found White Lands, in Great Hallingbury and several other places, Beet Lands, in Wormingford, Blood Lands, in West Hanningfield, and Lady Lands, in Willingale Spain and in Layer Breton. In Steventon (Berks), not enclosed until 1885, the survival of *lands* is to be expected. Broad Lands represented *Le Brodelond* 1390–91, Inchland was earlier *Ynchelond* 1439–40, possibly 'a holding assigned to an *enche,* a manorial servant or workman', and Verb Lands (*Verbylond* 1390–91) may represent *Forbyland* 'a pasture close cultivated independently of the general system of the township'. Four Long Lands and Fourteen Lands lack earlier forms, but Seven and Twenty represents the *Seven and Twenty Lands Piece* of 1654, consolidating that number of strips. In 1638 part of the vicar's holding in *Castle Pitt Feild* in Thurlaston (Leics) is entered as "12 lands together called Julians Wong", Julian being presumably the person responsible for the amalgamation.

Selions, the open-field holdings of individual tenants, were identified by their position within the various furlongs. In terriers such locations are expressed by a recital of the names of the persons holding land on all sides (often with compass-point references to the positions of the neighbours' selions), or by referring to particular landmarks on one or more sides. If selion names had been the rule (rather than the rare exception), it would have been more convenient to use them. *Lands,* in the plural, occurs frequently; some apparently singular forms may be due to misreadings of contracted words.

Apart from forms like Roylance 'rye lands', in Toft, and *Rylance* 1634, in Pownall Fee (Ches), with Ballance, in Dunchurch (Warks), and the isolated Ballards 'bean lands', in Ashby St Ledgers (Northants), other slight variants of *land* occur. Middle English *lond* often occurs in early forms, e.g. *Le Oldelond* 1331–32, in Speen (Berks), *Myndeleyslond* 1345, in Ash (Sur). Dialect forms are also found, e.g. The Loans, in Charlton Kings (Glos), *The Loones* 1691, in Leckhampton, and a wide variety in Cheshire, e.g. Loohon, in West Kirby, Loont, in Lymm, Long Loons, in Irby, The Laughans, in Horton, and Saloon Hey 'sallow land enclosure', in Whitby.

Middle English *heved* (OE *hēafod*) 'a head' survives into modern times in such forms as *Heads* and *Hades*. The turning of the plough at the end of a selion left a deposit of soil; this gradually became a mound, appreciably higher than the strip. Across the width of a furlong, these *heads* might constitute a *headland* and it appears from some field-names that the two terms were interchangeable. Oxfordshire examples include The Hades, in Brize Norton, The Hade, in Headington, with the variant The Hudes, in Crowmarsh and elsewhere. In Warwickshire there are early instances, such as *Hades* and *La Breche Hades* 1369, in Budbrooke, *Le Hades t.* Hy 7, in Maxstoke, and *Longfurlonghades t.* Hy 7, in Tysoe, and the more recent Rudgway Hads 'heads adjoining the Ridgeway', in Long Lawford, alluding to an old road still traceable from Leamington Hastings to Flecknoe.

Heved-land is found in many field-names, e.g. *Le Cleyheuetlond c.* 1290, in Newton by Chester, *Le Hauedlond* 1317, in Hoon (Derbys), *Heuedlond'* 1372, in Pamphill (Dorset), *Mucylhauetlond* 1321 'the big headland', in Churton by Farndon (Ches). In *Frontehoweudland'* late 12c. 'the front headland', in Normanby (Lincs), Old English *hēafod* has been replaced by Old Norse *hofuth*. That headlands were of sufficient size to be separately enclosed is indicated by such modern names as Headland, in Turnditch (Derbys), and The High Hadland, in Great Boughton (Ches).

SEPARATIONS AND ENCROACHMENTS

It is seldom possible to determine, from name evidence alone, the precise date of any feature, or to establish the chronology of any event the names implies. However, the use of certain terms may offer a little help in dating. Among surviving medieval expressions are *Inhoke* and *Inheche,* signifying the removal of the named land from the crop-rotation routines of the common fields, usually by a partial enclosure. Modern English *hitch(ing)* is used in the same sense, but names derived from this are recognizably so, e.g. *Hitch Croft* 1603–04, in Eye and Dunsden (Oxon), Hitching Acre (*Pewsey Hitching* 1609), in Milton Lilborne (Wilts), and Old Hitching, in

Astall (Oxon). *Inhechinges* 1280 is found in Ducklington (Oxon) and Inhedge in Badger and in Cleobury Mortimer (Shrops). *Oldland Innocks* 1700, in Gillingham (Dor), implies long-standing disuse, as *Eldelond'* here is on record on 1381. Wiltshire examples of *inhoke* include *Le Hinhoc* 13c., in Lacock, *Muchele Ynhok* 1397, later Innex, in Colerne, *Northynnoke* 1428, later Enox Piece, in Kington St Michael, and *Le Inhoke* 1495, in Zeals.

Intake, derived from Old Norse *inntak,* was essentially an improvement carried out by a few members of the community, by which they brought into the system land which was normally left unused. The name is often without a specifier, e.g. *le Intacke* 1665, in Wetheral, *Intacke* 1604, in Dacre (Cumb), Intack, in Mere (Ches), Egglescliffe (Dur), Cliburn (Cumb), Asby, Crosby Ravensworth, and New Hutton (Westm). Intake (*Crosbie Intacke* 1609), in Crosby Garrett, was a prehistoric settlement site, and its enclosure for pastoral use might have been a renewal of its role of thousands of years earlier. *Langintak* 1409 is found in Skelton (YN), and an even older example, *Intak*, in a 1230 deed for Naburn (YE). Later examples are Intack, in North Dalton and in Barmston, Intake, in Roos, and Intakes, in Warter (YE). There are many other instances in Midland counties. *Newtakyng* 1487 is found in Gnosall (Staffs), with modern examples New Takein, in Castle Eaton (Wilts) and The Newtakein, in Ampney Crucis (Glos).

Ofnam, afnám, ultimately from Old English *ofniman* or Old Norse *afnima* 'to seize', signify land removed from the regulated common-field system and let for rent, usually as pasture closes. Wainwright cites Evenham, in Newton with Scales (Lancs), as a good instance of field-name longevity, surviving through more than six centuries from the Cockersand Chartulary *Avenames c.* 1221.[6] Early examples in the North Riding of Yorkshire are *Ofnam* 1160, in Allerston, *Houenam* 12c., in Middlesbrough, *Ovenham* 13c., in Ormesby, in Newton Morell and in Fylingdales, and *Les Ofnames c.* 1200, in Cayton. In the former East Riding, Aunholme Flatt, in Everingham, was earlier *Avenum c.* 1300. Early spellings of Haynholme, in Draughton (YW), range from *Havenham* in the twelfth century, through *le Avenham* and *le Havenom* early 14c., to *Ainholme* in 1817. Ainholmes, in Grassington, was *the Aynham* 1611; other modern forms include Ainums, in Threshfield, Aynums, in Silsden, Ainham, in Gargrave, Ainams, in Hetton and in Conistone (YW), Ainims, in Milburn, and Aynam, in Skelsmergh (Westm). In Childer Thornton (Ches) *Afnames* is found in the early thirteenth century, and a Macclesfield example, *Offenomes*, occurs in 1358.

Encroachment on the common or waste was occasionally declared to be such in the field-name, e.g. Encroachment, in Stour Provost (Dor) and in Duffield (Derbys). Enclosure Plot, in Corfe Castle, and Old Enclosure, in Long Crichel (Dor), are pieces of land isolated by early piecemeal enclosure. Purpresture Meadow, in Haslemere, and Perposture Field (*Porpister Meadow* 1674), in Frensham (Sur), allude to the 'illegal enclosure of common property'. Such encroachment might be licensed by the lord of the manor, often after the event, on payment of a fine.

Land in private ownership and cultivated outside the common-field system was said to be *in severalty*, and field-names indicating this separateness occur in a number of places. *Seuerall Furlong* 1548, in Pangbourne (Berks), shows that an entire furlong might be detached. *Seuerall*, in Shaw cum Donington (Berks), is of approximately the same date. Other examples are The Several, in Collingbourne Kingston (Wilts), and Severalls, in Hardwicke (Glos) and in South Kelsey (Lincs). Sunderland, in Northenden (Ches) and in Roos (YE), Sunderlands, in Foston (Leics), and possibly Cinder Land, in Monk Hopton, and Cinder Meadow, in Church Stretton (Shrops), is 'land detached from an estate, or set apart for a special purpose'. Cindrum, in Crudwell (Wilts), has a long history, starting from a charter reference to *Sunderhamme* 974.

ASSARTS AND GROUNDS

Assart is also found in the early field-name vocabulary but is not likely to have been used in devising names of closes in the later period. The frequent personal-name forms confirm that the clearance of such intakes was primarily an individual rather than a communal activity. *Essarto Caperun c.* 1250, in Derbyshire, is compounded with a personal name, as also are the Nottinghamshire examples *in Essartum Theodbaldi c.* 1150, *Sarta Radulfi, Gocelini t.* Hy 2 and *Essarta Sotsuni t.* Hy 1, and Jennet's Assarts (*Le Gennette's Sarte* 1606-07), in Stonesfield (Oxon). Less desirable soils might be developed, e.g. Clay Assarts, in Leafield (Oxon). The plural becomes *Sarch* in Great and Little Sarch, in Puttenham (Sur).

Ground(s) often refers to large pasture fields, such as were created as a result of fifteenth- and sixteenth-century enclosures, though an earlier example occurs in *Grundes* 1281, in Eydon (Nthants). *Thrupp Grounds*, west of Norton (Nthants), were enclosed grazing lands converted from arable which had supported a community of about 100 persons, expelled in 1498 by the prior of Daventry.[7] In 1714, *Kents Ground*, in Great Linford Bucks, was pasture land covering eighty acres, and *The Horse Ground* was fifty-seven acres in extent. Other instances include Hurst Ground, in Monks Kirby, and Holbrook Ground (*Holdbrokemeade* 1549), in Stoneleigh (Warks), Uffmoor Ground, in Romsley, Garden Ground, in Cradley, and Lower Ground in Lapal (Worcs), *Lotte Meadow Ground* 1662, and May Pole Ground, in Whitchurch, Dry Ground, in Crawley, Pump Ground and St John Ground, in Burford, and Leasow Ground, in Enstone (Oxon). In Berkshire the term seems to have developed in the eighteenth century. The Waltham St Lawrence Tithe Apportionment has Coppice Ground, George Ground, Moot Ground, Pond Ground, Watering Place Ground and Graffadge Grounds (*graffadge* being 'a sort of fence used at the junction of two boundaries'). Examples also occur in Wiltshire, Dorset and Gloucestershire. It appears from many of these examples that *Ground*, like *Field, Close* and *Leasow*, eventually developed into a catch-all term.

CROFTS AND CLOSES

Croft, usually interpreted as 'a small enclosure', is often associated with a cottage or house, representing the personal or family plot to provide the needs of the household, in the vicinity of the dwelling. This is the sense when it is specified by a personal name or surname, but other elements may combine with *croft* to indicate a piece of land set aside for the growing of particular crops or for other agricultural or even industrial purposes. Crops are named in *Watcroft* 1502 'wheat croft', in Gnosall (Staffs), Peascroft, in Longhope (Glos), and *Benecroft* 1340, in Breadsall (Derbys), and Bancroft (*Bancroft* 1116) 'bean enclosure', in Yelvertoft (Nthants). Brick Kiln Croft, in Tetton (Ches), Kiln Croft, in Lambley (Notts), and *Kylcroft* 1634, in Alkington (Glos), exemplify the last-mentioned use. In some places, an enclosed croft might be cultivated by several tenants. In Ham (Glos), in the sixteenth century, *Redecroft, Bancroft, Litlecroft* and *Prestcroft* were so managed.[8] *Croft* in Cornish field-names refers to enclosed rough ground, usually containing furze grown high for fuel. References to wild vegetation (perhaps deliberately encouraged as in Cornwall) are found in *Gorsticroft* 1341, in Tabley Superior (Ches), Furze Croft, in Milborne Stileham (Dor), and Broomy Croft (*Bromicroft* 1287), in Goostrey (Ches), and to farm animals in *Gosecroft* 1464, in Cheltenham (Glos), and *Calvecroft c.* 1300, in Shudy Camps (Cambs). Professions and social ranks are combined with *croft*, e.g. *Frerecroft* 1367, in Methley (YW) *Munkcroft* 1388–89, in Abingdon (Berks), *Preste Crofte t.* Jas 1, in Winkfield (Berks) and Charlcroft 'the churl's croft', in Cold Ashton (Glos).

The spelling of The Craught, in Abenhall (Glos), and other *Craught* names in this county, probably represents the local pronunciation ('craft') used also in other southern and western counties. Stoney Croft, in Aldbury (Herts) was *Stonie Craft* in 1638 Glebe Terrier. Other variants of *croft* are found in Long Crote (*Langecroft* 1220), in Harpenden (Herts), Spittle Croats (*Spittlecroft* 1672), in Ardeley (Herts), Crate (*Le Croft* 1435), in Coombe Keynes (Dor), The Crate, in Lambourn, and Crouts, in Sandhurst (Berks). Association of ideas produced Scotch Groats, in Eastwick (Herts), from *Scotch Croft* (probably for *Scotts Croft*). Reduction to *Cutt(s)* occurs in Stubb Cutts (earlier *Stubb Croft),* in Harpenden (Herts). *Crifting* (OE *cryfting*) is formally a diminutive. Croften, in Hoveringham (Notts), is described in 1577 as a *little close called a Criftynge.* But the description 'small croft' is not answered by many modern fields bearing the name, and its use as a farm-name also implies considerable size. It may perhaps be concluded that *Crifting* is merely an alternative form of *Croft*, in much the same way as *Nooking* is of *Nook*.

The frequent *Close* names call for no special comment here except to say that the element is found in relatively few medieval examples. Early instances are noted in the EPNS surveys for Cambridgeshire (*le Close* 1409, *Tyleclose* 1465), Gloucestershire (*Priouresclos* 1373, *Symondesclos* 1483) and Warwickshire (*Le Oldeclos* 1316, *Stoniclos* 1336, *Le Summersclose* 1367).

APPORTIONMENT BY AWARD AND LOT

Later names recording the redistribution of land at enclosure include *Allotment*, which occurs in half a dozen places in Appletree Hundred (Derbys). Even more instances of (*The) Allotments* occur in the former East Riding of Yorkshire, where also are found Allotment Field, in Tickton, in Beswick, in Lund, in Great Driffield and in Long Riston. Street Allotment, in Claughton (Lancs), is beside a

Roman road. In Dorset there is an Allotment Pasture in Kinson. Ansty's Allotment, in Pimperne, has early associations, being possibly an enclosure granted to a member of the family of Stephen *Anestayse* 1332, of Durweston. Gravel Allotment, in Bincombe, provided materials for the upkeep of roads. Manorial Allotment occurs several times in Berkshire, e.g. in Tilehurst, in Sutton Courtenay and in Blewbury. In Woodley, Heath Allotment goes back to *Heath Pidells* 1603–04 (*Pidell* is a local form of *Pightel*), amalgamated to form the allotment.

Other field-names allude to the drawing of lots for the tenure of particular land, both arable and meadow. The distribution of arable land in this way is attested by Breeches Lot, in Milton under Wychwood (Oxon), but meadow being usually the most valuable land, *Lot Mead* and *Lot Meadow* are more common. *Lotmede* 1547, in Shaw cum Donnington (Berks), is recorded only slightly earlier than *Le Lottmeade* 1575, in Bledington (Glos), and *Lott Meade* 1577, in Dowdeswell (Glos). The Lott Mead, the Bagendon (Glos), dates from 1792; Lott Mead occurs in Northmoor (Oxon) and in Ampney St Peter (Glos) where *Smartes Lott Meade* 1639 suggests that the allocation was a semi-permanent one to a particular individual, perhaps for life or for a term of years. (The) Lot Meadow is found in Broadwell (Glos), in Milton (Berks), in Harpsden (Oxon), and in many other places. Some common grazing land, e.g. Town Close, in Meesden (Herts), was auctioned annually and the money distributed among the villagers.

In Churchill (Oxon), lots were drawn annually for shares in the four Lot Meads, each divided into Sets, and subdivided into Hides. The names given to the Sets indicate both locations and figures or symbols on the lots themselves, e.g. *Acres Set, Inn Mead Set, Way Acres Set* and *Broken Set* (containing *Duck* and *Drake), Blank Hide, Axtree Hide, Dunkpike Hide, Four Notches Hide* and *Knott Hide.* Though *Set* is found in other places, *Hide* in this sense does not seem to occur. With The Setts, in Whittlesey Rural (Cambs), may be compared *Pryors Setts* and *Settes Lotts* in the 1603 Survey of Whittlesey. The Lots (*The Lotts* 1604, *Cottenham Lottes* 1636), in Cottenham (Cambs), consisted of about 200 separate one-acre shares in the fens, one for each household, comparable with The Lots (*Fenground called Common Lotts* 1658), in Soham, and earlier examples, *Les Fenlotes* 1402, in Whittlesey, and *Les Lotes* 1446, in Elm. Individual shares are indicated in *The Lot or Dole of John Belwood* 1637, in Witcham, *The Lott Landes of . . . Edward Love,* in Sutton, and Hobb's Lotts, in Wisbech St Peter, referring to a family on record as early as 1335.

Dole, used as an alternative to *Lot* in *Lot or Dole of John Belwood*, just mentioned, is often combined with descriptive words, some of which (e.g. the frequent Dole Meadow) indicate that it was used of grassland rather than of arable. Changeable Doles, six separate closes, are found in Nailstone (Leics). Of The Dole, in Albury (Herts), it was reported that it "contains long mounds, suggesting . . . open field working".

Cut, frequent in Oxfordshire field-names but occurring also in other counties, has been discussed by Dr Gelling, who has concluded that *lot* is the probable equivalent. Examples include Broadcutt, in Aston Bampton, Longcut, in Charlbury, and Longcutt Furlong, in Hook Norton (Oxon). Ipsden, in the same county, has several instances – Bradcutt, Heathcutt, Crabcut, Kingcut and Smithcutt – suggesting the divisions of a single lot-meadow. Cut Meadow, in Altrincham, and Cutts Meadow, in Mobberley (Ches), may be further examples, though other interpretations have been proposed. The interpretation of such names as Parting Ham, in Buscote (Berks), and *Partinmeade* 1606–07, in Wootton (Oxon), is still problematic. Some of these, too, may allude to allocation by lot, e.g. Part Lot Mead, in Noke (Oxon), and the possibly related Partables, in Headon (Notts).

Cauel 'a division of land made by lot', is found in a number of field-names.[9] The word originally meant 'a piece of wood used in the casting of lots'. Modern forms include Cavil Field, in Lanchester (Dur), Cale Field, in Kingsley, and Middle Cale, in Adlington (Ches). Older instances include *Keueldale* 1199–1212 and *Kevelfeld c.* 1280, in Wolviston (Dur), *Kaulhul Meirs* 13c., in Penkridge (Staffs), and *Kevelfild* 1506, in Knaptoft (Leics). *Wandale*, found in field-names in the Midlands and the north of England, may be an indicator of apportionment by lot. The term is thought to be derived from Old Norse *vondr* 'a wand, a measuring stick' and *deill* 'a share, an allotment of land'. The wand may have been a means of determining the limits of individual shares. The term is found in *Wandoles* 1503, in Lamport, and there is a reference to *3 Wandells* 1632 of land in Stoke Albany (Nthants). Wandoles also occurs among the modern names in Desborough (Nthants). Two early Nottinghamshire instances are recorded – *Le Wandeles* 1233 and *Wandales* 1300 – but no later forms have been found. Other examples are Wandales, in Walesby (Lincs) and in Leake (YN), Wandles, in Duggleby, the Wandles, in Westow (YE), and Wandale, in Kirkleatham (YN), in

Hunmanby and in Garton on the Wolds (YE). The last three are traceable to *Wandayles* 12c., *Wandailes* 13c. and *Wandale* 12c. respectively.

REGIONAL TERMS FOR 'AN ENCLOSURE'

Tye is limited to south-eastern counties. In Essex the element (OE *tēag*) originally meant 'an outlying common' but was later applied to individual enclosures. Great and Little Tye are found in Stamford Rivers, Tye Field in Harlow, and Tye Pasture in High Easter. Burlong Stye Green Pasture (*Bourgoulonisteye* 1367), in Felsted, has initial *S* from the possessive form of the surname. In Surrey the element is confined to the east of the county, e.g. Brambletye, in Effingham, Rowtie (*Rowetie* 1578) 'rough enclosure', in Caterham, and Chalk Tye Mead (*Chalveteghe* 1312) 'calves' enclosure', in Limpsfield. Sussex examples include The Tye in Berwick, and *The Tye als. The Tyghe* 1567, in Hartfield, which later became Tye Farm.

A document of 1236 alludes to a field in Barfreston (Kent), called *Osmundesteghe*, and others named *Longetighe* and *Reteghe*, the last possibly 'enclosure at the river', strictly 'the at-the-river enclosure' (*atter ēa* misdividing as '*atte rea*'). An early fifteenth-century survey of Wye alludes to *Piriteghe* 'pear tree enclosure', and *Eastbrettegh* 'eastern broad enclosure'. *Beere Tyght, Scotten Tyght* and *Long Tyght* 17c. (*Longetheghe* 1381–82), in Deal, also contain the element. The only Berkshire instance is the medieval *Brembeltheye* 'bramble enclosure', in Warfield.

(The) Tining, or *Tyning*, is a term for '(fenced) enclosure', limited to some western and West Midland counties. Two Worcestershire examples, in Broadwas and in Bredicot, occur in the 1649 Survey. Modern Wiltshire examples are The Tinings, in Melksham and in Heytesbury, Gore Tyning, in Nettleton, and New Tyning (*The Tinning* 1608), in North Wraxall. Earlier forms include *New Tyning* 1640, in Bradford-on-Avon, and *Tyning t.* Jas 1, in Corsham. Gloucestershire examples include The Tyning (*The New Tynynges* 1632), in Leonard Stanley, Lower and Upper Tyning (*Newtyning* 1639), in Harescombe, and The Tynings (*The Tyneing c.* 1682), in Stonehouse.

Leasow, from Old English *lǣswe* 'at the pasture' (the dative singular of *lǣs*) preserves this sense in many names, but in the West Midlands it has acquired a general meaning. Back Lane Leasow,

Lime Leasow, Chapel Leasow, Clover Leasow, and Pit Leasow were all arable closes in the Romsley (Worcs) Tithe Apportionment of 1839, but Rough Leasow, Third Leasow and Steeps Bank Leasow were noted as pasture.

Leasow sometimes replaces other terms for 'enclosure'. Ox Leasow, in Bentley (Warks) from 1592, was *Ox Close* in 1540. Piggotts Leasow, in Aston (Warks), was *Piggotts Croft* in 1649, and Coalpit Leasow, in Cannock (Staffs), was *Coldpit Field* 1567. This one-way process, in which *Leasow* appears only in more recent forms, indicates the probable late sixteenth-century dating of the development of the broader usage of the term. *Horse Lesow* 1416 and *Ox Lesow* 1433, rare early forms in Warwickshire, with some instances elsewhere, have animal names as specifics, suggesting the sense 'pasture' at that time. Others may be noted, e.g. School Leasow, in Brocton, Gorsey Leasow, in Essington, Stonepit Leasow, in Huntington (Staffs), and Turnip Leasow, in Oldbury (Worcs). In the Glebe Terriers for Warwickshire and Worcestershire, the term appears only rarely and then usually in such names as *Ox Leasow* or *Cow Leasow*. Examples elsewhere and later include Barley Leasow, in Harley, Rye Leasow, in Church Pulverbatch (Shrops), Corn Leasow, in Oldbury, Oat Leasow, in Cakemore (Worcs), and *Wadlands Lessow* ('woad-lands leasow') 1666, in Weston under Lizard (Staffs). It replaces *Field* in Pit Leasow, in Knowle (Warks), which was *Le Pit Feelde* in 1692. Variations include *Leasoe, Leasure, Lez(z)er, Lezue* and *Lezza*. *Ye Vicar Leisure Peice* 1674, in a Glebe Terrier for Castle Donington (Leics), has the spelling *Leazure* five years later. Lower Lezar is found in Newbold Pacey (Warks), and Summer Leazons in Rollright (Oxon).

Apart from *Cangul* 1471, in Unstone (Derbys), Cangle Ing, in Warmfield (YW), and two Cambridgeshire examples, *Cangle* 'an enclosure' has been noted only in the south of England, e.g. *Cangle c.* 1300, in Goring (Oxon), Cangles (*Kangelfeld t.* Jas 1), in St Peter's (Herts), and Cangley Mead (*Cangle* 1466), in Croydon (Sur). *Le Kangel* 1222 is found in Navestock, *Le Kangel* 1381 in Stebbing, and *Kangelfeld* 1336 in Wethersfield and in Gosfield (Ess). Some of these survive, e.g. Cangley, in Gosfield.

The grandiose associations of the word *Park*, often thought of as an artificial landscape around a large house, have to be discarded when the term in used in field-names, where it often represents Old English *pearroc* 'an enclosed piece of land'. This usage is characteristic of Devon and Cornwall, and occurs sporadically elsewhere, e.g. Park Mead (*Parrocke Meade* 1585), in Mere (Wilts), Furzy & Green

Parks, in Horton, and perhaps The Parks, in Wimborne Minster (Dor). Devon examples are Broad Park and Stoney Park, in Ashburton, Lambs Park and Fore Park, in Blackawton, and Wheel Park, Miller's Park and Ash Park, in Newton Poppleford. In Bickleigh, which has Yellow Park, Broad Park, Down Park and Lane Park (each with two or three subdivisions), one group of *Park* names

Plate 2.3 Surveyors at work in the early seventeenth century, measuring with Gunter's chain, from Norden's *Surveior's Dialogue*, 1617

Plate 2.4 Surveyors depicted on the Enclosure Map of Henlow (Beds) *c.*1798 Gunter's chain is here used as a decorative frame.

seems to be recent: Great, Little, and Lower North Park were formerly part of fields known as *Bickfords*, from the name of a landowning family here in 1673.[10]

The Cornish word *Park*, which has been borrowed from English, is found principally in the four western hundreds of the county. *Park* is qualified in the same ways as *Close, Leasow*, etc. in other counties. Cornish specifiers include *Munys* 'little', e.g. Park Minnus, in Gerrans, *Banathel* 'broom', e.g. Park Bannel, in Paul, and *Jarden* 'garden', e.g. *Park an Jarns* 1649, in Constantine, and Park Jearn, in Paul. Anglicization of Cornish terms has brought about forms such as Park Crazie, in Perranzabuloe (Corn. *cres* 'middle'), Park Skipper, in Paul (Corn. *skyber* 'a barn, a hut'), and Park Drysack, in St Keverne (Corn. *dresek* 'brambly').[11] The specifiers are sometimes English words, e.g., Park Little, in St Keverne, Park Vine, in Crowan, and Park Saffron, in St Gluvias. The derogatory Park-an-Starve-Us, in St Keverne, has been given a superfluous Cornish definite article.

27

Park (ME *park* from Old French) 'a tract of land enclosed for beasts of the chase' is also found in field-names, this sense often being confirmed by references to a pale, e.g. *The Parke Pale* 1541, in Kelvedon (Ess), and *Le Parke Pale* 1592, in Bremhill (Wilts), to which may be added Pale Field (cf. *Le Parke Pale* 1466), in Lyme Handley (Ches), on the boundary of Lyme Park. *Park Feelde* 1587, one of the great fields of Holdenby (Nthants), was named from its proximity to the medieval park.[12]

NOTES AND REFERENCES

1. H.L. Gray, *English Field Systems* (Cambridge, Mass., Harvard University Press, 1915; repr, London, Merlin, 1959), uses the term 'Midlands' in this context to represent the band of territory running approximately from Co. Durham to the Isle of Wight but excluding the north-western and south-eastern counties and the whole of East Anglia.
2. Gray, p. 69.
3. Gray, p. 456.
4. M.M. Postan, *The Medieval Economy and Society* (Weidenfeld & Nicolson, 1972; Penguin Books, 1975), p. 147.
5. A. Rumble, 'The Merstham, Surrey, charter-bounds, AD 947', *Journal of the English Place-Name Society* 3 (1970–71), pp. 3–31, especially 29–30. See also Gray, pp. 366–7, 549.
6. F.T. Wainwright, 'Field-names of Amounderness Hundred', *Trans. Historic Soc. of Lancs and Cheshire* XCIX (1945), pp. 181–222, here p. 186.
7. J. Steane, *The Northamptonshire Landscape* (Hodder & Stoughton, 1974), pp. 174–5.
8. Gray, p. 89.
9. V. Watts, 'Place-name evidence for the allocation of land by lot', *Leeds Studies in English* XVIII (1987), pp. 247–63.
10. For the Bickleigh names I am indebted to Mr Paul Hartley.
11. See P.A.S. Pool, *Field-Names of West Penwith* (priv. pub., Hayle, 1990), the source of most Cornish examples in the present work, supplemented by information privately conveyed by Mr Pool.
12. M. Beresford, *History on the Ground*, 2nd edn (Gloucester, Sutton, 1984), p. 213.

CHAPTER THREE

Field-names and the landscape

THE PANORAMA OF LIVING THINGS

The current interest in the natural environment and the emphasis on conservation have done much to bring the term *landscape* back to implying an overall consciousness of the outdoor scene rather than meaning a momentary visual impression from a viewpoint, or a picture of what is there observed. It would be making a large claim to suggest that field-names provide more than a slight key to the complexity of the outdoor scene, but they do undoubtedly offer some evidence of what was present when the names were given, and are a record of human reactions to the life in the fields.

In the early seventeenth century, the names of five of the six common open fields of Lenton and Radford (Notts) related to features of the landscape: *Beck Field, Alwell Field,* alluding to an old well, *Morfeld, Red Field* and *Sand Field.* Five or more centuries of history can often be documented from the earlier forms of such names. Hard Meadows, in Newnham (Nthants), were no softer underfoot in the fourteenth century, as they were recorded as *Hardemede c.* 1375. Black Acre, in Lindsell (Ess), has an early counterpart in *Blakeacre* 1426.

PATTERN AND COLOUR IN THE FIELDS

Visual features of the rural scene include the patterns and colours offered by the surface of the land, both ploughed field and unbroken fallow, as well as by the variety of vegetation from woods and heaths to meadows and cultivated crops. In Gridiron Field, in Great Wakering and in Kirby le Soken (Ess), the gridded pattern in the furrows or among the growing crops would probably be smaller than that in Harlequin Field, in Timperley (Ches). In *Checkqr Cowpasture* 1598, in Marshchapel (Lincs), and Chequer Field, in Smallwood (Ches) and in more than a dozen parishes in Essex, the allusion is to the variegated appearance of the field. *Le Chequer* 1616 has been noted in Deal, and *Chequer End* 1616 in Sutton (Kent). The earliest name of this type seems to be *Chakborde* 1323, later known as Chequer Field, in Altofts (YW). A mottled surface may also be described as *pied*, a term found in the seventeenth-century name *Pyde Croft*, in Great Stanney, Pied Flatt, in Burwardsley, and Pyd Acre, in Wincham (Ches).

Another name type connected with pattern in *Rainbow*, eighteen examples of which were found in Surrey. A likely interpretation was first proposed in *The Place-Names of Essex*. The name is applied when the arc of a curving boundary is followed by the furrows nearby. Concentric curves make a most agreeable pattern on the autumn surface of arable land and obviously suggest the coloured bands of a rainbow.[1] Essex has in fact a very great number of closes called Rainbow Field (certainly more than fifty), and half a dozen instances of Rainbow Mead, as well as Rainbow Piece, in Corringham, and Rainbow Shot, in Wimbish, in addition to nearly a dozen pieces of land called simply Rainbow, found also in Burghfield and in Sandhurst (Berks), in Eversley (Hants) and in Stapleton (Shrops).

Catsbrain names have also long been regarded with interest. Catsbrain (Farm) (*Cattesbreyne* 1348), in Oakley (Bucks), and *Kattesbreyn* 1300 were noted in early EPNS county volumes, and *Catebraynehulle*, of approximately the same date, occurs in Cirencester (Glos). Oxfordshire examples include Cats Brain (*Cattesbrayn* 1315), in Enstone, and *Catsbraine* 1601, in Hanwell. Examples elsewhere include Catbrain, in Ludford (Shrops), Catbrain Piece, in Moreton (Berks), Cats Brain Furlong, in Whitchurch (Warks), and Catsbrain, in Hinton St Mary (Dor).

The explanation of *Catsbrain* usually offered, 'soil consisting of rough clay mixed with stones', is borne out by an inspection of some examples. It may be the small pebbles in the fields that are compared to cats' brains. The resemblance in size and appearance of some of these pebbles may be checked by reference to Plate 3.1, but stones of this conformation have not always been found in other *Catsbrain* fields.[2] It has been noted that "it was a common term in the quarry

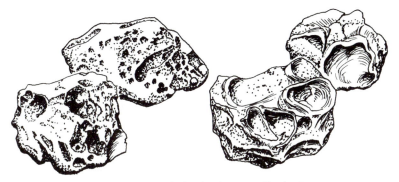

Plate 3.1   Pebbles possibly alluded to in the term *Catsbrain*
The pair on the left were collected by Mrs Ann Cole from Catsbrain Hill, South Stoke (Oxon) (GRSU 623832), those on the right from Catsbrain Farm, Oakley (Bucks) (GRSP 646099).

districts [of Gloucestershire] and it may have originated as a local word for certain types of oolitic fossil".[3]

Colour references are found in a great range of field-names. White Breaks, in Blyth (Notts), Black Lands, in Thundridge (Herts), Pink Belly, in Swarkestone (Derbys), Green Garth, in Gembling (YE), Grey Croft, in Bennington (Herts), Yellow Piece, in Buxton (Derbys), Purple Mead, in Chickerell (Dor), and Blue Leys, in Boughton (Notts), offer little difficulty in linguistic interpretation, though the contextual significance may not always be clear. Some, such as Grey Croft, may contain a surname. Many possibly describe the appearance of the soil, such as Dunland Hey (*The Dunland* 1562) which may be 'the brown selion', in Liscard (Ches). Others probably relate to features of the vegetation, such as the colour of flowers or of dying herbage. The diagnostic use of some colours is illustrated in an observation by Aubrey: "The watred meadows all along from Marlborough to Hungerford, Ramsbury, and Littlecot, at the later end of April, are yellow with butter flowers. When you come to Twyford the floated meadowes there are all white with little flowers . . . The graziers told me that the yellow meadowes are by much the better, and those white flowers are produc't by a cold hungry water."[4] Such knowledge probably went back many generations, and the colour-signals were doubtless better detected in a relatively hedge-row-free landscape. Robert Plot, writing in the seventeenth century, observes that in the Chiltern area of Oxfordshire, "if it be of that poorest sort they call white-land, nothing is so proper as ray-grass (i.e. rye-grass) mixt with Non-such or Melitot Trefoil".[5] Here, evidently, *white* ranked lowest in the table of fertility.

Red Field, in Flawborough (Notts), was *Red Feild* in 1629. In Stratfield Mortimer (Berks), *Reddelond* 1462 was evidently enclosed a little later, for *Reddelonde Close* was on record in 1552. A bilingual name is found in Chidlow (Ches): Red Gough means literally no more than 'red red', as the second element is the Welsh word *coch* 'red'. Pink Meadow, in Feckenham (Worcs), and Pink Field, in Lamberhurst (Kent), however, may refer to finches (OE *pinca*).

Greenness seems such a general quality of the countryside that references to it appear tautological. The freshness in colour of a piece of pasture may be worth recording, as in Green Meadow, in Monks Horton (Kent), and Green Ham, in South Cerney (Clos). In Sledmere (YE) an impression of Arctic geography is given by the names Greenland and Lapland; the latter is probably 'a selion on the edge or border'. Polglase, in Ludgvan (Corn), was *Parke Glase* 1664, Cornish for 'green field'. Grandborough, in Brixworth (Nthants), was *Greneberwe* 'the green hill' in the reign of Henry III. Green Field, in Buckden (YW), is in fact 'the green hill' as earlier forms confirm e.g. *Grenefell* 1338 (ON *fjall* 'a hill, a mountain'). Greena Meadow, in Malham, is 'the meadow on or by the green hill' (*-a* from ON *haugr* 'a hill, a mound'). These limestone hills are clothed in a fine turf of sheep's fescue grass which is responsible for the colour.

Blue Field, in Little Easton, in Chingford and in Writtle (Ess), and Blew Close, in Thatcham (Berks), probably refer to the colour of wild flowers growing in the fields, as may Sky Blue, in Chelmsford (Ess). Blue Piece, in Barlborough (Derbys), supplements other colour terms in the field-names of this parish: White Car, Black Acres, Green Close, Golden Greave and Silven (i.e. Silvern) Banks.

Yellow Ley, in Kings Hatfield (Ess), Yellow Croft and Meadow, in Bollin Fee, Yellow Field, in Mottram (Ches), and Yellow Piece, in Buxton (Derbys), would probably have been commended by Aubrey's informants, quoted above. The colour may be that of the bare earth, or of yellow flowers in the meadows, especially buttercups and the prolific dandelion family. This colour has been found significant elsewhere in Britain, and Gwynedd Pierce has noted *Hilly Yellowes, Little Yellowes* and *The Long Yellowes* 1622 among the field-names of Porthkerry (Glamorgan)[6] The relatively few *Brown* references include *Broundflaht c.* 1240 'the brown *flat*', in Brampton (Derbys), and *The Browne More* 1420, in Askham (Westm).

Field-names of the *Blacklands* type often indicate places of archaeological interest. However, the carbonation of organic material left in former habitation sites is not the only possible cause of blackness in soil. The moorlands and boggy areas referred to in *Blakemor* 1261, in Coventry (Warks), Black Mire, in Killington, Black Moss, in Holme (Westm), and Blackmoor Breach, in Hailey (Oxon), owe their coloration to peat or to their growth of heath rather than to previous habitation.

Hoar (OE *hār*) is normally used of features, such as woods or standing stones, rather than the surface of the fields. It means 'grey, especially through being overgrown with lichen', and any reference to a boundary-marking function requires support from other evidence; *Hoar* itself (often *Har-* in field-names and place-names) should not be regarded as proof. *Le Harestane* 1309 is in Willaston (Ches), on the boundary with Little Neston. Harwood (*Harwoode* 1606–07), in Bookham (Berks), is also near the parish boundary. Whore Stone Croft (*Horestonesfeld* 1354), in Tushingham (Ches), and Whoreston Furlong (*Horestan* 1227), in Desborough (Nthants), are pieces of land 'by or containing the grey stone' (which may or may not mark a boundary), *Grey* often refers to the colour of stones. Greystone Bottom, in Winfrith Newburgh (Dor), refers to the same stone as *Greystonesforlong* 1392, described as "*1 furlong' terre iuxta le Greyston*" 1461 'one furlong of land near the Greystone'. Inspection of the fields may help to determine the geological or other implications of names like White Field, in Essington (Staffs) and Worksop (Notts), *Whitelond* 1694, in Painswick and in Coberley (Glos). Whiteshord Tyning, in Upton Scudamore (Wilts), refers to an enclosure (*tyning*) by 'a white gap' or 'gash'. Blazes Field, in Agden (Ches), is probably from Old Norse *blesi* 'a white spot' or 'a bare spot on a hillside'. Wetlands, in Rimington (YW), seems to be self-explanatory, but *Quitelandes* 1240 shows it to be 'white lands'.

MARKS OF APPROVAL

Colour terms, especially *Gold(en)*, may be used by way of compliment, e.g. Golden Holme, in Rampton (Notts), Golden Square, in Knapton (YE), Golden Lands, in Burbage (Wilts), and Golden Acre, in Painswick (Glos) and in Wix (Ess). These may refer to rich pasture or to productive arable, the latter being probable in Gold Crop, in Hawkeswell (Ess). Golden Biss (*cultura voc' Bisse* 1454), in Beer Hackett (Dor), is derived from Middle English *bisse* 'fine linen'. Similar comparisons are made in The Golden Dress, in Shrewsbury

St Mary, and in Golden Placket, in Culmington (Shrops). Goldpit Runnel (*Goldpitteslade* 1286), in Warboys (Hunts), may have had an excavation of some kind, but as it was a *slade* it might have been a suitable habitat for marsh marigolds, which were also once abundant in Gold Mead (*Goldemede t.* Hy 6), in St Stephens (Herts). Gold Diggings, in Folkton (YE), is more cryptic. Like the close named Klondyke, in Milton Lilborne (Wilts), this may be good land, whereas the emphasis in other names related to the Canadian Gold Rush seems to be on hardship rather than good fortune.

Happy discoveries of hidden treasure are recorded in such names as *Goldhorde* 1251, in Wytham (Berks), *Goldhordesmos* 1293, in Haslington (Ches), *Le Goldhord* 13c., in Uppington (Shrops). The thirteenth century was evidently a good season for treasure-hunters; the family name of one of these successful men is recalled, by *Goldhordeslond*, in Streatley (Berks), in 1338, when Walter Goldhord was also mentioned in the document. Goldfinder, in Little Stretton (Leics) and in Timperley (Ches), may also be literal references. Silver coins were discovered in the The Silver Field, in Sowerby (YW). *Silver* enters the field-names vocabulary in early names such as *Siluergore c.* 1260, in Fulbourne (Cambs), *Selverland* 1223, in Stambourne (Ess), and *Selvercroft* 13c., in High Ongar (Ess). *Silver* as a term for 'fresh water' has been found valid for a number of instances of *Silver Street*, as the name of a small thoroughfare leading to a supply of pure water, and the same allusion may be found in some field-names. Silver Mead and Well, in Silton (Dor), seems to support this interpretation, as may Silver Well (*Sylver Well* 1319), in Brough & Shatton (Derbys). Buxton, renowned for its water supply, has a field called Silver Lands.

SOIL TYPES

Names specifying the type of soil occur in many places. The information would obviously be relevant to the choice of crops and to the availability of other economic products of the land. Sandy Field, in Burton Fleming (YE), states its nature unambiguously, as do Chalk Close, in Crowmarsh (Oxon), Clay Garson (*Cleygaston* 1575) 'clay paddock', in Weston Birt (Glos), *the Clayfeilde c.* 1580, in Cherington (Glos), North and South Clay Fields, in Brandesburton (YE), and Clayhill Field (*Clayhilfeld c.* 1605, going back to *Clayhull* 1300), in Watlington (Oxon).

Clay was dug for various purposes, including for the manufacture of pottery and bricks. Many clay-pits are referred to quite early, e.g. *Clayputt* 1278, in Farnham (Sur), and *Cleypetfelde* 1328, in Little Abington (Cambs). Clay Grounds, in Alderholt (Dor), not far from Old Clay Grounds, in Cranborne, point to a pottery industry here, attested by Potten Hill and Crockerton Hill, in Cranborne, Potsherd Piece and Old Pottery Kiln, in Alderholt. Larput Field (*Larepottfeld* in 1539–40), in Bolton Abbey (YW), contains Old English *leirr* 'clay' and Middle English *potte* 'a pit'. *Daub*, the clay or clayey mud used in earlier centuries to plaster the framework of dwellings, is referred to in Dob Hey, in Lymm, Dobhill, in Runcorn and in Hyde, and Dab Acre, in Werneth (Ches). Chalky soil has generated such names as Chalk Field, in Dagenham, in Hornchurch and in Upminster (Ess), Chalk Close, in Alderholt (Dor), Char Croft (*Chalcrofte Lande* 1548), in Blewbury (Berks), and Chalcroft, described as "a field gleaming white with chalk fragments . . . in Grubb Street . . . near Darenth in Kent".[7]

Great Lands, in Crosby Ravensworth (Westm), is not the size-name that it at first seems, but, as is indicated by early forms, e.g. *Gretelands c.* 1230, is in fact a derivative of Old English *grēot* 'gravel'. A similar succession of names is found in Newton by Toft (Lincs): *Gretland* 1230–15, becoming *Greatlandes* in the seventeenth century. The element in Grotten Close, in Woodland (Dor), is *groten* 'gravelly'. A variant, *grīeten*, is found in Grittenham, in Brinkworth (Wilts) 'the gravelly riverside enclosure'; it is beside Brinkworth Brook. Another term for gravel is found in *Chesilruge* 1533 'gravel ridge', in Oldbury upon Severn (Glos), and Chessell Field, in North Wootton (Som). *Le Chisele* 1344, in Coulsdon (Sur), was evidently a large piece of land, as modern names include Broad-, Long-, Ten Acre-, and Twelve Acre Chisel. Gravel Plough is found in Hartshorne (Derbys), Gravel Lees, in Stebbing (Ess), and *Gravell Filde* 1585, in Frocester (Glos). Gravelly Ground is one of several Thatcham (Berks) field-names alluding to soil types, others being Sand Close, Chalk Ground and Peat Mead.

The impediments to cultivation in Stony Lands (*Stonilonde* 1300), in Mappowder (Dor), Stony Croft (*Stancroft* 1436), in Watford (Herts), and Stony Furlong, in Tichborne (Hants), were as unwelcome in later centuries as they had been in the Middle Ages. *Stony Acre* and similar names can be found all over the country. The possible range can be seen from Essex examples: Stone Croft, in Writtle, Stone Field, in Widford, Stone Leys, in Hatfield Peverel, and Stone Shot, in Roydon. Old Norse *steinn* 'a stone' is found in some Danelaw names, e.g. *Stayn Moure* 1250–60 'stony marshland', in Habrough (Lincs), and *Stainflat* 13c., in Potter Newton (YW).

In certain areas, sandy soil is put to good use in horticulture rather than agriculture. Sandfield (*Sondfeld c.* 1220), in Churchdown (Glos), is within the market-garden area near Cheltenham. Sand Field, in Hawton (Notts), has been so called since 1650; the name also occurs in High Roding (Ess), and as the name of common fields in Wadsworth (YW) and in Welton (YE). The generics in Sandy Acre, in Stanford Dingley (Berks), Sand Furlong, in Headington (Oxon) and Sandy Furlong, in Ipsden (Oxon), suggest that these also date from pre-enclosure days.

THE ROUGH AND THE SMOOTH

Besides Rough Piece, in Hilton (Staffs), there were some earlier names in the parish with this specifier: *Le Rughurst* 1507, *Rough Rudding* 1546 'rough clearing', *The Roe Croft* 1653 and *Rough Leasow* 1653. *Rowebalk* 1254 'the rough balk' is noted in Sharnbrook (Beds). Rough Meadow, in Bishops Itchington (Warks), is traceable to *Rowemedwe* 13c. *Smythfurlong* 1312, in Chinnor (Oxon), is from Old English *smēthe* 'smooth, bare', found also in Smesmoor Close (*Smethemor t.* Hy 3), in Normanton (Derbys).

Crumbly Croft, in West Hoathly (Sus), and Crumbly Land, in Sproston (Ches), suggest dry soil with a good 'crumb', making for easy sowing. Instability of soil is indicated by such names as *Le Quakandlowe* 1390, in Macclesfield (Ches), Shivery Sham, in Marston (Oxon), Earthquake Plantation and Landslip Screed, both in Birdsall (YE), and Quake Field, in Darlton (Notts). *Screed* in the Birdsall names, like Screed in Stirton (YW), may be the Old Norse *skritha* 'a landslip, scree'. The soil in Dust Furlong, in Gilmorton (Leics), and in *Dustholme* 1624, in Barton Seagrave (Nthants), would be too permeable for good cultivation.

The characteristic alluded to in *Dirty Croft* 1617, in Hartington Upper Quarter (Derbys), is perhaps as little to be recommended as *dusty*. Muddiness is not unnaturally accepted as a normal feature of ploughed soil in a damp climate. Mud Field, in Hatfield Peverel (Ess), recognizes this, and Dirty Shanks, in Pilling (Lancs), relates the state of the land to the people traversing it. Dirty Bottom, in Pyrton (Oxon), alludes to a valley bottom, watered by a sluggish stream liable to flood from time to time. Other examples are Dirty

Land, in Raby, and Dirty Acre, in Whitby (Ches), Dirty Croft, in Lindwell (Ess), and Dirty Leasow, in Oldbury (Worcs).

Names literally descriptive of hardness include *La Hardacre c.* 1245, in Stapenhill (Derbys), Harding (*Le Hard Inge* 1572) 'the hard meadow', in Hoebury (YW), Hard Mead, in Dyrham & Hinton (Glos), Hard Meadows (*Hardemede c.* 1275), in Newnham (Nthants), and Hard Leys, in Flintham (Notts). *Le Longeirenhard* 'the long iron-hard piece of ground' is found in Hognaston (Derbys), and *Iron-hade Furlong* 1617 'furlong by the iron headland' in Great Alne (Warks). Steel Close, in Kirkby Overblow (YW), however, is 'a close with a stile'. Leatherlands Corner, in Whichford (Warks), and Leathern Acre, in Merrow (Sur), utilize a different imagery to express hardness of the soil.

Objectionable to the cultivator though hard soil may be, its opposite is also unwelcome. Soft, yielding ground is referred to in Featherlands (*Fetherlande* 1563), in Holsworthy (Dev), and Featherbed Field, in Dunham Massey (Ches) and in Chapel Allerton (YW). Feather Bed, in Scammonden, and Featherbed Moss, in Grassington, in Marsden, in Saddleworth (YW), in Tintwistle (Ches) and in Charlesworth (Derbys), all allude to spongy areas of moorland peatmoss. Featherbed Meadow, in Kemberton (Shrops), and Featherbeds Field, in Kelvedon (Ess), allude to similar land.

". . . FENS, BOGS, DENS, AND SHADES OF DEATH"

Terms such as *fen, marsh, bog* and *carr* are found in numerous field-names. *Fens* are extensive tracts of marshy ground; they are characteristic of, but not exclusive to, eastern England. Names alluding to them include Fen Acres, in Houghton le Spring (Dur), Fens Close, in Idridgehay (Derbys), Fen Moor and Big Fen Meadow, in Dadlington (Leics). *Turfen* 12c., in Witchford (Cambs), indicates an area of peat, and White Fen (*Whites Fen* 1656), in Benwick (Cambs), is an ownership name. *Fan* in *Fanfurlong* 12c., in Wendy (Cambs), Fan Field, in Great Waltham (Ess) (*Le Fanne* 1402) and in Ware (*Fanfeld* 15c.), and Fan Mead (*La Vanne* 1463), in Ashwell (Herts), is a dialectal variant of *Fen*.

Marsh is of wide application, e.g. The Marsh (*Le Mershe* 1455), in Winterbourne Stoke (Wilts), Marsh Moor, in Walton Inferior (Ches), Green Marsh (*Grenemersh'* 1418), in Frimley (Sur), *Merse*

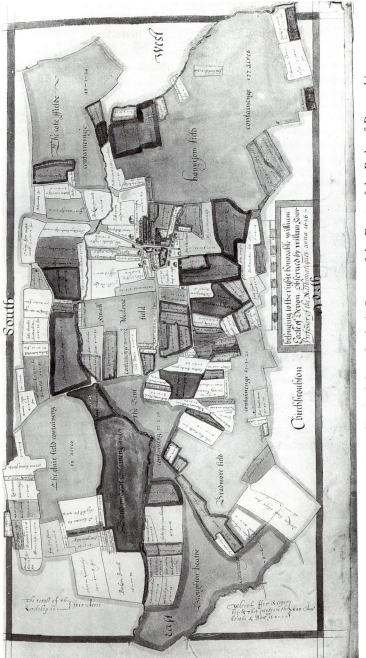

Plate 3.2 Field-map of Church Broughton (Derbys) from Senior's Survey of the Estate of the Duke of Devonshire Note the references to landscape and soil-types in *The Claie field, Bradmore field and Broughton Heathe.*

13c., in Sulhampstead, *La Mershe* 1372, in Cookham, and *La Marshe* 1552, in Binfield (Berks). Marsh Close (*Le Merssh* 14c.) is found in Eversden (Cambs), Marsh Meadow in Fledborough (Notts) and Broad Marsh in Flintham, but in much of the Danelaw, *kjarr*, the Norse term for 'marsh', is more common, as in Great Carr, in Hawksworth, Carr, in Southwell, Car Leys, in Lowdham, and Carr Close, in Girton. The Bogs, in Lapal and in Lutley, Bogs Close, in Romsley (Worcs), Bog Close, in Bushby (Leics), and Bog Field, in Heslington (YE), are clear enough. Waterlogged land is also indicated by other terms, e.g. *Redimire c.* 1234 'reedy mire', in Bingley (YW), Mirey Croft, in Malpas (Ches), Miredale, in Arncliffe (YW), Foul Slough (*Fouleslowe c.* 1350), in Colchester (Ess), Slop, in Colehill (Dor), Slop Field, in Great Canfield (Ess), Sloppy Field, in Basford (Ches), Slosh, in Appleby (Westm), and Quabbs, in Dymock (Glos). Rarer terms include *mizzick* 'boggy ground', found in Missick, in Tushingham cum Grindley (Ches), and *gog*, approximately synonymous with *quab* or *quag*, in Gog Ground, in Brinkworth (Wilts), in Shiplake, in Milton under Wychwood, and in Steeple Aston (Oxon). The disastrous fall implied in Slap Bang, in Chigwell (Ess), is not entirely at odds with the literal meaning of its earlier form, *Slapam* 13c. 'the meadow at a slippery place'. Old English *slǣp* 'a slippery muddy place' is found also in Tadslips Meadow (*Tadeslep* 13c.) 'the toad's slippery place'.

Clammy may express only a mild level of dampness but has an additional suggestion of unpleasantness. This is the sense of *Clam*- or *Clem*- names, used of 'wet, sticky, clay soil', found in Clem Park Meadow, is Brocton (Staffs), Clam Park, in Staveley (Derbys), Clamhunger Wood, in Mere, Clemonga, in Mobberley, Clamhanger, in Marthall cum Warford, and Clemley Park, in Little Longstone (Derbys), and in Yockleton (Shrops).

Squadge Field (*Queggemedwe t.* Ed. 1, *Quadge Medowe* 1608), in Wootton Wawen (Warks), has added an *S* to itself, perhaps to suggest the sound of human footsteps across waterlogged ground. Another echoic word, *quab*, is found in similar contexts, e.g. *The Quabbes* 1570, in Cannock (Staffs), and *The Quabby Moor* 1661, in Great Wyrley (Staffs). Names such as Quabby Leasow, in Cleobury Mortimer (Shrops), and Slough Field, in High Easter and in Hatfield Peverel (Ess), show that these fields were in the cultivated area, and in some seasons their soil was no doubt difficult or impossible to till. Terms relating to laborious cultivation, e.g. Stiff Field, in High Legh (Ches), were applied to land of this kind. A name of French origin, Malpas 'a bad or unpleasant passage', in Walton upon Trent

(Derbys) dating from the seventeenth century, evidently refers to muddy land. In the fourteenth century *Maupas*, in Theale (Berks), was an alternative name for a pasture called *Wydemore*, later Widmoor Common. The term also occurs in Malpas Meadow, in Rushbury, and Morpus, in Munslow (Shrops). Wet Foot, in Idbury (Oxon), is virtually an English translation of *Malpas*.

Characteristic vegetation of wet land may be referred to in field-names, e.g. the common *Rushy Meadow*. In north-western counties, *Moss*, the term applied to a peat bog, occurs as a specific element in a number of names, e.g. Moss Wood, in Appleton (Ches), Moss Ing, in Addingham (YW), Moss Bottom, in Hartlington (YW), *Le Moshulle* 1279, in Shap Rural (Westm), and Moss Field, in Shipbrook (Ches). *Carr* is regarded as a sign of the presence of alder trees, and *Alder Carr* is often found. Wirloons (*The Werne Londes* 1454), in Caldy (Ches), and Wern Meadow, in Alberbury (Shrops), are from Welsh *gwern* 'an alder swamp'; Warneck, in Camborne (Corn), contains the corresponding Cornish term *guern*.

Hell Hole, which frequently occurs, is a general term of disparagement. Places calling down such opprobrium include the vicinity of dark pools, damp hollows and secluded spots in uninviting scrubland. Some kind of menace was imagined among the trees of Hell Hole Spinney, in Odstone (Leics), and of Hell Hole Wood, in Whitewell (Westm). Variants include Hell Pit, in Welford (Berks), Hell Fire Piece, in Bibury (Glos), Hell Fire Gate, in Lower Swell (Glos), and Hell Gates, in Harlow (Ess).

SWEET AND SOUR LAND

However clear may be the meaning of the words, the significance of some picturesque names is not always obvious. Sour Ale and Sweet Ale, two fields in Cuxham, present a mirror-image of naming, like Sour and Sweet Middle Ground, in Pyrton (Oxon), and Sweet and Sour Field, in Alsager (Ches). The reference to ale may be to different varieties of grain crop used for brewing; medieval, and possibly later, ale was not necessarily made from barley malt, and hops were not universally used for flavouring. Older writers employ epithets such as *fat* and *lean* in their descriptions of soil. These terms refer to physical characteristics. Fatlands, in Baggrave and in Rotherby (Leics), probably refers to soil quality, whereas Fat Pasture, in Minshull Vernon (Ches), alludes to the richness of the grass.

Other favourable references to soil chemistry occur in Sweet Field, in High Legh (Ches), and Sweetlands, in Bingham (Notts). There are also instances of Sweet Bit in Lancashire, as well as Sweet Meadow, in Norbury (Staffs), Sweet Green, in Ash (Derbys), and Sweet Pot, in Claydon (Oxon), presumably alluding to the tastiness of the pasture, like Sweet Tooth, in Sandbach (Ches), and in Medlar and in Greenhalgh (Lancs). Earlier examples include *Sweetacre Medewe c.* 1386, in Baslow (Derbys). Knaresborough (YW) has both Sugar Hills and Sweeting, though they are not necessarily related. The former, if it is not a reference to robbers (OE *sceacere*), could be a reference to hills of conical (sugar-loaf) shape. Sugar Candy Close, in Appleby (Leics), may indicate stickiness or brittleness – either of which may be an attribute of sugar candy but less appreciated as a quality of the soil. Syllabub Close, in Whitchurch (Shrops), and Syllabubs Knapp, in Horningham (Wilts), suggest a delicious product, but the latter may be a playful reference to a milking-place, Dairy Coppice being found nearby.

Fanciful references to sticky soil in Glue Pot, in Crosby-on-Eden (Cumb), and Treacle Nook, in Spondon (Derbys), are unmistakable. The allusion in Plum Pudding Field, in Waltham St Lawrence (Berks), or in Plum Pudding Meadow, in Stapleford (Notts), in Ockbrook (Derbys) and in Stoke Dabernon (Sur), is also to sticky or boggy land. Plum Pudding Thorofare, in South Repps (Norf), is a close beside Plum Pudding Lane. Christmas Pie, in Wanborough (Sur), and Yule Pie, in Hornsea and in Bewholme (YE), also refer to soil of this consistency. The imagery is continued in Puddingholme (*Puddyngholm* 1438), in Sutton (Cambs), Pudding Yard Furlong, in Farnborough (Berks), Pudding Pye, in Inskip (Lancs), *Pudding Hole* 1664, in Tealby (Lincs), and Pudding Field, in Dagenham (Ess). Pudding Bag is found in Ashford Carbonell (Shrops), in Harston (Leics), in Kelham and in Selston (Notts). Pudding Bag Field occurs in Fryerning and in Little Leighs (Ess), and Pudding Bag Mead, in Widford (Ess). The synonymous Pudding Poke is found in Cuckney, in Laxton (*Puding Roods* 1625), and in Worksop (Notts), in North Elmsall (YW) and in Scarcliffe (Derbys), Pudding Poke Field in Melton Ross, Pudding Poke Nooking in Tealby, and *Pudding Hole* 1664 in Thorganby (all in Lincs), and the alliterating Pudding Poke Pightle in Great Bentley (Ess). Hasty Pudding, in Great Clacton (Ess), does not seem to occur elsewhere. Loblolly, in Wickham (Ess), alluding to a kind of thick gruel, and Hotch Potch, in Gawsworth (Ches), may also belong here, but not Dumpling Meadow, in Caldwell (Derbys), which was earlier *Dumples Meadow*

1661, from *dumpel* 'a deep hole or pit'. Other culinary metaphors for soft and sticky soil include Porridge Field, in Twemlow (Ches), Porridge Bottom, in Finchampstead (Berks), and Whey Porridge Close, in Solihull (Warks).

It is possible that some *Honey-* names refer literally to the production in the fields of either honey itself (in hives or in the nests of wild bees) or the nectar from which it was derived. Honey Hole, in Beckingham, and Honey Hole Close, in Laxton (Notts), may refer to the subterranean living quarters of bumble bees. But many of these names allude to an unwelcome stickiness in the soil. In Cambridgeshire, Honey Hill is found usually to occur in marshy areas, and early instances of other *Honey-* names in that county include *Honibuttes* 1228, in Stanton, and *Honiefelde* 1504, in Whittlesford. Names with a medieval origin, like instances of *Honiland* in Kent, may represent land held by the payment of a food rent of honey.[8]

Sourness, usually synonymous with 'the state of being waterlogged, badly drained', is complained about in a number of names, many early in origin. *Sureforlong* and *Sureland* 13c. are noted in Pyrton (Oxon), and *Le Surlond* somewhat earlier in Milford (Derbys). There are other examples, including *Sourerthe c.* 1275 'sour arable land', in Clifton (Ches), *Sourehul c.* 1260 'sour hill', in Thomley (Oxon), *Sourlond* 1317, in Cheselbourne (Dor), and *Sowerlands* 1578, in Wootton (Berks). The name *Furlong' vocat' Surecrofte* 1428 'the furlong called Sourcroft', in Arne (Dor), is justified by Barbara Kerr's account: ". . . over half was heath with patches of birch scrub and bog . . . The names of some of its closes reflect back-breaking labour, e.g. Bitters Gall, Furzey Vineyard, and Stoneyland."[9] In *Sourebuttes* 1343, in Tiverton (Ches), and Sowerbutts (*Le Sourbut c.* 1220), in Winmarleigh (Lancs), Sower Butts, in Staveley (Derbys), or Sour Butts, in Skelsmergh (Westm) and in Bingley (YW), it seems likely that *butts* 'remnants' are not the left-over pieces of the furlong pattern that merely happen to be sour, but, like Sour End, in North Stainley (YW), and Sourends, in Westby with Plumpton (Lancs), those left uncultivated because of this undesirable quality – fragments that, if better drained, might have been included in neighbouring furlongs. Sour Milk Field, in Bostock (Ches), may allude literally to the quality of the milk of cattle pastured here or to the muddy and sour state of the soil. The Galls, in Thirston (Northumb), *Gallcroft* 1558, in Welford (Berks), Gaul Leys, in Sutton Bonington (Notts), and Goal Meadow, in Galby (Leics), contain the Old English element *galle* meaning 'sore, a blister', the source of dialectal *gall* 'a wet spot', found in the common name Watergall, as in *Watergal Furlong* 1608, in Newbold Pacey (Warks). Early examples of the latter include *Watergalle(s)* 1200, in Moreton Pinkney (Nthants), recorded in 1200, in Ufton (Warks) in 1278, in Catton (Derbys) in 1327, in Yelvertoft (Nthants) in 1427, in Wellesbourne (Warks) in 1450, and in Cambridgeshire, where an example is noted in 1312. The element is found also in Rush Galls, in Blyth and in Ranskill (Notts). It is unlikely that galls on plants, as is sometimes suggested, are referred to by these names.

ELEVATION AND DEPRESSION

Hills and valleys are mentioned so often in field-names that the allusions pass unobserved. In parts of Craven, field-names occur such as Lingber 'heather hill', Peasbers (*Peaseber* 1649) 'pease hill(s)', and Rosber 'horse hill' (all in Nappa), Greenber, Lingber and Pearsber, in Newsholme and Vicarsber, in Paythorne (YW). These glacial *drumlins*, hillocks of about 100 feet (30 metres) in height and up to a quarter of a mile in diameter, each provided a suitable landscape unit for separate enclosure.

Names such as Hilly Field, in West Hoathly (Sus), in Farnham and in Windlesham (Sur), and in Little Bowden (Leics), may sometimes seem exaggerated, as there may be only a slight rise between one boundary and another. But to the cultivator of the land, without benefit of tractors, the slope would have represented an additional difficulty in his daily work. In the township of Brearton (YW) there are closes called Fall Hills, Gammer Hills, Gibb Hills, Hall Garth Hill, Jenny Hill and Limekiln Hill, as well as Barf Field (from dialect *barf* from OE *beorg*) and Brant Bank (from ON *brant* 'steep'). *Fall* may indicate a landslip; *Gibb* is from Middle English *gibbe* 'a hump'. *Gammer* 'grandmother' alludes to land endowed for the widow of a former owner. In some early forms *Hill* may be found as *Hull*, e.g. *Grethull* 1226 'gravel hill', in Appleton Roebuck (YW), or *Freschenou'hull* 13c. 'fresh enough hill', in Etwall (Derbys).

Hillocks might seem to be less of an impediment to progress, but their occurrence, especially in numbers, on otherwise level land might be as unwelcome as a more gradual slope on the side of a hill. Examples include *Hulloc* 1267, in Kintbury (Berks), *The Hillockes* 1611, in Wincle (Ches), Hullocks Nook, in Caldwell (Derbys), and Hillocks, in Idridgehay (Derbys), and the related *The Hillockie Feild*

1629, in Aston Iuxta Mondrum (Ches), and Hillocky Close, in Trusley (Derbys). High Hillocks, in Cranleigh (Sur), represents *Hulletlond* 1229 (OE *hylliht* 'hilly'). Old Norse *knottr* and the dialectal *knepp* both signify 'a hillock', e.g. Knot Hill, in Barton upon Humber (Lincs), Kneps, in Thornton, and Knepps, in Preesall (Lancs).

Mine Hillock, in Crich (Derbys), may represent spoil from an excavation. The numerous hillocks and depressions in Hills and Holes, in Barnack (Nthants, now Cambs), result from centuries of medieval quarrying for the ragstone used in the construction of many churches and at least two cathedrals throughout the east of England.[10] This name is also found in Darlton and in Warsop (Notts), as well as in Essendine and (now submerged) in Hambleton in Rutland, in which county also occur Hills and Hales, in Exton, Hills and Dales, in Ryhall, and Humps and Hollows, in Whissendine, denoting land where ironstone was obtained. A similar pairing is found in Hills and Gills (ON *gil* 'a ravine'), in Dacre (YW).

Slopes may be described as *hields* (OE *helde*), found in field-names such as Ellds, in Smethcott (Shrops), The Heald, in Bampton (Westm), The Heald or Yeld, in Derwent, Yelt Flat, in Killamarsh (Derbys), Heald Common (*Le Helde* 1600), in Thurlstone (YW), Heald Field, in Castleford (YW), Healds, in Tebay (Westm), Yields, in Blaisdon (Glos), The Yelds, in Blymhill (Staffs) and in Berrington (Shrops) (illustrated in Plate 3.3). Early examples include *Le Helde* 1302, in Bulkeley, and *Helede* 1357, in Acton (Ches), *Held* 1638, in Norton (Derbys), and *Philippsheld* 1392, in Titsey (Sur). Early names ending in *-helde* are sometimes 'normalized' to *-hill*, e.g. East Hill (*Le Esthelde* 1548), in Carshalton (Sur), or modified in some other way, e.g. Broomhall Mead (*Bromeld* 1500), in Caterham (Sur).

The Bank (*Le Banke* 1296), in Fooloe (Derbys), *Le Banke* 1550, in Swallowfield, and *The Olde Bancke* 1617, in Sonning, Bank Meadow, in Reading, Bankey Piece, in Hurley (Berks), Bankey Field, in West Hoathly, Banky Field, in Hurtstpierpoint (Sus), and Banky Leasow, in Minsterley (Shrops), all indicate land on a slope, or fields containing sloping portions. Noar Hill, in Newton Valence (Hants), includes *ora*, another Old English word for 'a slope'. *Noar* results from misdivision of Middle English *atten ore*, probably found also in The Nore, in Almondsbury (Glos). In similar names elsewhere, however, *Nor* (etc.) means 'north', e.g. Nor Croft (*Northcroft* c. 1200), in Eakring (Notts), and Normead (*North Meade* 1575), in Bitton (Glos). Rampant Down, in West Horsley, and Ramper

Down, in Elstead (Sur), seem to be adapted from *Romping* or *Ramping*, from the dialect word *ramp* 'to descend in a series of steps'. Rampshowe, in Orton (Westm), also contains this element, *howe* being from Old Norse *haugr* 'a mound'. *Rampart* 'an embankment, a raised road through a marsh' is found in Rampart Field, in Lexden (Ess), in Inskip and in Upper Rawcliffe, Ramper, in Thornton and in Wesham (Lancs), and Ramper Close, in Middle Rasen (Lincs).

The sloping nature of selions is expressed in the name *Rysynglondes* 1457, in Castleton (Derbys). *Bench*, relating to terraced hillsides, is found in Kates Bench Clump, in Maiden Bradley (Wilts), on *Kates Bench* (*Cattenbenche* 1385) 'wild cats' bench', a hill gently ascending to 700 feet (230m). Early examples of *bench* include *Benchacre* 1235, in Longbridge Deverill (Wilts), *Benchfurlung c.* 1240, in Sibford Gower (Oxon), *Gretebenche* 1332, in Calne, and *Benchefurlonge* 1570, in Bremhill (Wilts). Green Benches occurs in Chadlington, and Shepherds Bench in Shipton under Wychwood and in Wardington (Oxon). Old Norse *brekka* 'a slope' underlies *Le Breck* 1353, in Runcorn (Ches), Brecks, in Dewsbury (YW) and in

Plate 3.3 The Yelds, Berrington (Shrops)
The name represents Old English *hield*, 'a slope'.

Perlethorpe (Notts), Breck Field, in Poulton (Lancs), and Breck Top, in Warley (YW).

Hanging, either alone, e.g. *Le Hangynde* 1273, in Elsfield (Oxon), or as a specific element, e.g. *Le Honggyngelond*, in Tilston (Ches), alludes to land on a slope. The Hanging, in Eckendon (Oxon), replaces *Hangingfield* 1606; Hangings, in Staverton (Nthants), represents *Hangende Furlong t.* Ric. 2. Hanging Field is found in Walton Derbys), in Baguley (Ches) and in Ridge (Herts), and Hanging Furlong in Bathampton (Som). Old Norse *brant* 'steep land' is found in The Brants, in Airton, Brant Ridding, in Addingham (YW), Brantfield (cf. *Brantfeldwod* 1359), in Bowness on Windermere, Brant Pasture, in Preston Patrick (Westm), and Branthill Close, in Tur Langton (Leics). Brampers, in Bridge Hewick (YW), has developed from *Brantebergh* 12c. 'the steep hill'. Among fanciful names for steep land are Weary Banks, in Glusburn (YW), Tumble-down, in Upwey and in East Stoke, Stumbledown, in Chaldon Herring, and Break Neck, in Steeple (Dor).

In the northern counties of England, the termination *-low* indicates a hill, whereas in the Midlands and south such names were used of tumuli. In the single parish of Abney, in the High Peak area of Derbyshire, can be found Sickley (*Sickley Low* 1687), Bleak Knoll (*Blacklow* 1319), Upper Low, Nether Low, Long Low, Rough Low, Bright Low, Blindlow Flat (*Blind* means 'hidden, covered with vegetation') and Clusterberry Low (all possibly referring to tumuli), as well as other names, indicating 'a hill', such as *Cockehill* 1687, Head Knoll, Bank Head close and Birchway Hat, *Hat* being quite often 'a rounded or hat-shaped hill'.

Flat-topped hills are referred to by the term *Set-cop*, e.g. *Settecop c.* 1200, in Fiskerton (Notts), Setcop, in Martons Both, and Set Cops (*Sett-copps* 1685), in Halton East (YW), and Setcup, in Sutton (Derbys). The term, meaning literally 'seat-hill', has produced many different forms, including Sedcup(s), in Romford and in Kelvedon, Seed Cups, in Nazeing (Ess), Seed Croft (*Sedcop Close* 17c.), in St Paul's Walden (Herts), Set Croft, in Twyning (Glos), Seckup, in Warmingham (Ches), and Side Cops, in Scriven (YW).

Old English *clōh* 'a dell' is at the root of such northern names as *Clow* 13c., in Cranage (Ches), The Clough (*La Cloch c.* 1230), in Whittingham (Lancs), *Le Clogh* 1310, in Minshull Vernon (Ches), *Cloughpightell* 1557, in Wintersett (YW), and High & Low Cleugh, in Langdale (Westm). *Slack* (ON *slakki*) 'a valley, a hollow' is found frequently in field-names in the north of England. Slack occurs in Cabus, in Claughton, and in Stalmine with Staynall (Lancs), Slack

Field, in Crowley (Ches), Mirk Slack 'dark valley', in Whinfell (Westm), Low Slack, in Gluxburn (YW), and Slack Holes Close (*Slackhole Wonge t.* Jas 1), in Wheatley (Notts).

A valley may be deep, generating the field-name Deepdale, found in Kirby Underdale (YE), and in Kirkburn (YE), where its predecessor was *Depedale c.* 1200. *Depedale* 1293 occurs in Fulbourne (Cambs), in 1369 in Puddington (Ches), and *Deipdale* 1482 in South Stainley (YW). Deepdales (*Depedak* early 13c.) occurs on the boundary of Stallingborough with Keelby (Lincs). Debdale, in Islip (Nthants), was *Debbedale* in 1223, whereas the same modern name in West Haddon had the form *Depedale* in 1200. Other instances of Debdale occur in Evington and in Shawell (Leics). *Debden* (OE *dēop, denu*) is also found, e.g. Debden, in Croxton, and Debden Field (*Depedene* 13c., *Debdenfelde* 1494), in Ely (Cambs).

A *slade* is a shallow valley, a piece of greensward in a long depression in the fields, too marshy to cultivate. Field-name examples are *Le Slade* 1444, in Coombe Keynes (Dor), (The) Slade, in Worton (Oxon), in Oakthorpe (Derbys, now Leics), and in Quatford (Shrops), The Slade, in Coulsdon (Sur), dating from 1437, Slaid, in Steeton (YW), Slades, in Fishwick (Lancs), *Rixladesforlong* 1350, in Cirencester (Glos), overgrown with rushes, Broadslade (*Brodeslade* 1321), in Yelvertoft (Nthants), Waterslades (*Waterslade* 1458), in Great Totham (Ess), and Waterslade, in Toft (Cambs). A round depression may generate one of the *Frying Pan* names, or Punchbowl Field, in Meole Brace (Shrops) and in West Hoathly (Sus).

WATERCOURSES AND SPRINGS

Watercourses are important features of the landscape both practically and aesthetically, and are alluded to in numerous field-names. References to rivers are found in River Pasture, in Welford (Berks), *Ucford Meadow* 1591 'meadow by a ford on the river Ock', in Speen (Berks), Trent Meadow, in Newton Solney, and the same name is applied to a large meadow bordered on its north side by the Trent, in Foremark (Derbys), Wharfeside Pasture, grassland beside the river Wharfe, in Thorpe (YW), and Kennet Meadow (*Kenet Mede* 1547), in Enborne (Berks). Humber Furlong (*Humberforlonge* 1580–91), in Goxhill (Lincs), lies beside the Humber; it was one of the divisions of *Humber Field* 1667, the name of which did not survive enclosure.

Streams often made convenient parish boundaries and frequently gave name to common fields and furlongs. *Brook Field* is a great-field name in a number of places, and instances of furlong-names include *Brocfurlong c.* 1197, in Tetsworth, *c.* 1230 in Cuxham (Oxon), and Brook Furlong, in Alresford (Hants), in Berkhamsted (Herts) and in Rosliston (Derbys). Brook Close is found in Tibshelf and in Totley (Derbys), in Lubenham and in Houghton on the Hill (Leics), Brook Flat in Stretton (Derbys), and Brook Meadow in Crowley (Ches). In Sussex, and probably also in Surrey, the term *brook* is used of streamside meadowland, e.g. Brookland (*Broke-londs* 1592), in Forest Row, Brooklands (*Broclond* 1411), in Dallington (Sus), and The Brook (*Broclonde* 1315), in Bramley (Sur). *Yeldale Meade* 1522, the alternative name of Brook Mead (*Brooke-meade* 1522), in Merstham (Sur), indicates that a tax (OE *gield*) was levied on this land.

Beck (ON *bekkr*) occurs in the Danelaw, though it may be found alongside Brook in the field-names of a single parish. *Mylnbeck c.* 1225 is found in Eaglesfield (Cumb), Beck Close, in Pudsey, in Bardsey (YW), in Immingham, in Caistor and in Stallingborough (Lincs), and in Rampton, in Tuxford and in Stokeham (Notts). Fleets (*le Fleete* 1325), in Bratton (Wilts), is beside a small stream (OE *flēot*). *Burna*, another Old English term for 'stream', is found in *La Burnemed* 1182, in Reading, Burlands (*Le Burne Lands* 1547), in Peasemore (Berks). *Bornecroft* 1293, in Nether Peover (Ches), Burn Field, in Haltwhistle, and Burn Banks, in Campton (Westm).[11] A rarer term, meaning 'a watercourse' is found in Waterships, in High Laver, and Water Sheeps Field, in Great Parndon (Ess).

Spring in field-names may allude either to a small source of water or to a copse, and it is not always possible to distinguish one meaning from the other using documentary material alone. Clues are sometimes available, such as Spring Coppice, found in many places, or *Wood side called the Spring* 1609, in Lambley (Notts), pointing to the woodland sense of the term, whereas Spring Close, in Burley (Rut), and *Spring Meadow* 1652, in Church Eaton (Staffs), probably refer to a spring of water. *Sprink* occurs in Cheshire and Shropshire, and may possibly be found in other counties.

The term *Spa* refers to 'a therapeutic mineral spring'. Spa Close occurs in Ossett and in Lockwood (YW), in Thorpe Arnold (Leics) and in West Hallam (Derbys), Spa Meadow in Wrockwardine (Shrops) and in Brockholes (Lancs), Spa Well Meadow in Bexton

(Ches), and Spa Ing in Scammonden (YW). The name is taken from the town in Belgium, known and referred to in England since the sixteenth century. A curative well mentioned in *The Faerie Queene* "did excell and th'English Bath and eke the German Spau",[12] and it is Spenser's spelling of the word (reflecting the pronunciation used until the nineteenth century) which developed into the form found in Lower and Upper Spaw, in Wellington (Shrops), Spaw Well Brow, in Goosnargh (Lancs), Spaw Field, in Sandbach (Ches), Spaw Croft, in Tibshelf, and Spaw Close, in Alfreton (Derbys). The Middle English word *burbel* 'a bubbling spring' is found in Burbles, in Stirton (YW). The same definition applies to *purl* (OE *pyrle*), in Purl Piece, in Rugeley (Staffs). *The Pearlefield* 1611, in Rainow, Pearl (*Pearlfield* 1729), in Widdington, Pearl Field, in Audlem, Pearl Hill, in Buglawton, Big & Little Pearl (*The Pearl Field* 1725), in Christleton, and Pearl Meadow, in Chorley (Ches).

Well names often refer to springs or small streams rather than the pits normally alluded to by the term, though names like Well Garth, in Lawkland (YW), probably have the latter sense. Stinking Well Field, in Rylstone (YW), contained a sulphurous spring of the kind exploited by developers of spas. Flitwell Meadow 'spring of dispute', in Clipston (Nthants), is on the parish boundary. Caudle ('cold well') Meadow is found in Abberton (Worcs) and in Welham (Leics); variants such as *Caldwell, Caudwell, Caudiwell, Cord Well* and *Caldwall* occur, e.g. *Caldewallefeld c.* 1315, in Cannock, *Caldewallesmore* 1300, in Cheslyn Hay (Staffs). Old Norse *kelda* underlies *Cressekeld* 12c. 'cress spring', in Musgrave, *Kaldekelde* 1279, in Shap Rural, and Keld Croft, in Askham (Westm).

SIKES, DRAINS AND POOLS

Sich (OE *sīc*) or *Sike* (ON *sīk*) 'a small stream, especially one in flat marshland' is applied also to the marshy pasture land adjoining such a watercourse. Examples include *Le Quitesechemewdo* 1398 'the meadow by the white sike', in Basford (Ches), Seechcarr, in Layton with Warbreck (Lancs), *Sichefurlange* 1207, in Cowley (Oxon), West Sich, in Holmesfield (Derbys), Sich Bank, in Gnosall (Staffs), Whissage (*Le Whitesyche* 1432), in Great Sutton, Souche (*Le Souchus* 1500), in Rushton, *The Such Meadow* 1639, in Grange (Ches), and Sitch Meadow, in Brewood and in Acton Trussell & Bednall (Staffs). *Le Meresiche c.* 1300, in Lach Dennis (Ches), is 'the sike on a boundary'; Mar Syke, in Colston Bassett (Notts), is on the boundary with Langar. Scandinavian origin or influence can be detected in The Sick (*Syke* 1658), in Newbold & Dunston (Derbys), Ye Sikes, in Bigby (Lincs), *Balland Sick* 1638 'bean-land sike', in Galby (Leics), Kell Sikes, in Barton (Westm), Norman Sick, in Ruddington, and Sike Close, in Holme Pierrepont (Notts). In their account of the sikes in the West Field of Laxton (Notts), amounting to about twenty-five acres in the midst of the arable, the Orwins note that the lands on each side of these little valleys slope downwards to drain into them, and at the heads of the sikes the furlongs are at right angles to those lower down, again facilitating drainage.[13]

The drainage of the fields is referred to in self-evident names, e.g. Drain Field, in Tattenhall (Ches), and those derived from Old English *dīc* or Old Norse *dík*, e.g. *Oldfeldesdiche* 1346, in Rudheath Lordship (Ches), *Diche Mede* 1547, in Enborne (Berks), Ditch End Close, in Burton Overy (Leics), Hemp Dikes, in Bigby (Lincs), *Demesne Dyke* 1620, in Newstead, and Dyke Nook, in Monkridge (Nthumb). Some ditches performed additional functions, e.g. Gosditch, in Elkstone (Glos), favoured by geese, and Washdyke or Sheepdyke Close, in Burley (Rut), for sheep-dipping. Large excavations were sometimes ascribed to superhuman agencies, e.g. *Thorsdiche* 1327 'the giant's ditch' (OE *thyrs* 'a giant'), in Sparsholt (Berks).

Water Furrows (*Waterforowys* 14c.) occurs in Daventry (Nthants) and in Houghton le Spring (Dur), the Water Furrow Field in Norbury (Ches), Water Furrows Close in Owston (Leics), and Wet Furrows in Austrey (Warks). Various explanations have been offered for the name, e.g. spade- or plough-cuts across the furrows to facilitate drainage, but the most persuasive is that these were deeper furrows so ploughed in order to carry off surface water. They were conspicuous enough to pass into field-names, confirming that not every furrow (as might be concluded from some definitions) was a water-furrow.

Water Grip Furs (*Furs* here being 'furrows'), in Ebrington (Glos), confirms an early explanation of *water furrow* quoted in the *Oxford Dictionary*, which equates it with *gryppe* 'a drainage channel', occurring in Many Grips, in Hothersall (Lancs), Grip Tyning, in Bratton (Wilts), Grip Field, in Tollesbury, Gripe Field, in Bradwell-juxta-Mare (Ess), and The Grip, in Hullavington (Wilts), beside a small stream. The dialectal *gote* or *goit* (from OE *gotu*) ' a channel' is used in The Goat, in East Halton, Goat Car, in Cadney (Lincs), and Goyt Croft, in Mottram in Longendale (Ches).

Lache Meadow, in Featherstone (Staffs), Leach Meadow, in

Bispham (Lancs), Latchmoores, in Stansted, Latchmore Bank (*Lachemere* 1276), in Great Hallingbury (Ess), Litch Moor, in Hilton, Leachmere Leasow, in Church Eaton, Big & Little Letchmoor (*Leechmer* 1462–63), in Blymhill (Staffs), and Latchmoor Green (*Lechmore Green* 1739), in Rewe (Dev), contain *lache* 'a stream flowing through boggy land'. On Lechmoor Heath (*Lachemeresheth* 1299), in Aldenham (Herts), is a large muddy pond, which in earlier days possibly covered a greater area. The alternation of *-moor* and *-mere* in *Latchmore* names indicates the seasonal change between wet land and actual pools of water, which can often be seen on moors in winter.

Lake in field-names is likely to mean 'a stream' (OE *lacu*) rather than 'lake' in the usual modern sense, e.g. Dig Lake, in Lymm (Ches), in which *Dig* may be the dialect word for 'duck', and Duck Lake, in Walgherton (Ches). A small natural lake (ON *tjorn*) is referred to in *Tarne Flatt* 1539, in Shap Rural (Westm), Tarn Acre, in Pilling, Tarn Croft, in Barnacre and in Inskip, Tarn Field in Nateby (Lancs), *The Tarne Close* 1657, in Ormside, Tarnfield, in Brougham (Westm), and Tarnbanks (*Ternebanck* 1294), in Egremont (Cumb), *Pullforlonge* 14c., in Middlewich, *Pullmeduus* 1338, in Lymm, and *Le Pullondes* 1347, in Bulkeley (Ches), are from Old English *pull*, a variant of the more usual *pōl*, from which are derived Swanspool (*Swanepol* 1390), in Peterborough (Nthants, now Cambs), *Le Polmedowe* 1473, in Thornton le Moore (Ches), and Pollardine (OE *worthign* 'an enclosure'), in Ratlinghope (Shrops). References to ponds include Pond Ing (*Ponde Inge* 1592), in Binley (YW), Pond Field (*Pondacre* 1425), in Bushey (Herts), and Pond Meadow, in West Alvington (Dev). Fishpond Close, in Patrington, and Little Fishpond Fields, in Benningholme (YE), are not necessarily medieval. Puddle Field, in Sandbach (Ches), and similar names may refer merely to ill-drained fields, or to land containing pools of some dimensions.

The Flashes, in Gnosall (Staffs), Flash Croft, in Wincle (Ches) and in Upper Rawcliffe (Lancs), Flash Field, in Newbold Ashbury (Ches), Flash (*Flosh* 1742), in Brough, and Flosh, in Stainmore (Westm), refer to flooded grassland, e.g. where rivers have encroached on subsided land over salt-workings. Flax Meadow (*Flaskmedowe* 1524), in Lymm (Ches), also belongs with these names, which originate in Middle English *flasshe* or Old Danish *flask*. Dam 'a pool or pond', often made by stopping up a stream, is embodied in *Ye Damme Furlonge* 1577, in Croxton (Lincs) *Damfurlonge* 1586, in Theddingworth (Leics), Dam Field in Easington (YE), and Mill Dam Field (*Mylledame Flatte* 1570), in Baswich (Staffs). The Dam Fields, in Puddington (Ches), refer to a medieval water-mill dam. *Stanch* and *Stank* 'a dam' are found in Stanch Meadow, in Fotheringhay (Nthants), Stank Leasow, in Condover (Shrops), Stank Land, in Thorpe (YW), and Stanks Meadow, in Rowington (Warks).

Water supplies for canals, irrigation and the watering and dipping of animals may involve such equipment as reservoirs and pumping houses, or designated sections of streams and other watercourses. Such features are alluded to in Reservoir Field, in Welton, Pump Field, in Willerby (YE), Pumphouse Close, in Newton Solney (Derbys), Pumphouse Piece, in Chilcote (Derbys, now Leics), Pump Meadow and Sheepwash Meadow, in Rugeley, *Weare Meadow* 1599, in Church Eaton, Weir Meadow, in Forton (Staffs), Conduit Field, in Sturry (Kent), and *Le Waysshing Place* 1551, in Coleshill (Berks).

NOTES AND REFERENCES

1. Explained by P.H. Reaney, *The Place-Names of Essex*, p. 600, citing Hennell, *Change in the Farm*, p. 64.
2. The Gloucestershire EPNS editor cites W.J. Arkell and S.I. Tomkeieff, *English Rock Terms* (Oxford, 1953), p. 19.
3. Based on a private communication from Mrs Ann Cole, who kindly provided the pebbles illustrated in Plate 3.1.
4. J. Aubrey, *Natural History of Wiltshire* (ed. J. Britton, 1847), p. 56, quoted in E. Kerridge, *The Agricultural Revolution* (1967), p. 261.
5. From an extract from R. Plot, *Natural History of Oxfordshire* (1677), pp. 239–44, quoted in Gray, pp. 131–3, here p. 132.
6. G.O. Pierce, *The Place-Names of Dinas Powys Hundred* (Cardiff, University of Wales Press, 1968), p. 206.
7. A. Cole, 'The distribution and usage of the OE place-name *Cealc*', *Journal of the English Place-Name Society* **19** (1986–87), pp. 44–55, here p. 48.
8. N. Neilson, 'Customary rents', in P. Vinogradoff, *Oxford Studies in Social and Legal History* (Oxford, Clarendon Press, 1910), Vol. II, p. 8.
9. B. Kerr, *Bound to the Soil* (Baker, 1968), pp. 28–9.
10. See J. Stean, *The Northamptonshire Landscape* (Hodder & Stoughton, 1974), pp. 79–80 and Plate 11.

11. See A. Cole, '*Burna* and *brōc*', *Journal of the English Place-Name Society* **23** (1990–91), pp. 26–48.
12. E. Spenser, *The Faerie Queene*, I. xi. 30.
13. C.S. and C.S. Orwin, *The Open Fields* (Oxford, Clarendon Press, 1938, 3rd edn 1967), pp. 97–8.

CHAPTER FOUR

Woodlands and wild life

TREES IN THE LANDSCAPE

The temptation to dismiss as commonplace description some of the terms occurring in field-names is perhaps nowhere so great as with reference to woodlands. Seen today by the urban visitor as decorative contrasts to the severe geometry of virtually hedgeless arable fields, wooded areas are thought to be picturesque places that the plough cannot reach. A closer study of the history of woodlands in the landscape, and the significance of the terminology in place-names and field-names, will disabuse the observer of the notions of the accidental character of these attractive features or of the casual nature of many of their names.

Woodlands have been an essential part of the rural economy since before records of field-names began. They included what remained of the 'wildwood' as well as deliberately planted and systematically managed areas of trees, grown not merely for their timber but also for other products. Pigs fed on acorns and beech-mast; cattle could browse on young growth; rods from pollarded willows were used to weave basketry utensils of various kinds; oak-bark was used in tanning hides; fallen leaves were used as a manure and soil-conditioner; dead wood was used for fuel. Coppicing and pollarding also provided material of appropriate length and thickness for such tasks as hurdle-making, turnery and cleft-pole fencing. This list is by no means exhaustive, and many of these applications are referred to in field-names. But even modern names of copses and plantations invite a detailed exploration of their wide variety.

As the name of one of the common fields, *Wood Field* is found throughout the country. Great Wood Field survived into the nineteenth century in Epsom (Surrey), and *Wodefurlong* 1450 was almost certainly one of its constituent parts. *Wood* combines with a wide range of other generic elements, including *Acre(s)*, *Close*, *Holme*, *Ing*, *Land(s)*, *Leasow*, *Mead(ow)*, *Nook* and *Pightle*.

CLUMPS AND COPPICES

Besides providing a reference-name for adjoining fields, e.g. *Coppice Field* or *Plantation Close*, many groups of trees are themselves named. *Plantation* is a term found only in recent names, in some of which the term has been added to an earlier name which already implies this. Nockatt Plantation, in Longbridge Deverill (Wilts), may be compared with *Nocketts* 1591, in Oaksey (Wilts). These names probably represent Middle English *at then okette* 'at the clump of oaks'. Weskew Plantation, in Barton (Westm), is 'west wood', *skew* being from Old Norse *skógr* 'a wood'.

Trees are often planted on land unsuitable for arable crops. Some of the *Hungerhill Plantations* can be accounted for in this way. Bunker's Hill Plantation, in West Stafford (Dor), is doubtless utilizing land that had defeated other attempts to cultivate it. Similarly the soil of Honey Butts Plantation, in Owthorpe (Notts), would probably have been too sticky for normal cultivation. Land previously eroded by mineral excavations or put to industrial use might also be planted with trees. Chalkpit Plantation, in Woodditton (Cambs), is on and around a chalkpit in existence before the sixteenth century. Chalkdell Wood, in Knebworth and in St Peter's (Herts), are on old chalk diggings. Claypit Wood, in Farnham (Sur), is on or near *Clayputt*, recorded in a 1278 Rental. Other examples are Gravelpit Plantation, in Snailwell (Cambs), and Sandhill Plantation, in Carlton in Lindrick (Notts); *Sandpittis* were mentioned in Carlton in 1316. Peatpits Wood, in Tidmarsh (Berks), and Slatepit Plantation, in Barlow (Derbys), are among less common names of the type.

The terms *Coppice* or *Copse* occur frequently. The form *Copy* arose from taking as plurals such spellings as are found in, e.g., *Brockholds Copies* 1669, in Gretton (Nthants), or *Burye Copyes* 1542, in Salford Priors (Warks). The term has a technical meaning, 'woodland managed by coppicing, i.e. the removal of the main stem of the tree and harvesting the subsequent young growths', but is now used loosely for plantations in general, irrespective of the details of management. Clay Bank Coppice, in Wolford (Warks), was perhaps planted on land unsuitable for tillage, though *Clehullesland* 1224 suggests that it may then have been arable. The same soil seems to be found in Clay Copse, in Tilehurst (Berks), earlier *Clay Croft and Pightle*. Deadlands Copse, in Whittington (Glos), is a plantation on arable land which has gone out of use, perhaps because of infertility. There is an interchange with *Wood*, *Spinney* (discussed below) and *Plantation* in some places. Thornyfield Wood, in Nuneaton (Warks), was *Thorne Fild Copice* in 1591. Presgrave Copse, in Gretton (Nthants), was *Prestgrave c.* 1400 'the priest's grove' and became *Prisgrave al. Broadoke Copies* in 1609. The form *Grave* (OE *grāf*) is often found for 'grove'; another variant is *Greave*, from Old English *græfe*.

F.T. Wainwright noted the continued existence in Lancashire of hundreds of marl-pits, many surviving as ponds "or as pleasant dells with massive oaks to prove both age and long disuse".[1] Marlpit Plantation, in Catton (Derbys), and Marlfield Shaw (from OE *sceaga* 'a small wood, a copse'), in Coulsdon (Sur), are examples of tree-planting on such land. Marlpits are on record in two Sussex parishes where the name Marlpit Shaw occurs; there was a *Hye Marlyngpette* in 1519 in Salehurst and *Le Marlyngge* in Northiam in 1398. Marlpit Spinney, in Walton upon Trent (Derbys), may now be on the site of *Colens Marle Pyt* 1565. Marl Copse, in Aston Clinton (Bucks), however, is traceable to *Marrwell* 1639 'boundary spring', and is in fact on the parish boundary.

Quarry Wood, in Sherborne (Glos), is on the site of a quarry recorded in the thirteenth century. Brickiln Copse, in Braydon (Wilts), Brickkiln Coppice, in Purton (Wilts), Kiln Copse, in Swallowfield (Berks), Limekiln Plantation, in Widdington (Ess) and in Hodsock (Notts), and Limekiln Copse, in Cumnor (Berks, now Oxon), either adjoin the site of the kiln or occupy the land no longer housing it. Sandpit Copse, in Woodley (Berks), occupies the former *Sandpittes*, recorded in 1604. Lambpit Copse, in Woodborough (Wilts), is a former loam-pit. *Glassehouse Coppice* 1650, in Kenilworth (Warks), alludes to a *glasshouse*, which in the seventeenth century was a glass-works, not a greenhouse. The coppice would have been a source of charcoal for the furnace, as in Glazier's Copse, in Landford (Wilts).

In West Stafford (Dor), Sandy Barrow Plantation is by a tumulus. Some of the instances of *Cuckoo Pen*, which are often plantations of trees on the summits of hills, may be survivals of groves or other ritual sites, left uncleared and protected by the trees to prevent

Plate 4.1   Plantation on a former lime-pit, near King's Lynn (Norfolk)

desecration. There may be up to two dozen instances of *Cuckoo Pen* in Oxfordshire, more than a dozen in Gloucestershire, and it has been noted in other counties, particularly in central and southern England. Garden Copse, in the same parish, inevitably evokes Goldsmith's line "Near yonder copse, where once the garden smiled" but probably relates to a scene not nearly so melancholy. Prestfurlong Plantation, in Brailsford (Derbys), is evidently by or in a piece of land called *Prestfurlong* 'the priest's furlong', but of this there is no other record, though the form of the name suggests an early origin. Near Telegraph Plantation, in Alderholt (Dor), the remains of a telegraph are marked on the 6-inch OS map. These telegraphs were nineteenth-century structures, used for military signalling across the country. In the same parish Cripplestyle Plantation alludes to a barrier passable by sheep, one that could be crept through by them. Gallows Hill Plantation, in Arne (Dor), is where a gallows might be expected, namely where the road between Corfe Castle and Wareham crosses the Arne parish boundary with Corfe Castle.

A *spinney* is literally 'a plantation of thorn trees' but current usage allows the term to be more generally applied. Long Spinney Copse and Round Spinney Copse, in Kingston Lisle (Berks), may be associated with a pasture called *Le Espiney* 1234–35, *Le Spiney* 1241, very early evidence of the term *spinney*, not recorded in literature until 1600. Other modern examples include Spinney Close, in Netherseal (Derbys, now Leics), in Desford, in Kibworth Beauchamp and in Shangton (Leics), Spinney Field, in Biggleswade (Beds), and Spinneys Meadow, in Caldwell (Derbys).

Belt and *Clump* are terms for fairly small plantations, e.g. The Belt, in Shareshill (Staffs), Lower Belt, in Hilton (Staffs), and Lockinge Clump, in Lockinge (Berks). Maggot Clump, in Blandford St Mary (Dor), probably alludes to the magpie, under its dialect name. In Wiltshire and possibly other southern counties *Rag* is used of a small patch of woodland. Rag Mead, in Purton (Wilts), may be near *The Ragg* recorded in 1649. Rag, in Brinkworth (Wilts), occurs alongside other woodland-related names, such as Roundabout, Copid Ash, The Folly and Purlieu, on the edge of Braydon Forest. *Roundabout* names signify either small pieces of land completely surrounded by trees or, more often, a group of trees encircled by cleared land. A plantation of young trees may, as has been mentioned in the previous chapter, sometimes be described as a *spring*, e.g. Spring, in Wighill (YW), Sprink, in Blakenhall (Ches), Spring Coppice, in Brewood, Spring Coppice Piece, in Essington (Staffs), Spring Plantation, in Alderwasley (Derbys), Spring Wood, in Skegby (Notts), Springslade Wood, in Acton Trussell (Staffs) and Birk Spring, in Wothersome (YW).

Folly is occasionally used of clumps of trees, usually isolated plantations on hill-tops or on open land. Examples are Little Folly, a tiny plantation in Lockinge (Berks), and The Folly, in Napton on the Hill (Warks), in Eastleach Turville (Glos) in Hope (Derbys) and a number of other places. Both the derivation and the reason for the application of the term have been disputed, but *Folly* was first used to denote extravagant buildings and mock ruins in landscaped parks, and then the word was applied to some hill-top plantations resembling such structures. Folly Clump, in Childrey (Berks), is on a hill, and Folly Trees, in Steventon (Berks), is a small copse planted on a mound. Other examples are Folly Copse, in Stitchcombe (Wilts) and in Hartlebury (Worcs), Castle Plantation, in Cheveley (Cambs), earlier *Castle Folly*, like Hay Stack Folly and Red Gate Folly in the same parish, a small copse.

Commemorative names recalling people and events have often been given to plantations, e.g. Waterloo Copse and Wellington Wood, in Watchfield (Berks). In Teddesley Hay (Staffs) there are both Cromwell's Clump and Wellington Belt. Crimea Wood, in Hankelow, and Sebastopol Covert, in High Legh (Ches), commemorate the Crimean War. Jubilee Plantation, at Staunton in the Vale (Notts), was established in 1809. George III's jubilee had been celebrated on 25 October, the day before the commencement of the fiftieth year of his reign.

Jubilee Clump, in Chute (Wilts), was formerly called Whistling Ground, from its windswept location; the more dignified name commemorates Queen Victoria's jubilee of 1887, recalled also in Queen's Field in the same parish. Coronation Plantation, in Stratton (Dorset), was established in 1902 and named in honour of the crowning of Edward VII. "In the same year," observes Barbara Kerr, "Coronation Plantation, soon followed by other coverts, marked the end of grazing rights on the downland." Two of these 'other coverts' commemorate the war of 1914–18: Great War Plantation and (nearby) Prisoners of War Plantation. The latter alludes to a large camp for German prisoners at Dorchester in 1915–16.[2]

St Mary's Wood (*Seyntmariwode* 1345), in Fineshade (Nthants), alludes to the dedication of the priory, and Lady Wood, in Knossington (Leics), would have a similar reference. Ellen's Coppice, in Tarrant Crawford (Dor), may refer to Queen Eleanor, patron of the abbey. Queen's Coppice, in More Crichel (Dor), is in a detached part of Gussage St Michael, a manor held by a number of queens of England. King's Copse, in Swallowfield (Berks), commemorates the royal manor here in 1086. Earl's Wood (*Erleswode* 1285), in Syresham (Nthants), refers to the Earl of Leicester, the local lord in the reign of Henry II. Surnames of owners or their senior employees are found in some wood-names. Further and Hither Daggons Wood is named from the family of Richard *Dagon*, recorded in the Subsidy Roll of 1327. The name of Devil's Head Plantation, in Great Warley (Ess), has been playfully or unwittingly adapted from the surname of John Deville 1310, whose family owned land in Great Warley. Some descriptive names have been modified to resemble surnames. Birch's Wood, in Tolleshunt Knights (Ess), was merely *Birchwood* in 1588. Wynall's Copse, in Bucklebury (Berks), was *Wynde Hill Copis* in 1622–23.

Man Wood (*Manewode* 1235), on the boundary of White Roding

and Matching (Ess), is 'common wood'. Meanwood (*Menewode* 1270), in Whiteparish (Wilts), lies on the parish and county boundary. The first element (OE (*ge*)*mǣne*) signifies 'common or boundary land', to which also the frequent *No Man* names refer. Nomanshill Wood (*Nomannes Wode t.* Ed.3), in Sutton in Ashfield (Notts), lies at the junction of Kirkby, Blidworth and Sutton. Such land was often free of jurisdiction, and the alternative *Forswornewod* 1287 reflects the function of a 'nomansland' in the harbouring of outlaws. Woodlands on boundaries offer scope for territorial disputes, witness *Strifwode* 1316, in Shrewsbury (Shrops), and the various examples of *Threap Wood*.

Setting trees in regular rows will normally produce geometrical outlines which contrast with the lighter-coloured land adjoining plantations and invite the observer to identify them by their shape. More or less literal descriptions include Round Copse, in Cookham (Berks) and in Cranborne (Dor), which also has a Long Copse. Oval Plantation is found in Wareham (Dor), and Triangle Plantation in Bessels Leigh (Berks). Fanciful descriptive names abound, e.g. Half Moon Clump, in Castleton (Dor), Halfmoon Covert, in Lambourn (Berks), and Halfmoon Plantation, in Eckington (Derbys) and in Worksop (Notts), where there is also an Ale Bottle Clump. Elsewhere characteristic shapes are named in Swallowtail Wood, in Syresham (Nthants), Shoulder of Mutton Plantation, in Hooton (Ches) and in Greenstead (Ess), Spectacle Plantation, in Babworth (Notts). Cocked Hat Plantation, in Elkesley (Notts), Cocked Hat Copse, in Filkins (Oxon), Boot and Shoe Plantation, in Kirby Underdale (YE), and Horseshoe Plantation, in Aldwark (Derbys). Conventional symbols are alluded to in Heart Clump, in Hungerford (Berks), and Diamond Plantation, in Folkton (YE). Letters of the alphabet are also used as names, e.g. B Plantation, V Plantation and Y Plantation, in Blandford St Mary (Dor).

Other groups of trees may be named by their numbers. A pair of trees gave name to Two Thorn Fields (*Toothornefeilde* 1625), in Hope Woodlands (Derbys). Four Sisters, in Grovely Wood (Wilts), was *Rodnell alias the Foure Sisters Cops* in 1589. Four Oaks, in Beckley (Sus), is the recent name for *Brownsmiths Oaks*. Four Oaks also occurs in Dadlington (Leics) and in Berkswell (Warks). In Oxfordshire there are Five Ash Bank, in Idbury, and Five Oak Copse, in Wychwood. The numerical category also includes Seven Oaks, in Challow (Berks) and in Horsforth (YW), and Seven Ash (*Sevenash* 1326), in Kentisbury (Dev). Seven Sisters is the name of a group of elm trees in Lindrick (YW). In Greater London, *Seven*

Sisters and *Nine Elms* have given their names to neighbourhoods, though the elm trees themselves disappeared long ago.

REFERENCES TO TREE SPECIES

An oak tree is usually conspicuous enough to provide a landmark, and land containing or near such a tree will be named accordingly, e.g. *Ackfurlong* 1627, in Brewood (Staffs), Far & Near Oak Tree Close, in Desford (Leics), and Oak Meadow, in Castle Church (Staffs). Noke Field, in Abbots Langley (Herts), is formed by misdivision of *atten oke* 'at the oak'. Park Glaston (Corn. *glastan*), in St Clement (Corn), and Green Oak Meadow, in Netherseal (Derbys), refer to the holm oak (*Quercus ilex*). Old Norse *eik* accounts for such forms as *Aykwode* 13c. 'oak wood', in Stainton (YW). Cae Derwen 'oak field', in Clun (Shrops), is one of the Welsh names found in border parishes. *The Wookes* 1575, in Longney (Glos), reflects the local pronunciation of *Oaks*.

Individual or groups of oak trees, embellished with descriptive terms, are also referred to. Broad Oaks, in Solihull (Warks), is on record from the seventeenth century. The Pedlar's Oak, in Oakmere (Ches), stood by an old road from Eddisbury Hill to Crabtreegreen, and was doubtless a way-marker. Chapel Oak, in Salford Priors (Warks), is on land endowed for the benefit of Abbots Salford chapel, formerly held by Evesham Abbey. The Brundocks, in Occlestone (Ches), means 'the burnt oaks', and other *Burnt Oak* names are found elsewhere, e.g. *Burntoake* 1679, in Waldron (Sus), *Burned-oke* 1556, in Prittlewell, Burnt Oak Field, in High Laver (Ess), Burnt Oak Close, in Edgware (Middx), Brand Oak, in Leigh (Glos), and Bran Oak, in Pontesbury (Shrops). Shire Rack, in Bower Chalke (Wilts), probably for *Shire Ack* ('shire oak'), is at the meeting-point of the boundaries of Wiltshire, Hampshire and Dorset.

References to the ash (*Fraxinus excelsior*) are usually in easily intelligible forms such as Ash Tree Piece, in Somersal Herbert (Derbys), Ashfield Close, in Tirley (Glos), and Ash Furlong, in Fifehead Neville (Dor). Some of these may be plantations, rather than arable closes adjoining the ash trees. Ash Close Meadow in Brocklesby (Lincs), is identified with *Ashe Closse replenyshed with young Aishes*, mentioned in 1587, and the name *Ash Spring Close* is used for it in 1629 (*Spring* here meaning 'plantation of young trees'). Twizzle Ash (*Twizle Ash* 1623), in Grittleton (Wilts), alludes to a 'forked ash tree'. *Ashen* 'growing with ash trees' is seen in Ashen Croft (*Asshincroft* 1501), in Knowle (Warks) and in Ashnal, in Church Eaton (Staffs), the second element of the latter being *halh* 'a nook'. *Ascow* 1454 'ash wood', in Caldy (Ches), is a Scandinavian compound from *askr* with *skógr*. Eskholme Meadow, in Pilling (Lancs) is from Old Norse *eski* 'a place growing with ash trees'. Misdivision of Middle English *atten ashe* 'at the ash tree' has produced Nash Field, in Little Hadham (Herts), and Nash Hill, in Lacock (Wilts), referred to in 1331 as *locus vocatus* ['the place called'] *Atten Asche*. Modern names such as *Ash Yard* or *Ash Garth* probably refer to tipping places for domestic ashes rather than to the tree.

The birch may be referred to by the normal modern name, as in Birch Dale, in Picton (Ches), Birch Coppice, in Pimperne (Dor), and Birch Holt, in Unstone (Derbys). The termination in Birchet Field, in Charlwood, and Birchett Copse (*Byrchet* 1462), in Horley (Sur), means 'a copse', making the addition unnecessary. *Birchen*, found in Birchen Field (*Birchenfeilde* 1578), in Cannock, and Birchen Leasow (*Byrchen Leysoe* 1571), in Brewood (Staffs), means 'growing with birches', synonymous with Old Norse *birki*, found in The Birks, in Whitwell (Derbys), and Birks, in Morland (Westm).

Field-name references to the alder (OE *alor*), *Alnus glutinosa*, are many and varied, including Alder Leasow, in Brewood (Staffs), Aldersmead, in Spettisbury (Dor), Alders, in Bretby (Derbys), Allers (*Nallars* 1607), in Haselbury Bryan (Dor), *Le Ollerfyeld* 1424, in Norton (Ches), Owler Field, in Butley (Ches), Owlers, in Hathersage (Derbys) and in Weeton with Preese (Lancs), and Ollars, in Cleveley (Lancs). Eller Close, in Nether Wyresdale, and Ellar Field, in Pilling (Lancs), are from *elri*, the Old Norse word for 'alder'. *Aldercar* 'a marsh growing with alders', e.g. Alder Carr (*Alderfan* 1429), in Stebbing (Ess), *Ellerkere* 1345, in North Elmsall (YW), *Ellercar* 1540, in Askham (Westm), occurs so often that *Carr* (ON *kjarr* 'brushwood, a marsh') is regarded as indicating this tree. Cornish *guern* 'an alder' has a similar generalized meaning. Warneck, in Camborne, and Warnick, in Crowan (Corn), are based on the adjectival form of *guern*. Alracks (*Alrettefeld* 14c.), in Gestingthorpe (Ess), and Alder-woods (*Alderette* 1548), in Ash (Sur), signify 'a clump of alders'.

Outside the Danelaw, early forms in *Eller*, *Ellern* refer to the elder, e.g. *Elleforlang* early 14c., in Sturminster Marshall (Dor). Allusions to these shrubs (OE *ellern*) are usually recognizable from modern spellings *Elder* or *Eldern*, e.g. Elderns, in Henbury (Glos), Eldershaw Piece, in Essington (Staffs). Another Old English word, *ellen* 'elder', helps identification even where Scandinavian *elri* 'alder' forms are to be found, e.g. Ellenhurst, in Thelwall (Ches). A *hurst* (OE *hyrst*) is a tree-covered hill. In Little Neston (Ches) there are both Alder Graves and Elder Graves. Scawn Hill, in Pilleton (Corn), is from Cornish *scawen* 'an elder tree'. No problems are presented by the Elder Stubs, in Morden (Dor), in Banstead (Sur) (*Elderstubbe* 1618) and in a considerable number of other places. Elders Stumps is found at Ecton (Nthants). Neltro (*Le Eltrowe* 1345) '(at the) elder tree', in Bisley (Sur), like *Nash* and *Noke* names, preserves part of *atten* 'at the'. An alternative name for the elder is *bourtree* or *burtree*, occurring in field-names in the north of England, e.g. Burtyberry, in Thornton (Lancs), Burtree Bank (*Beurtrebanc c.* 1285), in Lowther, and Burtree Bush, in Brough Sowerby (Westm). *Bush* here has the sense of 'a bed (of shrubs or other plants), a copse'.

The aspen (*Populus tremula*) is not so well represented in field-names as are the alder, ash and oak, but it is found in a variety of spellings. *Aspen* is the adjective, the original form of the tree-name being *asp* (Old English *æspe* or *æpse*), found in Asp, in Chilcote (Derbys), Asps, in Albrighton (Shrops), and Asp Tree Croft, in Irby (Ches), to be compared with *Aspen Croft* 1635, in Forton, and Aspen Leasow, in Brocton (Staffs). Esps, in Baschurch, Espleys, in Eaton under Heywood (Shrops) and *Le Espenfeld* 1329, in Chidlow (Ches), are from the Mercian dialect forms *esp*, *espen*. Aspenny (*Asphanger* 1300), in Hullavington (Wilts), is 'aspen slope'. *Apse* forms are found in Apse Field, in Redbourn (Herts), in *Appsehey* 1580, in Cherington (Glos), and Apshanger (*Asphanger* 17c.), in Kingsclere (Hants). Apsleys, in Almondsbury (Glos), does not refer to the tree; it was earlier *Abbotisley* 1540 'the abbot's wood'.

The yew tree (*Taxus baccata*), planted in churchyards because, according to a seventeenth-century writer, "it attracts and imbibes putrefaction and gross oleaginous vapours exhaled out of the Graves by the setting Sun",[3] can also be found on or near agricultural land, despite its poisonous foliage and seed. Yew Platt occurs in Cadney (Lincs), Yew Tree Close in Crich (Derbys) Yew Tree Leasow in Weston Jones (Staffs), and Yew Tree Field in Sutton Downes (Ches), in Debden and in High Easter (Ess).

Poplar Tree Field, in Fingringhoe, Poplar Field, in Ashdon and in Bardfield Saling (Ess), Poplar Holt, in Immingham (Lincs), and Poplar Leasow, in Much Wenlock (Shrops) refer to the tree (*Populus spp.*), the Welsh name of which is found in Maes-y-Poblysin, in West Felton (Shrops). Other tree species are alluded to in Maple Copse, in Ashampstead (Berks), Maple Croft (*Mapullcroft* 1577), in Stebbing (Ess), and Beech Field (*Bechefelde* 1305), in Sandridge (Herts). Elm Tree Piece occurs in Sudbury (Derbys), Elbeam (for *Elmbeam*) Common in Elstead (Sur), and the adjectival form *elmen* in *Elmon' Stubbe* 1508, in Sturminster Marshall (Dor). Alm Slack, in Patterdale (Westm), is from Old Norse *almr* 'an elm tree', with *slakki* 'a hollow'. *Wychegrave* 1298, in Sturminster Marshall (Dor), alludes to a grove of wych-elms (*Ulmus glabra*). Wicken Meadow, in Over Alderley (Ches), and Wicken Pingle, in Hope (Derbys), refer to the rowan (ME *quiken*). Park an Gerthen 'rowan-tree field', in Ludgvan (Corn) is from Cornish *kerden*.

Trees marking boundaries had to be firm-rooted, long-lived and conspicuous; oak, ash, yew, and thorns were much favoured. Yew Tree Field is on the boundary of Cranborne (Dor) with Damerham (Wilts, now Hants). Old English *land-scearu* 'a boundary' is found in *La Stubbe vocat' La Landscharethorne c.* 1325 'the stump called the Boundary Thorn', in Buckland Newton (Dor). *Merethorn* 977 (OE (*ge*)*mǣre* 'a boundary') is a landmark in the bounds of Kingston Bagpuize (Berks). Mere Ash, in Bratton (Wilts) is on the county boundary. Mear Oak Field is on the boundary of Smisby (Derbys). Holy Oak Close, near the parish boundary of Donhead St Mary (Wilts), alludes to the ceremony of beating the bounds, to be discussed in a later chapter. Mark Oak Close, in Northington (Hants), is from *mearc*, another Old English word for 'boundary'. Cuckoo Oak is on the Cranage/Allostock boundary (Ches).

A pollarded or topless tree would be a recognizable landmark, e.g. in boundaries or as assembly places, as we are occasionally reminded by such minor names as *Copped Oak* and *Copthorn*. Copthorn, in Worth (Sus), goes back to *Copplethorne* 1437. Another Copthorne (*Coppedethorne* 1437) is found in Burstow, near the Surrey/Sussex boundary. *Le Coppedethorne* 1286 occurs in Shirley (Derbys), and *Copthornfeld* 1423 in Rickmansworth (Herts). Copton Bush, in Brightwalton (Berks), goes back to *Le Coppedethorne t.* Ed.1. Copythorn Cross, in Aveton Giffard (Dev), and Copy Thorn, in Dorchester (Oxon) and in Shrivenham (Berks), have probably been adapted from *Copthorn* or *Copped Thorn*, with which Copy Thorn (*Copped Thorn Furlong* 1677), in Seagry (Wilts), may be compared. Copytrough, in West Ashton (Wilts), is a fairly well-disguised form of 'copped tree'.

Sweet Willey Tree, in Ellerker (YE), and Sweet Willow Carr, in Brocklesby (Lincs), refer to the sweet-bay willow (*Salix pentandra*), which was cultivated or encouraged because a valuable infusion against ague could be made from its bark. The isolation of its active principle, salicin, led to the discovery of the properties of salicylic acid, the basis of aspirin. Osier Holt, in Lincoln, Osier Close, in Shearsby (Leics), and Ozier Ground, in Fifehead Magdalen (Dor), and in twenty or more parishes in Essex, are likely to refer to *Salix viminalis*, the true osier. Stream-side or pool-side cultivation of various kinds of willow is recorded in Wergen Pits, in Draycott Moor, Willow Bed Mead, in Welford (Berks), Sally Beds, in Toddington (Glos), Withy Bed, in Almondsbury, *Le Withie Beds* 1622, in Hanham Abbots (Glos), Withy Pits, in Longcot (Berks), Withlands, in North Kelsey (Lincs) and Withy Hayes (*Wythyheyes* 1540), in Lacock (Wilts). Regular harvests of pliant withies were obtained by the pollarding of such trees, providing raw materials for basketry, hurdle-making and other crafts. *Le Wiccres* 12c. occurs in Malham (YW), alluding to *wicker*, as in *wicker-work*, for material made from plaited withies.

Other members of the willow family are alluded to in *Wiligholm* 13c., in Immingham (Lincs), The Willow Ings, in Nettleton (Lincs),

Plate 4.2 Harvesting withies, Somerset

Sallow Close, in Buckminster (Leics) and in Freethorpe (Norf), and Salinge Meadow, in Lilleshall (Shrops). The dialect form *werg* is found in Worg Furlong, in Appleton with Eaton, *Wirge Furlonge* 1614, in Grove, *The Wirge* 1628, in East Hendred (Berks), *The Wergs* 1652, in Longford (Shrops), Wergs (*The Wirg* 17c), in Stratfieldsaye, and Wurgs Shaw, in Hartley Wespall (Hants).

There are numerous references to both wild and cultivated fruits. The apple is mentioned in field-names of all periods, e.g. *Appeltrebankes* 1270, in Crosby Ravensworth (Westm), Appelwraye (*Appelwra* 1296), in Torpenhowe (Cumb), *Bradappeldure t.* Ed.1 'broad apple tree' (OE *apuldor*), in Hurley (Berks), and Appletree Field (*Appeltonefelde* 1411), in High Easter (Ess). Allusions to the crab-apple include Crab Close, in Hammoon (Dor), Crab Tree Field (*Le Crabbetrowefeld t.* Ed.2), in Knebworth (Herts), Crabtree Field (*Crabtre Feld* 1440), in Peldon (Ess) and Crab Tree Pightle, in Cantley (Norf). *Crabbefurlong c.* 1300, in Elton (Ches), has a modern counterpart in Heath Chapelry (Shrops), where there is also Perry Meadow (OE *pirige* 'a pear tree'). Perry Field is common in Essex, going back, e.g., to *Pyryfeld* 1289, in Feering, *Pirfeld* 1363, in Stebbing, and *Peryfeilde* 1592, in Gestingthorpe. Other examples are *Piriteghe* 15c. 'pear-tree enclosure', in Wye (Kent), Perries (*Peryes* 1585), in Hale (Ches), and Pear Tree Field (*Piriefeld* 1332), in Ridge (Herts). Cherry Garden (*Chery Garden t.* Hy 8), in Wix (Ess), Cherry Crote Field, in Mucking (Ess), Plymebarrows, in Blakenhall (Ches) 'plum woods' (OE *plyme, bearu*), and The Mulberry Close, in West Rasen (Lincs), are among the other fruit trees named. Hazel Butts, in Whinfell (Westm), and Hazel Mead, in Sherington (Bucks), are clear enough, but Hesland (*Heseland* 13c.), in Desborough (Nthants), and *Heselscales* 1295, in Uldale (Cumb), are less obvious in meaning, being from Old Norse *hesli*. Bannut Tree Close, in Aylburton, Bannut Leaze, in Lydney, and Bannut Tree Orchard, in Dymock (Glos), refer to the walnut, named more conventionally in *Walnut Garth* 1666, in Tealby (Lincs), and Walnut Tree Close, in East Anstey (Dev). Old English *bēam* 'tree' (as in *hornbeam*) is found in Nut Bean Field (*Nubemefeld* [*sic*] 1436), in Watford, and Nut Binns 'nut trees', in St Paul's Walden (Herts).

CLEARINGS, STOCKINGS AND SCRUBS

Clearance of woodland is denoted by *ryding* 'a clearing', *stubb* 'a tree stump', and *stoccing* and *stubbing*, each of which means 'a clearing'. The frequency of the first in Hertfordshire and Essex testifies to the former extent of woodland in those counties. Hertfordshire examples include Reddings (*Reddinges* 14c.), in Abbots Langley, Readings (*Redyngs t.* Hy 6), in Aldbury, and Wood Readings (*Woderedinge t.* Hy 3), in Wheathampstead. There are more than twenty instances of *The Readings* in Essex, as well as Readings Field, in Kings Hatfield, and some other variants. Similar names in other counties include Over Ridding, in Sutton Downes (Ches), Ridding, in Claughton (Lancs) and in Eskdale (Cumb), Redin, in Birker (Cumb), *Rydynges* 1537, in Cowley, and Riddings (*Rydings* 1639), in Horsley (Glos). Old English *rod* 'a clearing' is found in *Rowrode* 13c. 'rough clearing', in Hunshelf, Little Rood, in Temple Newsam, and High Rods (*Heighrode* 1292), in Barwick in Elmet (YW); the dialect form *royd* (OE *rodu*) appears in *Julianroide* 1405, in Wakefield, and Wheat Royd, in Brampton Bierlow (YW).

Old English *stocc* 'a stump' is found in *Stocwit* 1316, in Bawtrey (YW). Names containing *stoccing* include *Stokynge* 1406, in Wakefield (YW), Stocken Flatt (*Stokenflatt* 1611), in Wincle (Ches), Stockings, in Badger (Shrops), and Stocking Ground (*Stockinge* 1231), in Oddington (Oxon). *Elderstubs*, mentioned earlier, is a common *stubb* name. Others are *Okenestobbe c.* 1301, in Siddington (Ches), *Elmestubbe* 1386–87, in Steventon, *Pyrstoub* 1339, in Bray (Berks), *Painistubing* 1218, in Stainton (YW) (which contains the Middle English personal name *Pain*), *Le Stubbyng* 1402, in Woolley, Stubbings (*Littelstubbings* 1330), in Worsborough (YW), and Steppings (*Le Newestybbing c.* 1400), in Cottingham (Nthants). *Stumblets* 1584 'a place abounding in stumps' occurs in Catsfield, Stumblets in Salehurst, and The Stumblets in Brightling (Sus).

Scrubland has generated various names, e.g. Nuns Bushes, in Chapel Ascote (Warks), Hubbards Bushes (*Hoberdyslonde* 1408), in High Ongar (Ess), Bushy Close (*Bushy Leasse* 1546), in Hanwell (Middx), Broomy Shoot, in Sutton Downes (Ches), Brush Park, in Ashreigney (Dev), Brushy Furlong, in Milton under Wychwood (Oxon), and Brushwood Croft, in Alderwasley (Derbys). From Old Norse *buskr* 'a bush' is derived Busky Close, in South Elmsall (YW). The Scrubs occurs in Kintbury (Berks), and Clipson Scrubs in Heath & Reach (Beds). Wormwood Scrubs, in Hammersmith (Middx, now Greater London), was earlier *Wormeholt* 1189–99 'snake-infested wood'; *Scrubbs* was added in the nineteenth century. Middle English *schrogge* is found in Wauldby Scrogs, in Swanland (YE), Little Shrog, in Altofts (YW), Shrogs, in Carleton and in Nateby (Lancs), Scroggsfield, in Corney (Cumb), and Shruggs, in Great Ness, in Sheriffhales and in West Felton (Shrops).

To these may be added *The Ruffe Grounde* 1684, in Chartham, The Rough, in Sturry (Kent), The Roughter (*Rowhton* 1339) 'rough enclosure', in Icklesham (Sus), and Ruffet, in Pauntley (Glos). The Queach (ME *queche* 'a thicket') occurs in Rickmansworth (Herts), Queeches (*Le Queche* 1349) in Eastwick, and The Queeches (*Le Queche t.* Ed. 3) in Watford (Herts).

The vegetation of such land would include gorse, heather, thorns, broom, holly, brambles and bracken. These plants are referred to in such names as Gorse Cover, in Burley (Rut), and Blackthorn Covert, in Cottesmore (Rut), which was formerly *Foxearth Gorse*. In addition to *Gorse* (OE *gorst*), the variants *Goss* and *Gorst*, locally *Gast*, as in Gastfield, in Dymock (Glos), both occur in field-names, as well as the synonymous terms *Furze* and *Whin*. *Furze* is found more in the Midlands and the south of England than elsewhere, e.g. Furze Cover, in Croxby (Lincs), and Furze Field, in South Mimms (Middx, now Herts). *Whin* is from Old Norse *hvin* and may be expected to be confined to the north and Midlands of England, e.g. *Quinhou c.* 1235 'whin hill', in Drigg & Carleton (Cumb), The Whin and Whin Field, in Storwood (YE), and Whin Cover, in North Dalton and in Thirkleby (YE). Old Gorse Cover, in Wistaston (Ches), was earlier *Whin Cover*. (*The*) *Gorse* or *Gorse* is approximately synonymous with *Cover(t)*. Instances include *Elenasgorstes* 1307–27 'Elene's gorse', in Churton by Farndon (Ches), The Gorse, in Pickworth (Rut), in Sanderstead (Sur), in Ashby Folville (Leics) and also in Bretby (Derbys), where it was earlier *Gorse Cover*. Parallel with these are The Furze, in Preston (Rut), *Whynnes* 1425, in Flitcham (Norf), and Whins, in Stainmore, in Ormside (Westm) and in Weeton (Lancs). Derivatives include *Gorsey*, *Gorsty*, *Gossy*, *Whinny*, *Furzey* and *Furzen*, varying freely among themselves. Gorsty Croft is found in Eaton, Gorsty Field (*Gorstie Croft* 1582) in Malpas (Ches), Gossy Close in Stretton (Rut), Winney Field in Sutton on Derwent (YE), *Whynny Close* 1539 in Gisburn (YW), Furzy Close in Hambleton (Rut), Furzey Close in Babcary (Som), Fuzzardy in Hinton (Glos), The Furzen in Alvescot, The Fuzzens in Prescote (Oxon), and Fuzzy Ground in North Newington (Oxon). Furry Close is occasionally found, e.g. in Kings Norton (Leics). *Furs* sometimes represents Old English *furh* 'furrow' in the plural.

The abundance of broom (*Cytisus scoparius*) is attested by frequent field-name references to it, such as *Bromecroft* 1322, in Yate (Glos), Broom Croft (*Bromecroftschote* 1380), in Acton (Middx), *Bromefelde* 1390, in Abbots Langley (Herts), Broom Lands (*Broomylands Close* 1662), in Caldwell (Derbys), *Bremehull* 1227 'hill overgrown with broom', in Chaldon Herring (Dor), Broom Park, in Beaford and in Ilsington (Dev), and Broom Close, in Heage (Derbys), in Chieveley and in Bucklebury (Berks). The random presence of holly in present-day hedgerows does not suggest orderly cultivation in the past. Its value as a winter feed, however, meant that supplies from wild trees were insufficient, and plantations were maintained in many places.[4] Examples include Holly Bush Close, in Cookham (Berks), in Stevenage (Herts) and in Hugglescote (Leics), Holly Leasow, in Myndtown, Hollindale, in Ercall Magna (Shrops), Hollinwood, in Newton (Ches), Holm Bush, in Hook (Dor), and Holmbush Piece, in Soberton (Hants).

Brambles, in Kinson, Bramble Close, in Stourton Caundle and in Langton Matravers, and Bramble Plot, in Steeple (Dor), allude to the blackberry (*Rubus fruticosus*), named also in about a dozen instances of Bramble Field in Essex, Bramble Grove (*Bramble crofte* 1538), in Cheshunt, Brambel Croft (*Bramblecroft* 1551), in Abbots Langley (Herts), and Bramelands, in Swinton (YW). However, Blackberry Fields (*Blakeborgh* 1393), in Winfrith Newburgh (Dor), has a different origin and means 'the black hill or barrow'.

Other shrubs to be found on neglected land or in hedgerows include those named in Briar Wood, in Kingsley (Ches), Briery Field (*Brierie croft* 1556), in Kings Langley (Herts), *Les Blackthornes* 1333, in Bretby (Derbys), Blackthorn Furlong, in Shipton under Wychwood (Oxon), Sloethorn Field, in Hunsworth (YW), and Barberry Fruss, in Ardsley (YW), in which *Fruss* possibly represents *frust* 'a fragment'. Galemoor (dating from 1637), in Frodsham Lordship (Ches), and *Le Wyrthorne* 13c., in Sturminster Marshall (Dor), probably refer to the bog-myrtle or sweet gale (*Myrica gale*).

Heathens Close, in St Michaels (Herts), was not the site of a pagan sanctuary, but from its earlier form, *Heath Herne* 1575, was evidently 'heath nook' (OE *hyrne*). *Heath, heather* and *ling* are well represented in field-names. The first (OE *hæth*), *Erica cinerea*, is to be found in the fairly common *Heath Close*, Heath Field (*Le Hethfeld* 1271), in Leese (Ches), and Heath Furlong (*Le Hethe* 1386–87), in Steventon (Berks). Heather (OE *hæddre*) is alluded to in Hather Hill, in Weston, Heathering Bank, in Alsager, Adderhill Croft, in Crewe (Ches), and Heather Field, in Elwick Hall (Dur). Compared with *Heath* names, those containing *Heather* are uncommon, unlike derivatives of Old Norse *lyng*, synonymous with *heather* (*Calluna vulgaris*), which is obviously restricted to the Danelaw and is represented by *Lyngefurlonges* 1422, in Cottesmore (Rut), Ling Field, Ling Croft and Ling Carr, all in Goosnargh (Lancs), Ling Leys, in Skelbrooke (YW), and Ling Close, in Ticknall (Derbys). Ling Knobs, in Ruddington (Notts), Lingy Hills, in Silsden (YW), and Lingber, in Nappa and in Newsholme (YW), allude to heather-clad hilly land. The plants give their names to typical landscape in The Heath (*Bruerie* 1229–37), in Acton (Middx), The Lings (*Le Lyngis* 1326), in Warsop (Notts), *The Lynges* 1612, in Glaston (Rut), and The Ling, in Storwood (YE). Pegs Ears, in Watlington (Oxon), originated in *Pekgesheth* 1300 'Pecg's heath'.

Heathland frequently produces much bracken, of little agricultural use except for composting or bedding litter. Most names relating to it are fairly easily interpreted, e.g. *Brackenflatt* 1373, in Methley (YW), Brackenber, in Great Strickland (Westm), Brackenburgh (*Brakenberch c.* 1210), in Great Limber (Lincs), both meaning 'hill on which bracken grew', Bracken Platt, in Clixby, Bracken Close, in Croxton (Lincs) and in Methley (YW), and Fern Close, in Spelsbury (Oxon). Weeds of hedgerows and neglected land include nettles, docks, thistles and plantains. These and similar plants are alluded to in *Neteli Croft c.* 1285, in Wallasey (Ches), *Nettlebed* 1545, in Dersingham (Norf), Great & Little Nettlehurst, in Sutton Downes (Ches) (*le nettelhurst* 1371), Nettledine, in Roddington (Shrops), Dock Field (*Dockcroft* 1638), in Aston (Herts), Docking Close, in Ardsley (YW), Thistle Croft, in Belchamp St Paul, in Great Yeldham and in Rivenhall (Ess), Thistle Field, in Ipsden (Oxon), Thistley Field, in Foulridge (Lancs), and Plantain Field, in South Skirlaugh and in Leconfield (YE). Cammock, or rest-harrow (*Ononis repens*), is a troublesome weed of pastures which taints milk and is difficult to eliminate. Names referring to it include Cammack Field, in Horndon-on-the-Hill (Ess), Cammick Hay, in Kington Magna (Dor), Cammick Redding, in Waltham Holy Cross (Ess), Keymick Croft, in Shrewsbury St Mary (Shrops). Other invaders of agricultural land include various fungi, those named in Mushroom Field, in Storwood and in Huggate (YE), and in Chinley (Derbys) being doubtless more welcome than most.[5]

Reeds, rushes and sedges are characteristic vegetation of streamside or waterlogged land. The first named are referred to in Great and Little Reeds, in High Easter (Ess), Reed Meadow, in Hockenhull, Read Meadows (*Le Reddemede* 1510), in Bruen Stapleford

(Ches), and Reed Fen, in Little Thetford (Cambs). Early spellings in *Rud-* are to be expected, e.g. *Le Rudiger* 1313 'reedy carr', in Mottram in Longendale (Ches), and *Rudlonde* 1518, in Idmiston (Wilts). Rushes (*Juncus spp.*) are mentioned in Rush Croft (*Le Rysshcroft* 1437), in Lea (Wilts), Rush Close, in Bushby (Leics), Rush Field, in Storwood and in Laytham (YE), and Rushy Pasture, in Houghton le Spring (Dur). In early names, *sedge* was used vaguely of several species of water-side plants. Modern usage restricts the term to members of the *Cyperaceae*, particularly plants of the *Carex* genus. Relevant field-names include Sedge Meadow (*Sedghay Meadow* 1600), in Frodsham Lordship (Ches), Seggy Carr, in Misson (Notts), Seggy Lands, in Melling with Wrayton (Lancs), and (from ON *sef* 'sedge') Seavy Carr (*Seyve Closes* 1590), in Eastrington (YE). Middle English *flagge* also vaguely referred to a range of water-side plants. Names containing this element include Flagg Holme, in Styrrup and in Harworth, Flag Carr, in Scrooby (Notts), Flaggy Doles, in Desford (Leics), and Flaggy Piece, in Stamford Rivers (Ess).

Wild plants are often referred to in field-names in popular form. The hairy willow-herb *Epilobium hirsuta*, for instance, is called *Apple-pie* in a number of field-names in southern counties, including Oxfordshire, which has Applepie Pightle, in Mapledurham, Applepie Corner, in Burford, and Applepie Piddle, in Nuffield. In Berkshire there is a location known as Applepie Green in Binfield, and Applepie Hill and Piece appear in the Tithe Apportionment for Compton. The same popular term is found also in Hampshire, in Applepie Ground, in St Mary Bourne, and Apple Pie Piece, in Milford. Hen and Chickens Furlong, in Ashwell (Herts), like Hen and Chicken, in Steventon (Berks), and Hen and Chickens, in Clifton Campden (Oxon), possibly alludes to the birdsfoot trefoil (*Lotus corniculatus*), endowed, as Geoffrey Grigson notes, with more than seventy names, from God Almighty's Thumb and Fingers to Old Woman's Toe-nails.[6] Blue Button Piece, in Diddlebury (Shrops), and Blue Button Field, in Mobberley, in Odd Rode, in Cheadle and in Nether Alderley (Ches), refer to *Scabiosa succisa* or *Succisa pratensis*, the Devil's Bit Scabious. This plant, prescribed in former times for scabies, worms, and even leprosy, had such a high reputation that the devil, envious of its success, is said to have bitten the root to try to destroy it. Thunderbolt Piece, in Quatt, and Thunderclaps, in Burford (Shrops), probably refer to the common red poppy (*Papaver rhoeus*), under its dialect name *Thunderbolt*.[7]

References to daffodils are by means of the separate components of the popular form *Daffydowndilly*, such as Daffy Leasow, in Ford (Shrops), Daffys Mead, in Bobbingworth (Ess), Daffydown Field, in Fareham (Hants), Dilly Wood, in Womersley (YW), and Dilly Bank, in Stoke upon Tern (Shrops); the entire form appears in Daffydowndilly Clump, in Middle Aston (Oxon), and the conventional name in Daffodil Pasture, in Great Easton and Daffodil Wood, in Writtle (Ess). Other variants include Havadrill Bank, in Blackden, and Hafodril Field, in Beeston (Ches). Some field-names containing *Gold* may be allusions to marigolds, e.g. *Goldeberge* 1187, in Bampton (Oxon), or Golden Green (cf. *the Gold Crofte* 1611), in Bollington (Ches). Rather more obvious is Marygold Field, in Terling and in West Hanningfield (Ess). Other flowers of field or hedgerow are named in Daisey Field, in Bollin Fee (Ches) and in Berrynarbor (Dev), Daisy Ley, in Mount Bures (Ess), Daisy Leasow, in Alderbury (Shrops), Bluebell Close, in Calver (Derbys), Primrose Field in Hunmanby (YE) and in Goosnargh (Lancs). and *Foxglove Hey* 1543, in Tabley Superior (Ches).

WILD MAMMALS

Overgrown land among the fields and in the waste on the edge of the parish sheltered wild mammals and game. Fox Cover(t) is frequent among the modern names of most English counties, applied to natural scrubland, to neglected rough pasture, or to deliberate planting of gorse and other shrubs to encourage game mammals and birds. The status of the fox is such, presumably, that it lends its name readily to such habitats.

Callor Fox Wood, in Werneth, and Cole Fox Meadow, in Norbury (Ches), refer to the same variety of fox, the *colfox*, as the one that, being "full of sly inquitee", so disturbed the lives of Chauntecleer and Pertelote.[8] References to foxes' lairs include Foxholes in Church Lawford (Warks) dating from the twelfth century; Fox Holes in Steeple Morden (Cambs), dates from the thirteenth. Early in the same century one of the three open fields of Cottenham (Cambs) was *Foxholefeld*. Foxhill, in Austrey (Warks), has developed from *Foxholes* recorded in 1213. Foxcote, in Ilmington (Warks), dating from 1607, is a less usual term for a fox's earth; another is found in Fox Grove Wood in Swinbrook (Oxon), probably from Old English *græf* 'an excavation'. The term *burrow* is found in Foxborough Close, in Foxton (Leics), Fox Burgh in Brooksby (Leics), Fox Burys, in

Watlington (Oxon). Foxburrow (*Foxbury* 1640), in Banstead (Sur), and Foxborough Copse, in Aldworth (Berks). *Fox-erthe*, an early compound, occurs in *Le Foxyorthes* 1478, in Wigland (Ches), Fox-yard Sike, in Dufton (Westm), and Foxearth Gorse, in Cottesmore (Rut). Other generics are also found, e.g. *Fox Feldes or Blak Earthes* 14c., in Bickerton (Ches), possibly the site of a former human settlement, and Reynard's Meadow, in Ellesmere (Ches), of interest in its use of the conventional literary term for a fox. Early references to hunting are found, e.g. Foxhunt Green (*Foxhunteslondes* 1435), in Waldron (Sus).

As the date of the introduction of rabbits into Britain has been much discussed, it may be of interest to note the earliest field-name allusions in the volumes of the English Place-Name Society. In Warwickshire and Nottinghamshire they date from the 13th century. The earliest reference in Cambridgeshire is dated 1287, in Derbyshire 1298, in Essex 1323, in Wiltshire 1383, and in Hertfordshire 1423. In the Middle Ages these animals were an important element in the agrarian economy. Not so hardy or so prolific as their modern descendants, they received loving care in the warren, sometimes to the extent that they even had burrows prepared for them. Historically, the word *rabbit* was used only of the young, and field-names containing the term are not numerous. Rabbit Croft occurs in Mytholmroyd (YW), Rabbit Field in Eddlethorpe (YE) and in Kirtlington (Oxon), Rabbit Ground in Pamphill (Dor), Rabbit Holes Meadow in Burton Overy (Leics), and Rabbit Burrows in Ryhall (Rut). Dying Rabbit Field, in Kirby Underdale (YE), was recorded about 1936, and so the name cannot allude to the great mid-century outbreak of myxomatosis.

Most field-names alluding to this animal are forms of Middle English *Coninger*, the 'rabbit warren'. The variants range from *Cannery* to *Gunnery* and include *Conery*, *Coning Earth* and *Coney Berry*. The interrelationship of *coninger*, *coning-erth* and *coni-garth* is illustrated by Coney Garth (*Le Conyger* 1425), in Middleton (YW), Coney Garth (*Conygreehill* 1686), in Farnsfield (Notts), Coney Green (*Conigarthe Closse c.* 1580), in Nettleton (Lincs), and Coney Gree (*Conyngercroft* 1376, *Conyngerth* 1540), in Sawbridge-worth (Herts). A warren was distinctive enough to be a landmark from which the furlongs, and even the open fields, were named, e.g. Cannon Grave Furlong, in Chadlington (Oxon), *The Great Felde otherwise called the Conyngrefeld* 1520, in Great Chesterton (Warks), and *Fallow alias Coneygree* 1605, a common field in Loughborough (Leics). South Field, in Waterstock (Oxon), was also *Coneygere*

Field in the eighteenth century. *Cony* compounded with other terms is found in Coney Close, in Aldborough (Norf), Coney Yards, in Pittington (Dur), and Cunaberries, in West Hoathly (Sus).

The term warren (Norman-French *wareine*) is occasionally found. Warren Mead, in Tetbury Upton (Glos), alludes to *Warenna de Tetbury*, appearing in local records from 1398 until the seventeenth century. *Ye Warren Thorne* 1427–28, in Bottesford (Leics), seems to have been succeeded by *Ye Coningree Lays* 1674, placed under the heading *Tethering Ground in ye Sands*, like Warren Heath, in Feltwell (Norf), a not unexpected landscape reference for a warren. Conversely, in Sowton (Dev), *Conynger* 1375 was eventually replaced by South Warren Close. Warren Close is found in Little Beddow, in Springfield, in Writtle (Ess), in Lubenham, in Holt (Leics) and in Kirby Underdale (YE); Warren Dale occurs in Londesborough, Warren Field in North Dalton (YE) and in Hadlow (Kent). Another term is found in Clapper Wood Hill (*The Clapurs* 1479), in Henley (Oxon), Clappers, in Hornchurch & Romford (Ess) and in Carrington (Ches), Clapper Field, in Freefolk (Hants) and in Alford (Sur), and Clapper Mead, in Amport (Hants).

The hare does not feature in many field-names. Examples include Hare Field, in Chigwell (Ess), *Haresfelde* 1560, in Rudheath Lordship (Ches), and Hare Croft, in Blaston (Leics). Monkey Corner, in Shiplake (Oxon), and Monkey Patch, in Condover (Shrops), refer to leverets, *monkey* being the dialect term for a young hare. References to the badger are frequently under the synonym *brock* (OE *brocc*), as in Brock Holes (*Brokholes* 1370), in Honly (YW), Brockholes Field, in Headington (Oxon), and Brockholes Carr, in Hardhorn (Lancs). Old English *brocc* 'badger' and *brōc* 'a brook' were sufficiently similar to bring about erroneous forms. Brookwell Hill, in Thames Ditton (Sur), seems to allude to a stream, but the 1548 form *Brokholehill* confirms a reference to a badger sett. Brock Hill, in Brigstock (Northants), however, was *Brokehill* in 1480, from *brōc* rather than *brocc*. Badger Meadow, in Stretton (Derbys), Badgers Leasow, in Alvechurch (Worcs), Badger Hey, in Marsden (YW), and Badger Field, in Kirkham (YE), probably refer to the animal.

Names alluding to the otter include Otters Field, in Chetwynd (Shrops), and Ottershayes, in Smallwood (Ches), in which the second element is *shay*, the dialect form derived from Old English *sceaga* 'a wood'. The wild cat is now very rare in England, but field-name references to it have survived. *Kathanger c.* 1200, in Woodend (Nthants), now gives name to Cathanger Farm. Catsbury Hill (*Cattesberewe* 1266), in Hartpury (Glos), was 'the cat wood' (OE *bearu* 'a wood'). Other examples are Cat Holes, in Hallaton (Leics), Catgreaves, in Moston (Ches), Cat Furlong, in Appleby (Leics), *Cat Acre* 1580, in Bulkeley (Ches), and Catch Field (cf. *Catts Grove* 1552), in Merstham (Sur). Catsprey (*Cattes Preye* 1586), in Chiddingfold (Sur), is 'meadow where wild cats were to be found', and *Wildecathisheuede t.* Ed. 1, in Betchton (Ches), 'wild cat's head(land)'. Catts Head Marsh, in Barking (Ess), resulted from a misreading at some stage of *Cattesmede* 1477. *Le Cattesmede* 1432, in Little Sutton (Ches), was alternatively *Cattesmete* 1398, and later Cat's Meat.

Cattle and sheep were preyed on by wolves as recently as the seventeenth century. Places where they lurked are indicated by *Wolueacres* 1372, in Haughton, and *Wlueshall c.* 1278 'the wolf's nook', in Church Coppenhall (Ches). References to the trapping of wolves occur in early names, e.g. *Ulpittes* 12c., in North Stainley (YW), and *Wolfepittes* 1608, in Marr (YW). Survivals and modern names include Woolpits Common (*Wolfputtes* 1287), in Cowley (Glos), Woolpit Field, in Boxtead (Ess), and Woolpits, in Furneux Pelham (Herts). Boarpits, in Shawbury (Shrops), is land on which wild boar were trapped. *Euerdenewode* 1482 'the wood in *Everdene*, i.e. the wild-boar valley', in Duffield (Derbys), and *Euerholt* 1337 'wild-boar wood', in Taxal (Ches), are also references to this animal.

The boundaries of a medieval deer park are faithfully followed by those of closes called Upper Park and Lower Park, in Cradley (Worcs).[9] Other parks are referred to in Deer Park, in Elsdon (Nthumb), in Belstone and in Stokeinteignhead (Dev), and Red Deer Park, in Stockton and in Montford (Shrops). References to deer include Stag Field, in Marple (Ches), Deer Acre, in Broadwas (Worcs), and Deer Pleck, in Hermitage (Dor). Deers Leap, in Brewood (Staffs), and Deerleap Copse, in Kingston Lisle (Berks), allude to a fence or hedge so constructed as to allow a deer to jump into a park but not out of it. *Bukstall* 1467, in Macclesfield, Bucksters, in Macclesfield Forest, and Buxtorstoops (*Buckstall* 1560, *Buckstostoope* 1611), in Rainow (Ches), allude to deer traps, *stolpi* 'a post' indicating the pole supporting the net in the trap. Does Piddle, in Stratfield Mortimer (Berks), and Doe Croft, in Odiham (Hants), allude to the female deer.

Among smaller mammals, mice are referred to in Mouse Furlong (*Musfurlong'* 1247–48), in Newbury (Berks), Mouse Field, in Lee-botwood (Shrops), and Mouses Nest, in Ringwood (Hants). Molde-warp occurs in Burton Lazars (Leics), Mole Field in Good Easter, and Moles Field in Tendring (Ess), but many references are to molehills, e.g. Molehill Mead, in Leaden Roding, Molehill Ley, in Thaxted, and Molehill Meadow, in Pleshey (Ess). Another popular name for the mole occurs in Want Field, in Chipping Ongar and in Matching (Ess). Names relating to hedgehogs include Urchin Furlong, in Claydon (Oxon), Urchins Dumble, in Ansley (Warks), *Urchins Mier* 1560, in Dersingham (Norf), and Hedgehog Field, in Willingale Doe (Ess).

BIRDS, REPTILES AND INSECTS

In addition to *Wren Park* and *Larks Lease* as terms for very small fields and very large ones respectively, literal allusions to these birds are also found in, e.g. Wren Shay, in Brackenfield (Derbys), and Lark Moor, in Great Witcombe (Glos). Bradtail, in Baschurch, Brunthill Coppice, in Bitterley (Shrops), and Firetail Covert, in Thornby (Nthants), allude to the redstart (*Phoenicurus phoenicurus*) under its various dialectal names. Tewit Hill, in Hartshorne (Derbys), *Pewytelowe* 13c. 'peewit hill', in Cleve Prior (Worcs), Lapperwing, in Hughley (Shrops), and Lapwing Hollow (*Lappinge-hallugh t.*Hy 3), in Eggington (Derbys), refer to the lapwing (*Vanellus vanellus*), as does Pyewipe Farm, in Lincoln. Tink Meadow, in West Felton (Shrops), contains *tink* 'a chaffinch', referred to also in Pink Ridding, in Shifnal (Shrops), and Pink Field, in Brereton cum Smethwick (Ches). *Queest, quist* or *cushat* (OE *cuscote*) 'a wood pigeon' are found in Quest Slade (*Quistslad* 1655), in West Dean (Glos), Quesse Wood, in Whitegate, Quis Croft, in Malpas, and Cushy Bank, in Bosley (Ches).

Corvids and other birds are referred to in Rook Field, in Hampstead Norris (Berks), Crow Nest, in Bingley (YW), Crows Nest, in Swindon (Glos), *Crows Nest Meadow* 1729, in Virginstow (Corn), Magpie Shaw, in Lamberhurst (Kent), Pye Close, in Hambledon (Hants), and Kite Meadow, in Lexden (Ess). The kite (OE *cyta, gleoda*) is also alluded to in *Le Gleyde Heye* 1507, in Nether Peover (Ches), where there is a more recent Kite Clough (*Cuythylcroft c.* 1300). The eagle (OE *earn*) is referred to in Eagle Leys, in Abdon (Shrops), Yarn Grove (*Yarne Grove* 1603), in Eastington (Glos), and Yarnwood Meadow, in Kinlet (Shrops). Hawks are named in Hawks Close, in Beausale (Warks), Hawkshaw, in Toft, Hawkeshaw, in Appleton, and Hawkshaw Meadow, in Peover Superior (Ches) (OE *sceaga* 'a small wood'), Hawk Moor, in Berrington

(Shrops), and Hawkesbarrow, in Bere Regis (Dor). A gap in woodland in which hawks could be flown for falconry was known as a *hawksherd* (OE *hafocscerde*), found in *Hawkeserde* 1362, in Brewood (Staffs), *Le Haukesherd* 1347, in Disley-Stanley, The Hawkesyord (*Hauekisherd* 1285), in Wincle, The Hogue Sherd (*Hauksherde* 1467), in Pott Shrigley (Ches), and Hawkshord, in Bradford on Avon (Wilts). Lapwing Field and The Lark Field, in Pott Shrigley, perhaps refer to the pursuit of those species by hawks, alluded to in *Haukesclogh* 1347.

Game birds are mentioned in Partridge Mead, in Cookham (Berks), and Pheasant Pingle, in Alderwasley (Derbys). There are numerous references to the glades and clearings where occur the territorial flights of the woodcock (*Scolopax rusticola*), known as *roding*, and *cockshoot*, the darting flight of these birds (or its location). The glades (oak coverts were preferred) were important enough to mark furlongs and headlands, e.g. *Cockshoot Furlong* 1780, in Kibworth (Leics), and *Le Cockshutehauedland c.* 1275, in Iddinshall (Ches). Other names include Cockerhead (*Cokerode* 1469), in Bridgstock (Nthants), Cockroad Close, in Sherfield English (Hants), Cockridden, in Horndon (Ess), Cockshute, in Leonard Stanley, Cock Shed, in Twyning (Glos), Cockshots, in Melling (Lancs), Cockshoot, in Shirley (Derbys), and Cock Shoot (*Kocsheth-erudyng* 1354), in Newton by Frodsham (Ches). *Cockshute Croft* 1553, in Lapworth (Warks), may be part of the land conveyed *c.* 1200 to William le Oiseleur (i.e. 'the Fowler') for a rent of *quatuor-widecocs* ('four woodcocks'). A *cock-shoot* was probably a natural glade, and a *cock-road* an artificial one. *Goldhwitenest* 13c. (probably for *Godwitenest*), in Middle Rasen (Lincs), seems to allude to the black-tailed godwit (*Limosa limosa*), a wading bird. The species formerly bred in eastern counties, and was caught and fattened for the table.

Duck decoys are indicated by Coy Ducks, in Brindley (Ches), Decoy Field, in Tolleshunt D'Arcy and in Worminford (Ess), Decoy Meadow, in Mouldsworth (Ches), and Decoy Pasture, in Felsted (Ess). *Enedewong c.* 1200, in Flitcham (Norf), is 'duck *wong*'. Goose Marsh, in Dedham (Ess), and Wild Goose Meadow, in Barnton (Ches), refer to feeding grounds. *Cuckoo Pen* names have been mentioned earlier. Non-fanciful references to *Cuculus canorus* include *Cuckow Park* 1727, in Colan (Corn), Cuckoo Close, in Blaby and in Wanlip (Leics), and in Heptonstall (YW), Cuckoo Field, in Langford (Ess), Cuckoo Thorn, in Gawsworth (Ches) and in Hursley

(Hants), and (the surely illusory) Cuckoo Nest, in Winkfield (Berks) and in Bingley (YW).

Reptiles and amphibians are named in Snakes Field, in Shellow Bowells (Ess), Snake Meadow (*Snakemead* early 17c.), in Winnersh (Berks), Frog Park, in Diddlebury (Shrops), and Frog Sick, in Crich (Derbys). Thatcham (Berks) has both Tadpole Meadow and Tadslips Meadow (*Tadeslep* 13c) 'slippery or muddy place haunted by toads'. Toads are referred to also in such names as Podmore, in Drayton in Hales (Shrops). Effets, in Eaton Constantine (Shrops), is derived from dialectal *eft* (OE *efet*) 'a newt', and Asker Dale, in Tranmere (Ches), from the dialect term *asker* 'a lizard'. Adder Holes, in Brewood (Staffs), Adders Field, in Harlow (Ess), Adder Meadow (*Two Adder Meadows* 1665), in Sandbach, Nadder Hey, in Ashley (Ches), and Viper Hills, in Baschurch (Shrops), allude to the adder (OE *næddre*). *Worm* in older field-names may mean 'a dragon' but 'an earthworm' in more recent ones, e.g. Wormy Loons (*Wormlandes* 1637), in Chorlton (Ches).

The most frequent allusions to insects are to ants, e.g. *Emetridge* 1626, in Englishcombe (Som), Pismire Hill, in Sudbury (Derbys), Anthill Ground, in Ashleworth (Glos), and Ant Tump Piece, in Church Stoke (Shrops). Wasp Field, in Tetton (Ches), and Bee Hole Meadow, in Chapel en le Frith (Derbys), are clear enough. Names containing *wig* may sometimes refer to a beetle or a similar insect, but some may be from the Old English personal name *Wicga* and others, particularly forms of *Wigmore*, may be from a supposed Old English word *wigga*, meaning 'that which moves', alluding to unstable ground, found in *Wygemor* 1248, in Midgham (Berks), Wigmoor (*Wiggemor* 1310), in Carden (Ches), and Wigmore, in Sparsholt (Berks). Delphin, in Kelfield (YE), and The Dolphins, in Pontesbury (Shrops), allude to the aphis or greenfly, popularly known as *dolphin*.

NOTES AND REFERENCES

1. Wainwright, 'Field-names of Amounderness', p. 191.
2. B. Kerr, 'Dorset fields and their names', *Archaeology and History* (*Dorset Nat. Hist. Soc. Proceedings*) **89** (1967), pp. 235–56, here p. 253.
3. R. Turner, *Botonologia: the British Physician* (1664), quoted in G. Grigson, *The Englishman's Flora* (Dent 1955, rev. edn 1987), p. 15.

4. See M. Spray, 'Holly as a fodder in England', *Agric. Hist. Review* **29** (1981), pp. 97–110.
5. Ketchup Piece, in West Haddon (Nthants), also alludes to mushrooms, made into ketchup in many homes in the neighbourhood.
6. Grigson, pp. 136–7.
7. Grigson, p. 49. The popular name is related to the belief that picking the flower provokes thunder.
8. G. Chaucer, *The Nonnes Preestes Tale of the Cok and Hen*, line 3215.
9. I owe this observation to Mr Peter Keate, who has also provided many field-names of the Halesowen area.

CHAPTER FIVE

A living from the land

"THE HEAVY STEPS OF THE PLOUGHMAN"

Ploughing the soil and harvesting the sun-ripened crops have always been regarded as essential features of the idyllic life of the agrarian worker, and, with the equally tranquil occupations of tending sheep and milking cattle, are virtually the only subjects of paintings of the daily life of the farm-worker. The workers take a less romantic view of their routine. A discordant note, such as *Break Back* or *Twistgut*, is occasionally heard among the field-names relating to the activities involved in wresting from the soil the raw materials for the food of the entire community.

The preparation of the land entails strenuous preliminaries. Clearance of woodland or scrub generates names like *The Rothe* 1380 (OE *rothu*) 'the clearing', in Englefield (Berks). The change of use from grassland to arable is noted in *Brokenemed'* 1278–79 'ploughed meadow', in Chesterton (Oxon). The term *breach* relates to the breaking of soil with the plough. The ploughing of hitherto unused land is clear from the early form of Breach Close, in Monks Kirby (Warks), which was *Brechslade* 1477, a *slade* (OE *slæd*) being 'a shallow valley', usually marshy and therefore brought into cultivation only when there was great need for more land. The names of the great fields of Scalford (Leics) in 1601 were (1) *Breach*, (2) *Clay & Redearth*, and (3) *Moorbeck*. Names similar to Breach Acre, in Whitegate (Ches), and Breaches (*Le Breche* 1332), in Essington (Staffs), can be found throughout the country. Variants include Short Breck and Breaks Close, in Styrrup (Notts), and Blackbridge (earlier *Black Breeches*), in Walthamstow (Ess), to which may be added Eleanour's Britches, in Stockton (Shrops). Names like Arable Close, in Rotherby (Leics), possibly imply that other piecemeal enclosure in the vicinity is for use as pasture. Since, by definition, ploughing was normal on arable land, such names as Ploughed Field, in Croxall (Derbys, now Staffs) and in Blackfordby (Leics), and Double Ploughed Field, in Capesthorne (Ches), point to some special circumstances. Ploughed Marsh, in South Moreton (Berks), is distinguished from marsh which was too wet for tillage, and from that which was used for pasture. Plough Ground, in Tubney, and Ploughed Ground, in Sparsholt (Berks), were perhaps previously pasture. Plough Crofts, in Eaton Bray (Beds), may be contrasted with other crofts which were either grass paddocks, as was *Grascroft* 1451, in Moreton (Berks), or, like Spade Tang, in Curbar (Derbys), were cultivated with the spade.

Recently broken ground might also be described as *New*, just as formerly used or worn-out land was called *Old*. *New Close*, *Newlands*, etc. occur frequently. The epithet in some examples was bestowed six or seven centuries ago. Newlands, in Shepperton (Middx), was *Newelond* in 1329, and in East Barnet (Herts) was *Le Newland* in 1296. If land had been permanently enclosed for cultivation, besides the commonplace *Arable Close* it might be given a name such as *New Taken in Close* 1596, in Duffield (Derbys), or *Newfoundland*, which may also have the sense 'remote land'. *Intake*, *New Taken In*, etc. do not in themselves indicate arable closes, but whether intended for ploughing or pasture, the preparation entailed in fencing or the planting of hedges would be considerable. Other variants are Newbrook or Newbroken Land, in Lower Heyford (Oxon).

The uniformity of ridges produced by ploughing was a sufficiently noticeable characteristic to be specified in field-names. The usual modern form in names is *Ridge* (OE *hrycg*), but in the north *Rig(g)* is found, being either the Scandinavianization of the English term or from Old Norse *hryggr*. Thus, Ridge Close, in Artington (Sur), and Ridge Field (*Le Redge* 1460), in Hitchin (Herts), may be contrasted with *Sandrig* 13c., in Tallantire (Cumb), Riggs (*Le Rigge* 1339), in Thorngumbald (YE), and Rigg Meadow, in Woodplumpton (Lancs). Middle English *hacken* 'to plough up the soil into ridges' occurs in Hack Croft, in Ollerton (Ches), *The Acking* 1572, in Moreton, Hacking, in Lepton, Hacking Croft, in Menston, and Lane Hackings, in Cumberworth (YW).

"OF DONG FUL MANY A FOTHER"

The spreading of manure, always laborious, must have become an oppressive way of life when practised on the scale recorded in some manors. In the thirteenth century, the service required in Forncett (Norf) was the carrying and spreading of twenty heaps of dung. In Petworth (Sus), thirty-six wagon-loads and eighty-three cartloads were purchased in 1347–48.[1] This essential activity is alluded to in such names as *The Dungfeld* 1650, in Rudheath Lordship, Dung Field, in Byley cum Yatehouse, and Old Dung Field, in Tabley Superior (Ches), Dung Croft (*Dongecroft* 16c.), in Reading (Berks), and Dung Cart Close, in Little Whittenham (Berks). The Denge (*Wren Parke alias Denge* 1484), in Great Bardfield (Ess), was probably a very small enclosure used exclusively to store manure. Muck Field, in High Easter (Ess), Muck'd Field, in Wettenhall, and Mucked Field, in Stapeley (Ches), and Dinge or Brookside Quarter (OE *dyncge* 'manured land'), in Kingham (Oxon), also refer to the spreading of manure.

Compass Meadow, in West Felton (Shrops), Compass Field, in Pattiswick (Ess), and Compast Field, in Beaumont (Ess), refer to *compost* or manure. A dunghill, also known as a sharnhill, midden or mixen, is referred to in Common Muckhill (*Mukhyl* 1521), in Peterborough (Nthants, now Cambs), Scornills Close (*Schornhilles* 1339), in Owsersby (Lincs), Dungmix Field, in Haslemere (Sur), *Mixine* 12c., in Bolton by Bowland (YW), *Mixenhull* 1350, in Rodmarton (Glos), and *Mixtenham* 15c., in White Waltham (Berks). *Le Foldecourse* 1549, in Barton on Humber (Lincs, now Humberside), refers to the oppressive requirement of having the tenants' sheep pasture in the lord's fold, one of the most bitter and understandable of medieval tenants' grievances.

Land needing manure may be described as 'hungry', which, with *Hunger*, frequently occurs, e.g. Hungry Park, in Withington (Glos), Hungry Acre, in Helsington (Westm), Hungry Home Close, in Ashby Folville (Leics), but especially with *Hill*, e.g. *Hungerhelle* 1204, in Standon (Herts), and Hungry Hill (*Hungerhull* 1469), in Brigstock (Nthants). The soil of Hungry Hill, in Walkern (Herts), is poor and stony, and it was said that Hunger Hill, in Harpole (Nthants), was 'very hungry and needed much manure'. Hungry Hall, in Bygrave (Herts), was earlier *Hungerhull* 1406. Hunger Hill, in Wootton Wawen (Warks), was earlier *Hangandehull* 1212 'hanging hill', i.e. a hill with a steep slope, which would cause drainage of nutrients from the soil. A spurious association with central Europe is implied in Hungary, in Twyford (Hants), Hungary Land, in Bere Regis (Dor), and Hungary Hill, in Awre (Glos), in Ripon (YW) and in Berkhamsted (Herts) (*Hungry Hill* 1525). Hungry Downs is found in Wenhaston (Suf), and Hungerdowns in many parishes in Essex, as well as in Brockenhurst and in Sheet (Hants).

Fields so well supplied with nutrients that they required no resting period received due recognition. "In the neighbourhood of Gloucester are some extensive common fields . . . cropped, year after year, during a century, or perhaps centuries, without one intervening whole year's fallow. Hence they are called 'Every Year's Land'".[2] This happy state of affairs was achieved partly by alternating grain crops and pulses, but presumably some contribution was made by the quality of the soil itself, fortified by judicious applications of manure. Marshall's "during a century" is supported by two Oxfordshire instances, Every Years Land (*Every Yeares Feild* 1679), in Kingham, and the same name in an undated Hanborough document probably of the seventeenth century. Everlasting Close, in Puddletown (Dor), may have a similar meaning.

OTHER NATURAL FERTILIZERS AND SOIL-CONDITIONERS

Bone-dust, or *bone-waste*, is alluded to in field names all over the country. Bone Dust Field, in Pott Shrigley, in Higher Bebbington and in ten other places in Cheshire, Bone Dust Bit, in Anstey (Herts), and Bonewaste Field, in Monks Coppenhall (Ches), refer to the phosphatic manure obtained from bones, either burnt or ground. The use of bones in some form is implied in Bone Field, in Hornchurch (Ess), Bonefield, in Beeston (Ches), Bones Field, in Letchingdon (Ess), and Bone Mead, in Southchurch (Ess). The grinding process would have been carried out in a mill such as that referred to in Bone Mill Garth, in Knottingley (YW). The practice is said to have begun when the beneficial effects on the soil were noticed on land near Sheffield, where bones had been stored for the manufacture of knife-handles. Home supplies proved insufficient for agricultural purposes, and during the nineteenth century bones were imported in large quantities.

The fertile soil known as *loam*, usually consisting of clay mixed with decomposed organic material, is alluded to in field-names such as Loam Close, in Wincle (Ches), and *Lomewood* 1572, in Wargrave

(Berks). In *Lutloomerssh*, *Micheloomerssh* 1355, in Ashampstead (Berks), *lȳtel* and *micel* have been prefixed to a compound of *lām* 'loam' and *ersc* 'ploughed land'. The geological map shows clay with flints and loam covering most of the parish. This desirable material would be dug from pits and spread on fields needing revival. Old English *lām-pytt* 'a loam pit' has given Lamb Pitts (*Lamput* 1321), in Hendon (Middx), Lampetts (*Lampetes* 1493), in Fyfield (Ess), Lampits (*Lampetfeld* 1383), in Hoddesdon (Herts). Lampitts Field, in Wickham St Paul (Ess), Lamb Pits, in Northenden, and the earlier *Le Lamputt* 1250–1300, in Middlewich (Ches). Lamb Pit, in Illston (Leics), was *Lamputis* in 1364. Many later names have the spelling *Lamb*, but another variant occurs in Land Pit Field, in Twinsted (Ess).

What was thought to be another organic fertilizer is referred to in The Diggings, in Steeple Morden (Cambs), the site of nineteenth-century excavation of coprolite, which was supposed to consist of the petrified droppings of prehistoric animals. It was regarded as very beneficial, a reputation enhanced perhaps by its presumed maturity. The material was even older than the dinosaurs, being natural phosphatic nodules.

Malm is a fertile mixture of clay and decomposed chalk, or sometimes consisting exclusively of the latter substance. Field-name references, which appear to be limited to southern England, include Malm, in Compton (Hants), Malms (*Le Mamey Pightle 1626, The Mawme* 1667, in Redbourn (Herts), Malm Close, in Bucklebury (Berks), Mauls Field (*Malmefeld* 1333), in Watford (Herts), Malm Furlong (*Le Malme t.* Hy 6), in Newbury (Berks) and in Little Wittenham (Berks) and Malm Ground, in Bournemouth (Hants, now Dor) and in Okeford Fitzpaine (Dor).

Malm Pits, in East Stoke (Dor), and *Malme Pitts* 17c., in Wallingford (Berks), indicate land from which malm was excavated, and Malm Quar Tyning, in Upton Scudamore (Wilts), would be an enclosure containing or adjoining a quarry.

Chalk has also long been used as a soil-conditioner, and excavation for this mineral to be applied to fields needing calcium, or improving the physical qualities of clay soils, is recorded in *Chalkput* 1255–90, in Bisley (Glos), *Cholk-Pitt-Shot* 1709, in Ringwould (Kent), Chalk Pit Ground, in Bucklebury (Berks), and Chalkpit Field, in Hinton Martell (Dor). Other names contain no explicit reference to a pit, e.g. Chalks, in Somerby, The Long Chalks, in Grasby, Chalk Lands, in Searby (Lincs), and Chalk Field, in Dagenham, in Hornchurch and in Upminster (Ess).

Chalk for treating fields would normally be brought no more than about a hundred yards. In Hertfordshire, Chalk Dell, in Lilley, Chalk Dell Close, in Stevenage, and Dell Field, in Sandridge, in Bushey, in Kings Langley and in St Peters (where *Le Delle* was recorded in 1332), allude to the practice in that county of excavating for chalk where it could be found within about 30 feet (9 metres) of the surface. It could then be spread over the surrounding land, the soil of which is either boulder clay or clay-with-flints. As lime and chemical fertilizers were brought into use, the disused pits collapsed and became pleasant hollows, colonized by a great variety of grasses and wild flowers. Early disuse seems to have occurred at Broken Dells (*Brokendale* 1519), in St Michaels (Herts). Names such as *Chalkdell Wood* refer to overgrowth of wild vegetation or deliberate tree-planting on disused excavation sites.

The Celts of pre-Roman Britain are known to have treated light soil with marl. This substance (or group of substances) consists of a mixture of clay and calcium carbonate.[3] Land granted by Turstin Mantel to Missenden Abbey in 1161 included arable and wood, with marl-pits. Maundins, in Kingshill (Bucks), is the modern counterpart of the medieval *Maldefurlong* in *Eldefeld* ('the old field'), one of the open fields there. Field-names, e.g. *Marleputt* 1376, in Barlborough (Derbys), provide evidence of the continuance of the practice during the Middle Ages. Marl Hill, in Church Knowle (Dor), is supported by an earlier reference to *quodam marlerio de Cnolle* 1268 'a certain marlpit of Knowle'. Marling is mentioned in *Marlyngcroft* 1393 and *Marlepytfurlong* 1450, in Winfrith Newburgh (Dor), where earlier *Marlyngput* is recorded in 1389. In Norfolk the name was in use even earlier; Marle, in Beechenwell, looks back to *Marledewong* in a document of 1218. Marlpits are referred to in early Essex names, *Marleputfeld* 1297 and *Le Marlhole* 1414, but the marling of bad land in the county is attested as far back as the reign of Henry II. Marling Place, in Wadhurst (Sus), is probably to be identified with *Le Marlyng* in the 1333 Court Roll. The alternative names Old Marled Field or Sandy Field, in Cogshall (Ches), allude to the soil and to its possible improvement.

Field-name references to the improvement of marshy land are numerous in the Macclesfield Hundred of Cheshire, e.g. Marled Field (*The Marledfield* 1610), in Disley-Stanley, and Marl'd Carr (ON *kjarr* 'brushwood, a marsh'), in Butley. Such treatment is hardly ever mentioned in narratives of the process of reclamation, which are usually concerned with the more obvious features of dams and drainage ditches. Settlement in the Forest of Arden was punctuated by marl-pits, the presence of which is attested by field-names such as Marlpit Close (*Le Marleputfeld* 1335), in Solihull, and in Shustoke, where there were *2 marl pits* in 1590, Marl Croft (*Le Marlede Croft* 1369), in Allesley, and Marl Field (*Le Marledecroft* 1369), in Fillongley (Warks). After the customary struggles, lasting for several centuries, between illicit marl-excavators and the lords, in early Stuart times Solihull freeholders were permitted to dig marl on the lord's waste provided "they shall either raile or hedge the . . . pitt sufficiently for the safeguard of cattell".[4]

Lime in field-names usually refers to quicklime, and there is no doubt about such names as Lime Piece, in Yeaveley (Derbys), *Lyme Lands c.* 1570, in Owersby (Lincs), and Limed Field (*Lymed Closes* 1604), in Heptonstall (YW), alluding to land to which lime has been applied to counteract acidity. The gap between natural conditioners and modern chemical additives is being bridged here. Lime has to be prepared by burning, referred to in Limekiln Nook, in Airton (YW), Limekiln Close, in Yeldersley (Derbys), and Limekiln Leasow, in Solihull (Warks), Lime Kiln Piece, in Calne (Wilts), near the *Limekilne* marked on a 1703 map. Turnditch (Derbys) has Lime Close and Limekiln Close. Limekiln Copse, in Cumnor (Berks, now Oxon), and Limekiln Plantation, in Widdington (Ess), indicate a source of fuel on or near the site of the kiln.

There may be confusion between *Lime* and *lyng* 'heather' or *līn* 'flax'. Linkfoot, in Helmsley (YN), was recorded as *Lime Pitts* in a survey of 1642 but had been earlier *Linfit, Lin(g)thwait*, and so is a *-thwait* compound with either *lyng* or *līn*. We are told that "the 1642 surveyor was a southerner who had constant trouble with place-names".[5] Conversely, The Lined Ground, in Pott Shrigley (Ches), is shown not to be from *līn* by *The Lymed Ground* 1735. Plaister Pit Close, in Ledston (YW), refers to the excavation of gypsum (calcium sulphate), used as a dressing on clover pastures.

FERTILITY BY FIRE AND WATER

The power of fire to destroy weeds and restore fertility has been utilized in various ways and is referred to in many different field-names. Furlong called Branderith, in Tealby (Lincs), is from Middle English *brand-erth* 'a field that has been burned over in preparation for tillage'. *Le Swithenis* 1260, in Ecclesfield (YW), is from Old Norse *svithinn* 'land cleared by burning'. *Brindestub* 1292, in Birker

(Cumb), *The Burnt Gorse* 1638, in Capesthorne (Ches), Burnt Heath (*Le Brenthet* 13c.), in Hilton (Staffs), Burnt Whin, in Upper Whitley (YW), Burnt Furze, in West Tilbury (Ess), and possibly Black Scrubs, in Chedworth (Glos), allude to the combustion of scrub. General or unexplained burning is referred to in Brandlands (*Brendelonde* 1428), in Standon (Herts), Burnt Lands, in Burford (Shrops) and in Broadwas (Worcs), Burnt Ground (*Burnt Close* 1725), in Cumnor (Berks), Burning Acre (*Brond Acare* 1610), in Newbold and Dunston (Derbys), Burnt Close, in Northolt (Middx) and in Sysonby (Leics), and Burnt Edge, in Laverton (YW); *Edge* in the last name is probably Old English *edisc* 'an enclosure, an enclosed pasture'. The ashes of various species of trees would have been used to improve land, but such incineration cannot be recognized with certainty from field-names. Ash-tree ashes, for instance, were recommended for the improvement of pasture, but there is no way of telling whether Burnt Ash, in Good Easter and in Mashbury (Ess), refers to the deliberate or merely accidental burning of these trees.

Soap Ashes, a field-name in Compton Abbas (Dor), alludes to ashes of oak and elm used in soap-making and subsequently spread as a manure. The value of this by-product was early realized, both for arable land and for grassland. In north Buckinghamshire, the Verneys so greatly appreciated the value of applying potash to their pastures that they "made a point of keeping at least one potash maker as a tenant. He was the only man given a long lease, and it included clauses specifying the provision of considerable amounts of potash every year and an option to buy his whole supply."[6] Soaphouse Ground, in Bisley (Glos), and Soaphouse Mead, in Holnest (Dor), also point to this activity. Other names in Holnest, Soapers Pool and Soapers Pools Coppice, show that soap-making there was some centuries old: *Sopornepole* 1555 is apparently 'soap-makers' pool' from *saperena*, the genitive plural form of Middle English *sapere* 'a soap-maker'. Soaphouse Field is also found in Stondon Massey, in Aldham and in Blackmore (Ess).

The proximity of the coppice for the ready provision of fuel is understandable, as is 'clearing', in Soap Ridding, in Mapperley (Derbys). The ashes of the fire provided potash, from which the essential alkaline constituent of soap was derived. This important element might be obtained by other means, and a number of names refer to its production, e.g. Potash Field, in thirty or more places in Essex, Potash Close, in Sulgrave (Nthants) and in Stanbridge (Beds), Potash Land, in Fawstead (Ess), Potash Four Acres, in Havant (Hants), Potash, in Milton and in Bradfield, *Pot Ash Ground* 1725, in Hatford, and Potash Mead, in Challow (Berks), in Stamford Rivers, in Stondon Massey and in Matching (Ess), as well as Potash Farm, in Priors Marston (Warks) and in Felsted (Ess).

The practice of paring and burning has generated a variety of field-names. The procedure required first the removal of turf or weeds ('paring') by means of a beating iron (an adze-like implement) or a breast-plough (a kind of pointed shovel pushed by the thighs of the user); next the herbage was gathered into beehive-like heaps to dry; finally the heaps were ignited and allowed to smoulder until only ashes remained, which were immediately scattered and ploughed or harrowed in. The breast-plough is said to have been used in Evesham market gardens throughout the nineteenth century, and in allotments in Gloucestershire and Suffolk until the Second World War.

There are only a few references to paring and burning in precisely those terms. Three fields in Yorkshire have the full phrase as their names: Pare and Burn Close, in Headingley, Pared and Burned, in Newall with Clifton, and Pared and Burned Close, in Yeadon (YW). Paring, in Bishop Thornton (YW), Paring Field, in Little Strickland (Westm), and Pared Field, in Glusburn (YW), are among the instances referring to the paring element. Some of the names of the *Burnt Close* type, mentioned above, may allude to the practice. Of more frequent occurrence are the *Burnbake* or *Burnbeak* names: Burnbeck, in Cranborne (Dor), Burnbake, in Ebbesborne Wake, in South Newton (Wilts), in Chaddleworth, in Draycott Moor (Berks) and in Ashmore (Dor), Burnbaked Piece, in Kintbury and in Didcot, Burnbake Piece, in Lockinge, and Burnbeak in Steventon (Berks). Burnbeak also occurs in Melbury Abbas (Dor), Burnbeak Mead in Folke, and Beak Land in Tufton (Hants). The Beak, in a number of Wiltshire parishes, is a further variant.

The breast-plough was also known as the push-plough, recalled particularly in Cheshire field-names such as Push Field, in North Rode, Push Plough, in Cheadle, Push Plough Field, in Bramhall, Push Ploughed Field, in Woodford and in Great Warford, Push Plow Meadow, in Picton, Little Pushing, in Gawsworth, and perhaps even the laconic Push, in Hattersley. The beating iron (in Devon dialect the *bidix* or 'beat-axe') was used in some other counties. The word *beat* (see below) accounts for such names as Beatlands, in Ilsington (Dev), Bourne Beat and Beat Leaze (*Batlese* 1539), in Puddletown (Dor), Beat-hamms, in Haslebury Bryan (Dor), and possibly Bean Beatings, in Hope (Derbys) and Beating Pasture, in Lea (Ches). *Beat* in these names has no connection with violent striking, strenuous though the operation undoubtedly must have been. It is derived

Plate 5.1 Breast-plough in use, Berkshire
The implement, also referred to in field-names as the *push plough*, would have been used in fields named *Burnbake*, *Burnbeat* and *Pared and Burnt*.

from an obscure word *beat* meaning 'turf'. Burnt Turf, in Dowde-swell (Glos), may also refer to this procedure.

The practice was particularly recommended on cold clay grassland that had been allowed to deteriorate, and it was also advised that the land should be dunged during the following winter. When used to excess, or on inappropriate soil, paring and burning could have a deleterious effect.

The technique was supposed to have originated in Devon, so that some names relating to it use the term *Devonshiring*. Devonshire Banks, in Betchton (Ches), Great Denshire, in Glen Parva (Leics), Denshire Field, in Hadlow (Kent) and in West Hoathly (Sus), and the slightly distorted Drencher, in Chirbury (Shrops), contain this term in its two most recognizable forms. The process was mentioned by Sir Richard Weston in the mid-seventeenth century, at about the time that *Denshirefeld* 1647, in Farnham (Sur), was placed on record. Dencher Field is found in Lingfield and in Merstham, and Denchers Meadow in Aston Flamville (Leics).

The term *water meadow*, in literary use, dates only from the eighteenth century, though the practice had an earlier origin and the expression was used in sixteenth-century field-names. Names such as Great Water Mead, in Tarrant Rawston (Dor), or *Waterclosse* 1554 and *Watermede* 1542, in Holnest (Dor), suggest pleasant riverside stretches of pasture, on which cattle or sheep feed in great content-ment, remote from anything that could be described as technological. This peaceful combination of the two elements of earth and water is also recalled in Water Mead (*Water Medowe* 1585), in Horningham and in Mere & Zeals (Wilts), and Water Meadow, in Bincombe (Dor), in Beenham and in Blewbury (Berks), and in Dewlish (Dor). Once again, things are not quite what they seem.

This apparently natural landscape is but the surface, quite literally, of an elaborate system of irrigation, utilizing water engineering of a considerable degree of sophistication. River water was diverted through channels traversing the meadows, controlled by sluices or hatches. The meadows, which took on the appearance almost of ridge-and-furrow land, were usually flooded twice a year, in winter to ensure an early bite for stock, and in late spring to produce a good crop of hay. Only wealthy landowners could afford to build the equipment required for the management of great volumes of water, and the financial co-operation, as well as the consent, of neighbours was necessary in the execution of such schemes.

Water Meadow, in Milton Abbas (Dor), had earlier counterparts in *Arnolds Water Mead* and *Whinch Water Mead* in 1659, recalling

Plate 5.2   Hatch for the water-meadows, Piddletrenthide (Dorset)

respectively one of the participants in the co-operative enterprise, and one of the pieces of equipment. Other field-names include *Le Flott* 1610, in Kimbolton (Herefs), Floated Meadow, in Myddle (Shrops), Floated Field, in Dore (Derbys), Floated Close, in Ripley, and New Floated Close, in Brackenfield (Derbys), Float Ing (ON *eng* 'water meadow'), in Kaber (Westm), and Floating Meadow, in Morningthorpe (Norf), and in Atcham and in Condover (Shrops).

Water Close 1592, in Netherhampton (Wilts), described in the document as an enclosure of 'wett ground', and *Wett Meade* 1605, in Broadchalke (Wilts), are further names possibly relating to water-meadows. To these may be added names containing *Flood*, e.g. Flood Gate Piece, in Rodsley (Derbys), which may allude to a hatch or sluice-gate, or *Weir*, as in Weir Piece, in Sutton on the Hill (Derbys), where there was also a Floated Close. *Le Flodgatemedewe* 1339, in Minshull Vernon (Ches), is much earlier than the recognized starting date for managed water-meadows, and may relate to a precursor of the more elaborate technique, or perhaps merely a local drainage system. There are also some *Floodgate* names in Warwick-shire, e.g. Flood Gate Leasow (*Le Floudyeat* 1544), Floodgate

91

Meadow, in Aston, Floodgate Field (*Fludgatemedow* 1490), in Packwood, and Floodgate Close, in Charlcote. The process of *warping* i.e. flooding the adjoining fields from a tidal river, has given rise to Warping Drain, in Hook and in Goole, Warpings, in Thorne, and Warped Close and Land, in Goole (YW).

GREEN PASTURES

The customary division of agricultural operations into arable and pastoral suggests that as grassland and its management play as large a role in the rural economy as arable land, pasture land and meadows will be as productive of names as is the tilled area. One problem of interpretation is that it is not always possible to discriminate between the divisions by means of the generics of existing field-names. Some of the regional terms employed, such as *Park* in the south-western counties, or *Leasow* in the West Midlands, primarily denote 'grassland' but are found to be used in a general sense for any piece of enclosed land. *Grass* is found used merely descriptively in names such as *Grass Close*, but also as a generic, with the sense of 'a piece of grassland', e.g. in Saltgrass, in Chester (*Saltegres* 1285) 'a salty pasture'.

Plate 5.3   Cattle in 'floated' water-meadows, Nunton (Wilts)

Even what appear to be references to grassland in the specific elements of names, for instance in Tithe Apportionments, are not always factually borne out in the information given in the 'State of Cultivation' column. Grass Lands (*Le Grasland* 1424–25), in Steventon (Berks), Grass Garth, in Bole (Notts), Grass Gore, in North Stoke (Som), and Grassey Close, in Chadlington (Oxon), seem to define their current use without specifying whether it is pasture or meadow. Pasture, in Foston (YE), Pasture Close, in Lockington (Leics), Feeding Pasture, in Folkton (YE), and Hay Field, in Garton on the Wolds (YE), appear to be more precise, but it is doubtful whether some of these names can be taken any more at face value than others already mentioned. The most than can be said is that at one time these fields were being so used. Old Pasture Close, in Gembling (YE), makes no commitment about its present use, though it implies that it has returned to arable cultivation. On the other hand, a note in an early EPNS volume observes that the medieval form *Horsacre* indicates that *-acre* "was not always used of arable land". The same may perhaps be inferred for *furlang* 'a furlong, a main division of an open field', in *Wetherfurlang* 1317, in Cheselbourne (Dor), the first element of which is *wether* 'a castrated ram'. To these examples may be added a later name, in Wiltshire, *Acra voc. Whitehorse* 1570, which may, however, actually have been arable and may allude to the figure of a horse cut in the turf of some nearby pasture rather than to a live, grazing animal in the '*acra*' itself.

Leasow 'pasture, meadow-land' is occasionally also used, as has been seen, for arable closes in the West Midlands. The same paradox occurs (less frequently) with *Leas(e)*, e.g. Oat Leaze, in Box (Wilts), Bean Leaze, in North Nibley (Glos), and *Wheat leese* 1575, in Alkington (Glos), and with *Mead*, e.g. Rye Mead, in Grafton & Radcot (Oxon). In eastern counties the term *Warlot* is occasionally found, e.g. *Warlottes* early 13c., in Newton by Toft, *Warlotes* 1256, in Immingham, *Warlett Close* 1717, in Worlaby, and Y^e Warlots, in Kilnwick (YE) and in South Kelsey (Lincs), and Warlotts, in Stallingborough and in Tealby (Lincs). Other names relating to pasture land include Eatage Close, in Tansley (Derbys). *Eatage* refers to grass, especially the aftermath, available only for grazing, and not for a further hay crop. *Summereaten Close* and *Midsummer Pastures* will be discussed later in the chapter. *Paddock* is a common name for a small grazing enclosure.

Angram Field, in Skipworth (YE), and Angeram Flatt (*Angramflatts* 1591) '*flat* by the grasslands', in Stillingfleet (YW), contain the postulated Old English word *anger* 'grassland, pasture', as opposed to heath, woodland and arable land. Names containing this element are plentiful in Yorkshire. An interesting variant is Anagrams, in Mappleton & Rowleston (YE). Old Norse terms for 'meadow' include *fit* and *eng*. The latter occurs frequently in the Midlands and the north of England, where many townships have pasture called simply *The Ings*. The term is also found in such field-names as *Inge Closse* 1615, in St John's, *Midle Ing* 1538, in Holme (Cumb), Ing Close, in Chilwell, New Ings, in Hayton, Thick Ings, in Laxton (Notts), Hard Ings, in Bonby, Fowlings (*Fuleng* 13c.) 'dirty meadows', in North Kelsey (Lincs), *The Ings* 1695, in Horton in Ribblesdale, Hallam Ings, in Tickhill, Hole Ing, Moss Ing and North Ing, in Addingham (YW).

Fit 'riverside meadow-land' is found in *Kirkefit t.* Ed. 3, in St John Beckermet, *The Fittes* 1597, in St John's, *The Fyttes* 1606, in Torpenhow (Cumb), *Braderfitlond* 14c. 'broader *fit* land', in Caldecott (Ches), Lady Fitts, in Warcop, Linefoot (*Langlynefitt* 1488) 'flax meadow', in Bampton, Peas Fitts (*Peasefitts* 1690), in Murton (Westm), Cockfit, in Dean (Cumb), Fit Close, in Roecliffe, and Fulfit Close, in Staveley (YW). The related term *fitty*, describing the outermarsh or land lying between the sea or Humber and the bank, is found in north Lincolnshire, e.g. Fitties, in East Halton and in Stallingborough, and Fitty Paddock, in East Halton, but also occurs in Cheshire, e.g. *Fittie Carr* 1611, in Rainow.

The very common element *Holme*, usually rendered 'water meadow', is from Old Norse *holmr*. The normal interpretation possibly suggests that managed water-meadows were far more widespread, and of much earlier origin, than they actually were. A better explanation 'stream-side meadow' might be adopted, alongside names from Old English *hamm*, to which this definition is also applied. Names embodying *holmr* include Sand Holme, in Litton, Mean Holme 'common meadow', in Steeton, and Sweet Holme, in Hetton (YW), perhaps a part of *Hetunholme* 12c., formed with the name of the township. Among Lincolnshire examples are Holmes Close, in Riby, Holme Garths, in Kirmington, and Holms Furlong (*Les Holmes* 1623), in North Kelsey.

Hamm, the Old English term meaning 'an enclosure' but particularly '(grass) land in the bend of a river', is the basis of many field-names terminating in *-ham*, which is sometimes interchanged with *-holme* in modern spellings. Examples include the simple form e.g. The Ham (*Le Hamme* 1399), in Bromham (Wilts), *Le Hom* 16c., in Basford (Ches). The Hams (*Ham Furlong* 1732), in Whitchurch

(Warks), but the element is also combined with various specifics, e.g. Nettam (*Nethlihommes* 1334) 'nettly meadows', in Leek Wootton (Warks), Broad Hams (*Brodehamme* 1445), in South Newton (Wilts), and Goose Ham, in Steventon (Berks). The Ham Field, in Shrewsbury St Mary (Shrops), is a particularly striking example (see Plate 5.4).

A meadowland term found in Surrey names such as Pray Field, in Cranleigh, Preylands, in Artingon, Pray Mead, in Betchworth, Pray Meadow, in Pirbright and in Wonersh, Primemeads, in Alfold, and *Oxpreye* 1444, in Chertsey, is derived from Middle English *pre(y)* (Old French *pre*) 'a meadow'.

CEREALS, GRASSES AND FODDER CROPS

The conventional classification of cultivated land into arable, pasture and meadow obscures certain facts of botany, land management and the usage of crops. The major arable crops grown in England – wheat,

Plate 5.4   Ham Field, Shrewsbury
Old English *hamm*, 'land in a river-bend', is well exemplified in this name.

barley, rye and oats – are botanically cereals (and therefore grasses). They are not all grown exclusively for human consumption and it is their annual cultivation above all which differentiates them and certain fodder plants from grassland. Names alluding to the cereals and other arable crops are to be found throughout this work in discussions of various generic elements, but a few variants may be conveniently noted here. Besides such common names as Wheat Field or Wheat Close, forms like Whatcroft, in Lymm (Ches), are also found. Forms with -*ai*- or -*ay*-, such as *Quaitelit c*. 1240 'wheat slope', in Lowther (Westm), are derived from Old Norse *hveiti*. Barley Close, Barley Field etc. are clear enough, but such names as Barcroft (*Berecroft* 1286), in Hurdsfield (Ches), are not so easily recognized. These allude to *bear*, or two-rowed barley, grown in the Midlands and the north; the term often combines with *hill*, as in *Berill* 1638, in Burton Overy (Leics), or Berryl Close, in Hatton (Derbys). Bigg Lands, in Meathop (Westm), is from Old Norse *bygg* 'barley'. 'Rye hill' or 'rye lands' are not readily detected in Royles, in Acton, or Rylance (*Rylondis c*. 1200), in Pownall Fee (Ches). Old Norse *hafri* 'oats' is found in Haveriggs, in Morland (Westm). Pillar's Croft in Brewood (Staffs), and Pillows Croft, in Siddington (Ches), are among the many forms referring to pilled oats (*Avena nuda*). Others are Pilot Field (*Pilatefeilds* 1638), in Falfield (Glos), and *Pillitlond* 1606, in Bruntingthorpe (Leics).

These and other arable crops were developed and improved from the sixteenth century onwards. Other advances included the systematic management of the pastures and the introduction of new species or varieties of grass. Bastard Leys, in Harleston (Nthants), refers to ridges that were not completely swarded over, as the leys were in the arable fields. Bastard Ley occurs in Toppesfield, and Bastards Ley in Black Notley and in Great Leighs (Ess). Improved Meadow, found in Bostock (Ches) and in Whitchurch (Shrops), possibly alludes to the execution of the recommendations of such works as Walter Blith's *The English Improver* – the ploughing of old pasture, appropriate manuring, and the sowing of such plants as sainfoin and clover.[7] Inoculated Meadow, in Cound (Shrops), Inoculation Close, in Snarestone (Leics), and the generic in Slough Inocculation (*sic*) and Wood Inoculation, in Purleigh (Ess), refer to the introduction of new grass by the rolling-in of clumps from old pastures during the winter, followed by a thin seeding in the following spring. This practice was introduced about 1812 but was (not surprisingly) discontinued when it was found to be slow and inefficient.

Catstail (*Le Cattestailles c*. 1500), in Napton (Warks), Cats Tail

Meadow (*Cattistaylesmede t.* Ed. 1), in Little Coggeshall (Ess), Cats Tails, in Orton (Westm), and Cat Tail Field, in Bramhall and in Clutton (Ches), refer to *Phleum pratense*. There are a few references to the alternative name, e.g. Timothy Close, in Bigby, Timothy Plat, in Wooton (Lincs), Timothy Flat, in Longford (Derbys), which is from Timothy Hanson, who in 1720 introduced it into the United States with great success and then exported it back to these islands. Quaker Close, in Killamarsh (Derbys), and Quaker Field, in Lymm (Ches), may allude to *Briza media*, or common quaking grass, known locally as Quaker grass.

Rye Grass Ground occurs in Shellingford and in Stanford in the Vale (Berks), Rye Grass, in Barnston, in Hempsted and in Radwinter (Ess), Rigrass, in Warmington (Warks), Rye Grass Close, in Glenfield (Leics), in Sudbury, in Marston Montgomery and in Alkmonton (Derbys), Rye Grass Field, in more than a dozen places in Essex, in Turnditch (Derbys) and in Peover Superior (Ches). Rye Grass Piece, in Sunningwell (Berks), was alternatively Ray Grass Ground. These names refer to the fodder crop *Lolium perenne*, much commended by seventeenth- and eighteenth-century agricultural improvers. A local name *eaver(s)* occurs in Eaver, in East Anstey, Eaver Grass, in Kingswear, and Hammersladeivor and Yondersladeivor, in Lustleigh (Dev).

Beswick, in Mobberley, and Busy Ditch, in Great Boughton (Ches), are probably derived from Old English *bēos, bēosuc* 'bent grass', but references to grasses of this group (*Agrostis spp.*) are more often in such names as Bents, in Blymhill, Bent Meadow, in Whiston (Staffs) and in Ingol (Lancs), Bent (*Le Bent* 1386), in Windley, Bent Pingle (*Le Bent* 1389), in Duffield, Benty Field, in Alfreton, Benty Close, in Bretby (Derbys), Benty Leasow, in Frodesley (Shrops), and Bennety Meadow, in Enbourne (Berks). Such names as Fog Close, in Seacroft, Fog Field, in Yeadon (YW) and in Edale (Derbys), *Foggy Field* 1611, in Sutton Downes (Ches), and Foggy Leasow, in Church Eaton (Staffs), are usually explained as referring to 'aftermath, long grass left standing in winter', but some may allude to *Holcus lanatus* or Yorkshire Fog, which has a little grazing value when young.

Tray Foin Intake, in Horkstow (Lincs), undoubtedly refers to clover or trefoil (*Trifolium spp.*). The spelling here is the converse of the confusion found in the numerous variations of *sainfoin*, discussed below. The spelling in Trefoil, in Prees (Shrops), and Trefoil Piece, in North Weald (Ess), is conventional, and there are Trefoil Close and Clover Close in Snelston (Derbys). The modern *clover* is found here and in Clover Leasow, in Acton Burnell (Shrops), Clover Lands, in Holwell (Dor), Clover Piece, in Cakemore (Worcs), and Clover Close, in Riby (Lincs), in Bushby and in Upton (Leics), but an earlier development of Old English *clæfre* can be recognized in *Claueraymedowe* 1432, in Huntington, and Clever Loonds (*Clefferlandes* 17c.), in Little Stanney (Ches). A variety of clover is alluded to in Dutch White, in Pontesbury (Shrops), and popular names for the plant are found in Sucklesome, in Catton (Derbys), Honeysuckle Field, in Upminster and in Chignall St James, and Honeysuckle Mead, in High Ongar (Ess), which probably refer to clover rather than to *Lonicera periclymenum*.

The spelling anomaly in *Tray Foin*, already mentioned, is multiplied in the orthographic history of *sainfoin*. The name means 'healthy hay' and normally refers to *Onobrychis viciifolia*. The similarity of sound of the French words *sain*, *saint* and *cinq* led to a variety of forms ranging from Sainfoin, in Walkington (YE), through the approximately right Sanfoin Close, in Spelsbury (Oxon), and Sarnfoin Close, in Wharram le Street (YE), to canonization in St Foin Ground, in Shrivenham (Berks). There are many similar examples, and mystification extends to versions like Cinque Foil Close, in Londesborough, and Sink Foil, in Duggleby (YE), which present the additional problem of possibly referring to cinquefoil (*Potentilla spp.*).

OTHER ECONOMIC PLANTS

Plants producing textile fibres of several kinds are referred to in field-names, as are the various crops subsidiary to textile manufacture. Flax (*Linum usitatissimum*) is a dual-purpose crop, producing both fibres suitable for weaving into a fine cloth and an oil which has valuable wood-preserving properties. Field-names referring to this crop include *Flaxhawe* 1317 'flax enclosure', in Cookham (Berks). *Le Flaxlondes* 1355, in Mouldsworth (Ches), Flaxlands (*Flaxeland* 1240), in Grafton Underwood (Nthants). *Flexfurlong c.* 1280, in Pyrton (Oxon), Flax Furlong (*Flexfurlong'* 1247–48), in South Moreton (Berks), and Flax Leaze (*Flexlegh* 1308), in Lacock (Wilts).

The first element in Leanworth (*Linworth* 1575), in Gotherington (Glos), is Old English *līn* 'flax', also commonly found in field-names. Lynworth, in Twyning (Glos), is probably also 'flax enclosure', as are, with greater certainty, Lime Holme, in Slaidburn (YW), Line

Garth, in Hoff (Westm), Line Lands, in Litton (YW), and Linnadine, in Hartlebury (Worcs). After harvesting, the plants were immersed in pools, e.g. *Fleaxe Pools* 1650, in Almondsbury (Glos). Flacks Field, in Takeley (Ess), was earlier *Flexmere* 1378, alluding to such a pool. Hemp, from which rope and coarse fabrics were made, was similarly treated – witness such names as Hemp Dubb ('hemp pool'), in Paythorne (YW). Being used by all the tenants, it would have been in a central location, as is suggested by a 1538 by-law of Great Horwood (Bucks), which required that each tenant 'shall clean his part of his ditch . . . as far as the Hemp Pool', without stating who was responsible for the cleaning of the pool itself.[8] This process of *retting* separated the fibres, which were then dried at *gig-holes*, in which a slow fire drove off the water from the retted plants.

Names referring to hemp include Hemp Field, in Marton (Ches), Hemp Flatt, in Whettenhall (Ches), Elbow Hemphay, in Beer (Dev), Hemp Land, in Littlebourne (Kent), Hemp Lands, in Buckden (YW), Hemp Leasow, in Stirchley (Shrops), and Hemp Croft, in Osleston (Derbys), in Newton (Ches) and in Dorchester (Oxon). Both hemp and flax were often grown in small enclosures near the dwellings, *Flax Plot*, *Hemp Pleck* and similar names providing abundant evidence. The plant named in Tasly (*Tasley* 1679), in Foxton (Leics), and in Tazle Field, in North Weald, Tazell Field in Salford, Tessil Croft, in Walthamstow, and Teazle Field, in Wethersfield and in Thaxted (Ess), in Leatherhead (Sur) and in Axminster (Dev), is the fuller's teasel (*Dipsacus fullonum*), the hooked seed-heads of which were customarily used in the combing of wool and to raise the nap on finished cloth.

There are numerous references to ozier beds. In Essex, Ozier Ground occurs about fifty times, and Ozier Field about twelve times. The young shoots from the pollarded trees were soaked in boiling water and then peeled, in readiness for basket weaving and similar crafts. The withies were also used in thatching and the preparation of hurdles for fencing and for drainage purposes.

FLAVOURINGS, FRAGRANCES, DYES AND THERAPEUTIC HERBS

Anise, or aniseed (*Pimpinella anisum*), a plant of Mediterranean or Near Eastern origin, has been grown in England since the sixteenth century. Anniseed Meadow, in Shrewsbury St Mary, and Annyseed

Meadow, in Middleton Scriven, are among the several Shropshire examples of field-names referring to this herb. Aniseed, in Little Longstone (Derbys), is another instance. Caraway (*Carum carvi*, the source of seed for seed-cake) was once grown in England. Among the relatively few field-name references are Carraway, in East Stour (Dor), and Carraway Piece, in Colne Engaine (Ess). A number of other Essex parishes have either Carraway Mead or Carraway Field.[9]

Dyleforlanges late 13c., in West Rasen (Lincs), and Dill Acres (*Dylfeld* 1356), in Baslow (Derbys), probably relate to the plant *Anethum graveolens*, cultivated in herb gardens and elsewhere for the carminative properties of the seeds. Some species of vetch were known locally as *dill*, especially in Gloucestershire, but this dialectal usage is not recorded before the eighteenth century. There are occasional references to parsley (*Petroselinum crispum*), e.g. Parsley Beds, in Ovenden (YW), Parsley Close, in Ticknall (Derbys), and Parsley Field, in Ardleigh (Ess).

References such as those in Mustard Field, in Helmstead (Ess) and in Sutton on Derwent (YE), and Mustard Close, in Tideswell (Derbys), may be to white mustard (*Sinapis alba*), grown as a forage crop, or to black mustard (*Sinapis nigra*), from the seeds of which the condiment is made. The latter is probably the allusion in Mustard Seed Piece, in East Tilbury (Ess).

Liquorice (*Glycyrhiza glabra*) was introduced into England in the Middle Ages. It was usually grown in market gardens near towns, from which plenty of manure could be obtained, but field-name evidence is country-wide. Its roots were harvested in the third summer after planting, but a good profit could be obtained to reward the long wait. Spanish Liquorice Ground, in Bere Regis (Dor), Liquorice Hill, in Linthwaite, Liquorice Close, in Ferry Fryston (YW), and Liquorice, in Eastham (Ches), testify to the wide distribution of the cultivation of this plant. Hirst Garth, in Pontefract (YW), is described as "a liquorice garth", and it was this area that was most renowned for the crop. Spanish Flat, in Norton in Hales, and Spanish Hays, in Cressage (Shrops), are further possible references.

The saffron crocus (*Crocus sativus*), not to be confused with the poisonous herb meadow saffron (*Colchicum autumnale*), was an important crop in Essex, where the twenty or thirty field-name references include Saffron Field, in Broxted, in Great Dunmow, in Margaret Roding and in Great Waltham, Saffron Garden, in Takeley and in Manuden, and Saffron Ground, in Debden, in Henham and in Thaxted. In other counties *Saffron Plott* 1546 is found in Cumnor

(Berks, now Oxon), Saffron Close, in Sall (Norf), in Ewelme (dating from 1605) and in Denton (Oxon), Saffron Hill, in Aylestone (Leics), Saffron Croft, in Lilleshall (Shrops), *Saffron Yard* 1564, in Higham Ferrers (Nthants), and Park Saffron, in St Gluvias (Corn). Gloucestershire examples include *Safronhay* 1470, in Beckford, *Safforne Hey* 1540, in Forthampton, and *Saffernehey* 1575, in Prestbury. *Safern Garden* 1602 occurs in Stapeley (Ches). Saffron Garden, near the priory in Maiden Bradley (Wilts), appears to be the only example in that county.

This versatile plant was used to produce an orange-yellow dye and to flavour food; it was a herbal remedy and was even said to kill or deter moths if spread among garments. It was reintroduced into England in the middle of the fourteenth century, and *Saffrongardyn* 1467, in Widdington (Ess), is possibly the earliest field-name reference to it. In the 1660s another plant, safflower (*Carthamus tinctorius*), began to be grown widely, particularly in Oxfordshire and Gloucestershire. This produced a pink dye and was alternatively known as 'bastard saffron' (though the two plants are not related). It is possible that some of the *Saffron* field-names in fact relate to this newcomer, and the alternative designation may lie behind such names as Bastards, in Felsted and in Stisted (Ess).

Maderlond 1247–48, in Newbury (Berks), *Maderton* 1332, in Fetcham (Sur), and *Le Maderyorde* 1370, in Shrewsbury St Chad (Shrops), allude to madder (OE *mæddre*, ON *mathri*) a plant (*Rubia tinctorum*) yielding alizarin, a red dye. From the dates of some of the forms it is evident that it was grown, presumably for this purpose, in medieval times. Attempts to grow it on a larger scale in the seventeenth century do not appear to have been referred to in many field-names. Madder or Mathers Garth, in Wetherby (YW), is a possible example, though *Mathers* may be a surname, apparently confirmed by *Mathers Football Garth* 1753. A related reference occurs in Crabmills, in Crayke (YN) 'mills for processing madder', in which the dialect *crab*, *crap* or *crop* is used, defined in the *Oxford Dictionary* as 'madder, especially the commercial product obtained by grinding the inner part of the root'. This term may be the source of Crapshill, in Great Easton (Leics), Crop Field, in West Hoathly (Sus), and Crab Croft, in Downham (Ess), though the last may be a reference to crab-apple trees. Moreover it would not be safe so to interpret a form earlier than the sixteenth century, when the French equivalent *crappe* was recorded. A 1792 quotation in the dictionary mentions "the herbs for dying [*sic*] as crap, woad and clary". *Clary*, *Salvia sclarea*, is alluded to in *Clarydole* 1674, in Gumley (Leics).

Plate 5.5 Old botanical illustration of an economic plant: madder, from J. de Kanter; *De Meekrapteler En-bereider* (Dordrecht, 1802)

Old English *wurma*, referring to a purple dye and to the plant from which this was extracted, occurs in a field-name, *Worminehalh* 1286, in an unidentified place in Macclesfield Hundred (Ches).

Woad, the source of the blue dye that might be said to have coloured the popular view of pre-Anglo-Saxon England (derived from the reports of Caesar and Pliny), was widely grown until the nineteenth century, when the introduction of indigo and cheaper chemical alternatives rendered its cultivation uneconomic. The plant (*Isatis tinctoria*), which belongs to the great family of Cruciferae, bears small yellow flowers. The dye is derived from the leaves after they have been ground and allowed to ferment.

References to this plant are found in all Midland counties, as well as occasionally in those further south. It was common in Northamptonshire, particularly in the vicinity of Kettering, where Wadcroft survives as a street-name. Spellings with *Wad-* preserve the Old English form *wād*. Some idea of the distribution can be gained from such examples as Wad Acre, in Moreton Valence, Woad Ground, in Aston Somerville (Glos), Wadlands, in Moreton Corbet (Shrops), Wadhills, in Saighton (Ches), Waddale, in Bakewell (Derbys),

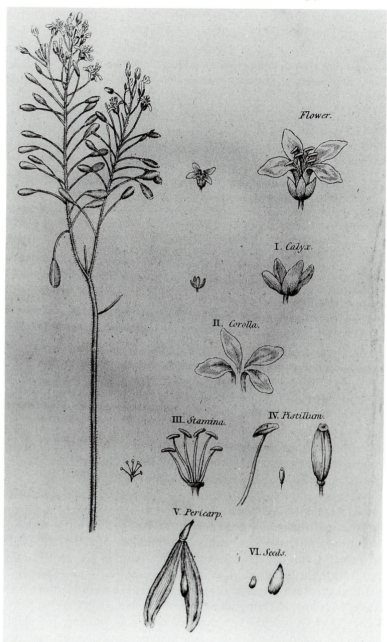

Plate 5.6 Old botanical illustration of an economic plant: woad, from Thornton's *British Flora*, 1812

Waddams, in Sutton Bonington (Notts), Wadlands Peice, in Foxton (Leics), The Woad Close, in Upton (Nthants, now Cambs), and *Wadbridge Furlong* 1739 (*Watbrech c.* 1185), in Hook Norton (Oxon). Medieval names without later forms include *Le Wadsike* 13c., in Shangton (Leics), *Wadbrech c.* 1240, in Steeple Barton (Oxon), and *Wadlandis* 1333, in Bretby (Derbys). The *breach* names, e.g. *Watbrech*, are of interest because of the cropping regime usually adopted. Woad was planted on newly broken or freshly manured land before wheat. Weld, or dyer's greenweed (*Reseda luteola*), is not often referred to in names, perhaps because it was intersown with other crops. Gaudy Ground, in Pontesbury (Shrops), is a probable allusion to this plant.

Lavender Acres, in Wimborne Minster (Dor), and Lavender Field, in Wargrave (Berks), allude to the fragrant shrubby plant *Lavandula vera*, cultivated for its flowers and for the essential oil derived from them. Lower Lavender, in Little Leighs, and Upper Lavender, in Great Waltham (Ess), are further references, and Lavender Field, in Mitcham (Sur), is in a place famous for its lavender production for the London market.

Tobacco Pipe Piece, in Essendine (Rut), is, at best, an indirect allusion, and need have no reference to the growing of the plant but may refer to a source of clay for pipe-making. The plant itself seems to have preferred the milder West Midlands – witness Tobacco Field, in Prees, Tobacco Piece, in Billingsley (Shrops), and Tobacco Plat, in Southam (Glos). There are a few examples in other counties, e.g. Tobacco Shot, in Wickham Bonhunt (Ess). Cultivation was prohibited by royal proclamation in 1619 but it was still thriving thirty years later, then further forbidden, tolerated subject to payment of excise duties, forbidden again, and finally suppressed (apart from in a few places) in the late 1650s.

Not all economic plants would necessarily be cultivated; wild shrubs would also be utilized and their location noted in field-names. Buckthorn (*Rhamnus catharticus*), for example, might yield a sufficient supply of its products without deliberate cultivation and might be located from such field-names as Buckthorn, in Hursley (Hants), and Buckthorn Meadow, in Ashford (Derbys).

Although Rush Meadow, in Hurley (Berks) and in Easton (Suf), Rushy Meadow, in Dalbury Lees (Derbys), and Rush Carr, in North Kelsey (Lincs), would have provided only poor grazing, the plants supplied a cheap means of domestic lighting. Rushes were also used as floor coverings and were plaited to make chair-seats. Reeds and sedge were used for thatching, the former being alluded to in Reed

Plate 5.7 Economic plants: harvesting sedge, Cambridgeshire

Furlong, in Burlington (Beds), Ready Furlong, in Breaston (Derbys), and Reed Fen, in Little Thetford (Cambs), and the latter in Sedge Fen (*Segghffen* 1431), in Swaffham Prior (Cambs). Segmar, in Ulceby (Lincs) 'boundary land where sedge grows', Segg Furlong (*Segfurlong* 13c.), in Flintham (Notts), and Segholme, in Lockington (Leics), show Scandinavian influence. Clearings or marshes from which thatching reeds could be obtained might be indicated by such general names at Thackthwaite (*Thacthwait* 1220), in Loweswater (Cumb), Thack Carr (*Thacker* 1339), in Burstwick (YE), Thackmire (*Thakmyre* 1524), in Beetham (Westm), Thatcholme (*Thacholmes t.* Ed. 3), in Bakewell, or *The Thatchin Marsh* 1640, in Castleton (Derbys).

DISPARAGEMENT AND DESPAIR

Unproductive land may be compared with that allotted to Cain, e.g. Cains Ground, in Heddington (Wilts), or to the fields of the Cities of the Plain, e.g. Gomorrah Close, in Snaith (YW), or Sodom Field, in Brampton (Derbys). Ill fortune is intensified by the biblical reference in Jonas Pasture, in Stanton by Dale (Derbys). Infertility may be attributed, or the land consigned, to the devil as in Devil's Own, in Norton Lindsay (Warks), or the various *Jack* names, e.g. Jack Tail, in Beighton (Derbys), Jack Flatt, in Coal Aston (Derbys). But Devils Bit, in Stoke Lyne (Oxon), is not derogatory but a reference to a flower, the Devil's Bit Scabious (*Scabiosa succisa*). Hell Hole, distributed fairly widely, e.g. in Elwick Hall (Dur), Farnsfield (Notts), Norbury (Staffs) and Elmley Castle (Worcs), seems to be a blunt expression of dissatisfaction at infertile or otherwise unattractive land. Variants include *Hell Hole Leases* 1674, in Countesthorpe, Hell Hole Close, in Odstone (Leics), Hell Hole Piece, in Cumnor (Berks, now Oxon), Hell Pit, in Lockinge (Berks), and Hell Gates, in Harlow (Ess). Perhaps early Victorian squeamishness about 'strong' language changed what was Hell Hole in 1813 to Hill Hole in 1841, in Newton by Toft (Lincs). Purgatory, a field requiring endless unpleasant labour, is found in Thatcham (Berks), in Wentnor (Shrops), in Forest Hill (Oxon), in Appleton (Ches), in Carleton and in Poulton (Lancs), and in Barlow (YW). This imagery is taken further in Long Purgatory Meadow, in Prees (Shrops).

A mixture of irony and descriptive realism is found in Wopses Castle, (i.e. 'wasps' castle') described as "a scrubby plot" on the parish boundary of Puddletown (Dor). *Castle* is used ironically in a number of derogatory names, e.g. Rats Castle, in Lechdale (Glos), possibly the site of a decayed building. Ill-favoured fields are described in terms of social unacceptability, e.g. Spendthrift, in Bingley (YW), Idle Field, in Great Shefford (Berks), Doubtful Piece, in Compton (Berks), Quarrelsome, in Clifton & Compton (Derbys), Spiteful Yards and Sullen Field, in Ipsden (Oxon). Normans Friend (for *No Man's Friend*), in Rawcliffe (YW), Good For Nothing, in Monks Coppenhall (Ches), Goodfornothing Acres, in Diddlebury (Shrops), Slovens Bank, in Great Hagbourne (Berks), and The Misbegotten, in Shardlow (Derbys). Kim Cams, in Montford (Shrops), means 'perverse'.

Other names allude to the physical and psychological effects of the recalcitrant land, e.g. Tedious Field, in Stisted (Ess), Weary Furlong, a large field in Wookey (Som), Hard Struggle, in Paul (Corn), Trouble Field, in West Parley (Dor), Troublesome, in Oldland (Glos), and Labour in Vain, which occurs fairly often. Break Back (*Breakebacke Close* 1662) is found in Treeton (YW), in Chetton (Shrops), in several places in Essex, and in Chaceley (Glos). The sense may be similar to Brokenback (*Brokenhyl* 1293), in Broughton (Hunts, now Cambs), or Broken Back (*Break Back Furlong* 1768), in Wroxton (Oxon), which may allude to the land itself, suggesting a mound which has been broken into in some way.

The various *Bedlam* names, for fields that only a madman would attempt to cultivate, also belong here. The name Bedlam occurs half a dozen times in Essex, Bedlam Field, in Cranham, and Bedlams Twelve Acres, in Tillingham; alone or with various generics the term is widely distributed in other counties. Unhappiness is represented by Little Content, in Milford (Hants), Breakheart Hill, in Chitterne (Wilts), and Sorrowful, in Wentnor (Shrops). The husbandmen of Dunham Massey (Ches) seem to have had plenty to complain about; fields there bear such names as Dreadful, Care Field, Terrible, Dangerous Acre and Sin Field. The last may perhaps not be a literal reference to bad behaviour, *Sin* being used in some names for 'seven'.

The pain of hunger (already touched upon in *Hunger Hill*, etc. names) is evoked in Famish Croft, in Sutton (Shrops), Pinchgut, in Northolt (Middx), and the contrast between feasting and fasting emphasizes the disappointment in Cold Christmas Field, in Thundridge (Herts). Hungerstarve Meadow, in Withington (Glos), Starve Gut Field, in Sible Hedingham (Ess), Starve Acre, in Didcot and in Lockinge (Berks), and Starvation Acre, in West Ham (Ess, now Greater London), have many variants in the context of inanition, including *Starveall*, *Starvecrow*, *Starve Goose* and *Starvelarks*. Lenten Field, in Godley (Ches), compares the diet enforced by an unproductive field with the traditional Lenten fast. *Langefriday c.* 1200, in Rowton (Ches), may be related in meaning to the last name, if it is derived from Old English *Lang-Frīgedæg* 'Good Friday', a day of rigorous fasting, and so suggesting a dearth of crops. In Denmark, field-names containing *Langfredag* are pieces of land upon which much effort has to be spent in cultivation. Friday was traditionally a day of ill fortune. Long Friday, in Wroxton (Oxon), however, seems to be partly a reference to actual length, as there were also Long Thursday Furlong and Short Friday Furlong in the same parish. Similarly fields called Long Fridays, in Stokesay (Shrops), adjoin others called Short Saturdays. These and other *Friday* names, such as Friday's Ploughing, in Neen Savage (Shrops), or *Frydaysham* 17c., in Ashton Keynes (Wilts), may be merely references to land on which manorial service was to be performed on Friday. Others, e.g. *Frydyescroft* 1319, in Churton (Ches), may contain the surname *Friday*.

There is an obvious connection between infertility and financial loss. This is expressed in such names as Little Gains, in Lambourne (Ess), and Small Gains, which occurs about a dozen times in Wiltshire, in Aston Bampton and in Chadlington (Oxon), in Sturry (Kent), and nearly a hundred times in Essex, with a good representation in many other counties as well. Small Gains, on Woolton Farm in Littlebourne (Kent), has been described by one with personal experience as a 'horrible, waterlogged field'. The Mistake, in Thingwall (Ches), Repentance, in Stamford Rivers (Ess), Hard Bargain, in Bitterley (Shrops), Sorry Bargain, in Waltham St Lawrence (Berks) and in Lelant (Corn), and The Cast Lost (i.e. 'the cost lost'), in Paul (Corn), indicate regret at a waste of purchase price. Similar in sense to these are Small Profits, in Greys Thurrock and half a dozen other places in Essex, and Small Profit, in Watlington (Oxon) and in Beer (Dev). Less and Less, in Penkridge (Staffs), suggests a downward slope in production. Dear Bought, a common derogatory name, occurs in Mobberley and in Chorley (Ches), in Newland and in Micheldean (Glos), in Kettlewell (YW), in Beetham (Westm), in Nether Wyresdale, in Pilling and in Wesham (Lancs). Early examples include *Derebouht* 13c., in Sall (Norf), *Derebocht* 1240, in Kirkheaton (YW), *Derebouth* 1240, in Chatteris, and *Little Deerebought* 1625, in Wicken (Cambs).

The expected outcome of continued use of such land is expressed in Hard Luck, in Thirston (Nthumb). Poverty Field, in Laindon and in Aythorp Roding (Ess), and Beggarall (or Buggerall), in Acton Round (Shrops). The resultant penury includes the discomfort and shame of Bare Arse, in Berrington and in Wroxeter (Shrops), in Nateby (Lancs) and in Hallaton (Leics); an early form of this name, *Barherse* 1342, occurs in Oxspring (YW). Bareblankets, in Wreay (Cumb), has unproductive patches. Reminders of physical suffering associated with poverty are provided by Pinch Poor, in Siston (Glos), Pinchgut, in Lacock (Wilts) and in Burghfield (Berks), Rawbones, in Tandridge (Sur), *Belly Ake* 1700, in Hugglescote (Leics), and Pine Belly, in North Elmsall (YW). Beggar's Banks, in Nackington (Kent), Beggar Bush, in Wardington (Oxon) and in Barton upon Humber (Lincs) and similar names in most counties refer to places actually affording shelter to mendicants, or to land that is likely to reduce the cultivator to indigence. Hang Dog Close, in Tealby (Lincs), and Hang Dog Leys, in Wigginton (Oxon), utilize the everyday expression *hang-dog* 'low, degraded' to describe worthless land.

Pickpocket, in Siston (Glos), Pickpockets Close, in Thorne (YW), and Piratical Field, in St Nicholas Hurst (Berks), equate the losses from the land with felonious deprivation of property. Negative names such as Hopeless, in Sandon (Ess), Carry Nothing, in Newbold Astbury (Ches), and Weighnought, in Ham & Stone (Glos), clearly allude to the amount of the harvest expected. Woworth, in Eckington (Derbys), seems like a cry of despair ('Woe worth the day!'), but it may be analysed into 'misshapen enclosure' from Old English *wōh* 'crooked' and *worth*. Literal expressions of disgust sometimes express more than those dependent on metaphor; the former include Bad Mead, in Hinton Parva (Dor), The Worst I Ever Came In, in Tilston, and The Worst That Ever Was Seen, in Duckington (Ches).

THE VOCABULARY OF SUCCESS

As images of famine prevail in names for infertile land, it is to be expected that the less numerous designations of productive land should utilize terms evoking abundance, such as Surfeets Meadow, in Hunsterson (Ches), Filhorn, in Marshfield (Glos), Feast Meadow, in Hinksey (Berks), and Cupboard Hill, in Stokenchurch (Bucks) and in Steventon (Berks). Restrained admiration is expressed in Pretty Field, in Siddington and in Tytherington, and Goodenough, in Peover Superior (Ches). Wheat Cake, in Beetham (Westm), implies a superior diet derived from fertile land, as do *Hony-cak Furlonge* 1625, in Bourton on the Water (Glos), Butter Cake, in Urkington (Ches), and Furlong Called Butter-cake-hill, in Tealby (Lincs). The satisfaction of agreeably tasting foods is suggested by Sweet Tooth, in Greenhalgh and in Medlar (Lancs), Yolk o' Egg, in Horsforth (YW), and Yolk of the Egg, in Woodford and in other places in Cheshire, and possibly Bacon and Beans Meadow, in Waterperry (Oxon). Bread and Cheese Lands, in Paddington (Middx, now Greater London), Bread and Cheese Meadow, in Huncote (Leics), and Banquetting Field, in Henley (Oxon), suggest pleasant picnics out of doors. Picnics there may have been at some time, but the leisure alluded to was restricted, as the names probably refer merely to the place where food was eaten during haymaking or harvesting, when bread and cheese were among the regular rations allowed to the workers.

Lucky Croft, in Barthomley, Make Good Hey, in High Legh (Ches), and Have a Good Heart, in Bishop's Castle (Shrops), expect, implore, or express thanks for, success. *Bliffeld* 1400 'pleasant field', in Peover Superior (Ches), and the frequent *Mount Pleasant* names may allude to the visual qualities of the landscape or to the tangible or abstract rewards from working on the land. The occasional ironic use of *Mount Pleasant* needs, of course, to be borne in mind.

References to the richness of milk may be found in the names of good pastures, e.g. Sweet Milk, in Bolton (Westm). Other complimentary terms for rich pasture include *Creame Poake Nooke* 1674, in Bigby, and *Creampoch Field* 1711, in Linwood (Lincs), Cream Pot, in Ketton (Rut), Cream Pots, in Stottesdon (Shrops), and Far Cream Pot, in Brewood (Staffs). Buttermilk Field occurs in Northern Etchells (Ches) and Buttermilk Hall in Prescote and in Barford (Oxon), Butter is also referred to in early names such as *Botereden* c. 1278 'butter valley', in Enstone (Oxon), and *Boterhale* 1354 'butter nook', in Poynton (Ches). Some names have a long history, e.g. Butterhill (*Buterhul* 1154–63), in Hook Norton (Oxon). Others lack early forms, e.g. Butter Field, in Isleworth (Middx, now Greater London), Butter Pasture, in Belper (Derbys), and Butterpatch, in Longworth (Berks).

Smarrow Hill, in Coaley (Glos), is from Old English *smeoru* 'fat'. *Fat* indicates good qualities in the soil or herbage, as well as the effect of both on the grazing beasts. Examples focusing on the fields themselves include Fat Pasture, in Minshull Vernon (Ches), Fatlands, in Baggrave (Leics), Fatland Field, in Lamberhurst (Kent), Fat Haden 'fat headlands', in Chinley (Derbys), and those referring to the fattening of livestock include Fat Ox (*Fatt Ox Close* 1607), in Haselbury Bryan, Fat Beast Close, in Muston (YE), Fattening Leaze, in Stoke Dabernon (Sur), *Fatting Leaze* 1664, in Hurley (Berks), Fatting Ground, in Pimperne (Dor), Fatling Pasture and Fatten Pasture, in Mayland, and Fattening Meadow, in Vange (Ess).

The advantages of early ripening are referred to in Earliest Croft, in Malpas (Ches), and also in some of the *Cuckoo* names, e.g. Cuckow Butts (*The Cuckow Butte* 1606), in Offerton (Derbys), which are said sometimes to indicate the production of a markedly earlier harvest than neighbouring fields. God's Gift, in Nateland (Westm), Providence, in Eaton under Heywood (Shrops), Blessing Field and Blessings Mead (*God-blessing* 1694), in Holt (Dor), Blest Acre, in Stockton (Shrops), and Thanky Furlong, in Milton under Wychwood (Oxon), express satisfaction tempered with a modicum of pious thankfulness. Garden of Eden, in Paul (Corn), applied to a group of garden plots on the cliff-top, is probably either an expression of hope of abundance with little or no labour, or a reference to a beautiful position; Canaan, in Worth Matravers (Dor), and Land of Canaan, in Tushingham cum Grindley (Ches), recall the land 'flowing with milk and honey' promised to the Israelites during their sojourn in the desert. Several centuries of building development make it no longer possible to ascertain the fertility of Land of Promise, in Shoreditch (Middx, now Greater London). There is a Promised Land Farm in Rowton (Ches), but Promised Land, in Kelfield (YE), seems to be a piece of wry humour, as it is annotated "Award withheld too long". Goshan, in Odd Rode (Ches), refers to the fertile part of Egypt which the Israelites were allocated. Beulah Field, in Ellerker (YE), looks back to another scriptural place of joy developed in *Pilgrim's Progress*.

Approval is expressed in Heaven Field, in Ashampstead (Berks), Heaven Gate Leaze, in St Briavels (Glos), Little Haven (*Lytill Hevyn* 1473), in Barkisland (YW), and perhaps Haven, in Sowerby (YW), for which a derivation from Old English *hæfen* 'a holding of land' has also been proposed, but it is interesting to note that there is a Hell Croft in the same township, indicating the local pattern of thought on the qualities of land. *Paradise* names are found quite early. They may refer to medieval pleasure gardens, may imply general satisfaction with the quality of the land, or may be ironic. Examples include *Paradis* 1309, in Earley (Berks), Paradise (*Parodys* 1337), in Clifton & Compton (Derbys), Paradise Croft, in Soberton (Hants), and Paradise Ten Acres, in Burnham (Som). An ironic example is Paradise, in Motcombe (Dor), which is a steep, bracken-covered hill.

Great Delight, in Austerson (Ches), indicates satisfaction at good fortune in a more general way, as do Happy Home, in Reighton (YE), and Happy Lands, in Steventon (Berks). Make Merry, in Ham & Stone (Glos), seems to be a piece of self-exhortation to celebrate (perhaps) a good harvest, and Easy Crook, in Appleby (Westm), possibly marks approval of land requiring little effort. Welcome, in Babcary (Som), and Pleasant Place, in Brightwell (Berks), seem to be general terms of approval, possibly referring to fertile land with an agreeable view, as may also be implied in Prospect Field, in Boreham (Ess). Adjoining a close called Paradise Meadow, in Goosnargh (Lancs), is another called Mount Pleasant. The ironic possibilities of some of these names have already been mentioned.

Names such as Gold Crop, in Hawkeswell (Ess), and Goldfinder, in Little Stretton (Leics), Rich Leasow, in Smethcott (Shrops), or Rich Field, in Great Waltham (Ess), may allude to the quality of the soil or of the product, or the monetary gain to be expected. Profitability is less obliquely mentioned in other field-names. These include Pay My Cost, in St Erth (Corn), Paywell Field, in Ashford Carbonell (Shrops), Great Gains, in Buscote (Berks), in Lambourne, in Rettenden and about a dozen other places in Essex (in contrast with many times that number of instances of *Small Gains*), Clear Gains, in Abingdon (Berks, now Oxon) and in Sherfield English (Hants), Long Gains, in Athorne (Ess), Make Me Rich, in Ferry Fryston (YW), Gold Finder, in Childer Thornton, and Turn Penny Field, in Buglawton (Ches). A return to good fortune is declared, or hoped for, in such names as Prosperity, in Sledmere (YE), Wealthy, in St Buryan (Corn), Profitable Field, in Lingfield (Sur), Hopeful Field, in Compton, God Speed Furlong, in Cholsey (Berks), and *God Speed* 1585, in Whichford (Warks).

DRAUGHT OXEN AND PARISH BULLS

A 1322 furlong-name in Hoby (Leics), *There the oxen were slaine* (written, in the original document, as a single word), has not lasted, but another fourteenth-century Leicestershire name, *ubi Godwynes-oxe morieabatur* ('where Godwin's ox died'), survived at least until 1679 as *Goodins Ox*, in the Great Bowden Glebe Terrier for that date. More famous than either of these is the thirteenth-century name *Thertheoxlaydede*, in Northall (Bucks), the name summarizing the despondency of the owner at the loss of perhaps his principal agricultural asset. Surviving names, such as Oxpasture, in Northolt (Middx), where there are also names alluding to bulls and cows separately, and Ox Leasow, common in Shropshire, are evidence of the importance of the ox as a draught animal until quite recent times. Other examples include Ox Mead (*Exemede* 1383), in Britford (Wilts), Ox Leys (*Oxeleasowe* 1585), in Balsall (Warks), *Oxehey Close* 1610, in Bushley (Worcs), *The Oxe Leasowe* 1628, in Prestbury (Glos), Ox Leasow, in Cradley (Worcs), and Ox Close, in Wirksworth (Derbys). A less obvious reference is found in Corby (Nthants), where Great and Little Excellent represents *Great and Little Exland*, recorded in 1580.

A late seventeenth-century document alludes to a piece of pasture

Plate 5.8 A medieval ploughman and his ox, from Crescentius, *Liber Ruralium Commodorum*, 1493

Plate 5.9   Ploughing with oxen in early twentieth-century Oxfordshire

called *The Constables Grass*, in Whittlesey Rural (Cambridgeshire), which was assigned to the village constables "for the keeping each of them a common Bull and Boar for the use of the Inhabitants". Elsewhere such custody was the responsibility of the incumbent. Joyce Godber has described conditions in eighteenth-century Bedfordshire. "In many parishes, such as Clifton and Steppingley, the rector still kept a bull and boar for parish use; for the ownership of such animals had to be determined, otherwise there would have been fighting on the common."[10] Bull Frith, in Walkington (YE), is laconically annotated by the school field-name collectors: "Parish bull kept here". In Lincolnshire, Bull Hill, in Cadney, is recorded as being held by the "Bylawmen for keeping a bull", and Yᵉ Bull Marfare, in South Kelsey, is described in 1767 as "meadow belonging to the Town for Keeping a Bull", providing further evidence of the 'common bull' practice. *Marfare* is from *marfur*, discussed below.

The frequent repetition in Westmorland of the name Bull Copy caused A.H. Smith to remark that "according to Caxton, *The game and playe of chesse* (1474) 112, 'a great bole is suffisid with right litil a pasture'." Though Smith recorded less than thirty examples of the name in Westmorland, other observers, in particular Mary Atkin, have reached a different total.[11] Mrs Atkin's records show that in the twenty-two townships of Kendal barony alone, there were forty-five fields bearing this name on the various farms; several townships had three or four each, and one (Helsington) had seven. Mrs Atkin also found that *Bull Copy* fields are often on large demesnal farms, on which field-names such as Hall Pasture, Lord's Pasture and Great Park might be found. Nearly all the *Bull Copy* fields were adjacent to the farmhouse, and often beside a track leading past the field towards outside pastures. It was convenient to keep the bull at a place where the cows could be brought to him for service. Most of these enclosures are known to have been former coppice land, the remaining trees providing some shade from the sun but not growing in sufficient numbers to cause problems from flies.

There are instances of *Bull Copy* in the West Riding of Yorkshire, mostly in the wapentakes of East and West Staincliffe, as well as the variant Bully Copy in Rawdon (Skyrack wapentake). Mrs Mary Higham has counted eleven examples in Tithe Apportionments, three each in Bentham and in Easington. She has also found the name in eight places in north Lancashire, one of which, Whittington, had as many as seven instances of Bull Copy on its separate farms.[12]

Though a close called Bull Copy must be small, it need not be minute, despite Caxton's opinion. Mrs Higham has found that these fields vary between two and five acres in extent. In Bull Marfur, in Stallingborough and other places in Lincolnshire, the local generic *marfur* 'boundary furrow' would be used of a not very extensive area of land. A variety of other terms in many different counties also suggest small plots of land, such as Bull Hern (from OE *hyrne* 'a nook or corner'), in Reading (Berks), Bull Acre, in Tabley Superior (Ches), and more significantly its antecedent thirteenth-century form *Bullehalith* ('the bull's *halh* or nook of land'), and, in Leicestershire, Bulls Nook, in Carlton and in Twycross, Bulls Pen, in Glen Magna, *Bull Gores*, in the open fields of Kings Norton. Bull Parlour, in Cadeby (*Parlour* usually meaning 'a secluded field'), has an area of just under two roods. But little weight can be put on the significance of some of these generics, because others such as *Crates*, *Croft*, *Dole*, *Field*, *Ings*, *Piece* and *Yard*, also used with *Bull* as specific, say no more and no less about their size. Bulls Tail, found in Wychwood (Oxon) and Donington (Leics), may be a small curved piece of land, named from its resembling the tail of the animal, or from the bull's being kept on a remnant or tail of land, of no particular size, projecting from another field. *Cow Close*, *Cowleaze*, *Cow Pasture* and so on are very frequently found, with appropriate regional variations. *Cow Carr* is found in the Fens, and *Cow Park* in the south-west. *Cow Leasow* may be expected chiefly in the West Midlands, though examples are found elsewhere, such as *Cowelesowe c.* 1360 in Shifford (Oxon). The idiosyncratic spelling of Coughgarth, in Hartley (Westm), puts a little variety into the listing of names derived from *Cow*. The name Cowleaze Thousand Acres, in Hampreston (Dor), must not be overlooked, though the field might well be, as it is very small. Cowgate 'the right of pasture for one head of cattle' is found occasionally, e.g. Cow Gait in Ashwell (Rut). Cowholding, in Glaston (Rut), embodies the rare term *holding*, i.e. land on which holding-stock or breeding cattle were kept. Cowhead occurs in Dunham Massey (Ches); Cowshade, in Arclid (Ches), may perhaps be broken down into *Cows-hade*, found also in Westmorland.

Cow Paddle, in Lincoln, adjoins the river Witham. *Paddle* in the sense of 'a wading place (for cattle &c.)' is not common but also occurs in Paddle Pit, in Heswall (Ches). Instances of Cowdam are found in Stallingborough (Lincs), meaning literally 'cow pond', but the specific connection with cattle seems to be belied by Horse Cowdam, found in the same Tithe Apportionment. *Dam Close* is found in a number of places, alluding to ponds of various kinds. Functional names in which the word *cow* is not used include Milking Close, in Abney (Derbys), and Milking Plot, in Fifehead Neville (Dor). In Soyland (YW), Baitings, from ON *beiting* 'a pasture', was the summer pasture for cattle in the medieval vaccary at Saltonstall. Fattening pastures have been mentioned earlier. Some names apparently referring to cows have other origins. Cowpits, in Horley (Sur), is plausibly to be identified with the sixteenth-century *Colpytt* 'a charcoal pit'. Cowcrofts, in Cottingham (YE), was earlier *Coltscroft c.* 1325, evidently intended for young horses rather than cattle. The term *Neat* (Old English *nēat*) 'head of cattle' is occasionally found in field-names, e.g. Neats Redding (OE *ryding* 'a clearing'), in Ashleworth (Glos), and Neat Field, in Matley (Ches). *Neat* is replaced in some Danelaw early forms by Old Norse *naut*. Neat Marsh, in Preston (YE), was *Notmersk* in 1344, and both forms survived in Neat *alias* Nodgarth, in Ambleside (Westm).

Field-names alluding to calves have a range of forms. There are numerous Calf Closes, but also Calves Close in (among other places) Windsor (Berks), in East Allington (Dev), in Breedon and in Tooley Park (Leics). In Calf Lears, in Witley (Sur), *Lears* is a dialectal variant of *Leaze*. Calf Garth (*Le Caluegarth* 1285–90) is found in Bampton (Westm). *Calurecroft c.* 1250, in Gloucester, and in the modern Calver Croft, in Alderwasley (Derbys) and elsewhere, originated in the plural possessive form OE *calfra* 'of the calves'; this form seems to be augmented by a superfluous possessive -*s* in *Calvers Close* in the 1626 Glebe Terrier of Medbourne (Leics), but this is probably from the term *calver* 'a cow in calf', found also in Calvers Croft dating from the seventeenth century, in Frodsham Lordship, and Colver Field, in Faddiley (Ches).

In Chilvers Lands (*Chilfurlonge* 1487), in Ashchurch (Glos), the Southern (West Saxon) form *cealf* has given rise to the *Ch-* spellings in both the medieval and the slightly altered modern forms. *Chalfhamstede* 1359, in Eaton Socon (Beds), probably indicates a cattle-breeding farm. *Chalfecroft* 1400, noted in an unidentified Sussex place, and *Chalvecroft c.* 1275, in Lambourn (Berks), both derive from *cealfa*, the possessive plural of this form, found also in *Chaw Parke* 1608 'calves' paddock', in Portland (Dor). Local dialect terms are found in some names, e.g. *Budcrofte* 1624, in South Leigh (Oxon), alluding to a yearling calf.

The impresssion is given, particularly when one is presented with a range of early name-forms going back seven or eight centuries, that cows have fed on *Cow Pasture*, calves in *Calf Nook*, bulls on *Bull Ings*, and horses on *Horsecroft*, uninterruptedly from time immemorial. For the fact that this is not so there is abundant documentary evidence ranging from medieval terriers, through seventeenth- and eighteenth-century leases to enclosure and tithe commutation documents, as well as sale particulars and estate maps of more recent times. In a 1611–12 terrier from the survey of Macclesfield Manor and Forest there is mention of "One other arrable called the Calfe crofts by estimation 3 acres". From this and a number of similar references it may be inferred that the use of the name of a grazing animal did not signify that the land was literally permanent pasture.

The daily and seasonal pasturing arrangements are recorded in various names. Pasture during the hours of darkness is described in Nightlands, in Long Sutton (Som), and Nightless (*Night Leaze* 1657), in Stanford Rivers (Ess). *Winter Pasture* 1611, in Staveley, and Winter Pasture, in Barlborough (Derbys), indicate land that was sheltered and well enough drained to be used in that season. Some pastures would be flooded or very muddy for much of the year, and the use of certain pieces of land was limited to summer, e.g. *Summerlesowe* 1225, in Houghton Regis, *Somerleys* 1746, in Billington (Beds), and Summercrofts (*Somercrofte* 1540), in Barrow upon

Humber (Lincs). *Somerheyse* t. Ed. 4, in Windsor (Berks), is 'a summer enclosure' (OE *(ge)hæg*). No early forms have been found for Midsummer Leas, in Market Rasen (Lincs), Summer Leaze, in Aldbourne (Wilts), Summers Dale, in Barham (Kent), or Midsummer Heads, in Twyning (Glos). Also to be noted are Summer Eating Ground, in Fifield (Oxon), Kirk Summer Eater Carr, in Bonby, and Summer Eaten Marsh, in Habrough (Lincs). Summerer, in Great Singleton (Lancs), is reinforced with *erg* 'a shieling'.

Transhumance, the transfer of animals to upland feeding-grounds during the summer, is recorded in some field-names. The Old Norse element *skali* 'a hut', normally referring to a shieling, is found in Skelsteads, in Newby, Scales, in Crosby Ravensworth (Westm), *Summerscales* 1680, in Silsden (YW), and *Scales Syke* 1578, in Aspatria (Cumb). *Swynsete* 1310, in Brigham, and Swinside, in Little Clifton (Cumb), contain another Scandinavian element, *sætr* 'a shieling', both examples referring to an out-pasture for pigs. *Gamellsarges in Bochland c.* 1220, in Bowland Forest (YW), combines *erg* (Old Irish *airghe*) 'a shieling' with the Scandinavian personal name *Gamall*. From the same term are derived Harrows, in Caldebeck (Cumb), *The Harowe* 1519, in Aldersey, possibly Cold Airs, in Eastham (Ches), Summerer, already mentioned, which covers a score of fields in Great Singleton, and Summerer Meadow, in Weeton with Prees, adjoining the Great Singleton fields. Great and Little Medler 'the middle shieling', in Preesall with Hackinsall (Lancs), was already more than 600 years old when it was entered in the Tithe Apportionment, going back to *Midelarge c.* 1215.

The custom of allowing the grazing of some meadows after the hay had been cut is recalled in such names as Lammas Close, in Catthorpe (Leics), in Whissendine and in South Luffenham (Rut), Lammas Mead, in White Notley (Ess), Lammas Meadow, in Biggleswade (Beds), in Essendine (Rut), in Bruntingthorpe and in Newton Unthank (Leics), The Lammas Meadows, in Neen Savage and in Neen Sollars (Shrops), and Lammas Lands, in Melksham (Wilts). *Lammas* is derived from Old English *hlāf-mæsse* 'loaf mass or festival', the first day of August, when newly gathered wheat was ground and bread made for blessing in a service of thanksgiving for the harvest.

The best use of limited grazing was sometimes achieved by tethering cattle, a practice referred to in the 1674 Glebe Terrier for Bottesford (Leics), on which are entered four parcels under the heading *Teathering Ground in ye Sands*; the sandy soil would probably produce only a sparse growth of herbage. Tethering would also be practised on marshy pastures and on pasture leys interspersed among arable strips, while the crops were still growing. Other examples are Teathering Leas, in Market Rasen, and Teathering Ground (*Pasture called Tethering Ground c.* 1550), in Goxhill, and Tetherings, in Barnetby le Wold (Lincs) and in Bessingby (YE).

The driving of cattle from home fields to out-pastures may generate the names of fields adjoining drove roads, as in Oxen Rake Meadow (OE *hraca* 'a narrow path'), in Malham (YW). Driving Road, in Brereton, Driving Lane, in Northern Etchells and in Mere, and Driving Lane Field, in High Legh, are Cheshire examples. *Drift* or *Driftway* is common throughout the Midlands and East Anglia. The names may designate the grass-grown tracks themselves, e.g. Cowrake, in Bampton (Westm). Neatgangs 'cattle tracks', in Goxhill (Lincs), consisted of 250 acres of pasture (later divided into six rectangular closes) beside the river Humber.

SHEEP AND OTHER FARM ANIMALS

Sleight, a term for '(sheep) walk, sheep pasture', is limited to southern counties, e.g. Sleight (*Atte Sleyte* 1333), in Corfe Mullen (Dor) and in Hilmarton (Wilts), Great Sleight, in Priston, Cold Sleight, in Corston, Sleights, in Wellow (Som), Sheep Slaight, in Dowdeswell (Glos), Slait, in Sherston, Sheep Sleights, in Easton Grey, and Sheep Sleight, in Draycot Cerne (Wilts). The usual term in the Midlands and the north of England, *Sheep Walk*, is found in Biggleswade (Beds) and in Dunholm (Lincs), The Sheep Walks, in Burton Fleming (YE), and *The Wold Sheep Walk* 1707, in Croxton (Lincs). Other names related to sheep include *The Sheep Haie* 1632, in Dowdeswell (from OE *(ge)hæg* 'an enclosure'), and the repetitive Sheppey Hays (*Schephay* 1369), in Horsley (Glos), Sheep Close in Neville Holt (Leics), Sheep Hill, in Baunton (Glos) and in Cliffe cum Lund (YE), and Sheepland, in Spettisbury (Dor). The dialect form *ship* is found in Ship Field, in Atcham (Shrops), Ship Croat, in Thorley (Herts), and Ship Mead, in Long Sutton (Som). Trip Field, in Belchamp St Paul's (Ess), contains the dialect *trip* 'a small flock'. *Sautheberch* 1200, in Eaglesfield (Cumb), is probably 'sheep hill', from Old Norse *sauthr* 'a sheep'.

Ram Meadow occurs in Bittesby, in Illston and in Kings Norton

(Leics), Tup Croft, in Stretton (Derbys) and in Marple (Ches), Ewe Field, in Holwell (Leics), Ewes Lands, in Margaretting and in Writtle, and Ewes Meadow in Great Easton (Ess). Eweleaze is found frequently in Dorset. Lambing ewes would be put into a convenient field, e.g. Eaning Close, in Badby (Nthants). Lambs Park is found in Blackawton and in Lustleigh (Dev), Lamb Croft in Kings Langley (Herts), Lamb Close (*Lambe Close* 1552) in Bingley, Lamb Garth in Ryther (YW), and Lamber Leaze in Ramsden (Oxon). The form in the last name is from *lambra*, the genitive case plural, meaning 'of the lambs'. Shear Hogs Close, in Illston (Leics), refers to lambs after their first shearing, the term being found also in Sharrag Hill, in Castle Ashby (Nthants). Dip Acre, in Shipton under Wychwood (Oxon), presumably alludes to a sheep-dipping place. References to goats are not numerous. Examples are Goat Close, in Lockington (Leics), and Goats Pightle, in Burghfield (Berks). Goatherds Close, in Odstone (Leics), is a related name.

Field-names relating to horses include Horse Pasture, in Carnaby (YE), Horse Croft, in Black Notley and in Abbot's Roding (Ess), Horse Close, in Tingrith (Beds), in Ringwould (Kent) and in Harewood (YW), Horse Gusson Close (*Horsgarstone* 1220), in Chinnor (Oxon), Horse Ing, in Bingley (YW), Horse Park, in Ashreigney (Dev), and Horse Plot, in Axminster (Dev). *The Mare and Foale* 1662, in North Kelsey, Mare and Foal, in Tealby, and Two Lands called Mare and Foal, in Nettleton (Lincs), may all allude fancifully to two fields of differing sizes (as in Nettleton), or to their use as literally described. Foal Paddock is found in Garton in the Wolds (YE), and Foal Close in Stretton (Rut). Functional and other classes of horse are referred to in various names, e.g. Coach Horse Leasow, in Shrewsbury St Mary (Shrops), Packhorse Ground, in South Stoke (Som), Palfrey Meadow, in Rainow, Naggs Pasture, in Cholmondeley, Hackney, in Buglawton, and Hackney Hey, in Bollin Fee (Ches). *Stone Horse Paddock* 1717, in Clixby (Lincs), and Stone Horse Patch, in Ford (Shrops), refer to stallions.

Land on which pigs were kept, or allowed to root, received such names as Pig Field, in East Allington (Dev), Hodge Stocking, in Kinndersley (Shrops), Hog Gaston, in Romsey (Hants) (from OE *gærs-tūn* 'a paddock'). Hog's Hole, in Lyddington (Rut), *Swyne Pytte Feld* 1551–52, in Ramsden (Oxon), and Swine Park, in Islington (Dev), and supplies of food would have been provided in Hog Trough, in Cookham and in Newbury (Berks). Domestic fowls are alluded to in Poultry Field, in Elloughton (YE), Chicken Field, in

White Roding, Chicken Croft, in Tollesbury and in Tolleshunt Knights (Ess), and Chickens Croft, in Inkpen (Berks). Upper and Lower Turkey Leys, in Tingrith (Beds), Goose Croft, in Hemel Hempstead (Herts) and in Beechamwell (Norf), Duck Field, in Bucklebury (Berks), and Duck Mead, in Witham (Ess) and in Hendon (Middx), are self-explanatory.

NOTES AND REFERENCES

1. H.E. Hallam, *Rural England 1066–1348* (Fontana, 1981), pp. 61–2, 88.
2. W. Marshall, *The Rural Economy of Gloucestershire* (1789), i., pp. 65–6 quoted by Gray, pp. 92–3.
3. Usage of the term was not uniform in different periods and places. In the eighteenth century, we are told, "The term 'Marling' was very loosely used, covering a number of systems of mixing subsoil with the surface soil. In the Isle of Wight it meant chalking, and may sometimes have been applied to the same process in the Weald" (G.E. Fussell, *The English Dairy Farmer* (1966), p. 102).
4. British Library Additional Rolls 11759–88, quoted by V. Skipp, 'Economic and social change in the Forest of Arden, 1530–1649', *Agric. Hist. Review* **18** (Supplement) (1970), pp. 84–111, here p. 96.
5. G.E. Morris and J. McDonnell, '"Thwaite" place-names on the North York Moors', *Ryedale Historian* No. 15 (1990–91), pp. 24–9, here, p. 27.
6. J. Broad, 'Alternate husbandry and permanent pasture in the Midlands, 1650–1800', *Agric. Hist. Review* **28** (1980), pp. 77–89, here p. 85.
7. See J. Thirsk, 'Seventeenth-century agriculture and social change', *Agric. Hist. Review* **18** (Supplement) (1970), pp. 148–77, especially pp. 158–9.
8. W.O. Ault, *Open Field Farming in Medieval England* (Allen & Unwin, 1972), p. 142.
9. Lord Ernle notes that in Essex in the late eighteenth century 'a peculiar crop, grown generally together, on the same land for three years together, consisted of caraway, coriander, and tea-zels' (*English Farming Past and Present* 6th edn, p. 193).

10. J. Godber, *History of Bedfordshire* (Bedfordshire C.C., 1969), p. 345.
11. This information is based on a personal communication from Mrs Atkin.
12. Details have been communicated personally by Mrs Higham.

CHAPTER SIX

Descriptions of size, shape and distance

An acre conteyneth in it .viii^{xx}. perches. An half acre conteyneth in it .iiii^{xx}. perches. The quarter of an acre (other wayes called a roode) conteyneth in it .x1. perches. An acre conteyneth in it .xl. dayworkes. A dayworke conteyneth in it .iiii. perches.

R. Benese, *Measurynge of all maner of lande* (1537)[1]

PAIRED AND GROUPED NAMES

Pairs or groups of names are normally formed on the basis of the relative distance, elevation or dimensions of the various components. *Great* is the usual term in field-names, whereas in the ordinary vocabulary it has been supplanted by *big* or *large* when applied to tangible objects. Though *Little* is the normal field-name term for its opposite, *Small* is sometimes found. Great & Little Gasson, in North Newnton (Wilts), form a division of *La Garston* 1570 (OE *gærs-tūn* 'a grass enclosure, a paddock'). *Big* is also sometimes found, e.g. Big Hoo Croft, in Hilton (Staffs), Big Cow Close, in Evington (Leics), and Small and Big Meers '(land on) the boundary', in Cricklade (Wilts). In other names, *Small* is used to mean 'narrow'.

From the name alone it is impossible to determine the size of a field called *Great Close, Great Meadow* or Big Field, and a difference of only a few acres may sometimes distinguish *Great Close*, etc. from its smaller counterpart. Two separate fields in Lubenham (Leics) were named as Great Close in 1843; one had an area of thirty-one acres and the other of sixty-five acres. Big Houghton Field, in Houghton on the Hill (Leics), measures fifteen acres; Little Houghton Field, nine acres. As Cornish fields are mostly small, notes P.A.S. Pool, many fields "of around four acres have been given the name Great Field without irony."[2]

HIDES, OXGANGS AND ACRES

A *hide* was originally about 120 acres in extent.[3] There are fields called the Hyde, in Ditton Priors (Shrops), Hide Field, in Loughton and in Theydon Mount (Essex), and Hyde Leys, in Arlingham (Glos). Even earlier than *La Hyde* 1305, in Reading (Berks), Hyde Farm, in Damerham (Wilts), may well represent the *1 hide in Dobreham* mentioned in Domesday Book. In Piddlehinton (Dor), *Cultura voc' Halfhide* ('a furlong called *Halfhide*') was placed on record in 1452. There is a Halfhide Field in Rivenhall, and Upper and Lower Halfhide in Tolleshunt d'Arcy (Ess). The *yardland*, or virgate, survives in some field-names. Head Three Yards, in Cheselbourne (Dor), may be the small area of land in the parish granted in a charter of 965. The unit (usually equivalent to about thirty acres) appears in another name in the same place, in a field called Head Yard. Preservation of an old terminology seems to have been a speciality of this parish, as yet another name, The Hundred Goad, in Shortlands, refers not only to what was presumably a furlong (a subdivision of the open field) but to a measure of area called a *goad*. Half Yardland, in Tilton on the Hill (Leics), was in two parts (Nos 58 and 61), totalling just over fifty acres at the time of the Tithe Apportionment, which also mentioned Half Yardland Meadow and Freemans Half Yardland (fourteen acres), and Taylors Yardland and Palmers Yardland (each of nearly ten acres).

An *oxgang* was an area of arable land varying between ten and thirty statute acres in different places. The term was used principally in open-field contexts, as in *Le Oxegung* 1391, in Shurlach (Ches), *Chapel Oxegange* 1541, in Ledsham (YW), *The Oxegang* 1556, in Shottle (Derbys), *The Twoe Oxgangs* and *The Three Oxgangs*, in Wrawby (Lincs), and the derogatory *Cursed Oxgong* 1334, in Weaverham (Ches). References to occupiers sometimes occur, as in *Habraham Hoxegange* 14c. 'Abraham's oxgang', in Ardsley, and *Pip' Oxegange* 1486 'the piper's oxgang' or 'the oxgang of a man named Piper', in Barwick on Elmet (YW). *More Oxgange* 1424, in Woolley (YW), is land on Woolley Moor. The term survived in some field-names after enclosure, e.g. Oxgang, in Langcliffe (YW). The

Norse term *stong*, variously 'a pole' or 'a rood', is found as a unit in Lincolnshire names, used descriptively in *Five stong of pasture called Teathering Ground* 1749, in Goxhill. The Forty Stong *(Le Fourtie Stonge Dale* 1548) occurs in Branstone & Mere. *Tenstang* is mentioned in a thirteenth-century Normanby le Wold document, and *Ye North Stong* occurs in the same parish in 1566. A similar unit of area, a *lug* 'a square pole or perch', is found occasionally, as in Hundred Lug, in Holt (Dor). Hundred Lace, in St Buryan (Corn), is measured in a local unit, 160 of which went to the acre. *Rood* is also found in field-names e.g. *Fowrtenerodewong* 1404 'the fourteen-rood *wong*', in Flitcham (Norf), *Le Twentyrodes* 1465, in Cleckheaton (YW), and Three Roods, in Barlborough (Derbys). These units were fractions of local or customary acres.

Acreage-names are among the most common in any list of post-enclosure field-names. There are many points for possible discussion, but numerous repetitions would be involved. One question that suggests itself is whether, as is sometimes said, a high proportion of them bear little relation to the actual size of the fields. Actual inspection will show that this is not so. The use of customary (or local), rather than statute, acres will account for some discrepancies. Alteration of boundaries will occasionally have left a larger or smaller piece of land bearing an earlier acreage name for the entire field. Acreage names are thought to be necessarily modern, but many medieval examples may be easily found. *Tenacre* and *Threacre c.* 1180 occur in Little Rissington (Glos). Twenty Acres Field, in Whitnash (Warks), represents *Twentiacreslade* 1221, and Eight Acres, in Cheselbourne (Dor), has a counterpart, *Eghteacres* 1317. Other instances range from *Halfacre* 13c. to *Fourtyacre* of 1376 in Hertfordshire, with many intermediate names.

OTHER UNITS OF AREA

In Oxfordshire, *far(un)del* (OE *feorthan-dæl* 'a fourth part') is used to mean 'rood' (a quarter of an acre), as in The Fardol, in Upper Heyford, and Ten Farundels, in Clanfield. A similar term is found in Farthing, in Bourton, and Farthing Field, in Charlbury (Oxon). There is a Farthing Meadow in Faddiley (Ches), but as there is also a Halfpenny Meadow in the same township these may be rents. Five quarters, in Paul (Corn), has an area of an acre and a quarter. The 1621 Glebe Terrier for Cadeby (Leics) refers to "one close to seaventeene Ridges called the Butt Close" and "one close called Brooke Forlong containeinge forty Ridges". Consolidations may be indicated by these units. In Ferry Fryston (YW), *Sexlandes* 'six lands', on record from 1320, was joined by *Neghenlandes*, alternatively *The ix Landes*, by 1558. With these may be compared *Neghenlandes* 1558, in Monk Fryston (YW), and *Le Fiftene landes* 1559, in Yeaveley (Derbys).

Other generics include *Dole*, as in Thirteen Doles (*Le Thryttene-dole* 1331), in Staveley (Derbys), and, rarely, *Selion* occurring in *Nineteen Selions* 1307, in Middlewich (Ches). *Acre* is used to mean 'selion' in Thirty Acres, in Storeton (Ches), where traces of thirty strips were still visible in 1896. Various numbers (usually from a half to about twenty) with such terms as *Yoking* means 'a stint of work performed by a ploughman', based on the time taken between yoking and unyoking his oxen. The term occurs in the Shropshire field-names Three Yokings, in Tugford, Four Yokings, in Stokesay, Five Yokings, in Hopton Castle, and Eight, Fifteen and Twenty Yokings, in Stokesay. Yoke Gate, in Nettleton (Lincs), going back to 1690, may have a similar meaning. *Daywork, Daymath,* etc. represented either the amount of arable land to be worked or the extent of grassland to be mown, respectively, by a single worker, or the number of days' service an individual field required. The type is well represented in Cheshire; instances in other counties include Three Days Work, in Corley (Warks), Four Day(s) Work in Edale (Derbys) and in Feckenham (Worcs), Six Days Work and Sixteen Days Work, in Solihull (Warks), Ten Days Work, in Crosby on Eden, and Twelve Days Work, in Walworth (Cumb). Variants occur, such as *Dark* and *Dork*. *Day's Work* was used in Kent to indicate a precise area, namely one tenth of a rood. Service in meadowland is alluded to in Nine Days Math, in Dowdeswell, Ten Days Math, in Coberley (Glos), and Twelve Days Math, in Fitz (Shrops). *Day Math* is contracted in, e.g. The Eleven Demath, in Tattenhall (Glos).

Meadow-land was sometimes measured in *swath(e)s*, e.g. *vnam swatham prati* 13c. 'one swathe of meadow', in Ely (Cambs), *Three Swathes* 1607, in Owersby (Lincs), *Six Swathes* 1699–1700, in North-moor (Oxon), *Seaven Swathes* 1674, in Desford (Leics), Eighteen Swathes, in Pontesbury (Shrops), and Twenty Swaths, in Rodbourne Cheney (Wilts). The *swathe* had a normal width of about ten feet, approximating to the reach of a scythe to the left and right of the mower. Details in a 1550 Meldreth (Cambs) document make this clear: "4 longe swathes prati ['of meadow'] in Longswathesmedow each of which swathis contain in breadth 10 feet". *Swath(e)*, as can be seen from this example, is also used with the general sense 'a piece of grassland', as in Long Swaths, in Elsfield (Oxon). A piece of glebe land in Kibworth Beauchamp (Leics) is described in the 1652 Terrier as "one halfe roode one [i.e. 'on'] *Carrs* called *The Swathes*". The usage of pasture has to be controlled, by limiting the numbers of beasts grazing upon it at any one time. The *cowgate*, an allotment of pasture for a single beast, is occasionally found, e.g. Cow Gate Marfur, in Ulceby (Lincs), *marfur* being 'boundary furrow', only a small area. *Neat* 'cattle' is found in *A Pasture called the Neitgath* 16c., in Goxhill (Lincs). But Horsegate Field (*Horsgate Quarter* 1601), one of the four great fields of Goxhill, probably alludes to a bridle-road. *Hundred Yowe Leasowe* 1652, in Poden (Worcs), was named from the number of ewes it could feed. Sheep Gates, in Nettleton (Lincs), was *Syepgates* in 1239. *Shepe Gatte* 1561, in Thornganby (Lincs), is defined: "One shepe gatte or the gatte of one hundrythe shepe".

NAMES FOR SMALL FIELDS

Small closes may be named from their actual size, e.g. Three Roods (frequent in Derbyshire), and (The) Half Acre, to be found in Sapperton (Glos), Stretton Parva (Leics) and many other places. An earlier instance is *Haulfe acre* 1617, in Charminster (Dor). *Halfacre* occurs in such names as *Le Longehalfacre* c.1301, in Macclesfield (Ches). *Pyked Half Acre* 1458, in Puddletown (Dor), would have been one that came to a point. *Le Longe Halflond* c.1286 occurs in Woodbank (Ches), and *Flaxhalflond* 14c. in Henbury cum Pexall (Ches). The exact sense of *Half*, used alone as a generic, is uncertain. It is found in *Longhalve* 1275, in Breamore (Hants), and in Wiltshire from the fourteenth century. Later names include Seven Halves, in Wilcot (Wilts), Halves, in Wheelock, and The Halves, in Northern Etchells (Ches).

Hundred Acres, applied fancifully to small fields, is well known. Doubts are still sometimes expressed about both the form of the name and the ironic intention. From many counties (but apparently not Cheshire or Yorkshire and one or two others discussed below) examples can be adduced of closes, usually each less than an acre in area, bearing this name. The explanation that the term is really a corruption of *Under Acre* cannot be sustained in the face of the vast numbers of instances. A selection is given in the Appendix.

The name (One) Thousand Acres is also given to very small fields, which are found to be no smaller and no larger than *Hundred Acres*, etc., most measuring one acre or less. Million Roods, in Temple Normanton (Derbys), and Billions Field, in Ramsden Crays (Ess), seem even more exaggerated. *Forty Acres* and, occasionally, *Fifty Acres* are also used ironically in some parts of the country. A very small field in Church Stretton (Shrops) is called Forty Acre, and The Forty Acres, in Kimbolton (Herefs), is also very small. Forty Acres, in Snareston, has an area of less than an acre and a half, and Forty Acres Close, in Lubenham (Leics), only about a quarter of an acre. Fifty Acre and Forty Acre in Hodnet (Shrops) were respectively a half and a quarter of an acre in extent. An 1804 document relating to Tealby (Lincs) confirms the irony by recording "a Little Close called Forty Acres". Forty Acres in this sense occurs also for a field eighteen perches in area in Widecombe, as well as in Bickleigh (Dev) and in west Cornwall, being found in Paul, in St Just, twice in St Buryan and in a number of other places, as well as in St Agnes, further east. Other acreages, chosen apparently at random, are also used for very small fields in Cornwall: Seven Acres, Nine Acres and Ten Acres are found in St Ives, in Lelant and in Towednack respectively.[4]

Smallness may also be indicated by generic terms. *Plot* is frequently met with in many parts of the country as a field-name generic. It is usually regarded as a neutral term for 'a piece of land', without any specification of size. *Plack* 'a worthless trifle, a small plot' and *pleck* (ME *plek*) 'a small patch of ground' both occur as names for small pieces of land. They tend to become confused, e.g. in Warwickshire and in Gloucestershire, particularly where *Plack* occurs in its West Midland dialect variant, as in The Plock, in Corley (Warks). In Surrey, Great and Little Spleck, in Abinger, and Spleck Coppice, in Thursley, present a minor variant. Hook (Dor) has Plick and several instances of Plot.

Other terms indicating small size include (The) Patch, found in Wormhill (Derbys), Down Ampney (Ches) and South Leigh (Oxon). The Patchet (*Le Patchet* 1488), in Marston (Oxon), has a diminutive suffix to emphasize its small size. The Scandinavian word *garthr* is regularly used in some counties of northern and eastern England. It is used of small enclosures, especially those near dwellings or with specialized uses, e.g. as milking yards or as gardens, or for the regular growing of particular crops. *Peertregarth* 1604 occurs in Appleby (Westm), Barley Garth and Grass Garth are found in Beamsley, Barn Garth in Copgrove, and Dairy Garth in Brearton

(YW). Hall Garth occurs in Cadney (Lincs) and in North Wheatley (Notts). The English word *yard* (OE *geard*) is also used in these contexts, e.g. Hopyard, in Everton and in Farnsfield (Notts), Milking Yard, in Yaxley (Suf), and Bull Yard, in Over Alderley (Ches).

Hoppet, either alone or as a generic, is given to small fields. Its use is limited largely to Essex, Middlesex and Hertfordshire, e.g. Hoppitts, in Eastwick, and Hoppit (*Le Hoppet* 1556), in Hunsdon (Herts) and in Hackney (Middx, now Greater London). There are fifty or more instances of *Hoppet* or *Hoppit* in Essex and a few in Surrey.

Spot, common enough in daily language ('a beautiful spot', etc.), is sometimes found as a field-name generic. In a 1625 document relating to Thoresway (Lincs) a piece of land is described as "a spot of ground called the *Little Churchyard*". A mill was sited on Mill Spot in Knossington, and there is another instance of this name in Tilton on the Hill (Leics), which also has Top Spot, with an area of just over three roods. The origin of Quillet as the name for a small field is obscure, but some connection in sense with *quillet* meaning 'a verbal trifle, a quibble' may legitimately be claimed. Examples include Quillet, in Sowton (Dev), in Saughall Massie, in Newton cum Larton and in Heswall cum Oldfield (Ches), Quillets, in Foleshill (Warks), and The Quillet, in Great Neston (Ches). In some places the term has the technically precise sense of 'portions of meadow marked by boundary stones'; in Cornwall it "is used to denote small garden type enclosures very seldom given individual names".[5]

In the Danelaw, Old Norse *brot* 'a fragment, a small piece of land' occasionally occurs. *Brotland*, in Canwick (Lincs), is found in a document of Henry II's reign. In Owersby (Lincs) *Brottes* 1358 survived until at least the seventeenth century as *the furlonge called the Brattes*. Bratts occurs in Rolleston, and Bratt Meadow in Fiskerton (Notts). Cross & West Broitch, in Nesfield (YW), are, like Broats, in Roecliffe, in the plural. Another Scandinavian term, *vrá* 'a nook', occurs as either *Wro* or *Wray*, e.g. Wray Field, in Poulton (Lancs), Wreay, in Shap Rural (Westm), and Wrays, in Nesfield (YW). *Roe* and *Ray* are also found. The English *nook* is also found, as in *Sandpitt Nooke* 1731, in East Halton (Lincs). Screed, in Kelham, and The Screed, in Kirklington (Notts), are examples of a name for a small, often narrow field, found also in The Screed, in Tealby (Lincs), Screeds, in Brandesburton, and Railway Screed, in Bridlington (YE). *Stitch* is found, particularly in southern and southwestern counties, meaning 'a small piece of land', often less than half an acre in area. Examples include Stitches, in Seagry, Water-stitch, in Winsley, and The Stitches in Langford (Wilts). Small Stitch, in Ilsington (Dev), clearly lays claim to no great size. The Cornish equivalent *leyn* occurs in such names as Lean Ridden 'bracken stitch', in Gwithian, and Leanheere 'long stitch', in Madron, with variants Linyers, in Lelant, Leniers, in Zennor, and Leanhiere, in Sennen. Earlier forms include the 1588 Sancreed names *Lene an Garrack* 'the rock stitch', and *Lene Nyendorwhy*, in which the second element appears to be adapted from the English phrase 'nigh the door way'.

The term *handkerchief* used to be heard in daily speech with reference to such matters as the area of domestic gardens but is seldom encountered today.[6] It suggests an approximately square shape as well as small size (reinforced in some examples by *Patch, Piece* and *Hoppet*) but does not always imply an extremely minute area; Handkerchief Piece, in the Tithe Apportionment for Cadeby (Leics), measures just over three-quarters of an acre, but Handkerchief Cross, in Clipsham (Rut), is more than four acres in extent. *The Handkerchief* is found as early as 1669 in Kemerton (Glos). Other examples include (The) Handkerchief Ground, in Arborfield (Berks), in Bisley (Glos) and in Hailey (Oxon), Handkerchief Hoppet, in Mashbury (Ess), and Handkerchief Piece, in Shinfield and in Inkpen (Berks), in Tackley (Oxon) and frequently elsewhere in the Midlands.

Wrens Park Shot (*Wrenparke* 1480), in Widdington (Ess), illustrates another figurative method of naming a small field. The small size of the bird combines with the pretentiousness of *Park* to underline the irony. The term appears quite early; besides the Widdington example, *Wren Park alias Denge* 1484 is the basis of Wren Park in Great Bardfield (Ess). Wren Park is also found in Easthampstead (Berks), in Piddington (Oxon), in Bulwell (Notts) and in more than a dozen places in Derbyshire.

Other fanciful names for small fields include Pinch, in Hodnet (Shrops), half an acre in area and about the same size as the ironic Many Days Work, in Whittingham (Lancs), and Thimble Hall, in Warsop (Notts). Thimble All, in Burton Pidsea (YE), was locally explained: "Tailor worked to buy field, and named it." Without further details, this can be neither rejected nor confirmed, but most anecdotal explanations of name origins leave out of account the existence of the same name elsewhere.

PIGHTLE AND PINGLE

Smallness is often regarded as the connotation of the elements *pightle*, *pingle* and *pingot*. Fields so called are not, however, necessarily very small, though in some places this is the sense of the term. In South Repps (Norf), former selions, with an area of about one acre each, are named Garden Pightle, Harmer's Pightle, Home Pightle, Middle Pightle and Temple's Pightle. In Morningthorpe (Norf), among other named pightles, one is actually called Acre Pightle. Pyghtle Close is a small enclosure near village buildings in Swanbourne (Bucks). Gray notes that at Shropham (Norf), there was a close of seven acres labelled 'formerly several pightles'.[7] Of four closes called simply Pightle, in Biggleswade (Beds), one has an area of nearly seven acres, one of just over five acres, one of about two acres, and the fourth of one acre and twenty-five perches. Two closes bear this name in Eggington (Beds); one is of just over two acres in extent, and the other about three-quarters of an acre.

Pingle, the nasalized form of *pightle*, usually found in the Midlands, occurs as far south as Surrey and Middlesex, e.g. The Pingle, in Hendon (Middx), though *Pightle* is the more frequent form in that county. Two examples in Wiltshire are also worth mentioning: Pingles, in Brinkworth, and *Pyngellis* 1503, in Highworth. There are examples of fields called *Pingle* with areas of about six acres, and no doubt the terms are often synonymous with *Bit*. Forms of *Pingle* in north-west England include *Pingo*, *Pingard* and *Pingert*. Elsewhere, a rare variant, The Pindle or Pingle, is found in Saxby All Saints (Lincs).

LONG, NARROW CLOSES

Narrow pieces of land are sometimes called *Strip* or *Stripe*, e.g. Long Strip, in Axminster (Dev), and East and West Stripe, in Exhall (Warks). The Stripe, in Naburn (YE), is described as "very narrow, long". Closes called *The Stripe* were often very small, one instance in South Luffenham being seventeen perches in area, and another in Barrowden (Rut) only eight perches. *Slip* or *Slipe* was also used of narrow fields. Slip Acre occurs in Liscard (Ches), *Slipe* in Berrington (Shrops), and upwards of a dozen examples of *(The) Slipe* in Essex. In Cambridgeshire are found Slipe, in Westley Waterless, Slipes, in Steeple Morden, and Long Slipe, in Balsham.

Sling is applied to fields shaped like the primitive weapon, i.e. of a narrow, slightly curved shape. The Sling, described as "a long, narrow strip", is found in Southwick (Wilts) and also in Fovant, in Oaksey, in Britford, in Langford, and in Whiteparish: Sling Field, in Winterbourne Dauntsey, in the same county, is said to be "a long strip by the road". The Sling (*Slinge* 1602) occurs in Great Wyrley; Slingett, in Westbury on Severn, Slingate, in Todenham (Glos). (The) Slinket, in North Newington, in Thame and in Wardington (Oxon), are from *Slinget*, with the same meaning.

Sling is closely related to *Slang*; both terms occasionally occur in the same parish, e.g. in Bredbury (Ches). In Desford (Leics) occur Top Slings Close and The Slang. *Slang* is found all over Shropshire, but *Sling* more often in the south of the county. *Sling* is found in Berkshire, but *Slang* appears to be absent. Though examples of *Sling* in Gloucestershire outnumber the occurrences of *Slang*, the latter occurs more frequently in many Midland counties. *(The) Slang(s)* occurs nearly forty times, and *Long Slang(s)* thirteen times in Cheshire. *Slang* frequently signifies a narrow piece of land beside a road or sometimes a river, though it may also be found away from such features, as in Oldfield Slang, in Kingsbury (Warks).

Spanglands 1674 was a long, narrow piece of land in the North Field of Countesthorpe (Leics). To this may be added Long Spong, in Bradden (Nthants), and the half-dozen instances of *Spawns* or *Sponds* in Shropshire. Plank Meadow, in Swerford and in Deddington, and Ash Plank Meadow, in Charlton in Otmoor (Oxon), express length and narrowness by a familiar analogy with a piece of timber. A thirteenth-century terrier for Bagworth (Leics) refers to "a golet of medow" there, and Evans Gullet, in Pulford (Ches), also seems to mean 'a narrow strip of land'. *Lag* 'a narrow, marshy meadow, usually by the side of a stream' is found in *Laggelee* 1270, in Swallowfield (Berks), Lag Mead, in Littlemore, Lag Meadow, in Prescote (Oxon), Lags, in St Nicholas Hurst, and The Laggett, in Fernham (Berks). Lagger, in Avening (Glos), meaning 'a narrow strip of land', is found also in The Lagger in Minchinhampton (dating from 1628). The Laggers, in Coaley, Laggar, in Old Sodbury, and The Legger, in Thornbury (Glos).

Shovel-Broad, found all over England and also in Scotland, means literally 'a shovel-breadth of land'. It is a veritably Protean term, with almost as many forms as there are instances of its occurrence, including Shelboard, Shell Broad, Shew Bread, Shew Birds, Shoe Broad (favoured in Derbyshire), Shaveley or Shovel Boards, in Coinsbrough (YW), Schoolbroad (*Scholebrod* 1273–74), in Claverton (Ches), Schoulbard, in Fleckney (Leics), and Shovelbroad (*Schouelebradlondes t.* Ed. 1), in Newton near Chester, Shuffle a Board occurs in Brinsworth, near Rotherham (YW). The second element (OE *brǣdu* 'breadth') accounts for the various later names ending in *-bre(a)d* (etc.), such as *Sholebreade Filde* 1575, in Welford on Avon (Glos), *Shelbreds* 1674, in Desford (Leics), *Showbreads* 1690, in Ab Kettleby (Leics), Shebreds, in Skipton, Shoe Bread Close (*Scovelbroad* 12c.), in Bramham. Shoe Briggs (*Shobrede* 1589), in Stirton, and Shoe Bridge, in Kildwick and in Steeton (YW). *Showlbread* 1620 occurs in Warkworth (Nthumb), and a Scots version, *Schuilbraidis*, in a 1599 deed relating to Eyemouth (Berwickshire). The name varies between singular and plural. Shovel Broads, in Treswell, was earlier *Shovelbroad Furlonge* 17c., and Shovel Broad Furlong, in Southwell (Notts), represents *Shovelebordes* 1619.

Abnormal length is implied in *Langet,* or one of its variants. In Wiltshire can be found (The) Langate, in Highworth, in Cricklade and in Rodbourne Cheney, The Langet, in Brokenborough and in Hankerton, and Langett in Purton, all in the north of the county. *Longe Langett* 1634, in Longhope (Glos), appears merely as Langet in the Tithe Apportionment. The name occurs as Langot in Alsager and in Broomhall (Ches).

GEOMETRICAL SHAPES

Literal shape names are used all over the country. The Angle, in Cardington (Shrops), is three-cornered, and a similar naming appears in Angle Dale, a triangular field in Holton-le-Moor (Lincs). Triangle, without addition, occurs quite often. Triangle Bit is found in Broughton Astley (Leics), Triangle Close, in Ashleyhay (Derbys) and in Stretton (Rut), and Triangle Croft, in North Rode (Ches). Duffield (Derbys) has both Three Corner'd Piece and Three Nook Piece. Three Nook(s) or Three Nooked is frequent in Cheshire, and is found in more than thirty parishes in Amounderness Hundred (Lancs). An early instance, *Thre Nocked Field* 1548, occurs in St Briavels, and an even earlier one, *Thracornardscroft* 1497, in Thornbury (Glos). *Parke Trye Corner* 1670, in Madron, and Try Corner, in Gulval (Corn), are hybrids combining Cornish *try* 'three' with English *corner*. Three-Point Field, in West Hoathly (Sus), uses a rarer term.

Triangular projections are often referred to as *peaks* or *pikes*, and land characterized by them is described as *picked* (rhyming with 'wicked'). Instances are numerous and include *The Picke* 1585, in Slimbridge (Glos), and Pikes, in Bramcote (Notts), dating from 1660. Peaked Piece, in West Parley (Dor), and Picket Close, in Steventon (Hants). Picked Close, in Puddletown (Dor), was the *Peaked Close* in 1625, and in the same parish occurred *la Pikedelonde* 1306 and *Pyked Halfe Acre* 1458. Other instances include *Atepike-delond c.* 1300 'at the pointed selion', in Denton (Oxon), and Piggledy Peers Croft (*Pykedeperefeld* 1306) 'a pointed piece of land with pear trees', in Coventry (Warks). Tram, in Barbon, in Firbank, in Mansergh, in Scalthwaiterigg, in Beetham and in Kendal (Westm), is the name applied to narrow, often tapering fields. Square Close, Square Meadow, etc. (often very approximate) occur frequently. A lozenge shape is indicated by Diamond, in Cound and in Cressage (Shrops), and Diamond Field, in Burton Fleming (YE). Five Corner Field occurs in Thirston and in Felton (Nthumb), Five Cornered Field, in Onston (Ches), Five Cornered Close, in Atterton (Leics), and Five Corners, in Wix and in Little Waltham (Ess). The Octagon is found in Gulval (Corn).

Circles, or more likely polygons are referred to by such names as Round Croft (*Roundfelde* 1413), in Stapleford (Herts), *Round Garth* 1717, in Claxby (Lincs), *The Round Half Acre* 1718, in Hougham (Kent), Round Piece, in Brooke (Rut), and The Circular, in Measham (Leics). Round Table occurs in Essington (Staffs), in Beausale (Warks) (*Le Rounde Table* 1544), in Ecclesfield (*The Round Table Meadow* 1660), and in Rotherham (YW), alluding to the Arthurian legend. Roundy Poundy, in Belstone (Dev), seems to be a playful expansion of *Round Pound*. Several names in Cornwall, including Park Round, in Gulval, The Rounds, in Paul, and Round Field, in Ludgvan, "contain or adjoin circular prehistoric features, usually fortifications".[8]

The Moon, in East Murton (Dur), is a large field, 176 acres in area. It is not clear from the name whether a complete circle or a crescent shape is intended in this or in Moon Mead, in Great Canfield (Ess), and Moon Piece, in Solihull (Warks), but a semi-circle or crescent is alluded to in The Half Moon, in Henley (Oxon), Half Moon, in Bowdon (Ches), and The Half Moon Close, in Tealby (Lincs). No reference to such shapes is intended by Park Moon, in Madron (Corn); this is derived from Cornish *mon* 'narrow'.

BUTTS AND GORES

Irregularly shaped patches of land were known as *butts*. The term, which occurs fairly frequently at all periods, sometimes has the more precise meaning of the shorter strips produced as two furlong boundaries converged. Typical examples of *Butt* names are Black-butts, in Elswick, Sowerbutts, in Winmerleigh, and Short Butts, in Carlton and in Thornton (Lancs), and Sour Butts, in Bampton (Westm).

Gores were the triangular remnants produced when the boundaries of two fields or furlongs met at a sharp angle. Depending on its size it might be treated as a unit, e.g. *The Goare* 1630, in Gloucester, or divided into selions, as in *Goreaker* 1524, in Pamphill (Dor), and is represented in post-enclosure names by Goore (*Gore* 1332) and Goore Mead (*Gore Mede* 1500), in Folke (Dor), The Gores, in Berrington (Shrops), Goores, in Ashchurch (Glos), Gore Corner, in Treswell (Notts), Gore Acre, in Purley (Berks), and Gore Field (*Gorefeld* 1403), in Takeley (Ess). Earlier examples are *Gore Acre c.* 1200, in Hasfield (Glos), *Goore Acre* 1557, in Sherburn in Elmet (YW), and *The Garra* 1625, in Canwick (Lincs). The equivalent Scandinavian term *geiri* produced *Gare* forms, e.g. *Le Gare* 1275, in Lincoln, and The Gares, in Stallingborough (Lincs).

The Middle English compound *gore-brede, gore-brode* 'the breadth of the gore' also occurs, e.g. in *Gorebrodefurlong* 1540, in Uckington (Glos), and Goarbrode (*Garebrode* 1261), in Oundle (Nthants). In Ascott under Wychwood (Oxon), *Le Garebrod* is found in an early fifteenth-century document; in Goring, in the same county, *Le Gorbrodacre* is recorded in 1349. Earlier still, *Garbradflatt c.* 1250 occurs in Tadcaster (YW). Also to be found are *Garbutt, Garbits, Gorbutt,* etc. derivatives of this, as may be seen in Garbutts (*Gorbrodefurlong* 1207), in Desborough (Nthants), Garbits, in Crosby Ravensworth (Westm), and Gorebutts, in Tideswell (Derbys).

Endelongelondes 1439–40, in Steventon (Berks), were 'strips lying alongside'. Pieces of land lying across others (or across roads, etc.) may receive such names as *Crosslands, Crossbutts, Cross Furlong* or *Cross Shott*. Cross Furlong, in Whitchurch (Warks), was *The Cross Furlong joyning too and hadeing part of Brook Furlong* in 1732, i.e. it adjoined and formed a headland for *Brook Furlong*. Crossfield, in Fulbourn (Cambs), has a different origin; early forms, e.g. *Corsefelde* 1293, suggest that the specific element is the Celtic word *cors* 'a marsh, a bog', which fits the topography of the area. Cross Leasow, in Edgton (Shrops), adjoins a crossroads, to which the name may directly refer, or it may allude to a cross which might be placed there. The interpretation of *Cross* names can seldom be certain, but there is no ambiguity about names derived from Old Norse *thverr* or *thvers* 'athwart', such as *Twerslondes* 1342, in Newton by Chester (Ches), *Twardolys* 1507, in Great Bowden, and Great Whart Lands (*Werthland* 1349–50), in Slawston (Leics). Therthwaite Meadow, in Underbarrow (Westm), crossed a small wood, and *Whartgates* 1638, in Galby (Leics), lay across roads.

OTHER IRREGULAR SHAPES

A piece of land with awkwardly twisting boundaries, or generally crooked in outline, may simply be so called. An early instance of the term is found in *Crokedflatts* 1200, in Thorpe Thewles (Dur). In addition to Crooked Croft, in Shelford (*Croked Croft* 1462), in Witham and in Great Leighs, there are in Essex more than a dozen instances of Crooked Field, a name found also in Houghton le Spring (Dur), Laverstoke (Hants) and Lamberhurst (Kent). The Crookad-eds, in Ashwell (Rut), is 'the crooked headlands'. The specific element in Wofurlong, in Weedon Lois (Nthants), is Old English *wōh* 'crooked', found also in Woe Furlong, in Malden (Sur), and in *Wowefurlong* 1306, in Windsor (Berks). In Woeful Long, in Newbold & Dunsden (Derbys), the same elements have evidently been misdivided. Old Norse *vrangr* 'crooked' is found in *Wrongelandes* 13c., in Shrewsbury (Shrops). Wranglands (*Le Wranglandes* 1339), in Preston (YE), and *Wranglandis c.* 1407, in Middle Rasen (Lincs).

Letters of the alphabet are sometimes used in names indicating shape; Round O has already been mentioned. Roman T, in Wrockwardine (Shrops), is a narrow field with two extensions at the boundary with the road. The same name occurs in Lilleshall, and similar examples include Tea Field, in Astley Abbots, T Meadow (*Tee Meadow* 1772), in Edgton (Shrops), and Tea Close, in Blaston St Giles (Leics). Another shape found in Shropshire names is exemplified in The L, in Clun, L Piece, in Boningale, Roman L, in Alveley, and Why Croft, in Onibury. To these may be added The Ell, in Tetton (Ches), Ell Close, in Christchurch (Hants) and in Billesdon (Leics), and L Field, in Great Kelk and in Skidby (YE). The Yes Field, in Swerford (Oxon), seems to allude to the letter *S*, and Wy Nook, in Wykin (Leics), to the letter *Y*.

Comparisons to the shape of tools and implements include Fire Shovel, in Horsley (Glos), Turf Spade, in Middleton by Wirksworth (Derbys), and Malt Shovel, in Swanland (YE). Hammer Head, in Bridgnorth (Shrops) and Chorlton (Ches), Hammerhead, in Walgherton (Ches), Anvil, in Bolas Magna, and Anvils Field, in Shrewsbury (Shrops), may allude to the shape of the land or to metalworking. Cleaver-Shaped Half Acres, in Tideswell (Derbys), explains itself. Edged tools and weapons are alluded to in Chopping Bill, in Lepton, Broad Axe Field, in Arksey, Butcher Cleaver, in Bradfield (YW), Striking Knife, in Bampton (Westm), and Chopping Knife, in Beighton (Derbys), in Aislaby (Dur) and in Stourpaine (Dor), which also has a close called Pickaxe. Broadspear occurs in Highclere (Hants), and The Dagger in Wansford (Hunts, now Cambs).

HOUSEHOLD GOODS AND MUSICAL INSTRUMENTS

The Old English word *tang* 'tong, forceps' appears in such names as Gorsty Tang, in Frodsham Lordship (Ches), for a spit or *pan handle* of land. There is likely to be some confusion with names derived from OE *tunge* 'a tongue', hardly different in meaning, to be discussed later. Fields with two angular turns may receive such names as The Handle, in East Hendred, and Grindstone Handle, in Hampstead Norris (Berks). A more elaborate shape is suggested in Teakettle Handlepiece, in Belper (Derbys).

Other domestic images are found in The Knitting Needle, in Whittington (Derbys), and The Spigot, in Twycross (Leics). Frying Pan Tail, in Dursley (Glos), probably alludes merely to the outline, but names like The Frying Pan, in Guiseley (YW) and in Hilperton (Wilts), suggest circular fields with central depressions. A triangular close in Newbold (Leics) is called Bottle Piece, and there is also Brandy Bottle in Great Longstone (Derbys).

Musical instruments provide the templates for Jew's Harp, in Lockinge, Jew's Harp Piece, in Ardington (Berks), Jews Trump, in Kilburn (Derbys), and Fiddle Neck, in Beighton (Derbys). The description of a sharp angle rather than the occupational hazard of violinists is expressed in Fiddler's Elbow, in Kennington (Berks). Fiddle Case, seemingly restricted to north-western counties, occurs in Claughton, in Nateby, in Preesall, in Goosnargh and in Clevely

(Lancs), and in Kendal and in Whinfell (Westm). The well-defined shape of a larger instrument supplies the comparison in Harp Field, in Little Totham and Little Bentley, and Harp Mead, in Great Dunmow (Ess). Welsh Harp Piece occurs in the Tithe Award for Woodley (Berks).

REFERENCES TO APPAREL

Many field-names allude to the shapes of garments and footwear. The Boot occurs in Verwood (Dor), Boot Close in Ilkeston (Derbys). The Boots in Ratby (Leics), and Boot Leg in Whitchurch (Shrops). *Shoelands*, found in the late sixteenth century in Aldenham (Herts) and Hendon (Middx), have a connection with shoes, but not to their shape. Earlier forms include *Scoland* 1177–86, in Wandsworth (Sur, now Great London), and *Shooland* 1610, in Puttenham (Sur). This is a "term . . . first used at the turn of the tenth century for land given to a monastic community to provide it with footwear".[9]

Stocking Foot is found as a name for an L-shaped field in Grimsargh, in Ingol and Cottam, and in Roseacre (Lancs). But Long Stockings and Short Stockings, in Duddington (Northants), allude to land formerly wooded but now covered with stumps. The Mantle with Strings, in Steeple Aston (Oxon), refers to a mantle-shaped piece of land with narrower strips adjoining. Stomacher, in Stoken-church (Bucks), Stomacher Patch, in Milton under Wychwood (Oxon), Stomacher Piece, in Studham (Beds) and in Sheepy Magna (Leics), Stomachers Bank, in Church Stretton, and Stomager, in Stoke St Milborough (Shrops), allude to an old garment. A *stomacher* was originally a waistcoat of mail, but the term was later used for a decorative garment worn by ladies under the lacing of the bodice. So it is not surprising that the *English Dialect Dictionary* should define *Stomacher-piece* as 'an irregular, awkward shaped piece of land'. Waistcoat Piddle, in Ruscombe (Berks), seems to be the only allusion to that garment.

Great Cod Piece, in Tachbrook (Warks), is perhaps a surprising analogy from the historic wardrobe, but an earlier instance, *Codpese* 1575, in Hinton (Glos), was contemporaneous with the use of the garment. The Tippet, in Branston and Mere (Lincs), recorded in the middle of the eighteenth century, may refer to a narrow piece of land by comparison with the scarf-like garment. Other examples, in Lincolnshire and in the West Riding of Yorkshire, confirm names of this type as garment analogies: *Hode and Tippit* 1601, in Thornton Curtis (Lincs), *Tippit* 1727 (*The Tippett* 1684), in Arncliffe, and an entry, 'Parcels of Ground called the Tippet & Hoode', in the 1764 Glebe Terrier for Kettlewell (YW), where the 1663 Terrier had the form *Tippitte and Hoode*. Another article of dress, the kerchief, found in Schorchief Nook, in Ripley (Derbys), may be mentioned as possibly equivalent in sense to *Handkerchief* in the naming of small pieces of land.

Headgear is alluded to in Old Hat, in Kintbury (Berks), presumably suggesting an indeterminate shape, Lady Hat, in Barnton (Ches), Dutch Cap, in Bradford Peverell (Dor), and Quaker's Cap Furlong, in Ashwell (Herts). Approximate triangles are designated Cocked Hat, in Ketton (Rut), in Farnsfield (Notts), in Durnford (Wilts), in Stoke St Milborough (Shrops), and in Holme, in Spofforth and in Almondbury (YW), Cockthat, in Bradwell (Derbys), Cock Up Hat, in Aston Brampton (Oxon), Cock'd Hat Field, in Plompton (YW), and Three Cocked Hat, in Irthington (Cumb).

Cheesecake names have been noted in many places in central England. These appear, from actual examples, to be wedge-shaped, and are doubtless named after the confection itself (or from individual portions). Other articles of food that provide field-names include Rye Loaf, in Blackwell (Derbys), which probably alludes both to shape and to convex conformation, the earlier form *Rye Lofe alias Cleft* 1690 suggesting a declivity in the surface similar to the cut made in the top of a loaf or a hot cross bun.[10]

ANATOMICAL NAMES

Features of human anatomy are referred to in Leg and Foot, in Hatherton (Ches) and Ellesmere (Shrops), Mans Leg, in Kendal (Westm), Lady's Leg, in Melverley (Shrops), and Leg Acre, in Bucklebury (Berks). The Leg, alluding to a long narrow field, occurs in Alvediston, and Leg Mead in Tisbury (Wilts). A parcel of land in Thorpe (YW) is called Fingers & Toes. A shape approaching a right angle is named Elbow, in Eggborough and in Sowerby (YW), Elbow Acre, in Boddington (Glos), Elbow Close (frequently), and The Elbows, in Ringwood (Hants). The Devil's Elbow, in Minchinhampton (Glos), alludes to something sinister about the feature. References to diabolical anatomy doubtless reflect additionally on the character of the land, and often the size of the feature. Devils Thumb is found in Matson (Glos), Devils Neck in Harpenden (Herts), and Devils Nick in Lamberhurst (Kent). Knees and Elbows occur in Upper Rawcliffe (Lancs), Knee Field in Winkfield (Berks), and Knee Croft in Stanton Lacy (Shrops). Spaldbone Close, in Knottingley (YW), derived from Middle English *spald-bone* 'shoulder blade', is a less usual example. *Bottom* in place-names and field-names is not an anatomical reference but alludes to the lowest part of a valley. Convex conformations are referred to in such names as Rumps and Buttocks, in Walworth (Dur), Great Buttock, in Compton (Hants), and Buttock Furlong, in Long Whittenham (Berks). Other anatomical references include Kidney Mead, in Hampreston (Dor), and The Heel, in Hamstead Marshall (Berks). In Shrewsbury St Mary, Swine's Sloat contains the local butcher's term, *slote*, for a hog's tongue. *Tongue*, already mentioned as a regular topographical expression, meaning 'a projecting piece of land, often between two streams', has almost lost its metaphorical force. Examples include The Tongue, in Elton, Tongue Field, in Haslington, and Long Tongue, in Bartington (Ches); in Shropshire, Tongue Sharp is found in Whitchurch, and Fleeting Tongues in Lydbury. *Tonghill* occurs in the 1638 Glebe Terrier for Husbands Bosworth (Leics). Snakelands, in Southam (Warks), may be identical with *Snaketunge* 1206, possibly a piece of land with a forked outline.

Shoulder of Mutton and (less frequently) *Leg of Mutton* are to be found all over the country and go back at least three centuries, used of pieces of land approximating to the shapes concerned. A patch of meadow-land in Sibson (Leics) is recorded as *Shoulder of Mutton Peece* in the 1638 Glebe Terrier. Shoulder of Mutton or Three Cornered Close, in Temple Newsam (YW), offers simultaneously a fanciful and a literal description of its shape. In Essex there are more than seventy instances of *Shoulder of Mutton* names but less than a dozen *Leg of Mutton* names. Cheshire has thirty examples of *Shoulder of Mutton* but only four or five of *Leg of Mutton*. In Berkshire there appear to be about six of the former but none of the latter.

GOOSE NECK, SWALLOW TAIL AND SPARROW BILL

Comparisons with animal anatomy, not directly related to meat technology, include Hare's Ears, in Alveley (Shrops), Glead Wing, in Kentmere (Westm) and in Ossett (YW), and Gledwing, in

Kirkheaton (YW), alluding to the wing of the kite. Goose's Foot occurs in Baschurch (Shrops). Goose Neck in Little Bromley (Ess) and in Merston (Sur), Goose Neck Field in Marleston cum Lache (Ches), and Goose Neck Meadow in Little Bentley (Ess). Swans Neck, indicating greater length and curvature, is found in Waltham Holy Cross (Ess), in Mobberley (Ches) and in Latton (Wilts), and Swans Necks in Navestock and in Roxwell (Ess). Mallards Tail, in Anderson (Dor), may refer to the wild duck but a surname is possible, as Mallards Close occurs in Morden, not far away. *Upper and Lower Pig Tailes* 1662 are found in Garforth (YW). The Bull's Tail, in Donington (Leics), is shaped like the letter *P*. Cats Tail Furlong occurs in Milton under Wychwood (where there is also Bulls Tail), and Snakes Tail Piece in Tackley (Oxon). Snakes Tail is found in Henbury (Glos), and Cowstail Pightle occurs in Swallowfield (Berks).

Cats Tail is found also in Knapton (Warks), in West Hoathly (Sus), in Chapel-cum-Pontesbright and in Wakes Colne, Cats Tails in Woodham Mortimer, and Cats Tail Meadow (*Cattistaylemede t.* Ed. 1) in Little Coggeshall (Ess); rather than alluding to shape it is likely that some *Cats Tail* names refer to the grass *Phleum pratense*, which has this popular name. Snigtail Meadow, in Sandbach (Ches), alludes to the tail of an eel. Swallow Tail, 'land in the shape of a forked tail', is found in Cound (Shrops) and in Little Strickland (Westm). *Twotayles* 1634 occurs in Bray (Berks).

The generalized term *tail* is so frequently used that, like *tongue*, its metaphorical origin is often lost sight of. Tail Field occurs in Willingale Doe and in High Easter (Ess). Old English *steort* has this significance, e.g. in *Stertefeld* 1332, the predecessor of Start Holes, in Ridge (Herts), and the 1269 forms of the Wiltshire names Stearts, in Sutton Benger, and Stirts, in West Kington, respectively *La Sterte* and *La Stirte*. Other modern forms of the name include Sturts, in Mappowder (Dor). Steart(s), in North Wootton and in High Ham (Som), and Starch, in Litchborough (Northants). *Le Qu c.* 1230, in Minchinhampton (Glos), probably from Old French *cue* 'tail', is an interesting variant. A more recent name, Lambsquay Wood, in Newland (Glos), alludes to a lamb's tail or to lambs' tails, this time using early Modern English *queue* for 'a tail', but may be a reference to hazel catkins, which are popularly called Lambs' Tails.

Another term regularly used in topographical contexts is *horn*, e.g. The Horns Arable, in Neen Savage (Shrops). The Horn, in Shurdington (Glos), dates from 1639, and Horne Field, in Waltham Holy Cross (Ess), has an early form *Upperhorncroft* 1408. Among

141

other early examples, *Hornforlong*, in Wendlesbury (Oxon), is named in a document dated *c.* 1270. Some names may be from the related *hyrne* 'a nook, a corner', as in *Horne* 1583, in Hampreston (Dor), an alternative for *paruo campo voc' Hurne* 1583 ('in the little field called *Hurne'*) later Herne Corner. Another related element is *horning* 'a bend, a corner, a spit of land', found in Horning (*Horning in Bosco de Ria* 1166–79 'Horning in Ryther Wood'), in Ryther (YW).

Sparrowbill Copse, in Brightwell (Berks), may be compared with Sparrow Bill Piece, in Kintbury in the same county, and with Sparable Clough, in Sowerby (YW). The shape here is that of a wedge, a *sparable* or *sparrowbill* being a 'small headless wedge-shaped iron nail', but the field-name application may, of course, be a direct allusion to the shape of the bird's beak. These names may possibly be analogous to Cockbills, in Rollright (Oxon), and *Cockbill*, in Southam (Warks), which can be traced back, through *Cockesbyle* 1252, to *Coccebyle* in a charter of 998. The area was a sharp projection of the boundary into the neighbouring parish of Radbourne, on the south-eastern edge of Southam. Not far away, Cockbillock, in Priors Hardwick, is located where the boundary of that parish makes a pointed intrusion between Radbourne and Priors Marston. Gogbill is the name of three fields in the south-west corner of Avon Dassett, which makes a short but sharp projection between the parishes of Burton Dassett and Ratley. In 1199 there was also reference to *Cockebile* in Stretton on Dunsmore.

LOCATIONAL REFERENCES IN FIELD-NAMES

The very common name Home Close (etc.), virtually standard throughout the country for the enclosure nearest the settlement centre or farmhouse, has a long history. Home Field, in East Barnet (Herts), has an early form *Le Homfeld* 1267, and the same name in Windsor (Berks) is found as *Le Homefeld* in 1363. Home Leasow, in Ashchurch (Glos), was *Whome Leasowe* in 1580. *Home* occasionally serves as a synonym for *Near*, and expressions like *Home Part of Seven Acres* sometimes occur. *Homer* is occasionally used to contrast with *Further*, particularly in the west of England. Sometimes, however, the term represents 'hollow mere'. Instances will be found of *Home/Holme* confusion. Home Field, in Hertingfordbury (Herts), was *Holmefeld* in 1441.

Naming by ordinal numerals is sometimes found. First Close, Second, Third and Fourth Close appear in Searby cum Owmby (Lincs), and Second, Third, Fourth and Fifth Field are named in a document dated 1919 for Shearsby (Leics). Sequences seldom go much beyond this. Some "remarkably unimaginative instances of such naming" are found in First Close, Second Close, etc. as far as Seventh Close, in Gulval, and First Field, Second Field, etc. to Sixth Field, in Ludgvan (Corn).[11] For all its apparent simplicity, this is no more convenient a means of identification than many others, since both the starting point and the direction of numbering have to be known. Moreover, unless there is a strict grid pattern in the boundaries of the fields, the sequence is difficult to trace, as anyone will admit who has ever had to identify named fields from numbers on a map.

Distance may be expressed in such names as Far Hill, in Duffield (Derbys), *Les Farrfields* 1593, in Leeds (YW); such names are often survivors from an earlier correlative system (*Far* with *Near*, etc.), Remoteness has generated numerous fanciful names, including the transferred place-names to be discussed later. Fargo, in Winterbourne Stoke (Wilts), and Distants (perhaps for *Distance*), near the boundary of Great Hucklow (Derbys), are transparent enough.

Many names express location by such terms as *Above, Below* and *Beneath* a topographical feature. Above Town, in Billesdon, Buff Town Close, in Market Bosworth (Leics), and Bufton, in Tugford (Shrops), locate the land on the higher side of the village (Old English *tūn*): *Beneathbeck* 1674, in Crosscanonby (Cumb), was on the lower side of the stream. *Tweemway Furlong* 1771, in Shrivenham (Berks), and Between Ways Close, in Monyash (Derbys), locate the land at a road junction, as did *Betwenyegats* 1355, in Darfield (YW), and *Betuynyegatis* 1364, in Illston (Leics), with Old Norse *gata* 'road'. *Betwes Ye Mylns* 1427–28 'between the mills' occurs in Bottesford (Leics), where also is found *Beneythcastellgatt* 1427–28, alluding to the road to Belvoir Castle. Phrasal forms used regularly include *Back of the, Front of the*, etc., e.g. Back o' th' House, in Aston (Derbys), Back o' th' House Field, in Almondbury (YW), and Front of House, in North Skirlaugh (YE). Although these phrasal forms seem to be characteristically northern, they are found in other counties, e.g. Back of the House Field, in Dagenham (Ess), and the more elaborate Field above the Garden by the Canal, in Northolt (Middx, now Greater London).

SECLUDED PLACES AND BOUNDARY NAMES

Seldom Seen, in Patney (Wilts), is in a remote part of the parish; the name is also applied to secluded fields in other counties. *Parlour* 'a secluded place, suitable for private conversation' evidently extended to remote fields. Bull Parlour, in Cadeby (Leics), illustrates the wisdom of keeping the bull in an out-of-the-way spot. A case has been argued for the interpretation of Puppys Parlour, in Barston (Warks), as a secluded courtship place.[12] This is also the sense of Cuckolds Parlour, in Corfe Castle (Dor) and in Hardwicke (Glos). Cupids Alley, in Duggleby (YE), and Cupid's Bower, in Stinsford (Dor), have a similar meaning.

Land on a farm or parish boundary is sometimes quite explicitly named: Boundary Field is found in Tytherington (Ches) and in half a dozen Essex parishes, including Chingford and Lexden. Boundary Piece occurs in Clifton & Compton (Derbys), Boundary Close, in North Repps (Norf), and Boundary Corner in Ashwell (Rut). Border Piece, in Kintbury (Berks), Border Close, in Arlington (Dev) and in Chaddleworth (Berks), and Border Pingle, in Ripley (Derbys), are also self-explanatory. Other terms for '(land on) a boundary' are *Rim, Margin, Edge, Skirt(s), Hem, Landshare* and *Mark*. Some *Cross* names also belong here. Cross Hey, in Ledsham (Ches), is probably the site of *Ledeshamcrosse* 1369, on the boundary of the parish. White Post Field, in Merstham (Sur), probably refers to a parish boundary-post.

The fairly obvious term *Rim* (Old English *rima* 'a rim, an edge') is found in some names for boundary fields, e.g. Rhyme Meadow, in Whitchurch (Shrops), and Rhyme Acre, in Northmoor (Oxon). Skirt is on the boundary of Bradley (Derbys), and another instance is on that of Offerton (Ches). Another boundary term is *Hem*, found in Hem Leasow, in Shifnal, The Hems, in Ashford Carbonell (Shrops), and Hem Paddock, in Taxal (Ches). The Rand occurs in Darrington (YW) and in Ellingham (Norf), and Rands, in Finningley (Notts), is on the county boundary. Marklands, in Limm (Ches), contains the Old English word *mearc* 'a boundary', found also in Mark Piece, in Highclere (Hants), and Mark Heys, in Westbury (Shrops). *Markylgroue* 1543, in Newent (Glos), on the Herefordshire border, alludes to a 'boundary hill', not to Marcle (Herefs), which is some miles to the north. Landshare Meadow (OE *landscearu* 'a boundary'), in Netheravon (Wilts), is on the river Avon, which here forms the parish boundary. Sharrow (OE *scearu* 'a boundary'), in Harleston (Nthants), marked the division between the East and West Fields.

The identification and preservation of boundaries was essential when documentation was scarce and maps all but unknown. The annual custom of beating of the bounds was widespread during the Middle Ages and is observed occasionally at the present time. Field-names generated by the old custom include the many examples of the *Gospel Close* type. Gospel Balk, in Ferrenby (YW), is near the Farnham boundary. *Gospel Crofte* 1587, in Kingsbury (Middx, now Greater London), was on the boundary of that parish with Hendon. Monwood Lea (*Monwood* 1426), on the edge of Ansley (Warks), has the western form *mon* for *man*, one of the usual developments of Old English *(ge)mǣne* 'common', sometimes used of land, etc. shared or lying between two parishes, as well as the sense of 'shared by the whole community'. No Man's Land (etc.) is frequently used for land on a boundary. At No Man's Heath, near Appleby Magna (Leics), the boundaries of Derbyshire, Warwickshire and Leicestershire come together. Leg, Higher and Middle Normans, in Cranborne (Dor), originating in *Nonemannes Lond* 1282, lie along the parish boundary. No Man's Land is on the boundary of Great Munden (Herts). In some places may be found the variant *Norman's Land* (etc.), as in Norman's Acre and Ditch, in Aston by Sutton, Norman's Hay, in Bromborough (Ches), and Norman's Field, on the boundary of Widford (Herts). *Ball* occurs in a number of boundary names; it may mean 'a rounded hill', as in Ball Hill, in Buckland Weston (Dor), at 825 ft (270m) the highest point in the parish.

The much-disputed term *balk* or *baulk* must receive more than a passing mention. It used to be argued that one of the worst aspects of the open-field system was the waste of land entailed by the existence of uncultivated balks between one strip and the next. It has now been shown, by the researches of many scholars including the Orwins, that individual field-names such as Baulk Field, in Kirby Grindalythe (YE), and Balk Close, in Eggborough (YW), in East Retford and in Edwinstowe (Notts), demonstrate that such balks as there were could be enclosed and constitute closes more or less of normal shape and size, perhaps by the inclusion of neighbouring arable within the new boundaries. Balks were to be found marking county boundaries, e.g. Shire Baulk, in Styrrup (Notts), Shire Baulk Furlong, in Ashwell (Herts), separating parishes, e.g. *Le Merebalk* 1507, between Doncaster and Wheatley (YW), and Gospel Balk, mentioned earlier, and marking the boundaries of premises, e.g. Kirk Balk, in Cudworth (YW).

Probably the most common term in the names of boundary fields is Old English *(ge)mǣre* or its derivatives, usually in the forms

Plate 6.1 The controversial term *balk* in the name of a famous field
Part of Broadbalk Field, Rothamsted (Herts), has been left uncultivated since
1882. Other portions have been regularly cropped without fertilizers for many
years.

Mear-, Mere-, Meer- or sometimes *Mar-. Le Merefurlonk* 1337–38,
in Slawston (Leics), and *Merforlong* 1309–19, in Steventon (Berks),
may have been on the edge of their respective parishes. The range
of forms is illustrated in the following examples: Mardale, in Braun-
ston (Nthants), Marlands, in Monks Kirby (Warks), and Meer
Meadow (*Le Mere* 1316), in Warwick.

In *Northmerenes* 1398, in Bromborough (Ches), two terms implying 'boundary' are combined: *(ge)mǣre* and *rein*, the Scandinavian
term for 'a boundary strip', which became the northern dialect word
rean. Rean is found in *The Gret Rane* 15c., in North Deighton (YW),
and *West Raine* 1695, in Dean (Cumb). Deep Reans occurs in
Claughton (Lancs), Reign in Linthwaite (YW), Long Rein in Haslington, and Rushy Reans in Shipbrook (Ches).

The boundaries of Twywell, Woodford, Islip and Lowick (Nthants)
meet almost at a point. Alenge is at the southern extremity of
Lowick; the neighbouring field in Islip is called Allege, and that in
Woodford Alage. The names are all forms of Middle English *alange*
'remote, lonely'. Three Shires, in Agden (Ches), is at the meeting-

146

place of the boundaries of Cheshire, Shropshire and Flint. The same name indicates the meeting-place of Gloucestershire, Wiltshire and Somerset, in Marshfield (Glos). Cheshire Acre is in a detached portion of Wirswall (Ches), located within the parish of Whitchurch (Shrops). Cheshire Fields, in Dodcott cum Wilkesley (Ches), are on the Shropshire boundary.

DISPUTED TERRITORY

Boundary land would sometimes be a matter of dispute between adjacent parishes or counties, though territorial quarrels could occur for other reasons, *Disputforlang c.* 1205, in Thomley (Oxon), can hardly be other than what it seems. Controvers, in Bere Regis (Dor), also seems to have this sense. Crowchills or Trowchills, not far from the boundary of Bennington (Herts), was *Strottishill* 1556, probably from Middle English *stroute* 'strife, dispute'. Struttle Mead, in Fencot (Oxon), may have a similar meaning. Street Field (*Strotefeld* 1312), in Titsey (Sur) was on the boundary of Titsey and Limpsfield, and Stroudhams (*Stroutham* 1548) was meadow land on the border between Byfleet and Cobham (Sur). An early form of Stutters Hatch, in Bayford (Herts) is *Stroutershacche* 15c., indicating an origin in Middle English *stroutere* 'a disputer'. The Callinge *(Calange* 1381), in Newton Solney (Derbys), is from *chalenge* 'disputed land', found also in *The Challenge Gosse Furlong* 1622, in Elvaston, *Callinghill Close* 1662, in Coton in the Elms (Derbys), and Challenge Moor, in Churchill (Oxon).

   Barettfelde 1476, in Northenden (Ches), may be 'field in dispute' or arbitration. Old English *baret* 'trouble, strife, dispute' is perhaps found also in Barratt Meadow, in Bollin Fee (Ches). Old English *threap* 'dispute' occurs in Threaphurst 'wooded hill in dispute', in Marple, Threap Meadow, in Grappenhall (Ches), Threapland (*Threpplandes* 13c.), in Cracoe. Threapleton (*Threapelands* 1602), in Wyke (YW), Threap Lands, in Newby, and Threap Lees, in Barton (Westm). An early instance is *Le Trepwood c.* 1130, in Dodcott cum Wilkesley (Ches). One cause of disagreement in connection with this place was that although geographically in Cheshire, the wood belonged to the Shropshire manor of Ightfield. Threapwood, on the Cheshire boundary with Flintshire, was regarded as in no county, parish, town or hamlet. No public authority or court had any jurisdiction, with easily imagined consequences of lawlessness.

Another element indicating disputed land is Old English (*ge*)*flit*, found in Flitlands (*Flyhtlond* 1390), in Yelvertoft (Nthants). The modern name also occurs in Ibstock (Leics) and in Rowland (Derbys). Flitlands, in Braybrook (Nthants), was earlier *Flithul* 1250, with which Flithill, in Northenden (Ches), may be compared. *Fliten* 'disputed' is found in *Flitenlonde c.* 1218, in Hampton Gay (Oxon). Some names with *Flit-* in their modern spellings, e.g. Flit Furlong (*Fletefurlong* 1212), in Toot Baldon (Oxon), may relate to a stream (OE *fleot*).

The Old English word *wroht* 'debated' appears in Wrautam (*Wrotholme* 1304), in Walsgrave (Warks), *Wroughthull* 1406, in Ashwell (Herts), and *Wrohthangran* 956, in Wootton (Berks). *Cheshull* 1228 and Chesland Wood, in South Wraxall (Wilts), contain the Middle English element *cheste* 'strife', found also in Chest Furlong, in Uppington (Shrops), and Chest Wood (*Chistewode* 1276), on the boundary of Layer de la Haye (Ess).

NOTES AND REFERENCES

1. Quoted in A.W. Richeson, *English Land Measuring to 1800: Instruments and Practices* (Cambridge, Mass., 1966), p. 37.
2. P.A.S. Pool, *Field-Names of West Penwith*, p.4.
3. An earlier sense of *acre* was 'a measure of land which a yoke of oxen could plough in a day', though the earliest meaning of the word was less specific: 'wild, undeveloped land' and then 'a piece of such land cleared for use'. There is a full discussion of *hide*, etc. in A. Jones, 'Land measurement in England, 1150–1350', *Agric. Hist. Rev.* **27** (1979), pp. 10–18.
4. Cornish examples have been kindly provided by Mr P.A.S. Pool, in a private communication.
5. Pool, p. 22.
6. The term has, however, been recently used of farms. An MP was quoted as asking, in a remarkable mixture of images, for help to British agriculture to "compete on the world stage, not to feather-bed pocket-handkerchief-sized homesteads" (*The Times*, 25 January 1991).
7. Gray, p. 312.
8. Pool, p. 86.
9. C. Hart, 'Shoelands', *Journal of the English Place-Name Society* **4** (1971–72), pp. 6–11, here p. 11.

10. In the seventeenth century, "Housewives who baked bread or cakes commonly cut the sign of the cross on top of the dough as a means of protection against evil influences", K. Thomas, *Religion and the Decline of Magic*, pp. 589–90.
11. Pool, p. 24
12. D. Torvell, 'The field-name Puppys Parlour', *Journal of the English Place-Name Society* **22** (1989–90), pp. 23–5.

CHAPTER SEVEN

Transfer and transplantation

REMOTENESS FIGURATIVELY EXPRESSED

A great variety of names, both literal and fanciful, may be applied to fields really remote from the dwellings. A location on the edge of a straggling village might give rise to a name such as *Flatteattetounende* 1320 '*flat* at the end of the village', in Monk Fryston (YW), corresponding to the frequent *Townsend Close, Lands* in *Lands End* names sometimes allude to selions on the edge of arable fields, as is confirmed by Lands End and Lands Heads, in Taddington (Derbys). Land's End, in Farnborough (Berks), seems particularly significant as it marks the meeting place of the parishes of Ardington, West Hendred, East Ilsley and Farnborough. Elsewhere, fields distant from the village, e.g. Lands End, in Chirbury (Shrops), may have been so named as seeming as far from home as is the place in Cornwall.

In many parishes, fields have been given the names of places in distant parts of Britain, or elsewhere in the world. The reasons for the adoption of such names include nostalgia, celebration, and occasionally a real or imagined similarity of climate or of topography. These transferred or transplanted names have been occasionally called 'nicknames of remoteness'. Some scholars have demurred at the term *nickname*, often employed for fanciful names of any kind, arguing that the designations are just as legitimate or 'official' as prosaic names such as *Wheat Close* or *Four Acres*. Moreover, the fields themselves may not be remote, though undoubtedly many are, and it may be more realistic to use a neutral term such as *transfer* for these names.[1] Investigation may discover whether the name is merely an arbitrary choice, or whether its selection was motivated by some topicality at the time the name was first applied; occasionally, it may be a mark of compliment or disapproval of the land so named.

Some transfers allude to an apparent similarity of location, or a likeness perhaps ironically observed. Others commemorate events at the original place bearing the name. Shanty towns were built by navvies who had served in the Civil Engineer Corps in the Crimea; they called one of these settlements Sevastopol.[2] Some feature of the soil or situation may be the basis for such names as Gibraltar, in Chelmsford and in West Hanningfield, or Gibraltar Field, in Little Beddow (Ess). Gibraltar Field is in a far corner of the parish of Flamstead (Herts). Gibraltar, in Rainow, and Gibralter Pasture (*sic*), in Hollingworth (Ches), may allude "to the great and costly siege of Gibraltar 1779–83", may be rocky or remote, or be pieces "of dear-won ground or just a new field broken in about 1783". Gibraltar Plantation is in a 'remote and constricted part of the parish' of Carburton (Notts), and the reason suggested for Gibraltar, in Fledborough (Notts), is "its situation at a definite narrowing of the width of the parish", suggesting the Strait rather than the Rock.

BRITISH AND EUROPEAN TRANSFERS

London is found in Heanor (Derbys), in Worth (Shrops) and in Gotham (Notts). Fields called Little London, in Alveley, in Munslow and in Oswestry (Shrops) were set aside for cattle drovers en route to London. This may be the reason for the name (often that of a hamlet rather than a field), in some other counties also. Birmingham, in Meltham (YW), may allude to some aspect of local industry or be derived from a surname. There is a Manchester Field in Willingale Doe (Ess). In Derbyshire are to be found Cumberland, Dublin Close, Manchester Land and North Britain. Cumberland also occurs at least twice in Shropshire, one instance being among the large group of town and county names on a single farm in Condover, in the company of Derby, Dorset, Durham, Gloster, Hampshire, Hereford, Huntingdon, Leicester, Northumberland, Nottingham, Somerset, Sussex, Warwick, Westmorland, Wiltshire, Worcester and York, with Shropshire added for good measure, though all these fields are within that county. Yorkshire occurs in Barking (Ess). The names of parts of London transferred to remote fields include Hide Park (*sic*), in Barbon (Westm), Westminster, in Madeley (Shrops), several instances of Pimlico in various counties, and three examples of Piccadilly in Wiltshire – in Grafton, in Hullavington and in Lacock. Piccadilly, in Boxwell (Glos), had the alternative name Picked Hay 'pointed enclosure', and other examples, e.g. that in High Easter (Ess), may have a similar origin. In Berkshire, in addition to two instances of *Piccadilly* – Piccadilly Common, in Winnersh, and Great Piccadilly, in St Nicholas Hurst – Pimlico is found in Denchworth, and Vauxhall in Winterbourne, Chelsea Park is found in Coal Aston (Derbys).

Isle of Scilly, in Coaley (Glos), may be explained in the same way as examples of Isle of Wight in Kennington (Berks), Colesborne (Glos) and Arnesby (Leics): a field with streams on three sides. Isle of Wight in Ratley (Warks) is an outlying field on the parish boundary. The Isle of Man occurs in Sheen (Staffs), and in the West Riding of Yorkshire in Glusburn and in Skipton (where it is recorded in 1690). *Isle of Mann* is described in the 1652 Parliamentary Survey of Bowland Forest as a "parcell of arrable land incompassed by the river Hodder". Isle of Man-Dale occurs in Long Marton in Westmorland, where also a field called Ireland is to be found. The latter name, like Ireland, in Wroxeter (Shrops) and in Croxden (Staffs), or Big & Little Ireland, in Alvechurch (Worcs), may have been land used for encampments by travelling Irish tinkers, or migrant builders of canals and railways. Other examples of Ireland occur in Barnston, in Lindwell and in White Roding (Ess), and there is a Great Ireland in Great Waltham (Ess). The home-towns of such peripatetic labourers may be recalled in names like Londonderry, in Oswestry (Shrops), Tipperary, in Brougham (Westm), Dublin Acre, in Shap Rural (Westm), and Kilkenn(e)y, in Poxwell, in Bibury and in Withington (Glos).

The ambiguity of *Scotland* names has long been recognized. Examples from Sussex, Devon and Northamptonshire were interpreted primarily as 'land subject to the payment of some tax or *scot*', but remoteness in the parish was also suggested. Scotland End, in Great Bowden (Leics), appears from its second element to be at an extreme point (Great Bowden itself being on the southern edge of Leicestershire). Scotland is also found in Hallaton and in Burton Overy (Leics). Scotland in Eaton & Alsop (Derbys) is near the parish boundary. Scotland Voyage, on the edge of Thistleton (Rut), refers to a journey that was at one time difficult and hazardous.

The allusions in Big & Little Italy, in Ellerton Priory (YE), or Barcelona, in Minchinhampton (Glos) and in Ecclesfield (YW), are likely to be to historical events as well as, if not more than, remoteness. In addition to Barcelona, Ecclesfield also included fields

called Geneva Leys, Madrid Close and Dunkirk. The last name is
also found in Eaton & Alsop (Derbys), in Bakewell (Derbys), in
Little Downham (Cambs), in Wethersfield (Ess), in Hawkesbury
(Glos), in Holwell (Leics), in Stanton (Staffs), in Strickland Roger
(Westm) and in Upper Whitley (YW). A document of 1669 relating
to Dishley Grange Farm (Leics) alludes to *Dunkirke Close*. This
name, used both for fields and for small settlements in England,
evidently has counterparts elsewhere. Rentenaar supplies a dozen
Dutch examples (one dating from the seventeenth century),[3] and
there are instances in Denmark. John Dodgson considered that
"some older examples of *Dunkirk* names in England could be
allusions to recusant staging-posts in Elizabethan and Jacobean
times", but decided that these names often refer "to the unfortunate
historical associations of the French place-name with English military
and political disaster". He concludes, in the glossary: "a name for a
remote scene of disaster, misfortune or discomfort" – phenomena as
well known, in their own way, in agriculture as in warfare.

Fraunce and *Normandie*, in Coxwell (Berks), are named in deeds
of the thirteenth century. Both names occur in other counties, e.g.
France (Field) in Cheshire and in Hampshire; on France Farm, in
Rushall (Wilts), there is a comment from the local school that it is
'so called because whichever way you wish to get to it you have to go
"over the water"'. But France, in Helion(s) Bumpstead (Ess), is
from a surname. Another early transfer is at Deerhurst (Glos),
where *Clerevowe* 1424 appears to refer to Clairvaux, and may
therefore have Cistercian connections. *Clereuaye* 1323, in Temple
Newsam (YW), has the same reference. Great & Little Orleans, in
Buscot (Berks), is near the parish and county boundary. Brittany, in
Stainmore (Westm), and Normandy, in Hillmorton (Warks), are
other transfers from just across the Channel, but elsewhere
Norman(s) Land, etc. is a variant of *No Man's Land*, e.g. Higher
and Middle Normans (*Nonemannes Lond* 13c.), in Cranborne (Dor).
Nomans Hill, on the boundary of Ladbroke (Warks), appears as
Normans Hill in the Tithe Apportionment. Normans Field, at
Pickworth (Rut), is on the border of that parish with Empingham.

Apparent allusions to Hungary have already been discussed.
Another phantom reference occurs in Mecca Brook, a field beside a
stream in Grange (Ches). This may be the name of the stream itself,
derived, like Micker Brook, in Cheadle Bulkeley, from Old Norse
mjúkr 'meek'. Bohemia, a close in a remote corner of Redlynch
(Wilts), was first recorded in 1820. The reference may be simply to a
distant country, but this was one whose remoteness and, indeed,

153

unreality were at that time enhanced by the roseate exhalations of Romanticism. Another possibility is that this name and Great Bohemia, in Hemel Hempstead (Herts), refer to gypsy encampments. This is often the significance of names alluding to Egypt, discussed below.

Transferred names relating to places in Switzerland are not often found. Geneva Leys has already been mentioned. Geneva and Berne occur among the Hollis names in Halstock (Dor), to be discussed later. References to lucerne are of course to the fodder crop rather than to the city. Names from Scandinavia and northern Europe occasionally occur. Finland, in White Waltham, and Pomerania, in Bradfield (Berks), are first recorded on the respective Tithe Apportionments, and Holstein Row, in Bamford (Derbys), appeared in 1840, at a time of constitutional problems in that duchy, occasioned by the accession of Christian VIII to the Danish throne in 1839. This was not, however, a deliberate creation but an alteration of an existing name – *Holston Row* – by popular etymology, doubtless influenced by events occurring at the time. *Holston* was probably a local surname. Poland, in Mottisfont (Hants), may be another example of this process.

Possibly because of its position on the eastern edge of the parish, a field in Darley (Derbys) is called Siberia Nursery. But Great Russia, Aston Russia and Home Russia, in Aston Bampton (Oxf), and Russia Field, in Golbourne (Ches), derive ultimately from Old English *risc* or *rysc* 'a rush'. The Cheshire land is named after Russia Farm, *Russhal* 'rush nook' in 1348, and the fields in Aston Bampton are associated with Rushy Weir nearby, *Hrisyge* 1069 'rushy island' developing to *Russeya* or *Russheya* from the thirteenth century onwards. Sledmere (YE) can offer both Greenland and Lapland; neither of these, however, is a transfer. Greenland (or Greenlands, as also in this parish and in Kirkby Lonsdale in Westmorland) almost certainly describes arable strips grassed over. Green Field, in Church Minshull (Ches), has an earlier counterpart in *Le Grenelond*, in a document of about 1304. Lapland is probably merely 'land on the edge (of an estate or parish)', from OE *læppa*. Apparent references to Holland must be similarly discounted; Netherlands, in Market Overton (Rut) and in Shinfield (Berks), may be 'lower arable strips', like Nether Lands, in Fareham (Hants), or *Netherlandes Lane Furlonge* 1591, in Pamphill (Dor). Holland Field, in Wethersfield (Ess), was *Holande* 1468 'land by a ridge'; Holland Flatt, in Weston Jones (Staffs), may have a similar origin. Twelve Hollands, in Burton

(Ches), is probably 'twelve headlands'. Amsterdam, in Carrington (Ches), refers to high dykes on the banks of the Mersey.

"BATTLES LONG AGO"

Many of the foreign place-names transferred to fields allude to battles. Blenheim, in Alverstoke (Hants) and in Bulwell (Notts), appears to be the only one of Marlborough's victories to lend its name for this purpose. Other military activities in the eighteenth century are remembered in names probably bestowed at enclosures taking place at that time. Carthagena, in Langworth (Berks), may allude to the capture of a treasure-fleet there in 1708, to the end of the protracted blockade in 1728, or to Vernon's successful attack in 1741. Carthagena Field and Portobello Tillage Field are in Norton (YE). Besides Portobello, in Badger (Shrops), there are Portobello Far Homestead, in Shirburn (Oxon), Portobello Field, in Rotherfield Grays (Oxon), and Portobello Wood, in Streatley (Berks). These names commemorate the successful assault on the place in Panama by Admiral Vernon in 1739. The fortunes of British forces in the Seven Years' War and other conflicts would have made these names current, to an extent, perhaps, that would be unusual in present-day conversation and correspondence. The shared experiences of every-day life in close-knit communities enabled eighteenth-century villagers "to give national events a parochial importance which made them of personal interest to every inhabitant".[4]

Maida Hill, in Nuneham Courtenay (Oxon), recalls the British victory over Napoleon at Maida in Calabria in 1806. Madrid Close and Barcelona, mentioned earlier, Busaco, in Worksop (Notts), and Malaga Slade, in Mickleton (Glos), were probably bestowed during, or soon after, the Peninsular War. Nelson's final victory has received little attention. Trafalgar Farm, at Temple Guiting (Glos), and Trafalgar, in Weaverham cum Milton (Ches), are the only examples that can be offered, but Nelson, in Elwick Hall (Dur, now Cleveland), commemorates the great admiral himself. Wellington's final triumph is remembered in Waterloo, in Kennington (Berks), Waterloo Copse, with Wellington Wood and Little Wellington Wood, in Watchfield (Berks), Waterloo Piece, in Stanton (Staffs), Waterloo Field, in Aveley and in High Easter (Ess), and Waterloo Close, in Cookham (Berks). East Stour (Dor) has a field called Waterloo and two others named Lowerloo and Middloo, adding a touch of levity to an otherwise sober memorial.

The horrors of the mid-nineteenth-century conflict in the Crimea are remembered in field-names. In Cheshire there are Crimea Wood in Hankelow, and Sebastopol Covert in High Legh; a plantation in Acton Trussell (Staffs) is called Inkerman Belt. Sebastopol also occurs among the names in Sudbury (Derbys). In Selston (Notts) two Crimean battles are commemorated – Alma and Inkerman; there are also Alma Fields, in Sledmere (YE), and Alma, in Dronfield (Derbys). Balaclava occurs in West Felton (Shrops).

Other transferred names from the continent of Europe include Flanders, in Willingale Doe (Ess), in Higher Whitley and in Antrobus (Ches), and in Stanton upon Hine Heath (Shrops), The Chantilly Gardens, in Earley (Berks), and Leghorn Parrock, in Underbarrow (Westm). The last name represents the anglicization (based on a dialectal form of the Italian word) of Livorno, in Tuscany. Hanover Corner, in West Woodyates (Dorset), like Hanover, in Romiley (Ches) and Rugeley (Staffs), possibly reflects the connection of the English Crown with that electorate and kingdom from George I to William IV. Hanover occurs also in Halstock, among the names given to his Dorset lands by the eccentric Thomas Hollis, who died in 1774.

REVOLUTION, REFORM AND BIBLICAL ARCHAEOLOGY

Hollis systematically renamed most of the fields on his estates in Halstock and in Corscombe (Dor). In the former parish he used the names of places and people connected with the Commonwealth Puritans or their overseas counterparts and forerunners, together with place-names with Puritan associations – New England, Boston and Massachusetts. In addition to continental place-names with Calvinist connections – Berne, Geneva, Limburg, Holland and Nassaw – there are also Northumberland, Shaftesbury and Oxford Coppice, seemingly alluding to the English places but in fact the titles of Commonwealth nobles. In Corscombe there are fewer place-name transfers (one being Piedmont Coppice, recalling the massacre of the Vaudois) but a number of references to jurists and to figures of the Reformation.

Hollis's nomenclature gives another dimension to transferred naming – the motivation of ideology. His selections include the names of a number of Greeks (including Solon, Socrates, Plato and Aristotle), but he omits Greece, which does occur elsewhere. However, Greece, in Crook (Westm), and Grese, in Blacktoft (YE), are in fact derived from Middle English *grese* 'stairs', indicating sloping land with terraces or steps.

Among biblical references, Jerusalem occurs in Westmorland, in the East Riding of Yorkshire, in Cheshire and twice in Cambridgeshire. In Coveney (Cambs), Jerusalem is on the parish boundary, but in Chippenham the field is part of the lands formerly *de domo Hospitalis Jerusalem*, and a number of other instances relate to previous ownership by the Knights Hospitallers. Jericho occurs in Lea (Ches), in Bolas Magna (Shrops) and, together with Jordan Beck, in Holme St Cuthbert (Cumb). In addition to Jericho Farm, at Cassington (Oxon), Jericho Field occurs on the very edge of Cliffe Pyppard (Wilts). A special sense of *Jericho* is found in the farming vocabulary, as an isolation field for sick cattle.

Sodom Field, in Brampton (Derbys) and in Holbeck (YW), seems to be emphatically derogatory and can be paired with Gomorrah Close, in Snaith (YW), as indicating blameworthy defects. There are fairly numerous names from *Bedlam* or *Bedlem*, earlier forms of *Bethlehem*. The primary sense is 'mad-house, asylum', from the London hospital of St Mary of Bethlem. *Bedlam* names may be of sites of hospitals for the insane but probably refer to land which only a madman would attempt to cultivate. Examples include Bedlam, in Wrington (Som), in Canewdon and in Messing (Ess), Bedlam Acre, in Onibury (Shrops), *Bedlam Pieces* 1717, in Swindon (Glos), and New Bedlam (*Bedlome* 1539), in Arthington (YW). The Swindon (Glos) land formed part of the endowment of the Hospital of St Margaret, Gloucester. This was a medieval foundation which presumably included the insane among its patients.

At the other end of the scale may be placed Paradise (in several counties), and Promised-Land Farm, in Rowton (Ches), with the synonymous Canaan Farm, in Rempstone (Notts), and Land of Canaan, in Tushingham cum Grindley (Ches), commendation being implied in this reference to the 'land flowing with milk and honey'.

Most examples of *Egypt* probably allude to land on which gypsies habitually encamp, e.g. Egypt, in Weston (Herts) and in Leckhampstead (Berks), Egypt Meadow, in Cressing (Ess), and Egyptian Marsh, in North Shoebury (Ess). Babylon, on record from 1618 as the name of an isolated piece of land beyond the river at Ely, had been referred to in 1419 as *tenementa ultra aquam*, the biblical reference perhaps arising not only from the topography but also from some melancholy aspect of the place. The names of a number of remote fields are with greater probability derived from the capital of another empire. These are Nineveh, in Hampton Lucy (Warks) and in Crook (Westm), Nineveh Close, in Holbeck (YW), Nineveh Farm, in Newnham Courtney (Oxon), in Idlicote (Warks) and in Great Preston (YW), and Nineveh Wood, in Kirkandrews Middle (Cumb). The Holbeck name dates from 1762, and other examples were first recorded in the early nineteenth century, before the Assyrian city was excavated by Sir Henry Layard. The name may have been topical many years before. As early as 1674 John Evelyn met "certain strangers, not unlearned, who had been born not far from Old Nineveh"; they spoke of fragmentary ruins, "but", he adds, "they could say little of the Tower of Babel that satisfied me". This visit by Assyrians could hardly have brought about the renaming of fields across the country, but the reputation of the area may have lasted somehow in popular memory. They delighted Evelyn with "the description of the amenity and fragrancy of the country for health and cheerfulness . . . So sensibly they spake of the excellent air and climate in respect of our cloudy and splenetic country."[5]

WIDER HORIZONS

Mention has already been made of Cartagena and Portobello. A Pyrrhic victory during the War of American Independence appears to have made an indelible impression on English minds, and occurs so frequently among minor names and field-name lists of many counties as to seem like a remedial incantation. Two examples are recorded in Cambridgeshire and two others in Warwickshire, three each in Nottinghamshire, in Cheshire, in Hertfordshire and in Derbyshire, and one each in Cumberland and in Surrey. Bunker Hill, in Ealing (Middx, now Greater London), has the precise form of the American place-name. Of the two Bunker's Hill Farms in Leicestershire, in Lubenham and in Seagrave, the second was probably laid out in 1775.

Besides *Bunker's Hill* names, references to places in the New World include America, occurring three times in Shropshire, in Handforth cum Bosden (Ches), in Barnston and in Little Canfield (Cam), in Great Dunmow (Ess) and in East Anstey (Devon). There is American Meadow, in Brimington (Derbys), American Field, in

Doddinghurst (Ess), and elsewhere are America Close, America Plantation and America Wood, as well as America Field, in Rayne and in Stisted (Ess), in West Hoathly (Sus) and in Tickton (YE), Big & Little America, in Sledmere (YE), Near, Far and Lower America, in Church Eaton (Staffs), America Butts, in Leighton Buzzard (Beds), and North and South America, in Helsington (Westmorland). South Carolina occurs twice in Derbyshire field-names. Other allusions to states include New Jersey, in Ugley (Ess), New York, in Melbourne (Derbys), in Bramham (YW), in Stanton Long (Shrops) and in Ilmington (Warks), North Carolina, in Ashover (Derbys), and Carolina, in Gosforth (Cumb). Georgia, in Little Leighs (Ess), and Georgia Spinney, in Osbaston (Leics), doubtless owe their names to the topicality of that colony in the mid-eighteenth century. It was founded in 1732 to provide for poor families from England. This and other American colonies would have links with the English countryside in the immigrants provided by families dispossessed or impoverished by the enclosures.

Pennsylvania occurs quite often. In Wiltshire there is one example in a remote corner of Monkton Farleigh, and another is found on the parish boundary of Market Lavington. There are others in Ufton Nervet (Berks), in Kingsley (Staffs), in Little Eaton (Derbys) and in Prees (Shrops). Philadelphia, in Hasland (Derbys), is a rare instance of the transfer of an American city or town name to a field. Potomack (*sic*), in Ludgvan (Corn), seems to be the only reference to an American river. It may be a general allusion, or may recall the British exploit in 1814 which culminated in the burning of the Congress buildings and of the presidential residence.

Shiptonthorpe (YE) has fields called California and Canada. California, in Worksop (Notts) and in Skirwith (Cumb), are on parish boundaries; California Plantation, in Whatton (Notts), is separated by a river from most of the arable land. These names, to which may be added West Indies, in Morville (Shrops), Barbados, in Berrington (Shrops), the three examples of Barbadoes in Derbyshire, St Kitts Island, in Britford (Wilts), and Antigua, in Alpraham (Ches), may be landowners' recollections of early manhood spent in slave-owning communities in warmer climes. Jamaica, in Ludgvan (Corn), is a memento of a trans-Atlantic visit by a local man, James Hoskin, who died in 1823. Mexico is among the field-names of Dufton (Westm).

Some examples of New England give rise to doubts about possible origins, as there is evidence that a few of these names represent earlier *Inland* and may therefore be 'land near the residence; land cultivated by the owner and not let to a tenant'. However, New

England, in Halstock (Dor), is in the company of Boston and Massachusetts, and so is probably a transfer. An instance of the similarly ambiguous name Newfoundland is near the southern extremity of South Knowle (Dor), which also has Terra Nova among its field-names. The ordinary sense of *new-found*, 'recently discovered, newly invented or brought into use', prevents unqualified acceptance, without early forms, of any *Newfoundland* name as a genuine transfer. Newfoundland, in Bloxworth (Dor), is near the parish boundary, and a field of the same name in Sturminster Marshall is particularly remote. However, Newfoundland, in Worth Matravers (Dor), is near the village and contains stone quarries, perhaps confirming the sense 'newly brought into use'. Newfound England, in Drayton in Hales (Shrops), belongs to both groups of names just discussed.

In the East Riding of Yorkshire, besides half a dozen fields called Canada (two in Laytham, and one each in Etton, in Lund and in Shiptonthorpe), Canada Field in Kirby Grindalythe, and Canada Plantation in Shiptonthorpe, there were others called Nova Scotia in Gembling, in Kelfield, in Naburn, in South Cliffe and in Withernwick. (The) Canada is found also in Kingsterndale (Derbys), in Great Easton (Leics), in Winterborne Strickland (Dor), in Avebury (Wilts) and in Rawdon (YW), and Upper and Lower Canada in Barking (Ess). The Canada adjoining Scotia Close, in Stretton (Rut), and Nova Fields, in Duggleby (YE), may have been originally Nova Scotia Fields. Novo Scota (*sic*) occurs among the field names of Thorington (Ess). Canada, in Highworth (Wilts), was reputed to be so named from good crops grown there.

Quebec Close, in Snelston (Derbys), is first referred to in 1824 but may have received its name much earlier. Other references to the city are in farm names. Quebec Farm, in Sileby (Leics), was built in 1760, a year after Wolfe's victory. Whitehouse Farm, in Great Budworth, and Arleyview Farm, in High Leigh (Ches), were each named Quebec some time before 1831. Quebec Farm, in Sileby (Leics), was established after the enclosure of the parish in 1760. Quebec Barn is on the northern edge of the parish of Upton Lovell (Wilts). Another possible Canadian reference occurs in Labradore Field, in Stoke-in-Teignhead (Dev).

In two Rutland parishes, Wardley and Hambleton, closes named Klondyke show that commemorative transfer of names was not limited to warfare. The name occurs also in North Wheatley (Notts), in Bretby (Derbys) and in Milton Lilborne (Wilts), where it was reported to be 'good land'. Gold was discovered on the Klondike in

1896, and these names preserve the memory of that event, though it is not always clear precisely what aspect of it the name implies – the hard labour and miserable conditions, the heartache and disappointment, the hope, or the gold.

'THE FATAL SHORE'

Not all visitors to what were then the British North American Colonies were happy about the experience. Before 1776 English criminals were regularly transported there, and some references may have a derogatory sense associated with the perception of the Colonies as places of punishment. After American Independence, transported felons were taken on a longer voyage – to New South Wales. Botany Bay, in south-eastern Australia, was so called from a first impression of abundant and diverse flora,[6] but its name took on a different connotation when it became the place of oppressive exile for lawbreakers who had escaped hanging for a variety of offences against persons and property, including rioting, machine-breaking and poaching. The name, which is of country-wide distribution, almost always occurs in the simple form, without generics, e.g. Botany Bay, in High Ongar and in South Weald (Ess), in March (Cambs), in Teversall (Notts), in Barlow and in Lepton (YW), in Pawston (Northumb), and in a dozen or more places in Shropshire. Botanybay Wood is found in Tabley Inferior (Ches), and Botany Bay Field in Little Baddow (Ess). Besides Botany Bay Close in Stisted (Ess), another instance adjoins Botany Bay Fox Cover in Billesdon (Leics).

Analogous names include New South Wales, in East Barnet (Herts, now Greater London), Australia Gorse, in Ridlington (Rut), Van Diemans, in Horton (Dor) and in Lyddington (Rut), Van Diemen, in Gretton (Nthants), Van Diemens, in Brinkworth (Wilts), Van Dieman's Land, in Hucknall under Huthwaite (Notts) and in Napton (Warks), Vandiaimans Land, in Fryerning (Ess), and Fan Damons, in Kemerton (Glos). The last examples allude to the pre-1853 name of Tasmania, where also a penal colony was established. The change of name to Tasmania was a direct result of revulsion against the evils of transportation generally, and the harshness of conditions in Van Diemen's Land in particular.[7] Its most notorious penal settlement is commemorated in Port Arthur Plantation, in Hinton Waldrist (Berks).

There were in these names several possible layers of meaning for Englishmen of the early nineteenth century. First, the named land is remote, just as Botany Bay and Van Diemen's Land are unimaginably distant. Malefactors are to be found there, just as they are in the Australian penal colonies, to which, thirdly, anyone apprehended on the named land might be transported. Details, based on letters and official enquiries, of the horrors of the voyage to Australia and of the subsequent inhuman treatment of the convicts, would have reached all sections of society. To rural workers of the 1830s, *Botany Bay* was no light-hearted renaming of remote or poor-quality land. It was a term that could strike terror in those that heard it, and its emotional resonances would have continued for several generations after transportation had been discontinued. New Zealand was not a place of transportation, but its remoteness was well understood. It occurs as a field-name in Shawbury (Shrops) and in Wiltshire, Cambridgeshire and Oxfordshire as well as in the far north-eastern corner of Harbury (Warks). In Harpenden (Herts) this name is said to commemorate the emigration of one of the farm workers, about 1880, to the Antipodes.

AFRICA, THE EAST AND THE ENDS OF THE EARTH

Apart from Egypt, already discussed, Africa is not much referred to in field-names. Barbary Field, in Whitwell (Westm), does not allude to the land of the Berbers but to the barberry (*Berberis vulgaris*). The Guinea, in Rodborough (Glos), Guinea Furlong, in Chetton (Shrops), Guinea Mead, in Boreham (Ess), and Guinea Field, in Allostock (Ches), may directly allude to the place or be expressing the rent in terms of the coin named from gold mined in Guinea. Half Guinea Pleck, in Ashford Carbonell (Shrops), refers to a coin, but whether to its small size or to a rent is uncertain.

The Cape, probably meaning the Cape of Good Hope, is an outlying field in the south of the parish of Warwick St Mary. In Lostock Gralam (Ches) Dodgson detects "perhaps a note of optimism" in the name of Cape of Good Hope Farm. Conflict in Southern Africa is recorded in a number of field-names. Zulu Land, in the far south-east corner of Marlborough (Wilts), and Zulu Barn, in Harwell (Berks), allude to a territory that was in the news from the late 1830s, though it became more prominent in 1879–80 when Britain made war on the Zulu king, Cetewayo. The Anglo-Boer War, at the turn of the century, is referred to in Ladysmith, in Hunmanby (YE), and Spion Cop, in Wheatley (Oxon) and in Littlebourne (Kent). The besieged town of Ladysmith was relieved, at a fifth attempt, on 28 February 1900. Spion Cop recalls the battle (by no means a glorious one for the British) which had taken place on 24 January of that year. Spy and Cop, recorded in the 1960s in Stonton Wyville (Leics), seems to bring to this name the outlook and predilections of the late twentieth century. Modder River Field, in Tanworth (Warks), was "so called because a dam in this field was being repaired when the Boers were driven back at the Modder River" (29 November 1899).

One of the rare Indian names, Calcutta Field, is found at St Nicholas Hurst (Berks); another is Bombay Lands, in Cressing (Ess). *Japan* occurs, so far as is known, only in Fareham (Hants). Nankeen Field, in Woodford (Ches), may relate to Nanking only by reference to the buff cotton material originally made there, and so possibly alludes to the colour of the soil in the field. *China* names form an interesting group in a number of Midland counties: China Field, in Alvechurch (Worcs), China Lands, in Curbridge (Oxon), China Leasow, in Childs Ercall (Shrops), China Mead, in Whitchurch (Oxon), and China Pasture, in Ashford (Derbys). There is also China Hall Meadow, in Writtle (Ess). Some of the examples may commemorate the Opium Wars and other events in China. China Island Mead, in Sunninghill (Berks), a unique instance of the toponymic recognition of the *Chinoiserie* movement, alludes to an island on the Duke of Cumberland's lake at Virginia Water, with its Chinese-style folly, built by ex-soldiers.[8]

Lastly, the most general 'remoteness' term possible, World's End (or Worldsend), is used as an extension of such terms as Town(s)end and Lands End. A Derbyshire example, *Worldesende*, dates from 1425. World's End is a lonely place in a remote corner of Ashprington (Dev); another instance is on the parish boundary of Westbury (Wilts), and the name also occurs in Pebmarsh (Ess), in Solihull (Warks), in Curbridge (Oxon), in Kingscote and in Ham & Stone (Glos), and in Rushton (Ches). Worldsend Gate is a spot on the Berkshire/Surrey boundary at Sunningdale, and Worlds End Wood is on the boundary of Clothall (Herts). Worlds End Ground occurs in Earley and in Theale (Berks), Worldsend Meadow, in Condover (Shrops), and Worlds End Piece, in Solihull (Warks). Utter End(s) is also found in a number of places and End of the World, in Clee St Margaret (Shrops), enriches this catalogue with a doom-laden resonance of finality.

NOTES AND REFERENCES

1. Robert Rentenaar has discussed the many terms suggested for this type of name, including *Wandernamen, Migrationennamen, noms transplantés*, and *noms transportés*, arguing for his choice of *eponym*. See his article, 'Die Zusätze *klein* und *nieuw* bei niederländischen Nachbennungsnamen', *Beiträge zur Namenforschung* NF 14 (1979), pp. 254–64, especially pp. 254–7.
2. T. Coleman, *The Railway Navvies* (1965, Penguin, 1968), p. 223.
3. R. Rentenaar, *Vernoemingsnamen* (Amsterdam, 1984), pp. 347–8.
4. B. Kerr, *Bound to the Soil*, p. 235.
5. W. Bray (ed.), *The Diary of John Evelyn* (Dent, Everyman edn, 1907), ii. p. 93.
6. Cook had much trouble in choosing a name, rejecting in turn "Sting-Ray's Harbour, Botanist Harbour, and Botanist Bay, before finally choosing Botany Bay on Sunday, 6 May [1770]", C.M.H. Clark, *A History of Australia* (Melbourne University Press, 1962), i. p. 49. Cook's first enthusiastic impressions of the area carried great weight when the decision about the convict settlement came to be taken some years later.
7. "Even its old name stuck to it like tar", remarks Robert Hughes, *The Fatal Shore* (Collins Harvill, 1987), pp. 590–1. He goes on to quote a journalist's remark in 1882 (nearly thirty years after the change of name) that "not one in a hundred" of immigrants knew the island as Tasmania. Hughes also points out (p. 170) that the number of poachers sentenced to transportation was not so large as popular legend has it. This does not affect the argument that fear of transportation would have been involved in the field-name connotations of *Botany Bay*, etc.
8. H. Honour: *Chinoiserie, The Vision of Cathay* (Murray, 1961), pp. 153, 162, 266–7, 269 and Figures 105 and 115; see also the excellent illustrations in O. Impey: *Chinoiserie* (Oxford University Press, 1977), pp. 141, 154.

CHAPTER EIGHT

Tenure and endowment

OWNERS, TENANTS AND THEIR NAMES

The name of a medieval tenant may occur in field-names recorded in the nineteenth or twentieth century. Davenports Meadow, in Sturston (Derbys), may be identical with *Daueneportcroft t.* Ed. 1, doubtless occupied by a member of the family of Christopher Dauenporte, mentioned in 1428. Saxeys Ham, in Wool (Dor), embodies a surname occurring in the Subsidy Roll of 1332 as *Sexi*, but this is not in itself evidence of continuity of occupation by members of that family. A generic may support an early association with the named family. *Croft* is not much used in the creation of recent field-names, and so to link Abraham's Croft, in Earles Colne (Ess), with Alexander Abraham, named in a Rental of 1395, is not straining credibility. Frequent references over a long period to a particular family in the parish also support a plausible connection between that family and the field-name, e.g. Browns Field, in Stebbing (Ess), has such earlier counterparts as *Brouneshalfyerde* 1424–27, *Browneslee* 1517 and *Brownesgrene* 1517, so that the likelihood of ownership by the family of Henry Broun 1287 must be allowed. The surname in *Skallardescroft* 1414, in Winstone (Glos), is that of John Skallard, mentioned in the same set of documents. A later occupier is referred to in a verbose entry in an 1840 deed relating to Middle Rasen (Lincs): "Close Formerly the Milking Hill afterwards the High Field but now better known by the name of the Barthorpe Closes", to which is added the comment "Formerly in the occupation of tenure of John Barthorpe".

Occasionally the endorsement of title deeds may serve as a guide to obsolete names, but seldom is the record as full as that of some land in West Sussex. Nineteenth-century documents relating to Buxted are deeds of "two pieces of new Assart land called Taylors in Hayerst Wood, late Minn's, before Watson's & Dray's, formerly Brunsden's". Evidently it had been the custom for the name of the current owner or occupier of the land to be applied to the land on his taking possession. It may be thought fortunate (by hard-working transcribers) that this practice was not more widely used.

Documents relating to parliamentary enclosure always contain many surnames, some of which will throw light on existing or later field-names. At much earlier periods, field-names embodying personal names and surnames will be of value for supplying evidence of particular families or individuals flourishing in the area, even though there may be no other documentary evidence. Another source of information is provided by the Tithe Apportionments, which list not only field-names but also the names of occupiers and owners. In the Apportionment for Essington (Staffs), the owner of Green's Upper & Lower Piece is named as Joseph *Green*, that of Quinton's Corner as Henry *Quinton*, and that of Vernon's Piece as Colonel *Vernon*. In the Tithe Apportionment for Horsley (Glos), Hilliers Hatherlings are named, and these can be identified as the hawthorn slopes forming land assigned to Christopher Hyller in 1629. Similar examples can be found throughout the country. Golden Staples, in Great Bardfield (Ess), appears complimentary, but early forms, variants of *Goldynesstaple*, occurring in the fourteenth and fifteenth centuries, point to an allusion to a 'post or pillar', doubtless a landmark, on property owned by a person with the Old English name *Goldwine*. In contrast, Old Kettle, in Elmstead (Ess), seems derogatory. Cristian *Ketel*, however, is named in the 1319 Subsidy Roll; the bearer of this surname, derived from Old Norse *Ketil*, would probably have been an Anglo-Scandinavian.[1] Another Essex name, Proverbs Green, in Great Dunmow, was *Prophetes* 1430, *Prophets Green* 1777, 1805, and is traceable to the family of John *Prophete* mentioned in records of 1368.

FIELD-NAME REFERENCES TO WOMEN

Women owners and occupiers of land are recorded in field-names of all periods. The modern Purn Croft, in Winfrith Newburgh (Dorset), is traceable to *Purnelcroft*, found in a series of records between 1392 and 1682 and probably derived from Petronilla or *Purnelle* de Bosco, who granted land to Bindon Abbey in 1280. Collice Field, in Islip (Oxon), goes back to *Cauda Aliiciae* 1233 'Alice's tail of land', the Latin name probably representing Anglo-Norman *Queue Aliz*, as it was recorded *La Quealiz* in 1235, and later *Cuwealiz, Cowaliz* and *Collis*. This Alice may also be referred to in *Alyce Mede* 1280, in Water Eaton (Oxon).

The person referred to in Queenborough, in Bampton (Oxon), first mentioned as *Queneburgheye* 1238 'Cwenburh's island', bore an Old English woman's name. Annis Wood, in the Sevenhampton (Glos) Enclosure Award, was in 1575 *Annyswoode*; the Middle English personal name *Anneis* was a variant of Agnes. Clemence Field, in Hurley (Berks), goes back to *Terra Clemence* 1304, which contains the Middle English female personal name *Clemence*.

Old Mary's Field, in Plomley (Ches), probably alludes to a seventeenth-century lady of the manor, Lady Mary Cholmondley, but it was probably a less renowned lady who gave her name to Old Mary's Yard, in Stanton upon Hine Heath (Shrops). Peggy's Croft, in Shrawardine (Shrops), is said to be named after Margaret Punch, who died in 1695. *Dame Isabell' Acre* 1465, in Torkington (Ches), refers to Isabel, wife of John De Legh, who cleared sixty acres of royal woodland here and built a moated manor-house about 1354. *Belldame Saares Heedland* 1440–41 and *Dame Sarysakyr'* 1465–66, in Steventon (Berks), allude to a certain Lady Sara, a female tenant of the period. *Margaretts Close* 1706 was the earlier name of Market Close in Billington (Beds). *Market* may be a development of the earlier name by popular etymology. Lady Wildman's Wood, in Newstead (Notts), was named after the wife of Colonel Wildman, who bought Newstead Abbey from Lord Byron in 1817.

Some names refer in general terms to the widow or dowager of an owner, e.g. Widow Pingle, in Skegby (Notts) and in Clowne (Derbys), and Widow's Allotment, in Carsington (Derbys). Grammum's Croft, in Woodford (Ches), was earlier *Grandmother's Croft* (1766), and may be compared with Grandmother Meadow, in Bollin Fee (Ches), Grandmother's Meadow, in Burrough on the Hill (Leics), and Grammers Croft, in Highclere (Hants). To these, which indicate remnants of land for the widow's benefit, may be added Old Woman's Meadow, in Marple, Old Woman's Field, in Butley (Ches), Old Womans Dowry, in Chapel en le Frith (Derbys), Gammers Rough, in Hulme Walfield (Ches), and Old Wife Ing, in Liversedge (YW), Heiress's Meadow, in Church Stoke (Shrops), is a slightly different allusion.

NICKNAMES AND PERSONAL-NAME/FIELD-NAME INTERACTION

More recent personalities are also remembered, occasionally under the familiar names by which individuals may have been known to their intimate friends. Nickeydan, in Routh (YE), is named from Nicholas Daniel Robinson, the village blacksmith, who owned the land between about 1890 and 1900. Such 'hypocoristic' or 'pet' names belong to an old tradition. Jenny Garth, in Wheatley (YW), was probably *le Jennys* in 1589, derived from *Jenny*, the pet form of *Janet*. Phyllis Croft, in the same parish, lacks earlier evidence. Collins Bank, in Hitchin (Herts), may represent *Colyncroft* 1409, containing *Colin*, the diminutive of *Col*, a hypocoristic form of Nicholas.

Many surnames, such as *Acres, Furlong, Meadows, Woods, Slade* and *Croft*, are clearly derived from field-names and minor names but do not identify the particular fields from which the families take their names. Given a context indicated in a documentary source, surnames can, however, be shown to be derived from the field-names of the place, or their earlier counterparts, and so support the antiquity of a particular feature in the place concerned. Associated with Orchard Mead, in Tixbury (Wilts), John *atte Norcharde* is cited from the 1333 Subsidy Roll. The Middle English *atten orcharde* is frequently wrongly divided in this way, just as *Atten Oke* and *Atten Ashe* become respectively *Noke and Nashe*.

Occasionally, what might be taken for an allusion to a natural feature turns out to have a personal-name origin. Myres, in Alston (Cumb), seems to refer to a marshy or boggy area, but this name has a different origin, since the field had been owned by Sir John Myers, a mining speculator in this district. Conversely, Knightleys, at Chirton (Wilts) appears to point to a man or family called *Knightley*, but a document of 1517 has *Nightleaze* 'night pasture', paralleled in Nightless, in Stamford Rivers (Ess), Nightless Field, in Capel (Sur), and Nightleys (*Night Lease* 1650), in Cheshunt (Herts). Rowbothams, in Offerton (Ches), may be either 'rough bottom-land' or the derived surname. Whitmarsh, in Winterbourne Earl (Wilts), could be a surname, but *Whitemersh* 1331 confirms a topographical origin. Ambiguities are numerous and include, e.g. Blackwell Meadow, in Prestbury (Ches), and Nash Field, in Little Hadham (Herts).

Bysshopesacr' 1411, in Minchinhampton (Glos), could be 'strip held by a bishop', but it is equally likely to have been named from the family of the fifteenth-century Isabel *Bysshop*. Persons Ham, in Woodsford (Dor), may be from the surname of William *Person(es)*, on record in 1332 and 1340. If the specifier is a possessive, with *Croft* and certain other generics, it is likely to be a personal name or surname. Occasionally, early forms cast doubt on what seem to be surname derivatives. Hollywells, in Penkridge (Staffs), appears to be from a surname *Hollywell*, but there was earlier a *Holiwallefelde* 1364, confirming the presence of a 'holy well'. Often, only a single modern form has been collected, but a medieval surname may support the possibility of some antiquity for the feature, if not for the name. Later names may also be of historical interest. Barrel Close, in Burton Pidsea (YE), is said to be named from a certain Beharrel, "a Huguenot, who once lived there". In fact, the Beharrels were Walloons.

MEMORIALS AND CELEBRATIONS

Besides the common practice of using surnames to indicate the ownership of land, personal names are sometimes given to fields by way of a compliment to a friend of the landowner or to celebrate famous people. The naming of Wellington Belt, a plantation in Teddesley Hay (Staffs), does not directly commemorate the military exploits of the great duke, but marks a visit he paid to Teddesley Hall. Similarly, Prince of Wales's Cover, in Baggrave (Leics), recalls a visit in 1871 by the then heir to the throne (later King Edward VII). The prince planted a tree on the land and sowed gorse seed, which unfortunately failed. Duck's Acre, in Rushall (Wilts), was given by Lord Palmerston to provide an annual dinner for the threshers of Charlton St Peter, in memory of Stephen Duck (1705–56), the 'thresher poet'. This largely self-educated man became rector of Byfleet in 1752, and was librarian to Queen Caroline. The provision of refreshments at harvest time was a general practice, and this endowment may merely have formalized a traditional perquisite of the labourers.

Many commemorations of victories are by means of the relevant place-names, but personalities are also recalled, sometimes alongside fields relating to their achievements. In Elwick Hall (Dur, now Cleveland), the Tithe Apportionment lists not only the field-name Waterloo but also others alluding to military leaders during the Napoleonic War. To the memory of the Duke of Wellington himself are assigned two fields, Wellington and Duke. Another field, Donkin, recalls an army officer under Wellington's command in earlier campaigns, but who was on the general staff in London in 1815. Also commemorated are Nelson (adjoining the field called Duke) and Blucher, referring to the Prussian general at the battle, also honoured in Blucher's Field, in Madron (Corn). Unexplained names here are St Peter, St David and Oxford, which by coincidence also occurs in Halstock. In Palethorpe cum Bindley (Notts) there are Duncan Wood and Vincent Grove. In Papplewick, in the same county, are Vincent Plantation and Howe Plantation. These names celebrate respectively Admiral Viscount Duncan, the victor of Camperdown (1797); Admiral Sir John Jervis, Earl of St Vincent, whose title derived from the Portuguese cape off which he defeated the French fleet in 1797; and Admiral Lord Howe, brother of the Bunkers Hill general. The last-named admiral's principal claim to fame was the victory off the Breton coast 'the Glorious First of June' in 1794. At the enclosure of the forest at Hatfield Broad Oak (Ess), by John Archer Houblon, plantations were named Elgin Coppice, after Lord Elgin, Houblon's cousin, and – perhaps to show that compliments of this kind should not be limited to the great and powerful – Hampton's Coppice, after his late farm steward. Maber, in Corscombe (Dor), refers to Thomas Hollis's steward.

Other personal names on Hollis's estate in Halstock and in Corscombe commemorate Greek philosophers and political theorists, such as Aristotle and Plato, ancient republicans and tyrannicides, such as Brutus, Cassius, Aristogeiton (spelt *Aristogyton*) and Harmodius, and later political theorists, including Bacon and Locke (whose name is given to a farm). Another farm is called Harvard, after John Harvard (1606–38), the first benefactor of the university which now bears his name; Hollis's great-uncle, Thomas Hollis, also made gifts to that university. Among statesmen and legislators celebrated here are Solon, Lycurgus, Pelopidas and Machiavelli (*Machiaval* to Hollis). Two fields on Sydney Farm honour the Puritan writers Prynne and Bastwick, each of whom was punished by mutilation. Bradshaw refers to John Bradshaw, who presided at the trial of King Charles I, and Cooke to John Cook, prosecutor at the trial. Hutchinson alludes to Colonel John Hutchinson, one of the signatories of the king's death warrant; Peters probably refers to Hugh Peter, hanged at the Restoration for his part in the execution.

In Corscombe the surnames are those of jurists and of leading figures in the Protestant Reformation. Bracton refers to Henry Bracton (died 1268), who wrote *De Legibus et Consuetinibus Angliae*

Nᵒ	Particulars	Qualᵗ	A	R	P
	COURT FARM				
	Robert Meech, Tenᵗ				
26	The Court House of the Manor of Corscombe; Abbas, Garden, Barton, and Moat		3	2	27
27	Cutbred	M	7	2	49
28	Abbots Orchard	M	2	1	23
29	Thane Godwin	M	4	3	34
30	Monks of Sherborne	P	12	0	41
31	Bishop of Salisbury	P	34	2	44
32	The Pope	P	33	1	17
33	Henry eighth	M	24	3	30
34	Cromwell	M	15	0	36
35	Edward sixth	M	25	1	21
36	Fermor	M	4	3	38
37	Reformation	P	27	3	29
38	Grass	M	2	1	02
	Total.		199	1	21

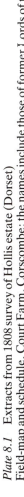

Plate 8.1 Extracts from 1808 survey of Hollis estate (Dorset) Field-map and schedule, Court Farm, Corscombe; the names include those of former Lords of the Manor.

('On the Laws and Customs of England'). Coke and Selden allude to legal writers of a later period, Sir Edward Coke (1552–1634) and John Selden (1584–1664). Wiclif and Tindal commemorate John Wyclif (1320–84) and William Tyndale (died 1536), translators of the Bible into English. Edward Sixth, Luther, Calvin and Knox require no explanation. Coligny and Jerome of Prague refer respectively to the Huguenot admiral who was a victim of the Massacre of St Bartholomew, and to the Hussite who was burned alive in Constance in 1416. Henry Eight Coppice and Stuart Coppice are exceptions, a piece of jocularity on Hollis's part, alluding to beheading.

In Lilburne Mead[2] Hollis acknowledged his debt to John Lilburne (?1614–57), the leader and spokesman of the Levellers. He would have relished Lilburne's words in praise of his predecessors, which sound like the roll-call of some of the Corscombe field-names: "The most faithful servants of Christ . . . being ever the greatest enemies to tyranny and oppression . . . as was John Hus in Bohemia, Jerom of Prague, John Wickliff in England, the Martyrs in Queen Maryes dayes, the Hugonots or Protestants in France, the Gues in the Lowe Countreyes", concluding by placing his own fidelity in the company of those he named.[3] Lilburne called Machiavelli (another Halstock name) "one of the most wisest judicious and true lovers of his country of Italies liberties and freedomes, and generally of the good of all mankind that ever I read of in my daies".[4] Brutus, among the tyrannicide names in Halstock, is honoured also in Ludgvan (Corn), in the company of Jefferson, recalling Thomas Jefferson (1743–1826). The blows struck for freedom by the man who became third president of the United States occurred just too late to be included among the Halstock field-names, as Hollis had died in 1774.[5]

THE ORDERS OF SOCIETY

Names referring to the king or queen are to be expected in royal manors. *The Kinges Close or Lordes Close* 1610 was in Chelmorton (Derbys), part of the royal manor of the Peak. Kings Close, in Hexton (Herts), first recorded in the late sixteenth century, is in a former St Albans manor which was held by Henry VIII for a short time after the dissolution of the abbey. An origin in the surname *King* is likely for a good many field-names of this type, e.g. Kings

Close, in Monks Kirby (Warks), traceable to Richard *Kyng* 1332, but a royal connection is certain in *Le Kynges Acre* 1507, in Halton (Ches), which was an honour of the Duchy of Lancaster. Lord's Acre, in Halton, dating from 1699, may in fact be the same piece of land. *Kinges Meade c.* 1605, in Benson (Oxon), also alludes to the Crown, as Benson was a royal manor. In confirmation of a royal allusion in *Kingescrofte* 12c., in Horton (Dor), the Domesday Book entry states "the king holds the best two hides [of the manor of Horton] in the forest of Wimborne". The definite article often supports the ascription of a name to a title or occupational name rather than to a surname. However, *The Kings Pingle* 1721, in Kirkby le Wold (Lincs), is not a royal reference, as 'Mr King' is named in the document.

Dukes Close, in Chickerell (Dor), refers either to the Duke of Cleveland or to the Duke of Bolton, each of whom once held this manor. *Le Erliswode* 1336, in High Legh (Ches) alludes to an unspecified earl. Earl's Mead (*Eorlesmed* 1393), in Arne (Dor), is named from either the Earl of Leicester or the Earl of Gloucester. The former held the manor in 1272; the latter in 1316. A less usual type is found in *Burgatesfeld* 1336, in Rettendon, and *Burgettfeild* 1596, in Rivenhall (Ess), which relate to the status of an Anglo-Saxon thegn or earl, who was permitted a *burh-geat* 'a manor gate' in the enclosure surrounding his defensible residence. Marshalsholm (*Mareshalholme* 1375), in Preston Richard (Westm), is more explicitly feudal, being part of a knight's fee held by Roger the Marshal, who flourished before 1283. *Le Louerdwod* 1332 ('the lord's wood'), in Gateforth (YW), *Lordesrydding* 1353 ('the lord's clearing'), in Dunham Massey, *The Lordes Close* 1611, in Hurdsfield (Ches), and *The Lords Mede* 1579, in Piddlehinton (Dor), to which may be added the Chelmorton example cited above, doubtless relate to the lord of the manor, an office and title which outlasted the feudal system. Maes Yr Arglwydd, in Oswestry (Shrops), is the Welsh equivalent of *Lord's Meadow*.

The significance of some names may at one time have been clear enough but after a lapse of many years it has now become obscured. Old Masters Meadow, in Adlington (Ches), is one of these, referring to land reserved for his own future use or profit by a retiring landowner, as may also be the sense of Grandfathers Croft, in Newbold Astbury (Ches). Gentleman's Mead, in Stanford in the Vale (Berks), is another name which is vague in its application. Country gentlemen are also alluded to in The Squire's Meadow, in Atcham (Shrops), The Squire's Field, in Utling (Ess), Esquire's

Meadow, in Ellesmere (Shrops), and both The Squire's Piece and Landlords Ground, in Spelsbury (Oxon). *Feeman Close* 1580, in Ripon (YW), embodies the rare term *feeman* 'vassal'. Madams Mead, in Goosey (Berks), and Madams Close, in Kingham (Oxon) and in Oakthorpe (Derbys, now Leics), allude to the wife of the landowner, as may some names of the *Lady* type, such as Lady's Lands, in Stondon Massey (Ess), Ladies Walk, in Odd Rode (Ches), and Lady Mead, in Chadlington (Oxon) but some of these names may refer to the Virgin Mary.

Colonel's Meadow and similar names are often found, perhaps suggesting ownership or occupation by rank-conscious retired officers. Admiral's Clump is found in South Dalton (YE). A surname, rather than the military rank, may be the origin of Colonel's Grove, in Oxenhall (Glos), as the family name *Columbelle* was found here in 1398. Major's Close, in Swanbourne (Bucks), was the property of Major Thomas Deveral at the time of the Civil War. The Deverals figure strongly in village history here, their name probably being a corruption of that of Robert de Veal 1278, alluded to in *Veal's Furlong* 18c., in Swanbourne. Captain's Close is not always a reference to military rank; *Captain* was often the name of the farm horse. In a document of the reign of Henry V there is a reference to *Lez Bondelandes*, in Brougham (Westm), from Old Norse *bóndi* 'a peasant landowner'. *Bondeth* 1296 'the peasant's heath', in Halton (Ches), may be a Scandinavian compound, the second element being Old Danish *heth* rather than Old English *hǣth*. *Le Bondmanwode c.* 1200, in Linwood (Lincs) 'the wood of the husbandman', is from the related Middle English term *bondeman* 'a customary tenant, an unfree villager or husbandman'. This term also occurs in the early form of Runnings (*Bondemanrennyng* 1464), in Boddinton (Glos), 'pasture-lands mown by the bondman' for the lord. Childs Lands, in Goring (Oxon), can be traced back to *Childeslond* 1366 'the land of the young nobleman', possibly found also in Childs Croft, in Sproston (Ches), though the surname *Child* may be present here.

Dawynlonde 1468, in Pamphill (Dor), alludes to customary tenants who owed one day's work each week to the lord of the manor – in this case the former royal manor of Kingston Lacy. The term is derived ultimately from Old English *dæg-wine* 'a day's pay'. Boors Meadow, in Marton (Ches), may be from Old English *(ge)būr* 'a peasant holding land in return for rent or services', possibly also found in Burland Field, in Pickmere (Ches). *Custumarii vocati Acremen* ('customary tenants called *Acremen*') are mentioned in a 1468 entry in Ministers' Accounts relating to Pamphill (Dor), where the field-name *Acremanlonde* is recorded at the same date. The term also occurs in *Akermanslande* 1538, in Cumnor (Berks).

Costicles Enclosure (*Cotseteles* 1331), in Colbury (Hants), and Cockshuttle Close, in Alne (Warks), allude to the successors of the Anglo-Saxon *cotsetla* 'cottager'. A term *cotsetl* has been proposed as an element in this group of names, meaning 'cottage-holding or the land belonging to it', about five acres of land held on condition that the *cotsetla* owed work to his lord on one day in the week. Among early instances are *Cotsettlemede* 1270, in Wanborough, *Cotsetelelond* 1363, in Colerne, *Cotsetlelond* 1374, in Durrington (Wilts), and *Cossettell Meade* 1548–49, in Buckland (Berks). The term survived, as Cossicles, into the Tithe Apportionment of Stratton St Margaret (Wilts), Cossicle, in Marcham (Berks), Cossakel, in Clifton Hampden (Oxon), and Cossical (*Cossetull* 1550), in Longworth (Berks).

Cotman 'a cottager' is found in *Cotman Forlonge c.* 1139, in Bletchingdon (Oxon), *Cotmannadole* 13c. 'the allotment of the cottagers', in Sharnbrook, and *Cotemanecroft* 15c., in Ascot under Wychwood (Oxon). The later term *cottager* also occurs, sometimes in the dialect form *Cotcher*. Cottagers Dales is found in Brocklesby Lincs). The Cottagers Part (*The Cottchers Parts* 1690), in Wrawby (Lincs), is distinguished from The Husbandman's Part. These holders of very few acres were also known as cottars (Old English *cottere*) and are referred to in Cotter Field, in Tarvin (Ches), and Cotter Lands, in Torkington (Ches), earlier The Cotter Lains 1697, a *laine* being 'a tract of arable land'. *Coterouspightel* 1317, in Selby (YW), is 'pightel by the cottager's house'. The status of *bordar* differed little from that of the cottar, and although *bordland* has sometimes been taken to mean 'demesne lands', it may refer to land held by these villeins. *Bourdlond* 1508 occurs in East Hendred, and *Bordelandes t.* Ed. 6 in Appleford (Berks).[6]

The one day's service was conventionally performed on Monday, and this may be the origin of such field-names as *Mondayeslonde* 1475, in Banwell (Som), Mondayland (*Mondai Londe* 1506), in Prestbury (Glos), *Mondayeslond* 1512, in Cheddar (Som), *Mondaylond* 1566, in Bremhill (Wilts), and *Mondaies Acres* 1599, in Spurstow (Ches). Mondays Croft (*Mundayes Crofte* 1575), in Frocester (Glos), and some others may be connected with the service only indirectly through the mediation of the derived surname *Monday*. Thirteenth- or fourteenth-century names are rather more certain to refer to the service, e.g. *Mondaylonde* 1346, in Castle Combe (Wilts), and *Mundayeslonde* 1398, several selions in Ince (Ches).

References to serfs are not plentiful in field-names. *Thralholm*

12c. 'the serf's meadow', in Killingholme (Lincs), is one of the few but remained in the records for less than a century. Old English *ceorl* 'a free peasant' occurs in *Churlgrave c.* 1180 'the peasants' grove', in Mapledurham (Oxon), *Cherluslowe c.* 1300 'the peasant's mound', in Alsager (Ches), and *Cherlefeld* 1349, in Henley upon Thames (Oxon). *Chorlemede* 1341, in Leeds (YW), last appears in the records as *Churll Medowe* 1540. Charlcroft is found in Cold Ashton (Glos), and Chirle Furlong in Churchill (Oxon). These men are more frequently remembered in names of the *Dead Churl* type, as in *Dedecherlesiche* early 14c., in Little Budworth (Ches), *Dedecherll* 1382–83, in Denchworth (Berks), Dead Charles, in Little Hallingbury (Ess), Dead Charl Field, in Abbots Anne (Hants), Dead Shells, in Welton (Northants), which was *Dedchurl* in the thirteenth century, *Dedecherle c.* 1285, in Cassington (Oxon), and in three separate places in Warwickshire. The possible manner of death is suggested in *Chokecherle* 1505, in Newton (Ches).

The parallel types, referring to dead men and women, are found in *Dedemanne* 1239–40, in Kintbury (Berks), Dedman (*Apud Le Dedeman* 1494), in Great Gaddesden (Herts), Deadmans Field, in Acton (Ches), which is said to be the burial place of fifty men killed in a skirmish in the Civil War, *Dead Woman's Bush* 1578, in Wootton (Berks), Dead Woman, in Birdbrook (Ess), Dead Woman's Piece, in Uffington (Shrops), and Dead Womans Field, in Fetcham (Sur) and in St Stephen's (Herts). There is an Anglo-Saxon cemetery in the vicinity of *Dedeman* 13c., in Grantchester (Cambs). Dead Man's Acre Copse may refer to a tumulus in Bibury (Glos). Dead Mans Slade, in Barton on the Heath (Warks), has an earlier form *Dedechurl* 1381. A more youthful demise is remembered in Dead Boy Plantation, in Aldermaston (Berks).

PROFESSIONS AND OCCUPATIONS

Occupational terms frequently occur as the specific element in the names of land held by the practitioners of various trades and professions, including of course the various rural specialities. There are many instances of such names as *Doctor's Close* throughout the country, and Cae Doctor appears in Oswestry (Shrops). Most are impossible to elucidate further, but the owner of Doctor's Field, in Shrewsbury, is known to have been Dr Robert Waring Darwin, father of Charles, who was born nearby.

Plate 8.2 Bark being removed from oak trees for use in the tanning of leather Some fields, such as *Barker Ing*, are associated with the process or the operatives.

Some terms are not easily recognized. *Heusters Croftes* 1462, in Egerton (Ches), were occupied by a *heuster* 'a dyer'. Simmister Croft, in Pickmere, contains the Middle English occupational name *Semester* 'tailor, seamstress', and Quisters Hey, in Dutton (Ches), was the enclosure used by a bleacher, earlier known as a *whitester*. Barker Ing, in Crigglestone, and *Barkerroodes* 1559, in Huntwick (YW), allude to the *barker* or tanner, who prepared the bark of oak trees to provide the tannin for the treatment of his hides. Sowter Butts, in Monyash (Derbys), is from Old English *sutere* 'a shoemaker', also referred to in *The Shoemakers Close* 1700, in Thorpe Arnold (Leics), and in Shoemaker's Croft, in Shrewsbury. Grammarian's Field, in Brereton-cum-Smethwick (Ches), may have been an endowment to provide funds for the schoolmaster's salary.

Out in the fields, certain locations might bear names relating to those supervising the game preserves or tending the grazing or browsing animals. *Warnerriding c.* 1200 was the assart occupied by the warrener.[7] *The Swinesherd Bushe* 1579, in Canwick (Lincs), need not have been more than his temporary shelter while guarding his pigs, corresponding to Shepherds Bush, in Dorking (Sur). Shepherds Croft (*Schepeherdcroft* 1450), in Normanton (Derbys), may be either the occupation name or the surname. Creedman's Close, in Bennington (Herts), was *Cribmans Close* in 1652, land allocated to a cowman who had care of the feeding-cribs of the cattle.

Smithishalfacre c. 1250, in Hassop (Derbys), would be the patch assigned to the smith by virtue of his craft. Customary services would not be required of him, but his duties included sharpening the scythes of other tenants. *Cartarflate* 1409, in Bilton (YW), alludes to the manor or parish carter. He too would be able to carry on agricultural activities only when not performing the duties of his trade, which might possibly keep him away from home overnight or for several nights together. Peatman Croft (*Petmarcrofte* 1547) in Appleby (Westm, now Cumbria), is from *peatman* 'a peat-cutter', or the surname based upon it. Goldsmith's Grove (*Goldsmiths Grave* 1652), in Halifax (YW), commemorates Richard Commons, a goldsmith and 'a common drunkard' who hanged himself and was buried at a crossroads.

Outsiders of various kinds are referred to either by their place of origin or by the name of their occupation. Welshman's Patch, in Ford (Shrops), would have been land set aside for cattle-drovers from Wales. Yorkshireman's Close, in Middle Rasen (Lincs), and Cheshireman's Meadow, in West Felton (Shrops), allude to incomers from neighbouring counties, and *Le Freynsshecroft* 1357, in Ardeley (Herts), to a foreigner from across the Channel. Tinkers Nook, in Gembling (YE), probably refers rather to a camping site of itinerant craftsmen than to an allotment in the fields. The same remark applies to Petty Royd (*Pedderroid* 1573), in Netherthong (YW), this being the clearing (OE *rodu*) where a pedlar might habitually stay overnight. *Girthman Close* 1579, in Ripon (YW), alludes to someone not by virtue of his profession or occupation but more from his predicament. He would have been a criminal who sought sanctuary at the Grithstone (*Grythstane* 1228), from Old Norse *grith* 'truce, sanctuary'.

NATIONAL AND LOCAL OFFICIALS

Chancilors Field, in Malpas (Ches), is probably identical with *The Chancellors Peice* 1694, alluding to Thomas Egerton, Lord Chancellor of England at the end of the preceding century, who owned land here. Purrance ('purveyance'), in Leafield (Oxon), reminds us of the frequent royal progresses of medieval monarchs. The duties of the royal *purveyor* included the purchase of provisions on terms advantageous to himself. Shreves Close, in Mundesley (Norf), may be derived from the surname *Shreeve*, a form of *Sheriff*, but Sheriff's Meadow, in Shrewsbury (Shrops) and in Forton (Staffs) (*Shereue Meadowe* 1320), almost certainly allude to a sheriff, and the land may have been charged with certain dues payable to that officer. *Croners Feildes* 1637, in Hale (Ches), were held by the coroner.

Manorial and parochial officers enjoyed exemptions and perquisites of various kinds, which perhaps offset their liability to penalties when they failed to punish others for misdemeanours against the manorial customs. But they lost these privileges when their parish was enclosed. The steward had the general oversight of all the lord's estates. Steward Ing (*Steward Inge* 1375), in Methley (YW), Stewart Meadow (*Le Steward Medeu t.* Ed. 1), in Staveley, and *Stewardes Acres* 1613, in Chaddesden (Derbys), are among field-names alluding to this important officer. On one Glastonbury manor a tenant, in 1189, held five acres "quia bedellus est", 'because he is the beadle', and in another document *Budellond* occurs as a field-name. Allocations of land to the beadle, who was responsible for the policing of the dwelling area of the parish, include *Budelham* 1295, in Upton (Berks), and *Bydellesmede* 1411, in Horsley (Glos), Beetles Mead (*Bydellismede* 1477), in Arne (Dor), Beadle Garth, in Tealby (Lincs), Beadles Eight Acres, in Tolleshunt Major, and Beadles Ten Acres, in Tolleshunt D'Arcy (Ess).

A *ferdel of land called Reeveland*, in Bleadon (Som, now Avon), belonged to the reeve *ex officio*. *Reveton'* 1278–79 'the reeve's enclosure' is found in Great Tew (Oxon). *Revemede* and *Revegore* 'the reeve's meadow' and 'the reeve's gore or wedge of land' are found in Ramsey (Hunts, now Cambs), where the reeve was free from customary duties and ate for part of the year at the lord's table. Other examples include *Le Reuehok c.* 1270, in Harwell, *Repham c.* 1280–90, in Kintbury, *Great Revehams* 1686, in Eaton Hastings (Berks), Reves Hay, in Crudwell (Wilts), and Reeves Ground (*Revelond* 1545), in Preston Bagot (Warks). The office of reeve, like other manorial appointments, was not much sought after, and in one place a special rent was paid by twelve virgaters, "that they may not be chosen for the reeveship". The corresponding official in a market town is referred to in *Portreeve's Acre* 1753, in Arundel (Sus).

Another official had the task of overseeing the proper conduct of activities in the fields. Haywards Hooks (*Haiwards Hooke* 1561), in North Moreton (Berks), was, like *Le Reuehok* already mentioned, *hookland*, separately cultivated and not following the cropping regime of the common field, in this case allotted to the hayward, who oversaw the management of arable, fallow and pasture. Nominally he cared for the hedges, which prevented grazing animals from straying on to growing crops. Hewards Swath, in Frodsham (Ches), was allocated to the hayward of the royal manor of Frodsham, and Haywoods Piece, in Kingsbury (Warks), may be the allotment of William *le Hayward* on the 1332 Subsidy Roll. Haywards Close and Meadow, in Frilford (Berks), may be derived from the surname *Hayward* rather than the official title. Pindar Close, in St Mary Bishophill Junior (YW), was held by the pinder, responsible for detaining stray beasts in the parish pound.

The bailiff's holding is remembered in *Campo voc' Le Bayly* ('(in the) field called Le Bayly'), in Newent (Glos), and *Bailicroft* 1310, in Spotbrough (YW). Among more recent names are Bailiffs Leasow, in Pontesbury (Shrops), The Bayliffes Brookes, in Lower Slaughter (Glos), and Bailiffs Marsh, in Soughminster (Ess). The holders of *Tythyngman's Acre* 1604, in Bucklebury (Berks), Tithing Mans Ground, in Islip (Oxon), Tythingman's Land, in Pimperne (Dor), or Tithingmans Acre, in Painswick (Glos), were the parish officers who carried out duties later performed by the police. *Cunstable Land* 1229, in Goring, Constables Ham, in Rousham, and Constable Plot, in Spelsbury (Oxon), refer to the functionaries under a different name, that of (*petty*) *constable*. The Bellman's Grass, in Whittlesey (Cambs), was to the bellman (the town-crier and/or watchman), also referred to in The Bellman's Swath, in Grove (Berks).

The tenure of Hangman's Croft, in Ravenscroft (Ches), was by service of providing an executioner to the barony of Kinderton; the execution place, last used in 1596, was Gallows Field, at the end of Lodge Lane, in Kinderton. Hangman's Acre, in Painswick (Glos) and in High Roding (Ess), were probably also lands granted to manorial hangmen.

Milnewardesforlonge 1327, in Catton (Derbys), was land allotted to the keeper of the manorial mill. A *woodward* or forester is referred to in *Wodewardesham* c. 1275, in Lydney (Glos). Forests were not under local jurisdiction, but land might be granted to officials permanently stationed in the locality. *Le Bowe Bearers Peece* 1596, in Duffield (Derbys), was land assigned to an under-officer in the forest, who had the duty of preventing trespasses affecting the deer and the vert (i.e. the vegetation serving as cover for the deer).

Marshalflate 1539, in Loweswater (Cumb), appears to refer to the marshal 'a servant who looked after the stables'. In the same parish there was also *Serganteshou* 1230 '(the) Sergeant's mound', referring to a man performing direct personal service to the lord.

MONASTIC AND OTHER CHURCH LAND

Many field-names refer to officials of the monastery, such as abbots or priors, or to the community itself as abbey, priory or convent. *Convent* was not restricted in meaning in the Middle Ages to female religious communities; *Le Convent Garden* 16c., in Bisham (Berks), was the garden of the Preceptory of the Knights Templars, taken over by the Augustinian Canons in 1337, and *Le Convent Land* 1601, in Thornton Curtis (Lincs), was probably Thornton Abbey property. *Bishop, Parson(s), Monk* and *Abbot* may also be surnames, but the definite article in *Le Abbottes Land*, in Daglingworth (Glos), argues against this containing the surname Abbot; it was in fact once owned by the Abbot of Cirencester. Abbot's Wood, in Branston (Lincs), occupies all or part of *The Abbotes Medowe* 1579, probably owned by the Abbot of the Cistercian Kirkstead Abbey. Abbotts Meadow, in Shurlach Ches), refers to the Abbot of Dieulacres, and *Abbotteshill* 1679, in St George (Glos), to the Abbot of St Augustine's Bristol. Abbey Lands, in Knossington (Leics), were a possession of Owston Abbey, not far away.

From the early Middle Ages to the immediate pre-Reformation period, the monasteries became greater and greater landowners. Grants, purchases and other transfers would all be carefully recorded. In addition to the estates surrounding the abbeys, and the granges or out-stations, there would be individual plots of land bequeathed to monastic communities by pious individuals. It is not surprising, therefore, that religious owners or occupiers are referred to frequently in field-names.

Prior Meadow (*Priory Pingles* 1539), in Worksop (Notts), was land owned by Worksop Priory. Priors Close, in Barton (Cambs), is explained by the fact that Merton Priory held the advowson, and Priors Croft, in Marlborough (Wilts), was part of the property of St Margaret's Priory. Prior's Wood, in Henham (Ess), probably alludes to the Prior of Dunmow, who held land here in 1235, but Prior's Wood, in Kelvedon Hatch (Ess), may be named from the family of Thomas Priour, who appeared in the records in 1337. *Priers Meadow*

1569, in Poulton (Ches), refers to Dieulacres Abbey, in Staffordshire; the abbey was originally sited in Poulton but the establishment
there became a grange when the monastery removed to Leek
(Staffs). Priors Field (*Priors Heye* 1554), in Moreton cum Lingham
(Ches) was a possession of Birkenhead Priory. *Prior's Grove* 1640,
in Shaw cum Donnington (Berks), was part of the priory of Crutched
Friars in Donnington. Priors Down (*Priours Mede* 1538, *Manor of
Pryors Hold* 1735), in Wantage (Berks), alludes to the manor which
belonged, with the advowson of the church, to the Abbey of Bec;
the priors of Ogbourne presented to the living until the dissolution
of alien priories by Henry V, so that the reference in the field-name
survived its origin for a longer period than names alluding to
monasteries dissolved by Henry VIII.

Monkes Landes 1544, in Bygrave (Herts), had been acquired in
the twelfth century by Adam, the cellarer of St Albans Abbey.
Monks Bottom, in Tyneham (Dor), was part of the manor of
Povington owned by the Abbey of Bec. Monks Acre, in Bowdon
(Ches) refers to the Benedictines of Birkenhead Priory. *Munke
Meade* 1607, in Haselbury Bryan (Dor), was the property of Glaston-
bury Abbey, and Monks Mead, in Therfield (Herts), belonged to the
Augustinian canons of Royston. Monk Ings (*Munkeng* 1364) 'the
monks' meadow', in Askwith (YW), alludes to the monks of Sawley
Abbey. Monkadine (*Monekedene* 1335) 'the monks' valley', in
Wallingford (Berks), refers to the Benedictine priory there, and
Munkendeane 1550, in Cholsey (Berks), to the monastery founded
by Ethelred the Unready, destroyed by the Vikings but later revived
as a dependency of Reading Abbey. Black Monks Mear (*Blake
Monke Mere* 15c.), in Lincoln, alluding to the Benedictines, is
noteworthy in stating the name of the order.

Pittance Croft, dating from the reign of Edward I, in Holborn
(Middx, now Greater London), was land providing funds to the
pittancer of St Giles's Hospital. Pittances were donations intended
to provide, on great festivals, additional food for the community; the
bursar or administrator of such funds was known as the pittancer.
The endowment might consist of a small estate, such as Pittensarys
Farm, in Bedwardine (Worcs), attached to Worcester Priory, or
pieces of land, e.g. Pittance Park, in Edwinstowe (Notts), under the
control of the pittancer of Rufford Abbey. The pittancer of Abingdon Abbey held *Le Pitensarie* 1585, in Abingdon (Berks).

The duty of distributing provisions or money to needy persons
devolved upon the almoner, who would draw upon endowed lands
for his funds. *Almoners Farm*, in Bedwardine (Worcs), is discussed

below. *Amners Orchard* 1535, in Tewkesbury (Glos) alludes to the almoner of Tewkesbury Abbey. The Alm'ners (*Le Aumeneresmede c.* 1250), in Chertsey (Sur), was part of the endowment of the almoner of Chertsey Abbey. Anmers Farm, in Burghfield (Berks), has a similar relationship to the almoner of Reading Abbey. Ampers Wick (*Anmerswike* 1539) 'the dairy farm of the almoner', in St Osyth (Ess), was owned by St Osyth's Abbey. Some of these names are hard to distinguish from those derived from *almerie* 'an ambry, a storehouse', among which are *Le Ambree Landes* 1601, in Thorganby (Lincs), Almsbury (*The Amerye* 1539), in Winchcomb (Glos), and Armoury Farm (*Almerey Land* 1468), in West Bergholt (Ess), which was on the estate formerly belonging to St John's Abbey, Colchester. *Almerelond* 1400, in Stisted (Ess), was owned by Christchurch, Canterbury. *Amery Lande* 1538, in Mitcham (Sur), relates to Merton Abbey, and *Ambrye Meade*, in Barton (Som), to Glastonbury Abbey. A 1649 survey of Hardwick, in Bedwardine (Worcs), included *Almoners Farm, Kitcheners Leasowe* and *Sextons Close*. The names referred to obedientiaries in the priory of Worcester. Cellar Flat (*Seller Flatte* 1540), in Halton East (YW), was held by the cellarer of Bolton Abbey. Reddons (*Sextensredon* 1452), in Barking (Ess), was an endowment of the sexton or sacristan of Barking Abbey.

Field-name references to *Canons* are normally to the religious orders of Canons Regular, and not necessarily to the chapters of cathedrals. *Canon Mede* 1491, in Bray (Berks), was owned by the Augustinian Canons of St Mary's Priory, Cirencester. Cannock Mill, in Colchester (Ess), was earlier *Canewykmelle* 'the mill at *Canwick (Wicam Canonicorum* 1158), i.e. the specialist farm of the canons', alluding to the canons of St John's Abbey. Cannons (*Canonfeld* 1536), also in Colchester, was owned by the Augustinian canons of a second monastery there, St Botolph's Priory. Canons Garth, in Tetney (Lincs), refers to the Abbey of Wellow, near Grimsby.

Chance Hays, in Huntington (Staffs), does not immediately suggest its being held by canons, but this is confirmed by *Channon Heys* 1575, *Chanance Heys* 1578, *le Chanons Hey* 1598, preserving the medieval form *chanoun*. Canonhams 'the canons' meadows', in Banstead (Sur), incorporates *Hamma c.* 1170, granted to the prior and canons of St Mary Overy, Southwark. Canfield Farm, in Stebbing (Essex), was *Cannonfylde* 1517, held from the thirteenth century by the Augustinian canons of Little Dunmow. Land referred to in the Missenden Cartulary as *Iminge* (for *Inninge*) *Canonicorum* 'the canons' innings' was owned by the community of Great Missenden Abbey, of the small Order of Arrouaise. This became Grange Farm, with fields bearing modern names, Grange Field and Grange Grove, nearby.

In Lostock Gralam (Ches), *Monchenehull* 14c. 'the nuns' hill' refers to the nuns of Chester who were granted land here about 1220. Minson Meadow, in Cookham (Berks), was *Munchenelesse* 1294 (OE *myncen* 'a nun'). In 1199 the Prioress of Clerkenwell Priory held a virgate of land, Minchins (*Mynchonys* 1504), in Great Dunmow. The same community held Mince Croft (*Mynchynhopes* 1480 'the nuns' little valleys'), in North Weald Basset (Ess).

Evidence of nuns in Cookham is afforded by the field-name *Nunpitts Fere* 1608 'the furrow by the nuns' pit'. *Nunne Medowe* 1521 was land held in Derby by the nuns of St Mary there, who also owned *Nunnefeld* 1514, now Nunfield Close, in Crich (Derbys). Nun Moor (*The Nun Moores* 1683), in Brewood (Staffs), and Nun Crofts, in Whiston (Staffs), were owned by the Benedictine nuns, the 'Black Ladies of Brewood'. Nuns Field (*Nonnesfeld* 1547) and Nuns Clough, in Trusley (Derbys), refer to the nuns of King's Mead, Derby; in 1236 an acre of wood in Trusley had been granted to Rametta, their prioress. The pre-Reformation ownership of *Nun Headland* 1579, in Thoresway (Lincs), has not been established.

Granges were the outlying estates in monastic ownership. Their agricultural management was distinct from the routine followed in the village fields. The arable land did not have to be divided into strips, and so could be cultivated as efficiently as a present-day farm. The pasture could be treated as a unit, and flocks and herds managed more economically. *Le Graungefeld c.* 1300, in Takeley (Ess), was owned by St John's Abbey, in Colchester. Grangefields, in Trusley (Derbys), were owned by the nuns of King's Mead, Derby. Cotesfield (*Grange of Cotes* 1254), in Hartington Middle Quarter (Derbys), belonged to Combermere Abbey. *The Grange* 1482, in Cookham (Berks), was owned by the Augustinian canons of Cirencester, who were granted an estate in Cookham by Henry I and retained it until the Dissolution. The *ambry* or pantry of this community was *Almery Grange*, in Cirencester (Glos), not far from the Abbey itself.

The word *friar* (ME *frere*) has a wider application in field-names than in modern usage, which normally limits the term to members of the religious orders of mendicants. Place-names and field-names including *Friar* may also imply ownership by such orders as the Knights Templars or Knights Hospitallers, and the term may occasionally be used of other non-mendicant orders. *Frerehage* late 12c. 'friars' enclosure', in Thurnscoe (YW), cannot allude to the mendicant friars, founded in the early thirteenth century. In Kingerby (Lincs), Friars Thorns adjoins a field called Canons, both probably alluding to the same community.

Friars Gap, in Weston (Herts), is possibly traceable to *Frerestokkyng* in documents of the reign of Richard II. No information is given in published sources about the orders alluded to in *Frerekarre* 1557, in Cantley, Friar Close, in Balby (YW), *Friarsmeadows* 1593, in Congleton (Ches), *Frerencroft* 1418, in Newnham (Glos), and Friars Field (*Frerefeld* 1497), in Grendon (Warks), which is attributed to 'the friars of Coventry', without qualification; there were both Carmelites and Franciscans in Coventry in the fifteenth century. Frier's Ground, in Gloucester, is the site of the premises of the White Friars, or Carmelites, who are also alluded to in Friary Closes, in Doncaster (YW). *Whyte Freers Close* 1546–47 lay among the fields of Warwick. The field-names Higher and Little Freary (*Le Frary* 1313), in Gillingham (Dor), probably refer to the Dominican friars known to have been in Gillingham before 1250.

Religious orders of knighthood belong to the age and outlook of the Crusades. The greater orders were very powerful; they were free of episcopal jurisdiction and their property was exempt from tithe. Although the Templars flourished in England for little more than a century and a half (*c.* 1155–1310), their name survives in many place-names and field-names. *Templeresforlong* 1464, in Southam (Glos), refers to this order, who held land at Newland, in Southam. Temperlands, in Moore (Ches), was earlier referred to as *Templecroft* 1547. Temple Field, in Copmanthorpe, and Temple Field, in St Mary Bishophill Junior (YW), show the more usual method of naming the property of this order. Temple Bottom Mead, in Ogbourne St Andrew (Wilts), is in Rockley in that parish, owned by the Templars. These and the early forms of other names, e.g. Templands (*Temple Cowe Leasowe, Temple Meade* 1578), in Andoversford (in Dowdeswell, Glos), suggest a preponderance of pasture. *Le Covent Garden t.* Ed. 6 and Temple Park, in Hurley (Berks), were part of the possessions of the Templars, who had a preceptory here. *Le Templecroft* 1277, in Little Sampford (Ess), later passed to the Knights of St John of Jerusalem; their land, *Le Freres* 1343, later became Frier's Farm. References to hermits and anchorites are less frequent. Allusions are to be found in Hermitage (*Ye Armitage* 1585), in Shrewsbury St Julian (Shrops), Hermitage Field, in Appleton (Ches), Hermitage Wood, in Whiteparish (Wilts), in Gawsworth and in Siddington (Ches), and Hermitage Close, in Loughborough (Leics). There is a thirteenth-century mention of an *Ermitecroft* in

Malham (YW), and *Le Ermettescroft* 1440 occurs in Ince (Ches). Armitt Field and Far Armitty are found in North Duffield (YE). *Hermytesbothum* 1384 'the hermit's valley bottom', in Disley-Stanley (Ches), points to the kind of secluded spot normally chosen by a hermit as his dwelling place, as does *Hermitesrane* 'the hermit's boundary land', in North Stainley (YW). An unusual example is found in Essex, Bedeman's Berg (*Bedemannesberga* 1177) 'the hill of the man of prayer', in Writtle. Anchor Mead, in Wimborne Minster (Dor), is supported by medieval references to an anchorite, e.g. *Toft ex Parte Boriali Anchoriste* 1427 'the toft on the north side of the anchorite's (dwelling)'; in the same place, St Catherines or Catherines Field was earlier *St Catherine's als. Le Hermitage* 1550. *Ancresynge* 1535 'the anchorite's meadow' is found in Sprotborough (YW).

Further evidence of anchorites is provided in such names as Ankers, in Comberbatch (Ches), Ankerage, in Tortworth (Glos), Anchor Field, in Greenstead and in Dedham (Ess), *Ankerhawe* 1497 'the anchorite's enclosure', in White Waltham (Berks), and Anker's Croft, in Horton (Ches). Abbey Grange, in Derwent (Derbys), was *One Mans House alias Abbey* in 1656; the land apparently had some connection with Welbeck Abbey, but the earlier references, beginning with *Wonemanfeld* in the reign of King John, point to occupation by a solitary or hermit. The first element in Anslow, in Albrighton (Shrops), may be Old English *ansetl* 'a solitary dweller'.

THE SECULAR HIERARCHY

In addition to the great possessions of the monasteries, church property also included land held by bishops, the chapters of cathedrals and collegiate churches, diocesan officials and the parochial clergy. Bishop's Wood (*Bysscopeswode* 1270), in Ruardean (Glos), extends across the Herefordshire border and was once a possession of the Bishop of Hereford. Bishop's Ground, in Market Lavington, and Bishop's Wood, in Redlynch (Wilts) refer to the Bishop of Salisbury, who held land in West Lavington and was lord of the manor of Downton. Bishops Leys, in Woodmancote (Glos), alludes to the Bishop of Worcester; it is in the Hundred of Cleeve, which was a liberty of that bishop in the Middle Ages. *Bisschopishaye* 1353 'the bishop's fenced-in enclosure', in Tarvin (Ches), was the park owned by the bishops of Lichfield, Lords of the Manor of

Tarvin in the Middle Ages. Bishopric (*Bissopeswyke* 1219), in Stebbing (Ess), developed from the earlier name, meaning 'the bishop's dairy farm', by association with the ordinary term *bishopric*, meaning 'the jurisdictional area of a bishop'.

Chapter and diocesan offices and officials are alluded to in such names as Treasurer's Garth, in Ripon (YW), from the chapter treasurer there, referred to in the earlier name *Tresorer Wall* 1533, Other names include The Prebend, in Avon Dassett (Warks), which provided the stipend of one of the Lichfield canons. Prebendal Farm, in Bishopstone (Wilts), similarly supported one of the canons of Salisbury. Such a farm would often consist of separate enclosures scattered through the open fields, like the glebe of an individual parish. Dean's Meadow (*Deanes meadowe* 1574), in Acton Trussell (Staffs) alludes to the Dean of St Mary's, Stafford. Dean and Chapter Lands, in Harlethorpe (YE), or The Deans Canonical Farm, in Lincoln, has developed from *The Deanes Orchard* 1649. Deans Field, in Chester, is probably to be identified with *Le Denefeld* 1360, owned by the Dean and college of the church of St John the Baptist, Chester. The Latin field-name Laudamus (perhaps elliptically for *Te Deum laudamus* 'We praise thee, O God') is ecclesiastical in tone, perhaps expressing a prayerful thanksgiving for the outcome of some land transaction. Archdeacon Meadow (*Pratum Archidiaconi Glouc'* c. 1230), part of Mean Ham, in Longford (Glos), beside the Severn, belonged to the Archdeacon of Gloucester.

Collegiate churches were served by communities of secular priests, not members of religious orders. College Copse (*The College Mede* 1686), in Chiddingfold (Sur), is part of the land granted in 1481 as a chantry in St George's Chapel, Windsor, which was a collegiate church. College Leasow, in Morville (Shrops), was evidently owned by the community responsible for the collegiate parish church there. College Meadow, in Thorpe (Sur), was part of the possessions of the Dean and College of St Stephen's, Westminster. Occasionally *College* names refer to monasteries, e.g. College Field (*Colledge Fields* 1536), in Dodcott cum Wilkesley (Ches), earlier the property of Combermere Abbey.

THE PRIEST AND HIS CLERK

Priest Field, in Sutton Downes (Ches), dating from 1611, was supplemented by *Gleabe Riddinges* 1611. *Ye Preiste Leas* 1625, in

Canwick (Lincs), was probably also part of the glebe. Churchfield, in Cookham (Berks), is 'field belonging to the church' rather than 'near a church', as it was formerly glebe land of the Abbey of Cirencester. The glebe was the holding, originally in the common fields, attached to the parish priest's benefice. This is land about which much documentary evidence is available in the form of Glebe Terriers dating from the late sixteenth century. These terriers provide information on neighbouring land-holders, the names of open fields and furlongs, and sometimes details of subsequent enclosure.

The glebe originally approximated to the holding of a rich peasant, one or two yardlands. *The Parsons Closes* 1706 was probably all or part of *Le Kirkeoxeganges* 14c., in Bolton by Bowland (YW). There were exceptional cases. When Leicester Abbey appropriated Hungarton church, the Archbishop of York stipulated that the vicar "was to have a good and befitting house, a glebe of three virgates of land, with meadows and pasture".[8] Whether cultivated personally or by a tenant, the glebe represented a part of the income of the priest. It was often, at the enclosure, left as isolated closes in the previous locations in the former common field, e.g. in Gimingham (Norf), where individual pieces of glebe land include Parson's Close, Glebe Pightle, Sermon Acre, Second Thoroughfare and part of Sawing Pits. Closes of glebe land in other counties include *The Gleebe* 1650, in Eynsham (Oxon), *Glibe-Shott* 1709, in Ringwould (Kent), Glebe Field, in Chettle (Dor) and in Fingringhoe (Ess), Glebe Close, in Alexton (Leics), and The Parsonage or Glebe Homestall, in Kirtlington (Oxon). God's Croft, in Charlton (Wilts), was formerly glebe.

Prestridding 1523, in Cawood (YW), 'the priest's clearing or assart', was possibly a useful addition to the land owned by the incumbent, who already had *Le Personerigge* there in 1414. Fieldnames with this reference often have *Prest* or *Pres(s)* as their first element, e.g. *Prestfild* 1360, in Mottram in Longendale (Ches), Press Field (*Prestefelde* 1461), in St Michael's (Herts), Press Croft, in Great Canfield (Ess). Press Mead, in Wimborne Minster (Dor) 'the priest's meadow', has earlier forms *Prestemede* 1411, 1552, *Presse Meade* 1591, 1598. In Cheshire, *Prustesfeld* 1343, in Capenhurst, shows a local dialectal feature, in contrast to *le Prestisfeld* 1360, in Malpas, and *Prestfeld* 1360, in Mottram in Longdendale. Priest Meadow, in Ely (Cambs), goes back to *Prestesmedwe* 12c.

The original feoffees of *Preestland* 1426, in Gateforth (YW), can actually be identified as John de Rycall, chaplain, and William Pace, vicar of Ricall. *Prestland* 13c., in Lincoln, was given by the Vicars Choral of the Minster to Nocton Priory. Other examples are Priests

Field (*Prestisland* 1367), in Felsted (Ess), Priest Top (*Prestefeld* 1153–54), in Hook Norton, and Priestlands, in Bloxham (Oxon). In some names the incumbent was called the *Parson*, e.g. *Personeshamme* 1410, in Steventon, *Parsonisfurlong* 1519, in Ashbury, Parsons Croft, in Cookham (Berks), and *The Parsonage Pingle* 1611, in Thorganby (Lincs). Gwerglodd yr Offeiriad, in Llanyblodwel (Shrops), is 'the parson's meadow'.

Another term alluding to the incumbent may be noted in Vicar Banks, in Appleby, *The Vicars Carr* 1578, in Barton, Vicar's Croft, in Clifton (Westm), Vicar's Close, in Thornton Curtis (Lincs), and Vicars Two Leys, in Swanbourne (Bucks). Earlier examples include *Vikerclos* 1368, in Tanshelf (YW), and *Vickers Wonge c.* 1635, in Brentingby (Leics), later *The Parsons Clos* 1700. *The Vicarage Ground* 1580, in Barrow upon Humber (Lincs), was glebe land there. Vicarage Coppice, in Coombe Keynes (Dor), about a mile from the vicarage, is probably a development from *Le Vicaryshegge* 1448 'the vicar's hedge', on the parish boundary, which it was probably the incumbent's duty to maintain. Vicarage Mead, in Horfield (Glos), was *The Vicaryes mede* in 1540. Bread, in Long Buron (Dor), was *Vicar's Breade'* 1405 (OE *brǣdu* 'a broad piece of land'). *Vicarage*, like *Parsonage*, frequently has the sense of 'benefice' and alludes to glebe land.

Local arrangements for the commutation or allocation of tithes made possible the naming of such fields as Tithe Lands, in Beaford (Dev) and in Bibury (Glos), or *Tithes Meadow* 1739, in Mouldsworth (Ches). The tithe meadow in Clifton upon Dunsmore (Warks) was allocated to the lord of the manor "in lieu of the tithe of hay due to him as lay rector".[9] Queen Anne's Bounty was a perpetual fund for the augmentation of poor livings, alluded to in some unexplained way in Queen Ann's Bounty Field, in Willaston (Ches), and in Queen Anne's Bounty, in Hailey (Oxon). This fund was produced by the amalgamation of monies previously received for the first-fruits and tenths payable to the Pope, but annexed to the Crown by Henry VIII.

Clerkslond in Englefield (Berks), referred to from 1401–02, was land assigned to the parish clerk, as were Clarkes Field (*Clerkes Feld* 1475), in Marton (Ches), The Clerks North and South Half Acre, in Beer Hackett (Dor), and *Clerks Bitts* 1729, in Rousham (Oxon). In Linwood (Lincs) the significance of the name is clarified in a terrier of 1822: "a close called the Clerks Yard for the benefit of the Clerk". Sexton's Glebe, in Beaumont (Ess), was a three-and-a-half-acre plot, assigned to the parish clerk for the time being. Sextons Meadow, in

Great Bentley, and Sextons Field, in Colne Engaine (Ess), may be similarly explained.

CHANTRIES AND OBITS

Names of the same type as Chantry Piece, in Chadlington (Oxon), are worth bringing to the attention of local historians and medieval archaeologists. Chantries were foundations endowed to support a priest who was obliged to celebrate daily or weekly masses for the souls of the donors. A chantry was founded in 1325 by Simon Wulstan, for the soul of Geoffrey le Smyth, the masses to be said in the chapel built in 1295 on the bridge at Biddenham, Beds. The *chantry* was the charity itself; the fields may be merely part of the endowment. However, field-names of this type have been applied to the sites of chantry houses (in which the chantry priests lived) or of chapels. Chauntry Field, in Englefield (Berks), was *The Chauntrye Lande* 1555, supporting the Chantry of St Mary in the parish church. Chantries, in Shalford (Sur), were woodlands forming the endowment of the Norbrigge Chantry in Trinity Church, Guildford. The Chantry, in Burrough Green (Cambs), was owned by *Batemannes Chaunterie* 1445, founded by John Bateman, the parish priest, in the chapel of the Conception of Burgh. The Chantry, in Harlow (Ess), belonged to *the chantrie of St Parnell the Virgin* 14c. *Chantree Moore* 1628, in Middle Rasen (Lincs) refers to the Chantry of St Mary, West Rasen, which since before 1376 had held "4 marcates of land in *Middelrasyn*". Less recognizable modern forms include Chantley Field, in Woodford (Ches), Chanter Land, in Barham (Kent), and Chanter Lands (*Estchaunturland, Southchaunturland* 1408), from Middle English *chauntour* 'chantry priest', in Cottingham (YE). East and West Chandry Piece (*Le Chauntery Pece* 1514), in North Moreton (Berks) belonged to the Stapleton Chantry, founded in 1299. Occasionally a saint's name is used as an alternative name for the land, as in *The Churche Laundes or St Katherin Launds* 1548–49, in Ardington (Berks, now Oxon). Prestons, in Ashurst (Sus), was "sometimes in the tenure of the Chantry Priests of Steyning".

Not all chantry land was explicitly named. In Stainforth (YW) such land included "ij a. of medowe in one close called *Medyllherst*, one roode medowe in *Pyghell*, j closse, called *Bouthom* . . . and one roode lyeng severall in the *Est Inges*". Many of the holdings would have been lands in the common fields, e.g. in Hatfield (YW), where the "Service of our Lady in the paryssh churche of Hatefelde" was maintained from the income of "v rowdes of land lyeng in *Furfelde* . . ." and "an acre and a halfe of lande in *Mylnfelde*". Whereas a chantry imposed a daily or weekly obligation of prayers or masses for the deceased, in perpetuity, another form of regular intercession also existed. *Obits* were prayers said or masses celebrated on fixed days in the year. The maintenance of the priest was provided by lands such as *Obite Lande* 1559, in Aston, and *Obit Lands* 1559, in Braithwell (YW). Only the donor's name survived in the modern form of Almonds, in Saffron Walden (Ess), which was *Almans Obeit Launde t.* Hy 8. After the Reformation the term was used for funds for general charitable purposes.

CARE OF THE PARISH POOR

Field-names bear witness to assistance given to the village poor from bequests of pieces of land, the rents from which provided the necessary funds. Some benefits in cash or kind (bread, fuel, etc.) might be provided on specified annual occasions or supplied regularly to the indigent. There might also be casual payments to those fallen on hard times. These compassionate objects are reflected in names such as Charity Close, in Bushwood (Warks), and Charity Butts, in Withington (Shrops).

In some parishes, the local Overseers of the Poor were recorded in earlier documents as trustees of the land, from the income of which they made grants in cash, or which they used as a site for a workhouse. Poor House Field, in Newhall, and Workhouse Field, in Pownall Fee (Ches), are examples. The Overseers of the Poor owned Charity Close, in Rotherby (Leics). There are Charity Pastures, in Burghfield (Berks), Charity (*Charity Close* 1684), in Thurnscoe (YW), Charity Field, in Laytham (YE), and Charity Piece, in Wokingham (Berks). Charity Mead, in Mappowder (Dor), administered by trustees, was let commercially and the rent applied to the poor-rate fund. Elsewhere, the incumbent was responsible for making annual payments on specified dates. The rent of Money Croft, in Therfield (Herts), provided funds for a bread charity. Income from Bonnets Close, in Soham (Cambs), was originally used to provide bonnets for the poor of Isleham. Testament Ground, in Horsley (Glos), was endowed to provide schoolchildren with copies of the New Testament. Sermon Acre, in Mundesley (Norf), pro-

duced 10s 6d per annum, used for providing bread for the poor,
though originally intended as a fee for a sermon. Some examples of
Gospel Close, etc. were endowments for such purposes as the
education of village children. Harmony, in Bures (Ess), is said to be
a corruption of *Almonry*, a copse which furnished lop-wood to
certain recipients.

Poors Piece (etc.) is to be found in many places, e.g. *Poureslond*
1480, in Arborfield (Berks), Poors Land, in Crowton (Ches), Poor
Folks Close, in Hayton (Notts), and Poor Folks Closes, in Bletchingdon (Oxon). Poors Piece, in Little Baddow (Ess), is held by the
parish council on behalf of the poor. Poor Land, in Rampton (Notts),
is administered by the Charity Commissioners. The purpose of Poor
Allotment, in Winterborne Kingston, in Upwey and in other places
in Dorset, is clarified by an 1863 document referring to the land in
Upwey: "the Poor's plot . . . on which the poor . . . exercise the
right of cutting furze for fuel". This confirms that such names as
Poor's Furze, in Ogbourne St George (Wilts) and in Lambourn
(Berks), refer to this purpose.

The land allotted often seems very small. The Overseers of the
Poor in Toynton St Peter's (Lincs) received one acre, ten perches in
the 1773 Enclosure Award. In 1786 Poor Land, in Sidestrand (Norf),
an enclosure of two acres, produced £1 14s annually.

Some names alluding to the poor may refer to allotment gardens,
sometimes specifically awarded by Enclosure Commissioners for the
use of poor people in compensation for the loss of fuel or other
rights on the common. Labouring Poors Allotment, in Cottisford
(Oxon), is one of these. Happy Lands, in Barrow upon Trent
(Derbys), represents a bequest to provide small-holdings for poor
people. Each tenant was to hold one-and-a-half-acres of arable and
three acres of meadow with additional grazing rights.

Parishes were empowered by the Select Vestry Act, 1819, to
obtain up to twenty acres of land by lease or purchase, for the benefit
of the poor, to whom it might be leased in individual allotments. A
further Act, in 1831, increased the area to be enclosed to fifty acres.
The Poor's Allotment, in Brington (Nthants) and in Frilford (Berks),
Allotment for Labouring Poor, in Pyrton (Oxon), and Cottage
Orchard and Allotments, in Compton Beauchamp (Berks), are
examples of this. The land might be in a neighbouring parish:
Faringdon Poor Ground was in Shrivenham (Berks); the needy in
Shrivenham were catered for in the Poors Ground there. Poors
Gardens is found in Tarrant Keynston, Poors Land in Haslebury
Bryan (Dor), in Crowton, in Disley-Stanley, in Leftwich (Ches) and

in Barley (Herts). In some counties, *Potato Gardens* or *Potato Grounds* might be let to the poor by individual farmers, sometimes at four times the rent they paid themselves, getting the land manured and dug into the bargain.

RENT AND OTHER PAYMENTS

Pennylands and similar names often refer to holdings for which a rent was paid. Penny Rent, in Wem (Shrops), declares itself explicitly. Penny Croft, in North Stainley (YW), was first mentioned at *Pennigescroft* in 1303 and was recorded frequently for more than 500 years. Penny Croft, in Takeley (Ess), is traceable back to *Peny Croft* 1422. Penny Lands (*Penyland c.* 1560), in Winchcombe (Glos), were plots in the common field paying a penny rent. In the late Middle Ages *penny* (OE *pening*) was used of money in general, so that *Pennylands*, etc. may refer not to an actual rent of one penny but merely to the fact that such land was held against a money payment rather than in return for manorial service. A 1575 Survey of Over (Cambs) refers to "copyholds called *Penny Lands* formerly of the demesne let by copy of court roll to such as would give most rent and farm to hold them". Some names, e.g. The Halfpenny, in Padworth (Berks), Halfpenny Meadow, in Lower Swell (Glos) and in Kempsey (Worcs), Halfpenny Catchpiece, in East Ilsley (Berks), and Halfpenny Croft, in Whitchurch (Shrops), allude to the overnight pounding of drovers' cattle at a charge of a halfpenny per beast. Halfpenny Field (*Halpenyfeilde* 1336), in Elm (Cambs), represents a local tax for dyke maintenance.

Sometimes the value in (pre-decimal) pence is given, as in Tippenny, in Ormside (Westm), Tippenny Meadow, in Bloxham (Oxon), Twopenny Close, in Hartshorne (Derbys), Threepenny Field, in Wistaston (Ches), Sixpenny Patch, in Balking (Berks), and Forty Penny Meadow, in Gawsworth (Ches). There are forms in *-worth*, e.g. *The Ninepennyworthe of Ground* 15c., in Newhall, Eighteen Pennyworth, in Altrincham, and *Fourty Peniworth* 1611, in Hurdsfield (Ches).

Half Crown, in Chelmarsh (Shrops), alludes to a coin of the value of two shillings and sixpence (12.5p), in use until a little before the introduction of decimal coinage. These also appear *Le Fore Shillings Acre* 1551–52, in Dorchester (Oxon), Five Shilling Meadow, in Evington (Leics), Five Shillings Piece, in Bampton (Westm), Nine

Shillings Meadow, in Myddle (Shrops), Ten Shillings Field, in Whitchurch (Shrops), and Forty Shilling Close, in Rowington (Warks). The noble (equivalent to six shillings and eightpence or 33.33p) is mentioned in Noble Croft, in Pontesbury (Shrops), and Three Nobles Hay and Seven Nobles Hay, in Lea (Ches), where also *Five Nobles Hey* was recorded in 1698. This coin was current from the reign of Edward III until the seventeenth century. Examples of *guinea* (originally equivalent to a pound but later regarded as worth twenty-one shillings) include Half Guinea Pleck, in Ashford Carbonell, Guinea Furlong, in Chetton (Shrops), and Guinea Mead, in Boreham (Ess). Higher amounts are also found e.g. (The) Five Pound Piece, in Shavington (Ches) and in Rotherfield Greys (Oxon), Ten Pound Field, in Rudheath Lordship (Ches), Ten Pound Piece, in Foston (Leics), and Twelve Pound Meadow, in Easthope (Shrops). *Pound*, unqualified by a number, will almost certainly refer to the manorial or parish enclosure in which stray animals were kept until released on payment of a penalty. *Penning*, a derivative of *pen* 'an animal pen', is found in (the) Pennings, in Hamfallow and in North Nibley (Glos), Penning Mead, in Coulston, and Well Penning, in Amesbury (Wilts).

Farthing Croft and similar names from *farthing* (OE *feorthung* 'fourth part') are regularly used to indicate land land which is divided into four parts, or more specifically which has an area of a quarter of a virgate. But Farthing, in Steventon (Berks), was *Ferthyngesmed* in 1410, pointing to possible rents charged for stints of grassland. In Rainow (Ches), Thursbitch (*Thurresbacheker* 1384 'marshy place at the demon's valley') was recorded in 1620 as *the Farthinge or Furbachcarr meadow*; it is likely that this was an assart. Farthings-land, in Cann (Dor), appears to argue for a surname derivation, seemingly confirmed by there having been a Roger Ferthing in the parish in the fourteenth century. In the sense 'a quarter of a virgate', *ferling* was used in some places, resulting in possible confusion with *furlong*. *Peppercorn* names, as in Pepercorn Hey, in Tintwistle (Ches), relate to the liability for a peppercorn rent, at a time when a 'consideration' of some kind, however trivial, was required to validate certain kinds of transaction.

LORDSHIP, TENURE AND LOCAL IMPOSTS

Demesne land, occupied by the lord of the manor and not let to tenants, was identified by such names as *The Lords Mede* 1578, in

Piddlehinton (Dor), Lords Close (*The Lorde Close* 1568), in Kendal (Westm), Lords Wood, in Allostock (Ches) and in Byley cum Yatehous (Ches). Mains, in Barbon and in Beetham (Westm), Mesne Close, in Mansfield (Notts), and Mesne Field, in Curbar (Derbys). *Goodmans Field* 1645, in Chorley (Ches), and Goodman's Close, in Galby (Leics), may also be land occupied by the owner, and *good-wife* to that held by the lady of the manor, e.g. Good Wives Hey (*Godewif Heyes* 1580), in Appleton (Ches). A particular kind of encroachment by a lord of the manor, in this case from a royal forest, is described by the term *approvement*, found in *Thapprove-ment of Rudheth* 1471, in Byley (Ches), the land having been 'approved', by Dieulacres Abbey, out of the royal waste of Rudheath. *Approvement* usually implies an enclosure of waste, leaving part for the continuing use of the commoners.

Pater Noster Bancke 1719, in East Hendred (Berks), was held in 1283 by Johannes Pater-noster by the serjeanty of saying a daily *Pater-noster* for the king's soul. *Le Pater Noster'* 1227, in St Briavels (Glos), *Paternostreland* 13c., in Hazlewood, and *Paternoster lands* 1660, in St John's (YW), are also said to be lands whose rent paid for the saying of paternosters. Copyhold Close, in Benson (Oxon) and in Hope (Derbys), and Copyhold Field, in Corringham and in Willingale Doe (Ess), relate to tenure authenticated by a copy of the court roll. Chatter Holt (*Charterhold* 1650), in Eynsham (Oxon), means 'land held by charter'. *Moland'* 1262, in Rivenhall, *Mollemed* 1415, in Wix, and *Molefeld* 1382, in Stapleford Tawney (Ess), Molmons Marsh, in Barking, Mowlands, in High Easter and in White Roding, and possibly Mow Mead, in Aythorpe Roding, and Mow Field, in Little Waltham (Ess), allude to copyhold tenure held by payment of a quit-rent on the land and commonly freed of all labour service. *Cheetland* 1347, in Methley, and Cheeting Field, in Bradfield (YW), was *escheated* land, i.e. land which reverted to the lord when there was no qualified heir.

Property transferred as payment for damages is recorded in *Hundebite* 13c., in Wighill (YW), alluding to land made over in compensation for the bite of a dog. *Gavelerth* 1459, in Pucklechurch (Glos), and *Gauelmed* 1299, in Bristol, were arable and meadow land respectively, liable for *gavel*, which might be a duty to be performed or money paid in commutation. *Gavelerth* required the ploughing by a tenant of a specified amount of the lord's land. *Gavelmead* was a similar duty of mowing in the demesne meadow. A tax of some kind is also indicated in *Geldfeild* 1651, in Crowley (Ches). In Lincolnshire, *Warnoth* or *warnot* indicated a rent which incurred a penalty for non-payment. If not settled by the appointed day, an amount double the original rent became payable, on the third day a three-fold amount became due, and so on. The term is found in *Wardnoth* 1219, in Croxton, *Warnot* 1428, in Osgodby, and *Warnott* 1445, in Cabourne (Lincs).

Names of the 'morning-gift' (OE *morgen-giefu*) type allude to the Anglo-Saxon custom of granting lands by a husband to his wife on the morning after marriage. A tenth-century charter relates to five hides of land in Fonthill (Wilts) as the *morgen-giefu* of a certain Ætheldryth. Some of these names survived into later centuries, e.g. *Moreyngcroft* 1547, in Purley (Ess), and *Moregeve* 17c., in Mayfield (Sus), and even into modern times, e.g. Morgay Wood, in Guestling, Morgay Farm (*Morgtheve* c. 1240), in Ewhurst (Sus), Morrif (*Le Moreyife* 1411), in Foleshill (Warks), Mooray (*Morwyeve* 1428), in Chilmark (Wilts), and Moor Farm (*Moruefelde* 1469), in Woodham Ferrers (Ess). Earlier forms not surviving include *Moriyenesfeld* 12c., in Layer de la Haye (Ess), *Moreyf* 13c., in Westbury (Bucks), *Morwyevecroft* 1363, in Grimstead (Wilts), and *Morughyenewode* 1416, in Checkendon (Oxon). Dowry Close, in Groby (Leics), Dowry Meadow, in Aston Subedge (Glos), and Great Dowry, in Sandbach (Ches), were pieces of land assigned to a woman on her marriage.

Names such as Smock Close, in Blaston (Leics), have sometimes been taken to be shape names, referring to the garment known as a smock. Forms such as *La Smokacre* 1276, in Broadchalke (Wilts), and *Smokacres* 1326, in Andover (Hants), indicate how the spellings in *Smock-*, found even in *Smockacre c.* 1260, in Longlevens (Glos), have come about. The reference is to *smoke-silver*, a tax paid in lieu of tithewood to the incumbents of certain parishes. The most common generic is *acre*, as in the names already mentioned and in *Smocaker c.* 1220, in Hilmarton (Wilts), *Smokesacre* 1268, in Standish (Glos), and Smockacre, in Ewelme (Oxon) and Codford (Wilts). Smoak Lands is found in Brookthorpe (Glos) and in Martyr Worthy (Hants), Smock Close in Welham (Leics) and in Pentrich (Derbys), Smock Field in Wanstead (Ess), and Smoke Piece in Buscot (Berks). Other exactions include *Royalty*, found in a limited number of field-names. This is defined as 'a payment to an owner by a lessee' (the owner being not necessarily the Crown) and is found several times in Cheshire: Royalty, in Alvanley, in Kingsley and in Tarporley; Royalty Plantation, in Little Stanney; Royalty Wood, in Acton. To these may be added Great & Little Royalty, in Branston (Lincs), and Royalties, in Waddington (Lincs). The Fifteens, in Upton &

Signet (Oxon), is part of the Burford property known as The Fifteen Lands, first mentioned in 1382, held in trust for the purpose of relieving the burden upon the town when a tax of tenths of fifteenths was levied.

NOTES AND REFERENCES

1. J. Insley, 'Addenda to the Survey . . .: Personal names in field and minor names', *Journal of the EPNS 10* (1977–78), pp. 41–72, here p. 43.
2. It will be observed that his is one of the few names devised by Hollis to receive the addition of a generic.
3. J. Lilburne, *The Just Defence of John Lilburne, Against Such as Charge him with Turbulency of Spirit* (1653), quoted by W. Schenk, *The Concern for Social Justice in the Puritan Revolution* (Longmans, 1952), p. 24.
4. Lilburne, *The Upright Mans Vindication* (1653), quoted by Schenk, p. 34.
5. 'What did the inhabitants of Halstock think of these outlandish and hard-to-pronounce names?' asks a modern historian of the parish. 'It is to be supposed that they largely ignored them among themselves, sticking to the familiar 'Cowleaze' or 'Furzy Ground'. Nonetheless, when the Tithe Map was produced in 1841, all the Hollis names were there, and what's more they are still in use today. He would have been pleased about that' (P. Lemmey, *A History of Halstock*, Halstock, privately published 1964). For a list and discussion of the names, see J. Field, *Compliment and Commemoration in English Field-Names* 2nd edn (Hemel Hempstead and Edinburgh, 1986), pp. 19–23.
6. See A.J.L. Winchester, 'The distribution and significance of "Bordland" in medieval Britain', *Agric. Hist. Rev.* **34** (1986), 129–39.
7. Located in Farnley (YW).
8. B. Elliott, 'The appropriation of parish churches', *Downside Review* (January 1986), pp. 19–24, here p. 21, citing W. Hamilton Thompson, *The Abbey of St Mary of the Meadows, Leicester* (Leicester, 1949), p. 150.
9. A. Gooder, *Plague and Enclosure: A Warwickshire Village in the Seventeenth Century* (University of Birmingham and Coventry Branch of The Historical Association, 1965), p. 10.

CHAPTER NINE

Buildings, transport and manufacturing industry

In addition to features of the natural landscape, man-made structures are also frequently referred to in field-names. Many allusions are to agricultural buildings but there are also references to buildings not directly connected with agriculture, to roads, and to street furniture and minor structures. Ruins and surface indications of archaeological sites also receive attention in a wide variety of field-names. Even before towers and spires became usual, churches would have been larger than other buildings nearby, and apart from what would have been seen as their centrality in the life of the community, this physical conspicuousness was a good reason for their mention in field-names.

CHURCHES AND CHAPELS

Church Field is a frequent early alternative to compass-direction names for the great fields of a number of parishes. A 1278 deed refers to land *in campo quod vocatur Kirkefeld* ('in the field which is called *Kirkefeld*'), in Thriplow (Cambs). Other examples are *Cherchfeld* 1370, in Cannock (Staffs), *Ly Chyrchfeld* 16c., in Hinxton (Cambs), *Le Churchfeild* 1617, in Bradfield (YW), and *Church Feild* 1679, in Norton-juxta-Twycross (Leics). In Church Field, one of the three great fields of Moor Monkton (YW), the place of worship stood alone and quite apart from the habitations.

From the generics in Church Furlong, in Spelsbury (Oxon) and in Baggrave (Leics), and Church Hades (cf. *Chercheshot* 1376), in Bidford (Warks), it is reasonable to conclude that they date from before enclosure. Instances recorded only from that period include *Chercheforlang* 1342, in North Moreton, *Churchfurlong* 1447, in Sunningwell (Berks), *Church Headland* 1665, in South Ferriby (Lincs), and *Church Furlong* 1729, in Rousham (Oxon). Church Meadow, in Pott Shrigley (Ches), is associated with *Le Chapel Yerde* 1492, the inconsistency being explained by the fact that St Christopher's Church was formerly *Our Lady of Dovnes Chapell in Pott* 1472.

In areas settled by Danes or Norsemen, field-names alluding to churches frequently utilize the form *Kirk*, either directly from the Old Norse *kirkju* or as a Scandinavianized form of English *Church* with which it occasionally interchanges. *Kyrke Field* is named in a document of *c*. 1426 relating to Frickley (YW). Church Field, in Lenton (Notts), is named as both *The Churche Feild* and *Le Kirkefield* in 1609. (*Le*) *Kirkefeld*, in Kendal, was recorded with *Kirk*- or *Kyrk*-spellings until 1699, but *The Churche Feild* intervened in 1556 and *Churchfield* in 1697. English and Scandinavian terms alternate in the records of Flitcham (Norf), where *Chirchewong* 1386 is followed by *Kyrkewong(e)* 1434, 1443, *Chirchewonge* 1468, and *Kyrkwong c*. 1508. Kirk Meadows, in Glassonby (Cumb), preserve the memory of the ancient church of Addingham, which stood close to the Eden and was submerged when the river changed its course. Church Butts (*Kirkbutts* 1460), in Burton (Westm), belonged to the vicars of Burton. Church Wong, in Tickhill (YW), was *Kirkewong* in 1373. A different origin is suggested for Church Leys, in Hankelow (Ches), explaining the absence of a place of worship in the vicinity; the first element in *Chircheleges* 13c. is taken to be Old Welsh *cruc* 'a mound or barrow'.

Fore Litton, in Basildon (Berks), is 'before the churchyard', from Old English *līc-tūn* 'corpse enclosure', found also in Litton Close, in Ilkestone (Derbys). Churchyards may not be *fields* in the agricultural sense, though sheep may as safely graze among the burial plots as on other pastures. Related names are *One Close called the Churcheyarde* 1546–47, in Princethorpe (Warks), the Kirk-Yard Close, in Brodsworth (YW), and Church Yard Orchard, in Sotwell (Berks). Graveyard Field, in Mobberley (Ches), is named from the neighbouring cemetery, The Quakers' Graveyard.

Chapel Field (*Le Chapelfeld* 1349), in Tushingham (Ches), adjoins St Chad's Chapel, possibly a chantry chapel, on the site since the fourteenth century. Chapel Wood, in Catcliffe (YW), was referred to as *Capulwod* as early as 1379. *The Chappelfeld* 1480, in Haslingfield (Cambs), owes its name to *The Chapel of the Blessed Virgin*

Mary Whightehill in Eslyngfeld, mentioned a few years later. The chapel had been founded in 1344; *Whightehill* has now become Chapel Hill. *Le Chappell Croft* 1548, in Acton (Ches), was the site of a chapel referred to in the fourteenth century. Chapel Field (*Chapell Field* 1683), in Eshton (YW), is the site of St Helen's Chapel (*Capella Beate Elene de Essheton* 1429), adjoining a holy well of the same dedication. Chapel Close, in Sturminster Newton (Dor), is named from the former Bagber Chapel (*Capellam de Bakebere* 1340). Chappel Field, in Mottram St Andrew (Ches), was probably the *fild wherein the Chappell of Mottram standez* 1504. Chapel Mead, in Stourpaine (Dor), is the site of the church (dedicated in 1331) of the decayed settlement of Lazerton.

P.A.S. Pool, noting that *Chapel* in field-names normally indicates an ancient site, e.g. *Hale Chaple* 1588 (*hale* meaning 'rough, uncultivable ground') in Sancreed (Corn), as well as other instances already discussed, adds that modern Nonconformist chapels generate such names as Preaching House Field, in Madron and in St Buryan (Corn), each of which adjoins a Methodist chapel.[1] Meeting House Four Acres, in South Repps (Norf), is near an old Nonconformist graveyard. Two fields called Meeting House Pightle are found in Ludham (Norf); one is opposite the Methodist chapel, the other is the site of a demolished Baptist chapel. Englands or Meeting House Ground, in Sherborne (Dor), was *Meeting House Close* in 1802; *Englands* is evidently from the surname of a former owner, as there is a reference to a *Cottage . . . heretofore Englands* in 1677. Other instances include Meeting House Croft, in Clifton & Compton (Derbys), Meeting House Ground, in Bucklebury (Berks), The Quakers Meeting House Close, in Houghton Regis (Beds), and The Methodist Nook, in Out Rawcliffe (Lancs). Ranter's Field, in Shrewsbury, alludes to the Primitive Methodists (dating from about 1810), who were customarily so called. Antichurchman's Field, in Shinfield (Berks), possibly also refers to religious dissenters.

"BELLS ON THE UNDULATING AIR"

In earlier centuries there would have been no clocks in private possession, and church bells were used more often than they are today. They were rung to summon the people to mass and other services, and to formal meetings of the community on purely temporal matters, held in the church as the only public building with sufficient capacity. Alarms would be sounded by the ringing of the bells. The routine operations in the fields were also timed in this way by the parish priest or clerk, who rang to define the hours of daylight and darkness which limited many activities, such as gleaning, the picking of peas, or even the taking of a cart into the arable fields. The curfew was a reality; after it had been signalled, the seriousness of certain crimes greatly increased, and strangers found wandering among the houses might be arrested. Even in the eighteenth century, "Frequently pealing bells kept the village in touch with the world. They announced that the king had returned safely from his travels, that a princess had married, that victories had been won, and even that creditable attempts had been made, such as Vernon's unavailing attack on Cartagena."[2] So it is not surprising that funds should be required for the frequent renewal of bell-ropes, specifically referred to in Bell Ropes (*Belleropes* 1320), in Harlestone (Nthants), Bell Rope Close, in Scarscliffe (Derbys), and Bell Rope Field, in Reigate (Sur). *Bel Rope Meadow* 17c., in Framlingham (Suf), was "given to provide Ropes for the Bells, when they were in number five".[3] The rent of Bell Ropes, in Biggleswade (Beds), a field of forty-one acres, presumably provided ample funds for its declared object. The term *bellstring* occurs in *Belstringelande* 1559, in Braithwell, Belstring Flatt, in Mexborough, and Bell String Acre, in Adwick le Street (YW). Land given to provide bell-ropes in Coln Rogers (Glos) received the name The Church Land.

A piece of land in South Luffenham (Rut) was allotted to the parish clerk there, in recompense for ringing the church bell at 5 a.m. and 8 p.m. daily from Michaelmas to Lady Day. This bequest of Bell-ringing Close was said to have been made by a benighted lady traveller who was guided to the village by the sound of the church bells. Beanfield, in Sawbridgeworth (Herts), was alternatively Bell Mead. The original purpose of the endowment was that beans grown on the land should be strewn on the floor of the church. *The Bell Acre* 1540, a parcel of ground in the Netherwood Meadow of Canford Magna (Dor), was so called because it "hath byn alwayes apperteyning to the maintenance of the said bells", namely those of Wimborne Minster. Local informants noted that Bell Acre, in Langford (Wilts) "was traditionally used by the Sexton as payment for the bellropes he was called upon to provide". Bell Field, in Bletchingley (Sur), seems to have been originally *Belacre* 1229, becoming *Belcroft* by 1546. A deed of 1586 refers to "*Belcroft* . . . for providing beel-ropes for the said church". Bell Croft also occurs in Shrewsbury (Shrops) and in Smisby (Derbys). The proximity of

Bell Field, in Routh (YE) to All Saints' Church there makes it likely that this, too, was endowed land. Bell Field also occurs in Sutton on Derwent and in Harlethorpe (YE), and in twenty or more parishes in Essex. The 1806 Glebe Terrier for Gimingham (Norf) records that the rector "has 1a. 1r. of land, left by Widow Browning, for a sermon on St Stephen's day" and that "An acre is charged with providing bell ropes". Knell Field, in Abdon (Shrops), "was perhaps given for the tolling of a curfew bell".[4] Tinkletong Field, in Burton Leonard (YW), and the possibly unrelated Dingle Dongle, in Great Ness (Shrops), have all the appearance of playful inventions or alterations of other names. However, the seriousness of the similar name Ding Dong is guaranteed by the Enclosure Act for West Rasen (Lincs), in which this land is fully described: "that said Piece or Parcel of Old Inclosed Land called Ding Dong . . . to pay the clear Rents and profitts thereof to some poor Parishoner of the said Parish of West Rasen for ringing a Bell in the said Parish Church at a certain Hour during some part of each and every year for ever". *Chyme Silver* 1578, a wood on Brownsea Island, in Studland (Dor), is also likely to have been land endowed to provide a bell fund.

THE FURNISHING OF THE CHURCH

Other church equipment and supplies were also maintained from the rent of endowed land. The Chalace, in Fairford (Glos), probably provided funds for the purchase of sacramental wine, like Chalice Field, in Hurstbourne Tarrant, and Chalice Pightle, in Heckfield (Hants). Lamp-acre, in Churchill (Oxon) and in Salperton (Glos), and *Lamp Acre*, recorded 1548–49 in Yattendon (Berks), 1606–07 in Wootton (Oxon), 1617 in Beighton (Derbys), and 1711 in Watlington (Oxon), refer to endowments to provide lamps in the respective parish churches, as do Lamplands, in Broughton Poggs (Oxon), Lamp Meadow, in Ilkeston (Derbys), and Lamp Plot, in Pirbright (Surrey). *Lampeland* 1540, in Cirencester (Glos), was "given . . . to finde and maynteigne in the said church oon lamp burninge". *Lampforeheade* 1575, in Frampton on Severn (Glos), was described as land "geven to maintaine Lampes & lightes to burne in the church of Frampton". This was also the purpose of the income from Near, Middle, Top and Far Lights, in Lapley (Staffs), and from Vestry Light, in Bruern (Oxon). *Our Lady's Meadow*, in Great Easton

(Leics), was an old endowment to maintain a light in Great Easton Church.

Le Taper Land vel St James Land 1575, in Quedgeley (Glos), earlier *Taperacre t*. Ed. 3, may be identical with the later Candle Patch, land producing rent to provide candles. A similar meaning attaches to Candle Ground, in Bibury (Glos). Church Acres, in Sutton Veny (Wilts), was endowed to pay for candles in the (now ruined) St Leonard's Church. *Judas Gardin* 1629, in Wareham (Dor), was land "given to the mainteynance of a light called Judas light", i.e. the very tall central branch of a seven-branched candlestick, on which the Paschal Candle was placed at Eastertide.

Many endowments for altars and altar lights were made in the Middle Ages, but records of them are of Reformation or post-Reformation date, mainly because the systematic enumeration of the objects concerned took places when their use was about to be abolished. Their memory lingered in the names of the endowed land, and some of the funds passed over to other charities whose origin is often stated to be unknown. Land producing £2 1s per annum was vested in the chuchwardens of North Repps (Norf). It was noted in 1786 as "not known when or by whom given", but the rent had been used "for ornamenting the church for 100 years past".

The rent of Clock Close, in Grove (Berks), paid for the upkeep of the church timepiece. Endowments for the maintenance of the chancel are alluded to in The Quire, in Broadwell, *Le Quere c*. 1290, in Toot Baldon (Oxon), *Seyntuary Close t*. Hy 8, in Oxford, and *The Seyntury Land* 1576, in Reading (Berks). *Chauncell Close* 1608–09, in Watlington (Oxon), however, may belong to the *Cangel* names discussed in an earlier chapter, and names like Apshanger, in Kingsclere (Hants), are more likely to refer to aspen trees than to the apse of a church. *Porchecroft* 1341, in Tabley Superior (Ches), provided for the maintenance of that part of the church. Other parts are alluded to in Steeple Furlong, in Berrington, Bobbington Steeple Piece, in Claverley, and Roof Leasow, in Stoke St Milborough (Shrops).

SCHOOLS, COLLEGES, ALMSHOUSES AND HOSPITALS

Gifts and bequests for the founding of parish schools are frequently encountered in local records. An interesting sequence is to be found in the documentation of School Garth, in Aberford (YW): *The Parsonage Fould* 1635, a piece of glebe land, *The Foot-ball Garth* 1675, and *The Vicars Close or Football now called the School Garth* 1764, which may be the same as *The Vicarage Fold commonly called the School Fold*, from the charity school built there in 1716. School-ham close, in Cotgrave (Notts), was *Scholewong* in 1585. In addition to School Field, in Bollin Fee (Ches), there is also Schoolmaster's Meadow, presumably his perquisite. School Field, in Wath upon Dearne (YW), probably alludes to *The Schoolhouse*, referred to in 1748. Fields adjoining the school, or on which the school buildings were sited, are alluded to in such names as School House Field, in Willerby (YE) and in Bere Alston (Dev), and Schoolhouse Sykes, in Kirmington (Lincs).

College field-names refer to land owned by collegiate churches and by the colleges of Oxford and Cambridge universities, or occasionally by public schools. *The Colledge Ground* 1664, in Dowdeswell (Glos), was the property of Corpus Christi College, Oxford. College Farm, in Writtle (Ess), was land given by William of Wykeham to New College, Oxford, which also held Scholars Dale (*The College alias Schollers Meadowe* 1649), in Barrow upon Humber (Lincs). College Fields, in Alston (Lancs), belonged to St John's College, and College Down, in Upavon (Wilts), to King's College, Cambridge. College Copse, in Ash (Sur), was owned by Winchester College, College Close, in Owston (YW), by University College, Oxford, and College Wood, in Little Bentley (Ess), by Gonville and Caius College, Cambridge.

Medieval guilds, both secular and religious, invested in land, e.g. *2 gardens still known by the name of Corpus Christi* 1774, in Wareham (Dor), formerly the property of "a fraternity, gild, or chantry, called Corpus Christi", and *Parcell called the Trynyty Gilde* 1547, in Kendal (Westm). Some names refer to the guildhouse, either because the land was the site of the building or because the rent contributed to the maintenance of the headquarters of the guild. Gilbert Flat, in Marske (YN), is shown by its early form, *Gyldhousflat* 1408, to be '*flatt* near the guildhouse', an allusion found also in *Gilhusmor* 14c., in Whitby, *Gildusclif* 1284, in Middlesbrough (YN), and *Gildhustoft* 1158–67, in Hooton Pagnell (YW), 'moorland', 'a hill or cliff' and 'a toft', in the possession of the guild. A guild-hall is referred to in *Yieldhall Green* 1761, in Wokingham (Berks). Pottmanns Brook (*Portmanebroc* 1253–54), in Reading, was, like Port Mead (*Le Portmede* 1285), in Oxford, meadow belonging to the merchant guild.

Shelter for paupers was provided in various establishments, alluded to in such names as Old Workhouse Mead, in Boreham, Workhouse Meadow, in Great Braxted and in Rivenhall (Ess), and in Westbury (Shrops), where the land adjoins the old Workhouse. Workhouse Field occurs in Doveridge (Derbys), in Codicote (Herts) and a dozen or more places in Essex. There are also Workhouse Pightle, in Swallowfield (Berks), Poor House Field, in Newhall (Ches), and Union Field, in Berrington (Shrops). The *Union* was a combination of parishes brought about by the Poor Law Amendment Act of 1834. The earlier sense of *Workhouse*, 'a workshop, a factory', probably applies to Workhouse Close (*The Workhouse Croft* 1552), in Gomersal (YW).

Another old institution was that referred to in Almshouse Leasow, in Shawbury (Shrops). Almshouse Hawes, in Corfe Castle (Dor), were enclosures beside the almshouses there, on record since the seventeenth century. Almshouse Meadow, in Puddletown (Dor), was owned by Napper's Almshouse in Dorchester, founded by Robert Napper in 1615. Almshouse Wood, in Saffron Walden (Ess), was first mentioned in 1605, and there are fields called Almshouse Meadow, in Purleigh, and Almshouse Field, in Chipping Ongar, in Langford and in Barnston (Ess). *Bedhusland* 1226, in Appleton Roebuck (YW), alludes to a *beadhouse* 'prayer-house', so called because the inmates, sometimes termed *beadsmen*, had the duty of praying for their benefactors.

Even more ancient was the hospital or spital, which might be either a hostel for poor people or an institution for the care of the sick. Hospital Shaw, in Aveley (Ess), was part of the land owned there by St Bartholomew's Hospital in London. Hospital Close, in Bawtry (YW), was attached to Bawtry Spittle, recorded in 1535 as *Capella Sancte Marie Magdalene juxta Bautre vocat' le Spittell* 'the chapel of St Mary Magdalene near Bawtry, called The Spittell'. *Spittelfeld'* 1421, in Castle Church (Staffs), alludes to the Hospital of St Leonard, in Forebridge. Hospital Farm, in Newport (Ess), probably includes *Hospitallfeld* 1549; there is a reference in 1597 to *St Leonard's Hospital* there. *The Spittil Felde* 1540, in Chester, relates to the leper hospital of St Giles, founded in the late twelfth or early thirteenth century and managed by St Werburgh's Abbey. *Spittle Hill Meadow* 1548, in New Windsor (Berks), was named from the hospital for lepers, first referred to in 1339. There was another leper hospital in Maldon (Ess), St Giles's Hospital, the possessions of which included *Spytelland* in 1540.

The houses of the Knights Hospitallers were also known as

hospitals, and some field-names refer to land owned by this order, e.g. *Hospitale Rode* 1617, in Bingley (YW), which belonged to the Knights Hospitallers of Beverley. Hospital Plot, in Wareham (Dor), had probably been held by the Hospitallers, but there was another hospital, *Spytle* 1590, which gave its name to *Claus' voc' Spittle* 1593 'the close called *Spittle*'. The well-known Spitalfields, in Stepney (Middx, now Greater London), was previously *Lollesworthe* 1278 'Lull's enclosure'. The name was *Spittellond* in 1399. It was a large field behind the churchyard of St Mary Spittle, founded in 1197. On its surrender to Henry VIII by the Augustinian canons who served it, the hospital contained 180 beds "well furnished, for receipt of the poor; for it was an hospital of great relief".[5]

Pest House Close, in Northolt (Middx), is mentioned in 1806 but is not referred to earlier or later. This pest-house, a hospital for sufferers from infectious diseases, was on the land belonging to Samuel Hoare at Wood End. Another Pest House Close is found in Saffron Walden (Ess). Pest House Orchard occurs in Houghton Regis (Beds) and Pest House Field in Epping and in nearly a dozen other places in Essex, as well as in Steeple Aston (Oxon).

DOMESTIC AND FARM BUILDINGS

References to domestic buildings are frequent, particularly in the Tithe Apportionments, where House Close may occur more than once in any one township, and Cottage Close perhaps many times. Some instances are early, e.g. *Housebanke* 1468, in Roecliffe (YW), and *Le Netherhouse Mede* 1552, in Stratfield Mortimer (Berks). References to various types of dwellings include Turf Cote Croft, in Church Minshull (Ches), and Blue Slates Field, in Ellerton Priory (YE), near the first farmhouse in the district to have a slate roof. Cottage Carr, in Horkstow (Lincs), and Cottage Piece, in Peckleton (Leics), may refer to land in the tenure of cottagers rather than proximity to the cottages themselves. *Cotstowe c.* 1197, in Tetsworth, *Costowe* 1239, in Claydon, and Castors (*Costowa* 1268), in Great Tew (Oxon), mean 'the site of a cottage' (OE *cot-stōw*), the term, or its synonym *cot-steall*, being found also in Costhill Field (*Costoll* 1606), in Warborough, Costard Furlong, in Horspath, and Custard Mead, in Dorchester (Oxon).

Hall normally refers to the seat of the lord of the manor, e.g. Hall Garth, in South Stainley (YW) and in Thoresway (Lincs), Hall

Garths, in Azerley (YW) and Hall Croft, in Offcote (Derbys) and in Middleton (YW). Hall Room, in Mobberley (Ches), was an allotment on Lindow Moss belonging to Mobberley Hall, the generic *Room* meaning 'space, clearing' (OE *rum*). Hall Field, in Rudheath Lordship (Ches), dates from 1650, and the name is also found in Warslow (Staffs) and in Wistaston (Ches). Land so named may be close to the hall or be part of the manorial demesne. However, grassland called *Hall Meadow* will normally not be adjacent to the manor-house. The name is found in a number of places, and early forms include *Le Hallemede* 1352, in Cumnor (Berks, now Oxon), *Le Hallemedowe* 1415, in Belper (Derbys), and *Halmede* 1453, in Congleton (Ches). Two or more manors in a parish or township are distinguished by such prefixes as *Old, New, Upper, Nether*, etc., e.g. *Le Netherhalleorcharde* 1384, in Weston (Ches).

Subsidiary dwellings and other buildings are referred to in Gazebo Piece, in Egham (Sur), and Summerhouse Field, in Clacton (Ess). Lodge Close, in Biggleswade (Beds), in Frisby, in Illston and in Baggrave (Leics), would be near the lodge at the entrance to a park or the grounds of a big house. *Dye House Close*, in a 1747 document relating to Wareham (Dor), refers not to the craft of dyeing but to a dairy (ME *dey, dey-hus* or *deierie*), other relevant names being Day Meadow (*Le Deymedowe* 1354), in Peckforton, *Deyhuscroft* 1357, in Frodsham, *Darie Croft* 1670, in Cholmondeley (Ches), Dairy Close, in Shawell (Leics), and Dairy Ground (*Le Deyfurlonge c.* 1420), in Helmdon (Nthants). Apple House Field, in Bisham (Berks), alludes to a fruit-store. Brewhouse Close Furlong, in Leighton Buzzard (Beds), refers to a domestic rather than a commercial brewery. Food preservation in earlier centuries depended on the Ice House, referred to in the Tithe Apportionments of Ealing (Middx) and of Upminster (Ess). Ice House Field is found in Chigwell (Ess), Ice House Meadow in Ludford (Shrops), and Ice House Mead in Gosfield (Ess). This was an insulated store into which ice was packed, at a convenient distance from the dwelling. It was constructed in a sheltered location, wholly or partly underground, often among trees, as is confirmed by Ice Cellar Plantation, in Latton (Ess), and Ice House Plantation, in Mere (Ches).

The pigeonhouse, dovehouse or dovecote was often a substantial building adjoining the manorial hall and was an appurtenance of the lord. It was usually a circular building with a turret or lantern. A revolving ladder pivoted on the central pillar of the building allowed eggs to be taken. The value of the pigeon as a source of fresh meat was early realized, especially in winter when other meat was scarce, and specific provision for their feeding was sometimes made from the arable crops. In Kettering in 1294, for instance, a tenth of the barley was set aside for the pigs, fowls and pigeons.[6] Here, as elsewhere, the birds would also have taken their fill, when allowed, from the grain crops in the fields.

Dove (OE *dufe*), *Pigeon* (OFrench *pijun*, originally meaning 'young dove') and *culver* (OE *culfre*) are found indiscriminately in field-names, the number and variety of which testify to the frequent occurrence of these structures. Pigeonhouse Field (*Pidgeonhouse Field* 1664) appears in Hurley (Berks), *Culverhouse Croft* 1444 in Shrewsbury, and Pigeon Close in Neen Savage (Shrops). Pigeon House Croft, in Blacon cum Crabwall (Ches), was *Dove House Yard*, in 1620. Dove-house Close, in Claydon (Oxon), probably alludes to the dovecote of the Gilbertine Priory of Clattercote. Dovehouse Leasow is found in Shifnal, and Duffers Yard, with the contracted form of *Dovehouse* frequently found in field-names, in Broughton. The 1585 form, *Duffehouse Lesowe*, of Dove House Leasow, in Blymhill (Staffs), clarifies the contraction, found also in Duffers, in Furneux Pelham (Herts) and in North Lopham (Norfolk). Ducket, in Dalston (Cumb), is a known site of a dovecote. *Dovecote* is the favoured term in Derbyshire, as is shown by Dawcourt Yard, in Barlborough, Dovecote Close, in Wingerworth, and Dovecote Meadow, in Whittington. In some names, *house* is implied, e.g. Culverhay, in Cheltenham (Glos), Culverhays (*Culverheye* 1570), in Alvediston (Wilts), and *Culverclose* 1544, in Charminster (Dor), 'pigeon enclosure'.

Farm buildings include the barn, generator of a multitude of names, and sheds, often unspecified as to their purpose. *Barn* without further qualification occurs in such names as *Barnacre, Barn Close* and *Barn Croft*, in many parts of the country. *Bere-ærn* means 'a barley building' but other uses may be indicated, e.g. *Le Haybarne* 1339, in Minshull Vernon (Ches), or *Le Wheteberne* 14c., in Church Minshull (Ches). In the area of Scandinavian influence, *laith* is encountered (from ON *hlatha* 'a barn'), as in *Latebot'* 1250–60, in Stockbridge, Laith Butts, in Askham (Westm), *Lathplatt* 1652, in Sowerby (YW), *The Laith Close* 1652, in Thoresway (Lincs), Laith Breck, in Worksop (Notts), Laith Close, in Aston, Laith Croft, in Ovenden, and Laith Holme, in Marsen (YW), and *Le Lathested* 1557 'the site of a barn', in Doncaster (YW). *Tendelaythehyerd* 1439, in Skircoat, and Tithe Laith Close, in Adwick upon Dearne (YW), refer to the yard and to the close of a tithe-barn. Granary Close

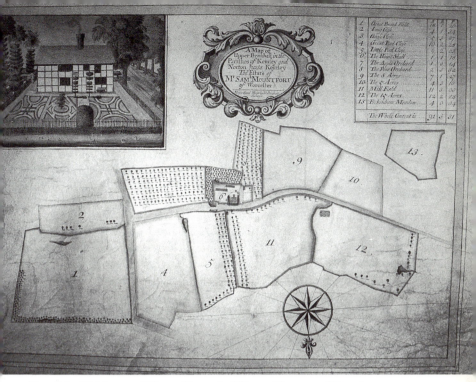

Plate 9.1   Field-map of Upper Broomhall Farm, Kempsey (Worcs)

occurs in Northolt (Middx), in Bradfield (Berks) and in Cliffe cum Lund (YE).

Other outbuildings of various kinds are also alluded to in field-names, e.g. *The Hennhouse Close* 1593, in Potter Newton (YW), Shed Field, in Ellerton Priory and in Beswick (YE), Shed Meadow, in Brailsford (Derbys), Cart House Close, in Northolt (Middx), and Waggon Hovel Close, in Packington and in Dadlington (Leics). A *Hovel* may be either a shed or a framework on which a rick or stack is constructed. The Office, in Shelve (Shrops), and Office Field, in Newhall (Ches), allude to a 'house of office', i.e. a latrine. Other terms are not readily recognizable. Hulke Meade, in Ozleworth (Glos), is 'the meadow with a shed', the specifier being from Old English *hulc* and not the same as *hulk* 'a flat-bottomed ship'. A related term, *hulu*, is found in Hull Piece, in Poulton (Glos). *Belfreygarth* 1558–79, in Walesby (Lincs), is from the dialect term *belfrey* 'a lean-to or shelter-shed'. A southern dialect expression for 'a shed, an outhouse' occurs in Skilling Close, in Norton, Skilling Ground, in Rowde, and Skillam Mead, in Brokenborough (Wilts). Wheelhouse Close, in Ashwell (Rut), alludes to a building (normally circular) containing a horsewheel as motive power for threshing machines, etc. The siting or housing of other farm machines also found a place in field-names, e.g. Engine Piece, in Heather (Leics), Engine Close, in North Luffenham (Rut), Machine Close, in Cadeby (Leics), Whimsey, in Shawbury (Shrops), and Whimsey Piece, in Coleorton (Leics).

Animal shelters also give their names to fields. Scapegoat Hill, in Golcar (YW), was *Ship Coat Hill* in the early nineteenth century and referred to nothing more dramatic than a sheep-cote, found also in *Shepecotestede* 1320 'site of the sheep-house', in Monk Fryston (YW), *Le Shepcotefielde* 1409, in Hemingford (Hunts), *Shepecoate Royde* 1624 'sheep-cote clearing', in Warley (YW), and *Sheepcoate Croft* 1600, in Great Stanney (Ches). *Le Shephous upon the Mersh* 1395, in Frodsham (Ches), was a shelter for the flocks of Vale Royal Abbey grazing on Frodsham Marsh. The same term is found in *Schephousforlong* 1340, in Speen (Berks). *Lamcote* 1436, in Great Tew (Oxon), was a house or shelter for lambs. Easter Croft, in Sprotborough (YW), The Easter Field, in Much Wenlock (Shrops) and in Wilsden (YW), Oyster End (*Oystreherne* 1382), in Little

Plate 9.2   Upper Broomhall Farm: the farmhouse today

Hadham (Herts), The Oysters, in Culmington, and The Yesters, in Baschurch (Shrops), are probably all from Old English *eowestre* 'a sheepfold'. From the dialect terms *boose, boosing, boosy* (OE *bōs, bōsig*) 'a cow-stall' are derived such names as Boose Field, in Beeston (Ches), Bowzing Ground, in Dowdeswell (Glos), Boozing Croft, in Doveridge (Derbys), and Boozy Pasture, in Agden (Ches), in Smethcott and in Cound (Shrops). An alternative term for 'cowshed' is found in *Le Shypon Croftes* 1417, in Edleston (Ches), Shippen Park, in Billesdon (Leics), and Shippon Field, in Plumley, in Allostock (*Sheponfeld* 1465), in Congleton (Ches) and in Great Marton (Lancs).

Dog Kennel Close, in Herriard (Hants), in Bucklebury (Berks), in Yeldersley and in Church Gresley (Derbys), may refer to structures of some substance and even architectural interest. The housing of numbers of hounds required buildings of considerable size. Dog Kennel Mead occurs in Tilehurst (Berks), Dog Kennel Field in Aldershot (Hants), in Chiddingfold (Sur) and a dozen times in Essex, and Dog House Field in Appleton (Ches).

Another important building in the medieval landscape was the mill. There is usually good documentation, sometimes in Domesday Book, to support field-name references. *Milnefeild* 1587, in South Ferriby (Lincs), alludes to a windmill, an early reference to which is *Molendinum de Ferriby* 1167. The mill often gave name to one of the great fields before enclosure. If such names do not survive after the mill has gone, there may be references to traces of it, e.g. Mill Post Field, in Northolt (Middx).

FIELD-NAMES AS ARCHAEOLOGICAL INDICATORS

Hundreds of field-names may be described as of archaeological interest, but it does not follow that every field bearing such a name will necessarily produce archaeological remains. "After all, only the site itself, and sometimes only the excavation of the site, can prove whether the testimony of place-nomenclature is reliable or misleading."[7] There may be recorded or potential archaeological associations with many of the names seen in earlier chapters, referring, e.g., to windmills, dovecotes, early pits and quarries, chapels, gold-hoards, and mounds. Even plant-names (and their field-name derivatives) may be significant in this context; a growth of nettles, for instance, is an indication of a high phosphate content in the soil and so, possibly, of former human habitation.

The possible archaeological significance of field-names of the *Blacklands* type has already been mentioned. Blacklands, in Swalcliffe (Oxon), has a considerable depth of discoloured soil, which may indicate Romano-British habitation. Substantial discoveries have been made in Blackmiles (*Blackemylde* 1320) 'black mould', in Medbourne (Leics). Field-walking finds here have included flint flakes, cores and scrapers, considerable amounts of Roman pottery, and some Anglo-Saxon and medieval pottery.[8] *Blackmiles* also occurs in the 1674 Glebe Terrier of Bottesford (Leics). In the eighteenth century Hucclecote (Glos) had both *Blackland* and *Crockmeads*, possibly alluding to the finding of Roman or other pottery. In Mildenhall (Wilts) the hamlet of Cock-a-Troop Cottages is near Black Field (*Blacke Fyeld* 1578), the site of the Celtic settlement of *Cunetio*. Cock-a-Troop developed from *Crockerestrope* 1257 'hamlet of the pot-maker', probably from the numerous sherds revealed by ploughing in Black Field.

Quarrying during 1926 in Black Piece, in Clipsham (Rut), uncovered Roman material, including slag (from iron-working) and pottery. Investigation in advance of ironstone excavation in Black Holm, in Thistleton, and the adjoining Black Wong, in Market Overton (Rut), also revealed a Roman site.[9] In Dorset, Blacklands is found in Buckland Ripers, in Corfe Castle, in Wyke Regis, in Chickerell and in Swanage, where there is also Chesties (OE *ceaster*, interpreted in field-names as 'a fortification, an earthwork'), reinforcing the suggestion of the *Blacklands* name. Chester Field, in Treales (Lancs), is also a *ceaster* derivative.

Isolated stones are sometimes alluded to in the names of neighbouring fields, particularly if they are markers of some kind. Hone Ground, in Hinton Martell (Dor), from Old English *hān* 'hone, sharpening stone', is near a boundary stone marked on the 6-inch Ordnance Survey map. Alex Stone, in Lilleshall (Shrops), is said to refer to a Roman milestone on Watling Street, nearby. There are occasional field-name references to ploughed-up or scattered masonry or heaps of stones. These, too, may indicate archaeological features. Half-buried buildings (whatever their nature) or even natural stones on the surface are sometimes referred to as 'sunken churches', e.g. Sunken Church Field, in Great Abington (Cambs), Sunkenkirk, the site of a stone circle in Millom (Cumb), *Sonkinkirk* 1415, in Windley (Derbys), Kirksink, in Gargrave (YW), the site of a Roman villa, and *Sunkenchurche t.* Hy 3, in Brixworth (Nthants),

where there is also *Dedmansbyryellys* 14c. Great & Little Cross Field
(*The Crosses Croft* 1630), in Sandbach (Ches), allude to local Anglo-
Saxon crosses. Some references to walls may point to ancient
earthworks or buildings. Wall Farm, in Saintbury (Glos), is near
some ancient entrenchments. Wall Furlong, in Bryning (Lancs), was
associated in a thirteenth-century document with a small fortress.
According to John Bridges, the historian of Northamptonshire, at
Burntwalls Farm (*Les Brendewalles* 1255), in Daventry (Nthants),
"many loads of stone, of ruined walls and foundations have been
digged up"[10]

Field-names of the *Chestles* type (OE *ceastel* 'a heap of stones')
sometimes indicate such remains, though, if only a modern form is
available, the possibility of derivation from *ceosol* 'gravel' must not
be overlooked. Chestles is found in Nettleton (Wilts), and Chestles
Field in Rolleston (Wilts), which is near the site of an ancient village.
Roman coins have been discovered at Chessels, in Lower Slaughter
(Glos). The same name also occurs in Wick and Abson, where "three
large druidical stones" were said to have been found, with remains
of a Roman villa, and in Old Sodbury, near which is the site of a
Roman camp, but none of these ancient features is associated with
the field itself. Early names in Wiltshire which have not survived to
the modern period include *Chastles* 1317, in Alderton, *Le Chastle* c.
1400, in Malmesbury, and *Chesteldeene* 1518, in Damerham. *Chesthill Acres or Chestrenhill* 1712, in Stonesfield (Oxon), appears to
offer a choice of derivations. *Chesthill* may be from *ceastel*; *Chestrenhill* may be from *ceaster*, another derivative of which, *Chestrefelde*
16c., in Nettleton (Lincs), is in a parish in which Romano-British
pottery has been found.

These names must also be distinguished from those derived from
Middle English *castel* 'a castle' but extended to mean 'an earthwork',
etc., e.g. Castle Meadow (*Castell Meade* 1551–5), in Banbury
(Oxon), *Casteleslond* 1392, in Upper Slaughter (Glos), alluding to a
mound nearby, and *Castell* 1461, in Badgeworth (Glos), where there
are ancient remains. Castle Croft and Castle Field, in Gulval (Corn),
contain remains of prehistoric settlements. Great Stone Castle occurs
in Shrewsbury St Mary (Shrops), and earthworks are referred to by
names such as Castle Trenches, in Quatford, and Castles, in Much
Wenlock and in Shifnal (Shrops). In Berkshire, *Castleton* 1517, in
Hamstead Marshall, and Castle Meadow (*Castelmede* 1340–41), in
Speen, probably allude to three mounds in Hamstead Park. There is
an ancient earthwork in Castle Fields (*Castelfeld* 1455), in Hartfield
(Sus). Illusory references also occur. Castle Moss, in Tintwistle

(Ches), refers to outcrops of rocks thought to resemble ruined castles.

Cornish field-names of the *Round Field* type have been discussed in an earlier chapter. Round Hill (*Roundhillfeilde* 1636), in Ferry Fryston (YW), contains an Anglian tumulus, apparently superimposed on a pre-English burial. Similar names in other counties may also have archaeological significance. *Ringedyke* 1562, in Barton (Westm), is a circular diked enclosure, also known as *King Arthur's Round Table*, where the Roman road crosses the river Lowther. Ring, in Out Rawcliffe, and Ring Field, in Carleton (Lancs), are among those listed by Wainwright as often referring to ancient circular enclosures, especially to stone circles.[11] He adds Wheel Meadow, the name of five separate fields in Newton with Scales, where there are four others called Wharlicar (OE *hwyrfil* or ON *hvirfill*). Warley Carr is found in Leaven (YE). *Cringlands* 1720, in Caldbeck (Cumb), from Old Norse *kringla* 'a circle, a ring', may be placed with these, as well as Cringle Field, in Hambleton, Cringle, in Scalthwaiterigg, Cringle Carr, in Thornton, Cringle Syke, in Clifton with Salwick (Lancs), Cringlemer Meadow 'the circular boundary', in Dean, Cringling 'ring meadow', in Millom (Cumb), and Cringle Meadow, in Beetham (Westm). Old English *trun* or *turn* 'circular, round', describing topographical features of such a shape, may sometimes indicate a man-made stone circle. Turn Rough, in Carrington (Ches), merits examination, all the more so because *Rough* sometimes designates stone-strewn ground of archaeological interest.

The Old English word *burgæsn* 'a burial place', later 'a cairn', is sometimes used of heaps or surface scatters of stone at archaeological sites. Borrownes, in Crosby Ravensworth, contains the remains of an ancient village settlement, and at Borrans (*Borhan c.* 1240), in Lowther, there is a Long Cairn. Burwens, in Kirkby Thore, is the site of the Roman fort of *Bravoniacum*, and at Gibbon Borrans, in Clifton (Westm), there is a small rectangular mound. Other examples include Borrens, in Bradleys Both (which also has a field called Stone Rings), Borran Fold, in Dent (YW), Burwains (*Le Borewanes* 1366), in Cliburn, Borran, in Tanwath (Westm), and Borrans (*Ye Borren of Stones* in 1410), in Cleator (Cumb).

Tumuli may be indicated by the Old English words *beorg* and *hlāw* and the Old Norse term *haugr*, but all these elements are also found in names of natural hills. The use of Old English *hlāw* or *hlǣw* for 'a tumulus' is limited to an area from the West Riding of Yorkshire to the south coast.[12] *Brokenebereue c.* 1250, in Garsington (Oxon), and

Brokenboroughe 1552, in Reading (Berks), refer to barrows which have been invaded by robbers, whose entry is normally traceable by a trench or hollow on the top of the mound. From current forms of field-names it is not easy to distinguish between *beorg* 'a hill, a barrow' and *burh* 'a fortification'. *Hethenebergh* was alternatively *Hethenebouruwe* in thirteenth-century forms of Heathen Bridge, in Blackthorn (Oxon). *Goldeburwe Hauedlond* 1402, in Nether Seal (Derbys) is probably from *beorg*, alluding to a tumulus, rather than from *burh*. Ancient earthworks are alluded to in such names as Aulbury Field (*Aldbere* 13c.), in Westmill. Albury Common (*Eldburimore* 1398), in Bengeo, and The Aubreys (*Aldeburys* 1529), in Redbourn (Herts).

Two field-names in Essex Tithe Apportionments may contain the element *wīc-hām*, normally found in major habitation names: Wickhams, in Chigwell, and Wickham Ley, in Little Waltham.[13] Chigwell is traversed by the Roman road from London to Dunmow and has a major Romano-British settlement, *Durolito*, in its north-west corner. At Little Waltham several Roman roads converge at a point where there is "extensive evidence of Romano-British settlement". Whicum Close, in Nettleton (Lincs), is on the site of the lost place of Wykeham, in the southern part of that parish.

Tunstead and *Tunstall*, both meaning 'a farmstead, (the site of) a farm and its buildings', suggest earlier settled sites, sometimes even ancient ones. Once again, the name may be regarded as a possible indicator, not as infallible evidence of archaeological remains in the land so named. Tunstead is found in Barton, in Fishwick, in Out Rawcliffe and in Whittingham, Tunsteads in Barnacre and in Thornton (Lancs). Forms with *Dun-* are also found, e.g. Dunstall, in Sproston and in Little Stanney (Ches). Dunshill Close, in Gumley (Leics), was *Dunstall* in 1674. With Little Tunstall, in Bradwall (Ches), is associated *Tunstudemor* 1330, which has the local form of a *-stede* ending, replaced by *-stall* in the modern name. *Tunstudemor'* and *bruera de Dunstal* 1272 'heath of *Dunstall'*, in Elmdon (Warks), bear out Foxall's remark (based on Duignan) that these names occur on the "borders of ancient wastes, as if they had been outlying farmyards without homesteads".[14] How ancient they were is a matter for archaeological judgement, but that some of them, e.g. *Tunstall* and *Overtunstall c.* 1200, in Rowton (Ches), were merely sites in the Middle Ages suggests that their activity had ceased several centuries earlier. Motterstall, in Odd Rode (Ches), seems to mean, from the late thirteenth-century form *Maltonstall* 'farm site where speeches were made', perhaps an assembly place in Anglo-Saxon times on the site of former settlement.

A compound of *-stede* with *abbey* occurs in a compact group of three fields in Upper Rawcliffe with Tarnacre (Lancs), two sharing the name Great Abbeystead and the third being Little Abbeystead. Using these names as a starting-point, F.T. Wainwright argued a case for this large piece of land in a loop of the river Wyre being possibly the site of the lost Wyredale Abbey.[15] The termination is sometimes combined with other words, e.g. *Churchestude* early 13c., in Lambourn (Berks), and *Le Oldemulnestede* 1409, in Frodsham (Ches), the sites respectively of a church and a mill. *Kerster Flatt*, in Lowside Quarter (Cumb), seems to contain *kirkju-stathr*, the Scandinavian equivalent of *Churchstead*.

Field-names such as *The Town* and (*The*) *Township* often mark the sites of deserted medieval villages, although they may elsewhere refer to part of the common field nearest to the settlement, e.g. Town Furlong, in Newbold Pacey (Warks). The earthworks of streets and houses in the depopulated settlement of Chalford, in Enstone (Oxon), are visible in the fields called *The Towns* on an eighteenth-century map.[16] *Stodfold* names must also be mentioned. Old English *stod-fald* means literally 'a stud-fold, a horse enclosure', but it often refers to an ancient earthwork or a Roman walled enclosure, not because these had in fact been used for this purpose but because in the Middle Ages they were considered to resemble them. Stotfold, in Elwick Hall (Dur, now Cleveland), has been on record since about 1200. Studfold (*Stodefald* 13c.) occurs in Horton in Ribblesdale (YW), where also may be found another instance of Borrins (*Borweyns* 1581), and which was near a supposed Roman road. Other examples are *Stoodfall-Lees* 1578, in Eskdale (Cumb), Stud Fold, in Ness (Ches), and Studfold, in Embsay (YW).

A possible link with Romano-British agriculture is to be found in fields known as Great and Little Comps, in Bray, Lower and Upper Comps, in Earley, Camp (*Compe* 1292–93), in Hurley, and *Campeden* 1367, possibly identical with the modern Camp Close, in Newbury (Berks), Thorn Comp (cf. *Estcompe* 1225), in Houghton Regis (Beds), Campsfield, in Kidlington (Oxon), and perhaps Quomp Corner, in Kinson (Dor, now Hants). These names contain the Old English word *camp*, meaning perhaps 'an enclosed piece of land', a loan-word from Latin *campus* 'a field'. Camp Dale, Camp Bottom and Camp Covert, in Folkton (YE), allude to The Camp, a local earthwork. The element here, however, is not Old English *camp* (which is found only in the south of England), but Middle

English *camb* 'a bank or ridge of earth'. Modern *camp*, meaning 'encampment', is found in Roman Camp Piece, in Bisley (Glos). Not all names qualified by *Roman* or *Danish* necessarily relate to those invaders, but it is a matter of record that a hoard of bronze spears was found in the field called Bloody Romans, in Bishops Castle (Shrops).

References to former quarrying occur in names of the *Hills* and *Holes* type, discussed in an earlier chapter. Medieval fishponds, often more than one at any one site, have been discovered in appropriately named fields. A string of ponds can be traced through Fish Pond Fields, in Teigh (Rut). Ponds were also traced in Hall Close, in Empingham (Rut), the manorial centre. Of course, names such as Fishpond Leasow, in Wattlesborough (Shrops), or Fishpond Close, in Beechamwell (Norf), do not necessarily indicate medieval ponds.

DRAGONS AND THEIR HOARDS

In the reign of King Edward I there was an enquiry into "certain treasure trove found at *Goldenlowe*", in Dunstable (Beds). This name, recorded in 1286, resembles a number mentioned in Chapter Three, which may have originated in similar discoveries, otherwise unrecorded. Allusions to treasure guarded, according to the Anglo-Saxons and their successors, by a dragon (OE *draca*), may be found in other field-names, such as *Dracenhord* 1222, in Yanworth (Glos), Drake North (*Drakenorde* 940–46, *Drakenorth Coppice* 1539), in Damerham (Wilts), and *Drakehordforlong'* c. 1260, in Garsington (Oxon). 'Dragon mounds' not including references to hoards are also named, e.g. *Drakenhowe* 1328, in Flitcham (Norf), *Drakelowleyes* 1357, in Lower Bebington, Drakelows, in Thornton Hough (Ches), and *Drakehov*, c. 1220, in Kirk Smeaton (YW), in which Old Norse *haugr* replaces the English *hlāw* of the other names. Drake Hill Close (*Drakehowe* 1335), in Maltby (YW), the early form of which also contains *haugr*, possibly alludes to a tumulus marked on the first edition of the 1-inch Ordnance Survey map. Drakestones (*Drake-stone Side* 1651), in Stinchcombe (Glos), is near an ancient camp, and there are many scattered stones on the surface. Dragons Ford, in Newland (Glos), is surprisingly near a hill-top. The name is derived from *Drakehord* 1337, the later *Drakenford* 1618 having been possibly affected by a misreading of *Drakensord* in an intermediate source no longer extant. The supposed presence of a dragon did not necessarily imply the existence of buried treasure; it may have been merely a warning of possible danger if the barrow were explored.

Neolithic finds have been made in the area of the lost name *Goldwhurd*, in Titsey (Sur), and it is not improbable that gold or other treasure was once found there. Goldencross, in Rochford (Ess), was *Goldhord* in 1248, from which the present name is indirectly derived through a personal name *del Goldhord*, in *Goldhordescros* in 1425. *Golthortes* 1313 occurs in Weston Underwood (Derbys). Associated with Gollard Farm, in Amport (Hants), are the personal names *La Goldhord* 1248 and *atte Goldhord* 1327, pointing to a similar origin to that of the names already mentioned. The farm is about half a mile from the Roman Port Way. *Goldhorde* 1252 is found in Wytham (Berks); though nothing is known about any archaeological finds here, or elsewhere in the parish, some unidentifiable features known as The Five Sisters are marked on small-scale Ordnance Survey maps. *Goldhurd* 1548, in Shere (Sur), was probably not far from the Roman villa at Farley Green. *Hordberia* 13c. 'treasure barrow' occurs in Shipton (Glos).

Roman pottery has been found in or near *Crockemede* 13c. 'pottery meadow', in Brockworth (Glos). Crockmead, in Hucclecote (Glos), has already been mentioned. Crock Hole, in Portland (Dor), alluding to a hollow where potsherds were found, occurs in a parish where Roman remains have been discovered. *Pavement* names may refer to a tesselated Roman pavement but occasionally refer to a stretch of paved road, which may of course also be of archaeological significance, e.g. Pavement Field, in Rudheath Lordship, The Pavement Croft, in Eccleston, Pavement Hay, in Poulton (Ches), and Pavement Croft, in Preston Gubbals (Shrops).

ROMAN AND OTHER ROADS

A location beside a road or a canal is one of the easiest to describe in field-name terms, as either of these features is likely to constitute one of the boundaries. *Street* in major place-names and in field-names often refers to a Roman road. Street Field, in Thorpe Salvin (YW), alludes to the ancient Worcester–York road known as *Rikenild Street* but locally called Packman Lane or Road. This road forms the western boundary of the township, which was *Richenildtorp* in the thirteenth century. Street Field, in Caddington (Herts, now Beds), probably refers to the Icknield Way. Street Close, in Musgrave (Westm), lies by the Roman road from Stainmore to Brougham (now the A66). Street Acre, in Dunham Massey, Street Field, in Sale, and Street Hey, in High Legh (Ches), allude to the Roman road from Chester to Manchester which bears the spurious name *Watling Street*. The Roman road conventionally so called is named in Watling Field, in Wistanstow (Shrops). Street Flatt, in Newton Kyme (YW), alludes to the Roman road known as Rudgate. Fore Street Eweleaze, in Winterborne Kingston (Dor), is beside the Roman road which crosses the parish. Other instances, some of which may well refer to roads of post-Roman construction, include Street Field, in Albrighton (Shrops), Street Garth, in Fridaythorpe (YE), Streetway Piece, in Brocton (Staffs), and Street Moors (*Le Stretemore* 1370), in Halton (Ches).

Many centuries after the Romans left, roads provided by Turnpike Trusts are recalled in such names as The Turnpike, in Empingham, Turnpike Field, in Belton (Rut) and in Cheadle (Ches), Turnpike Meadow, in Chaddleworth (Berks), in Billesdon and in Arnesby (Leics), and Field next the Turnpike, in Upwey (Dor). Maintenance of these thoroughfares was financed by payments made by wayfarers at fixed points, near which were fields bearing such names as Toll Bar, in Ayston, Tollbar Close, in Glaston (Rut) and in Rivenhall (Ess), Tollbar Croft, in Hattersley (Ches), Tollgate Meadow, in Foston (Leics) and in Clifton & Compton (Derbys), and Turnpike Gate Field, frequent in Shropshire.

Other references to thoroughfares include Roadfield, in Wokingham (Berks), Road Furlong, in Steventon (Berks), Kingway, in Winterborne Zelstone (Dor), and Kingway Field (*Kingwey* 1426), in Almer (Dor), both referring to the Roman road from Dorchester to Badbury. *Harpway* (OE *here-pæth* 'a military road, a highway') is found in Harpway Furlong, in Hinton Martell (Dor); this refers to the Wimborne–Cranborne road, beside which are also fields called Wimborne Turnpike Road, in Hinton Martell, and Wimbourne Turnpike, in Chalbury (Dor). The road is probably that referred to in *Regiam Viam vocat' Herpath'* 1448 'the royal way called *Herpath*'. Eady Croft (*Edeway Shott* 1673), in St Paul's Walden (Herts), adjoins Icknield Way, traversing the parish from west to east. *Edeway* is from *Thede Way* 'the people's road', misunderstood as *Th[e] Edeway*. Eadway Close, in Eggington (Beds), also lies alongside *Edeway*. The Idways, of the same derivation, in Warmington (Warks), are beside a track leading to Napsbury Camp.

Some roads were laid out, of course, long before the enclosure of the named land. There are pieces of land, e.g. Portway Close

(*Portewey t.* Hy 7), in Tysoe (Warks), beside the *portways*, roads of some antiquity leading to a *port* or market-town, such as *Poortwey* 1434–35, in Steventon, and *Portway* 1778, in Balking (Berks). The Portway (*Portweis Furlong t.* Ed.6), in Appleford (Berks), is beside the road that led to Wallingford. There are closes named Upper & Lower Portway, in Church Eaton, Portway, in Haughton, Port Field, in Huntington, and Upper Port Leasow, in Bradley (Staffs). Port Lane Close, in Shapwick (Dor), is beside 1449 *venell' voc' Portlane'* 1449 'the street called *Portlane'*. Both *Portway Furlong* and *Street Furlong* occur in a 1652 survey of Greetham (Rut). *Portweis Furlong t.* Ed.6, in Appleton, adjoined the road to Wallingford (Berks). In Cambridgeshire, Portfield, in Balsham, adjoins the Icknield Way. Port Way Furlong, in Eltisley, alludes to an ancient trackway linking the Cam valley with Ermine Street. Other ancient roads are referred to in Portway Close, in Melbourne, and *Portweyefeld* 1346, in Teversham. *Portweyedole* 1398, in Graveley, alludes to the road (known as Roman Way) marking the former county boundary between Cambridgeshire and Huntingdonshire.

Packmen, the pedlars who made long journeys on foot bearing heavy loads of small goods, followed their route along ancient tracks and across open moors by means of way-marks, particularly in the form of posts, to which reference is made in such field-names as Stoop Break, in Carleton, Stopes Meadow, in Austwick, and Sutton Stoop, in Steeton (YW), from Old Norse *stolpi* 'a post'. Some *Guide Post* names may also refer to such way-marks. References also occur in such track-names as *Packman Lane*. Way Stones, in Rishworth (YW), indicate places where markers ensured a safe passage across country that was especially dangerous when covered by deep snow. Traders using packhorses are referred to in such names as Packsaddle, in Swannington (Leics), and Packsaddle Bank, in Weston (Ches).

Field-names occasionally refer to an adjacent road by the name of one of its terminal points, e.g. *Leisterway Hades* 1674, in Castle Donington (Leics), or Wimborne Way Close (*Wymborneway Furlonge* 1591), in Shapwick (Dor), adjoining the road leading to Wimborne Minster. A furlong called *Over Coventry Way* 1679 is found in the Glebe Terrier for Sharnford (Leics). Crawford Way Field, in Winterborne Tomson (Dor), lies beside the Roman road from Dorchester to Badbury, named on the Ordnance Survey map *Crawford Way*, referring to Great Crawford in Spottisbury. *Tween-way Furlong* 1771, in Shrivenham (Berks), and *Quarrefours c.* 1190, in Darrington (YW), allude to road junctions. Gate Saddles, in

South Elmsall, and Gate Shackles, in Walton (YW), are derived from Middle English *gate-shadel* 'a crossroads'. Other names in which two or more streets are involved include Boveways, in Coombe Keynes (Dor), *Bytwynewayes* 1519, in Ashbury (Berks), Tween Gates, in Greetham (Rut), and *Inter Vias* 13c. ('between the ways'), in Bagworth (Leics), a Latin entry in a demesne terrier in which most of the other names are in English.

Allusions to local paths and lanes include Cart Lane Close, in Balby (YW), Thieves Lane Leasow, in Brewood (Staffs), beside a road known as *Theveslone* as early as 1401, Lane Head, in Hepworth (YW), Ormsrake (*Ormesrake* 1468), in Saddleworth (YW) 'Orm's rough path', Outlet Field, in Woodcott (Ches), Outgang Close, in Balby (YW), in Rampton, in Blyth and in Kneesall (Notts), and Out Gates, in Gembling (YE). Other names include Bridle Pad Field 'land with or beside a bridle path, i.e. a by-way suitable for a ridden horse but not for a vehicle', in Barrowden (Rut).

Names referring to paths and ways across the fields themselves include Footpath Field, in Arborfield (Berks) and in Skipwith (YE), Footpath Ground, in Bucklebury (Berks), and Trod Field, in Garton on the Wolds (YE). Cross Lane Field, in Tetton (Ches), refers either to a link between two roads or to a lane across the agricultural land. Footpad Piece, in South Luffenham, refers to the same path as Footpad Field, in Morcott (Rut). *Crossegate* 1638, in Church Langton (Leics), and Footgate Close, in Barlborough (Derbys), show Scandinavian influence in using *-gate* (ON *gata*) instead of *-road*. In Rake Hey 'enclosure by or with a path', in King's Marsh (Ches), the first element is the dialect term *rake* 'a rough path'. Rake Side, in Saighton (Ches), is the common name for a series of fields beside Saighton Lane, formerly *Black Street Lane*, from which neighbouring fields were named *Blake Streets*. *Outrake* is used in south Shropshire for land between the fields and the open pasture, where the herds owned by various farmers were sorted after returning from the hills. Variants are found, such as Out Strake, in Chelmarsh, and Outstreaks, in Highley (Shrops). Outrake also occurs in Warcop (Westm). *Le Grenelane t.* Ed. 6, in Appleford (Berks), Green Lane Field, in Fridaythorpe, and Green Lane Field, in Garton on the Wolds (YE), embody *Green Lane* 'an occupation road giving access to the selions in the open fields'. *Chaseway*, with a similar meaning, is found in Essex field-names.

WAYSIDE FEATURES, CAUSEWAYS, BRIDGES AND FORDS

Items of street-furniture, such as signposts, are also referred to in field-names. The dialectal variants for 'a direction post' can be observed in the following miscellany of forms: Guide Post Lock (*lock* means 'an enclosure'), in North Wingfield (Derbys), Guide Post Close, in Foston, in Fridaythorpe (YE), in Rawcliffe (YW), in Crich and in Belper (Derbys), Guide Post Field, in Skipwith (YE), Handing Post Piece, in Charlbury (Oxon), Hand Post Ground, in Broughton Poggs (Oxon), Hand Post Piddle, in St Nicholas Hurst, Hand-Post Pightle, in Winnersh (Berks), Handpost Field, in Stanford Rivers, in Berden and in a number of other places in Essex, Signpost Close, in Hampreston (Dor), Signboard Piece, in Inkpen (Berks), Finger Post Field, in Wettenhall (Ches), and Fingerpost Close, in Frolesworth (Leics). The Hand and Post, in Upton (Oxon), makes sense if the 'hand' is the horizontal sign, separate from the 'post' which supports it.

Whereas direction posts were used almost solely at crossroads, milestones marked regular distances along a road and provided supplementary information about the direction of and distance from places on the route. Perhaps because they are less conspicuous than signposts, milestones are not referred to so often in field-names. Milestone is found in Branksome (Dor), Milestone Field in Remenham (Berks), in Langton Long Blandford (Dor), in Norton Mandeville, in Chipping Ongar, in High Ongar and in Rayleigh (Ess), Milestone Piece in Hinton Martell (Dor) and in Radley (Berks), Milestone Ground in Hurley (Berks) and in South Stoke (Som). Other structures in the countryside included, at the beginning of the nineteenth century, the telegraphs erected for military communications. Telegraph Plantation, in Alderholt (Dor), is named from the remains of one of these structures. A name associated with cross-country electrical cables, Pylons, occurs in Whitchurch Canonicorum and in Lytchett Minster (Dor).

A mound or dam across marshy land was earlier known as a *causie* (from Norman French *caucie*), and the track or road upon it as a *causey-wey*, from which developed the modern *causeway*. Field-names show all stages in the development of the term. The basic term appears in *Le Cawsey* 1578, in Haslington (Ches), Short Causey (*The Cawsye* 1579), in South Kelsey (Lincs), Causey Close, in Whitgift (YW), Causey Croft, in Mere (Ches), Causey Meadow, in Larbreck (Lancs), and The Carsie, in Shephall (Herts). The current form is more frequent, e.g. The Causeway Rough, in Brewood (Staffs), Causeway Field, in Acton and in Checkley (Ches), in Theydon Gernon and in Great Sampford, Causeway Mead, in Havering (Ess) and in Stratfield Mortimer (Berks), and Causeway Pightle, in Arborfield (Berks), with a further alteration in Coarse Way Field, in Thornton le Moors (Ches).

Names alluding to bridges are usually of the same form as Bridge Close, in Burton Lazars (Leics), Bridge Field (*Breggefeld* 1558), in Peldon (Ess), Bridge Piece, in Windsor (Berks), or Bridge Meadow, in Elstead (Sur). In early usage the term might apply to causeways, as well as to bridges as we know them today. Old Norse or Scandinavianized forms are found in the Midlands and the north, e.g. Brigg Close, in Hook (YW), Brig Meadow, in Poulton (Lancs), and Briglands, in Bampton (Westm). References to the material of which the bridge was made include Stonebridge Pingle, in Totley (Derbys), Stone Bridge Field, in Harrowden (Nthants), Stone Brig Carr, in Newton with Scales (Lancs), and Clod Bridge Acre, in Marple (Ches), referring to a causeway made from trampled clods of earth. Greece Bridge, in Northenden (Ches), is probably 'a bridge with steps' (ME *grese* 'a flight of steps'). *Quitstobbrugge c.* 1220 'the bridge at the white tree-stump', in Tabley Superior (Ches), names a landmark which might be appropriate for a causeway across marshy ground. Wettenhall Lane Bridge, in Wettenhall (Ches), was earlier *Ankers Plat* 'the anchorite's plat or footbridge', using a term found also in Platt Bridge Meadow, in Dodcott cum Wilkesley, and Platt Field, in Warburton (Ches).

Field-name references to fords are found in appropriate locations. Some examples are Ford Field, in Dodcott cum Wilkesley (Ches), Ford Mead, in Purton (Wilts), Ford Piece, in Shenton (Leics), and Ford Meadow, in Cheadle (Ches), in Bushby and in Stockerston (Leics). Twyford Meadow, in Mobberley (Ches), refers to a 'double ford'. Saltersford, in Kinderton, beside a brook south-east of Middlewich (Ches), was evidently on a route taken by salt-merchants. Smithy Crofts, in Bridgemere (Ches), may be associated with *Le Smithiford* 1313. Winterfoot, in Tilstone Fearnall (Ches), is 'winter ford', regarded as important since the depth of water at many fords in winter would be too great for safety. Fields adjacent to ferry landing-places are duly named, e.g. Ferry Field, in Bollin Fee, in Cheadle and in Pownall Fee (Ches). References are sometimes to the vessel providing the service, e.g. Boat Field, in Shrewsbury Holy Cross (Shrops) and in Warburton (Ches). Horse Boat Fields, in Shrewsbury St Mary (Shrops), referred to the ferry used to convey the draught horses to the other side of the Severn at a point where the towing-path changed to the other bank.

CANALS, RAILWAYS AND AIR TRANSPORT

Navigation Close, a clear reference to land beside a canal, is found in Findern (Derbys), which abuts the canal formerly known as the Grand Trunk Navigation. The same name occurs in Barrow (Rut), referring to the disused Oakham–Melton Canal, and in Lubenham (Leics). Canal Meadow is found in Copford (Ess), in Brooksby (Leics) and in Ingol (Lancs), Canal Close in Glen Parva (Leics), Near & Far Canal Piece in Rugeley, and Canal Field in Essington (Staffs), in Catterall and in Claughton (Lancs). Tunnel Field, in Barnton (Ches), adjoins Saltersford Tunnel on the Trent & Mersey Canal. Lock Brow Wood, in Dutton (Ches), is named from a lock on the Weaver Navigation; Lock Brow and Meadow, in Barnton (Ches), adjoins Saltersford Locks. Other canal-related names include Wharf Fields, in Market Overton (Rut) and Incline Field, in Sutton Maddock (Shrops).

Many railway routes were being established in what might be called the 'Tithe Commutation period', the 1830s and 1840s. It is therefore to be expected that in the Apportionments such references should occur as Station Field, in Etton (YE), Railway Field, in Acton (Middx, now Greater London), Railway Meadow, in Crich (Derbys), and Railway Close, in Swannington and in Cossington (Leics), in Skelton (YE) and in Grazeley (Berks). Often such land consists of narrow stretches beside the line, or fragments of fields divided by the railway engineers. Some of the generics indicate this, e.g. Railroad Piece, in Marholme (Nthants, now Cambs), Railway Piece, in Crich (Derbys), in Bollin Fee (Ches) and in Ullesthorpe (Leics), and Railway Screed, in Bridlington (YE). Line Field, in Berrington (Shrops), adjoins the route of the Severn Valley Railway. In Rutland The Line Field is found in Ketton, and Bradshaw's Railway Field in Oakham. Station Fields in Morcott adjoin Line Fields in South Luffenham, and in Essendine and in Barrow there are fields called Over The Line. Viaduct Close, in Seaton (Rut), is at the northern end of the spectacular crossing of the Welland valley. Signal Field, in Scampston (YE), may refer to a railway signal nearby. Tunnel Close is found in Swannington (Leics), and Tunnel Field in Merstham (Sur). Cattle Arch, in Barrowden (Rut), adjoins a tunnel allowing cattle to pass through the railway embankment. The names of adjacent pieces of land occasionally refer to military and civil airfields, e.g. Aerodrome Field, in Elloughton (YE).

INDUSTRIAL USE OF LAND

Names of the *Hills and Holes* type have been explained as relating to stone-quarrying in the Middle Ages and later. Field-names also mark the use of neighbouring land for the mining or quarrying of other minerals, for handicrafts of various kinds, and for general industrial development. Names like Forge Meadow, in Penkridge (Staffs), Papermill Meadow, in Stanton upon Hine Heath (Shrops), Smithy Field, in Higher Whitley (Ches), Factory Yard, in Laxton (YE), and Warehouse Field, in Thelwall (Ches), are to be found in many parts of the country. Fields called Rope Walk, such as those in Derby, in Castleton, in Bakewell (Derbys) and in Bollington (Ches), are usually regular but quite narrow rectangles of land. *Le Gleshousfeld* 1311, in Cholmondeley (Ches), and Glasshouse Meadow, in Mucklestone and in West Felton (Shrops), allude to the manufacture of glass.

The preparation of timber by hand is recalled in Sawpit Field, in Firby (YE), and Sawpit Close, in Hungerford (Berks), in Broughton Astley (Leics) and in Bruern (Oxon). Cloggers Leasow, in Drayton in Hales, and Cloggers Croft, in Stoke upon Tern (Shrops), refer to the localities where itinerant teams of Lancashire cloggers would prepare wood from neighbouring alder-copses for the making of clogs. In Essex, Cold Bakers, in Loughton, alludes to charcoal-burners, and Cutlers Green (*Cutlers Grene* 1336), in Thaxted, commemorates the medieval cutlery industry there.

Textile manufacture was widely dispersed all over the country long before the factory system was introduced. Spinning, weaving and dyeing were essentially cottage industries and were not apt to generate field-names. Vegetable crops producing dyes (mentioned in an earlier chapter) needed the dedicated or casual use of pieces of land, and some processes were outdoor operations or required open-air treatment of their materials. Bleaching, for instance, is referred to in *Blechefeld* 1425, in Kaber (Westm), and Quisters Hey, in Dutton (Ches), from early modern English *quister*, *whytstar* 'a bleacher'. Dyeing is alluded to in Dyer Lands, in Kirkoswald (Cumb), and Dye House Meadow, in Kettleshulme (Ches).

The *walking* or *fulling* of cloth is referred to in such names as Walk Close, in Babworth (Notts), Walk Meadow, in Enbourne (Berks), in Beaford (Dev) and in Hallow (Worcs), Walk Field, in Havant (Hants) and in Cound (Shrops), and Walk Ground, in Charlcote (Warks). Walkmile Croft (*Walkmylne Croft* 1529), in Ashford (Derbys), alludes to a fulling mill. There is an instance of such a mill, *Le Walkmylne* 1415, in Wirksworth, and there may be earlier relevant field-names elsewhere, as the mills were introduced in the late twelfth century. Examples in other counties are Walkmill Field, in Nether Knutsford (Ches) and in Whitchurch (Shrops), Walk Mill Brow, in Barnacre (Lancs), and Walkmill Bank, in Oxspring (YW). Another term is used in Tucking Mill Mead, in Stourton, and Tuckingmill Mead, in West Tisbury (Wilts). After fulling, the cloth was stretched (or *tented*) and dried on outdoor frames, to ensure evenness of shape and to prevent shrinkage. *Tenter* names are often found, e.g. *Tentarleas*, in Aberford (YW), Tenter Bank, in Haltwhistle (Nthumb), and Tenter Field (*Teynterplot* 1535), in Great Coggeshall (Ess). Essex examples of this name (nearly twenty in number) are mainly in Lexden and Hinckford Hundreds, the centre of the old woollen industry of that county. Early names in this area include *Tentouriscroft c.* 1400, in Stisted, *Teyntourcroft c.* 1425, in Finchingfield. and *Le Teyntorfeld* 1544, in Dedham. Tenterfield (*Tentar Bank* 1553), in Kendal (Westm), is reminiscent of the manufacture of the coarse cloth known as Kendal Green. In 1582 the burgesses ordered a watch to be kept on the tenters. Variant forms are found, e.g. Tainty Field, in Horley (Sur), Tentry Field, in Marden (Ches), Taintry Field, in Cheswardine, Tuntree Meadow, in Neen Savage, and Tean Tree Croft, in Hodnet (Shrops), as well as Frame Field, in Hinton Ampner and in Titchfield (Hants), and Frame Yard, in Kenley (Shrops). Frame Field, in Tolleshunt d'Arcy (Ess), does not belong here; it was earlier *Frerenefelde* 1398 'the field of the brethren', alluding to the community of Beeleigh Abbey, who owned this land.

The loss of twenty-four yards of cloth "off from the Racks" was reported in the *London Gazette* in 1678. These contrivances, which seem to have differed from tenters in having a mechanism for applying additional tension, are referred to in Rack Close (*Rackemeade* 1562), in Dursley (Glos), in Sandhurst (Berks) and in Box (Wilts). Rack Ground, in North Nibley (Glos), *Racke Close* 1640, was described as having "Rackes to dry clothes".

The tanning of leather is recorded in field-names. Bark, especially that of oak-trees, was stripped from the trunks as near as possible to the place of felling. *Tanhousmede* 1539–40, in Reading (Berks), Tanhouse Close, in Wistanstow (Shrops), *The Barkhouse Garth* 1535, in Barwick in Elmet (YW), and *Barkhowse Meadowe* 1609, in Haslington (Ches), denoted the premises where the bark was steeped in order to extract the tannin. There is a reference in 1578 to *The Tanne Howse* in Haslington. A later name, Skin Pit Field, in Marton (Ches), probably also relates to a tannery.

References to the processing of salt are frequent in Cheshire and neighbouring counties, e.g. Salthouses Field, in Bispham with Norbreck (Lancs), Salt Piece, in Mainstone (Shrops), and Wychhouse Meadow, in Eaton (Ches). Brine Pit Field and Wych House Field were adjacent pieces of land in Sandbach (Ches). Eating House Meadow, in Nantwich (Ches), is not a place for taking refreshments; early forms, such as *Heatyng House Yorde* 1575, indicate premises in which brine was boiled.

MINES, QUARRIES AND OTHER EXCAVATIONS

Clay, limestone, chalk and sand might be excavated for agricultural purposes, already described, but some of these materials would have other uses, including building, exemplified by such names as Mortar-Pit Field, in Fridaythorpe (YE), and Brickhill Butts, in Southwell (Notts). The last name alludes not to a hill but to a kiln, showing a development from *Bricke Kilne Close* 1694 similar to that found in Brickhill Baulk, a former brickyard in Bessingby (YE). The extraction of gypsum is indicated in Plaster Pit Field, Ratcliffe on Soar and *Plaister Pitt* 1686 in Tuxford (Notts). *Sperstanerig c.* 1200, in Kirkby Thore (Westm), contains Old English *spær-stān* 'gypsum'. Other materials are referred to in Ironstone Close, in Cottesmore (Rut), and *Alum* 1578, in Studland (Dor), adjoining a copperas mine. Copperas Ground, in Brightlingsea and in Walton (Ess), alludes to a mineral used in dyeing and for the treatment of scab in sheep. Rock salt was dug from Rock Pit Field, in Wincham (Ches), and Woad Holes, in Above Derwent (Cumb), was land from which black lead or plumbago (dial. *wad*) was obtained.

Unspecified excavation is referred to in *Le Quarels* 1315, in Mansfield (Notts), and *The Quarrell Close* 1535, in Aberford (YW), which use the form of the word *quarry* frequently found in older field-names. *The Quarrell Close* 1592, in Methley (YW), has an earlier form, *Warell Close* 1490. Warrel Close is found in Wyke (YW). Another form occurs in The Quor, in Elmley Castle (Worcs), Quar Bush, in Camerton, and Quar Furlong, in Stanton Prior (Som). The current term appears in Quarry Close, in Kingswear (Dev), in Hermitage (Dor) and in Billesdon (Leics), Quarry Field, in Arnold (Notts) and in Thorpe Bulmer (Dur), and Quarry Shaw, in Lamberhurst (Kent).

Old English *(ge)delf* 'a quarry' is found in The Delph, in Broseley (Shrops) and in Feltwell (Norf), Delf Closes, in Brighouse (YW), and Delft, in Crook (Dur). *Stanidelf* 1352 (OE *stān-gedelf* 'stone quarry'), in Shrewsbury St Clad (Shrops), and Stony Delph, in Coventry (Warks), may refer to early excavations. Standal's Pit Furlong, in Chadlington (Oxon), is a likely example, and other names of this origin include Standhill (*Stondelfeld* 1556), in Hitchin (Herts), Standles, in Gretton (Nthants), and Upper and Lower Standles, in Alne (Warks). Gravels, in Brimington (Derbys), is from Old English *græfel* 'a quarry'. Stonegravels (*Le Stongravel* 1310), in Chesterfield (Derbys), has another early form *Stondelf* 1315, showing the substitution of a better-known term for a rare one, though the name reverted to *Stone Gravel* in 1563.

Red Chalk Hill, in North Willingham (Lincs), probably refers to *raddle* (otherwise *reddle* or *ruddle*), a red ochre used in the marking of sheep. It is not chalk but a mixture of iron oxide and clay, "in a state of impalpable subdivision", the *Oxford Dictionary* tells us. Sources of this material are indicated by Radling, in Wootton (Sur), Raddle Pit, in Braithwell, Riddle Pits, in Hepworth (YW), Riddle Potts, in Kendal (Westm), Ochre Hole, in Fixby (YW), Ocre Mead, in Chignall St James (Ess), Far Ochres, in Knapton (YE), Ochre Ground, in Forest Hill (Oxon), and possibly the otherwise unexplained The Occopits, in Hopton Wafers (Shrops).

References to coal mines are to be expected in the names of neighbouring pieces of land. Many instances other than the following may be found in the relevant areas. Coal Pit Leasow occurs in Weston Jones (Staffs) and in Stapleton (Shrops), Coal Pit Close in Middleton (YW), in Billesdon (Leics) and in Beighton (Derbys). Coalgill Sike in Hartley, Coalpit Sike in Asby (Westm), and Coalpit Meadow in Wervin (Ches).

Bellond Field, in Hathersage, and Belland Yard, in Stoke (Derbys), contain the dialect term *belland* meaning 'lead poisoning caused by powdered ore', not unexpected in an area where the metal was mined. Other references to minerals and mining in this county include Allotment Mine Hillock, in Eyam, Calamine Piece, in

Brassington, and Calamini Close, in Cromford (alluding to *calamine* 'zinc oxide'). Adit Field, in Lelant, and Adit Croft, in Morvah (Corn), allude to drainage-tunnels in Cornish tin mines. Park an Shafty, in Towednack, and Park Shaftis, in St Ives, were fields containing mine-shafts, the English word having been given a Cornish dress.

The digging of peat for fuel is recorded in such field-names as Turf Close, in Tur Langton (Leics), Peat Close, in Bradley (Derbys), Peet Hey, in Werneth (Ches), Peat Wick, in Setmurthy (Cumb), Turf Pits, in Hattersley and in Walton Inferior (Ches), Turpets, in Nettleton (Lincs), and Turf Pit Leasow, in Lydham (Shrops). Peat Delf, in Elstead (Sur), means 'peat digging' (OE *(ge)delf*), and Peat Pots, in Stainmore (Westm), 'peat holes'. Turkers, in Gembling, and Turker Butts, in Foston (YE), allude to 'turf carrs'. The more formal expression meaning both 'the right to cut peat' and 'place where peat may be dug' is found in Turbary Croft, in Warmingham (Ches), and possibly Turfberry, in Cliburn (Westm). The moorland or boggy types of landscape are referred to in Turf Fen, in Ely (Cambs) and in East Dereham (Norf). Peat Moor, in Kintbury (Berks), *Mospitt Meadowe* 1610, in Horton cum Peel, *Moss Pitt Flatt* 1663, in Tarvin (Ches), Peat Moss Field, in Dufton (Westm,), *Flaught Howe* 1578, in Nether Wasdale (Cumb), *Flayelond* 13c., in Elton, and Fleed Moss, in Kingswood (Ches). The specific terms in the last two names mean 'flayed' or 'pared', used in the north-west of England with reference to the stripping of peat, an individual sod being known as a *flay*, found in *Flaybrick Heays* 1645 'sod slope enclosures', in Claughton cum Grange, Flea Flat, in Anderton, Flays, in Cotton Edmunds, Fleas, in Norley and in Saughall Massie, and The Fly's (*sic*), in Moreton cum Lingham (Ches).

NOTES AND REFERENCES

1. Pool, *Field Names of West Penwith*, pp. 43, 84.
2. Kerr, *Bound to the Soil*, p. 35. The author adds in a footnote that in Bere Regis in 1739 a shilling "was paid for ringing the bells after a rumour that Carthagena had been taken".
3. J. Booth, *Nicholas Davenport and his Neighbours* (Framingham, Mass., 1935), p. 24, quoting R. Hawes and R. Loder, *History of Framlingham*, 1798.
4. Foxall, p. 15.

5. John Stow, *A Survey of London* (1598) (Everyman's Library edn), p. 150.
6. H.E. Hallam, *Rural England*, p. 107.
7. Wainwright, *Field-Names of Amounderness Hundred*, p. 193.
8. This information has been kindly provided by Peter Liddle of Leicestershire Museums Service.
9. See A.E. Brown, *Archaeological Sites and Finds in Rutland; A Preliminary List* (Department of Adult Education, University of Leicester 1975).
10. J. Bridges, *History and Antiquities of Northamptonshire* (ed. Whalley), i, pp. 42–3, quoted in *The Place-Names of Northamptonshire*, p. 20. For a plan and brief account of the Burnt Walls site see A.E. Brown, *Early Daventry* (University of Leicester, Department of Education, 1991), pp. 81–2.
11. Wainwright, p. 194.
12. Examples in Abney (Derbys) are discussed on pp. 48–9, above.
13. M. Gelling, 'English place-names derived from the compound *wīchām*', *Medieval Archaeology* XI (1967), pp. 87–104, also (with an addendum) in K. Cameron (ed.), *Place-name Evidence for the Anglo-Saxon Invasion and the Scandinavian Settlements* (Nottingham, EPNS, 1975, repr. 1987), pp. 8–26, here p. 26. Wickhams, as Dr Gelling notes (*Signposts to the Past*, p. 74), may be derived from the surname of an owner or occupier.
14. Foxall, p. 56, citing W.H. Duignan, *Notes on Staffordshire Place-Names* (Henry Frowde, 1902), p. 53.
15. Wainwright, pp. 196–8.
16. Cf. Beresford, *History on the Ground* (1957, repr. Gloucester, Sutton, 1984), p. 105.

CHAPTER TEN

Religion, folk customs and assembly places

LOCAL RIGHTS AND LIMITS

Social organization is no novelty. Medieval communities of all levels, from those of the manor and the parish to that of national administration, conducted their affairs with varying degrees of efficiency. The identity of local communities entailed a precise recognition of territorial boundaries. In early charters, as well as in many later land documents, boundary clauses described in detail the topographical features marking the edges of the estate or manor being granted. There would be regular inspection of the boundaries by means of processions or perambulations.

Because of the importance of the boundaries in civil, and not merely ecclesiastical, administration, these ceremonies were excluded from the post-Reformation prohibition of religious processions. The incumbent depended on tithes for his income, and so the precise location of the land of the parish had to be publicly known. It was also important to define the limits of the responsibility of parish officials such as the constables and the beadle. The parish was responsible for the care of its own poor, and so it was necessary to know on which side of a boundary the pauper was born.

Among the instances of *Holy Well* many are on parish boundaries, but their title is probably from their traditional qualities or powers and does not depend on their being halting places in perambulations. Names such as *Procession Pit Furlong* 1714, in Kinwarton (Warks), recall that, during the perambulation, boys of the parish, or sometimes a curate, would be immersed in a pool or held upside down in a well, just as boys would often be beaten, as part of the mnemonic function of the ceremony. Gospel's Knap, in Little Compton (Warks), is a hillock (OE *cnæppa*) on the parish boundary. Gospel Hillocks, in Kingsterndale (Derbys), are actually prehistoric burial mounds. *The Gospel Knowle*, in Castleton (Derbys), was on record in 1688. Gospelsich, in Stretton on Fosse (Warks), is a boundary stream which gave its name to *Gospellsyche Furlong* in 1585. Some names specified by *Holy* possibly also belong here, e.g. Holy Bush Furlong, in Turkdean (Glos), Holy Baulks, in Sutton Bonington (Notts), with perhaps *Hallowed Close* 1610, in Scarcliffe (Derbys), and Halilands, in Bollin Fee (Ches).

The ceremonies took place in Rogation Week, beginning with the Gang Days or Rogation Days (Monday to Wednesday), but sometimes might take place on Ascension Day, the Thursday of that week. Gang Monday Land, in Edgcott (Bucks), refers to a prescribed day under this title. Some names explicitly allude to a procession, e.g. Perambulation Way, in Great Snoring (Norf), Procession Field, in Battle (Sus), The Processioning Pieces, in Longcot (Berks), *Processionway* 18c., on the Morningthorpe/Fritton boundary (Norf), *Procession Waye* 1551–52, in Banbury (Oxon), and *Procession Waye* 1603–04, in Sonning Town (Berks). The same name was found in Higham Ferrers (Nthants).

Banners had been a feature of the medieval processions for the blessing of the fields, but their use was proscribed in the perambulations. They are remembered in the field-names Bannerings, in Sutton Meddock (Shrops), Banner Cross, in Eccleshall Bierlow (YW), Banners Style, in Overpool, on the boundary with Whitby (Ches), and *Banners Stoope*, a lost name in Middlewich (Ches), a boundary post (ON *stolpi* 'a post') thought to be at the limit of the town's salt-boiling rights, though the *Banners* element suggests a connection with the beating of parish bounds.

The scriptural readings and prayers in the ceremony are alluded to in the numerous *Gospel* names such as Gospel Stone, in Hathersage (Derbys), as well as in references to the Old Testament, e.g. The Psalms, in Bromfield (Shrops), and The Proverbs, in Boningdale (Shrops). But Proverbs Green, in Great Dunmow (Ess), does not belong here; it was *Prophetes* 1430, *Prophets Green* 1777, traceable to the family of John *Prophete* 1368. *Psalm Oak*, referred to in 1552 as "an ould oke marked with a crosse at Foxley Heathe" and apparently also known as Gospel Oak, stood at the spot in Smitham Bottom where Croydon, Sanderstead and Coulsdon parishes meet. The Lord's Prayer would be recited at least once during the perambulation, and some *Pater Noster* field-names allude to the Rogation-

Plate 10.1 The Gospel Stone, Hathersage (Derbys), marking a point on the route of the Rogationtide processions, referred to elsewhere in such field-names as *Gospel Close* or *Procession Field*

tide ceremonies. In Essex there are at least four examples: Pater Noster, in Upminster, Paternoster Heath, in Tolleshunt Knights, Paternoster Croft, in Chapel, and Paternoster Meadow, in Wix. The location of *Pater Noster Bancke* 1719, in East Hendred (Berks), is unknown, as are *Paternoster Yarde* 1578, in Brassington (Derbys), a little later referred to as *Croft called le Paternoster* 1583, and *Le Pater Noster*' 1227, *La Paternostre c.* 1275, in St Briavels (Glos).

There is some evidence that prayers were concluded at particular spots on the route. Amen Pingle, in Spondon (Derbys), is an exceptional form of names which normally have *Corner* as their second element. At Amen Corner (London SW17) the Tooting/ Mitcham boundary makes a right-angled turn. Amen Corner, in Binfield (Berks), in Babworth, in Edwinstowe and in Rufford (Notts), are described as being on or near the parish boundary. In Gussage All Saints (Dor) there is a local tradition of an ancient chapel, which need not be inconsistent with the interpretation proposed.

Some names emphasize the part played by trees, both individually and in groves. Gospel Greave occurs in Ashford, in Osmaston and in Wheston (Derbys), *Gospell Greve* 1612 in Kinnersley (Staffs), and there is a Gospel Greave Land in Butterton (Staffs). A *greave* (Old English *grǣfe*) 'a grove, a copse, a thicket' would be a sufficiently noticeable feature to serve as a landmark, and would need to be safe from damage. Gospel Tree is found in Cannock (Staffs) and Ashover (Derbys). There are in Wormhill (Derbys) two Gospel Greaves and also a *Gospel Tree* 1275–1445; these are not on the parish boundary but on the route of the perambulation to the mother church at Tideswell.[1] The fact that the procession came to a temporary halt is marked by the specific *Resting* (from Middle English *resting* 'a place where one can rest'), as in *Resting Greaves* 1668, in Whiston (YW), *Resting Bush* 1662, in Wickersley (YW), Resting Oak Hill, on the western boundary of Barcombe (Sus), and a fourteenth-century *Restingthorn*, in Northamptonshire. Resting Stone (*Restyngstanes* 1205–11), in Lawkland (YW), is a boundary stone on the top of Black Hill where five townships meet.

The longevity of thorn trees made them particularly suitable to mark boundary points, and they are mentioned in a number of names, e.g. Gospel Thorn, in Bolsover and in Callow (Derbys), in Crosby Ravensworth (Westm), in Brierley and in Pontefract (YW). The significance of Gospel Greave, in Green Fairfield (Derbys), is explained in a deposition dated 1666: "a Green Thorne tree called Gosspell greaue and there the minister did read a Gospell to the village of Hamblett of Cowlowe".

The oak is also notable for long life, and the massive size of ancient trees invokes respect and adds to their usefulness as markers. Gospel Oak is marked on the 1:100,000 administrative map at the boundary between Oxenhall and Newent and Dymock. The name also occurs in Avington (Hants) and in Whitbourne (Herefs). Gospel Oak, on the Hampstead–St Pancras boundary (Middx, now Greater London), cut down long ago, gave its name to a district. In Selston (Notts) this is the name of a close one field away from the parish boundary, where possibly a single piece of land has been divided into two. It occurs also in Hanborough (Oxon). In Wychwood (Oxon), Gospel Oak is located on the edge of Wychwood Forest near the borders of Leafield and Ramsden parishes. On 23 June 1652, John Evelyn, riding from Tunbridge Wells to London, was attacked "within three miles of Bromley, at a place called the

Procession Oak" by "two cut-throats".[2] This would have been one of the oak trees marking the Kent/Surrey boundary.

In addition to *Procession Oak* and *Gospel Oak*, the species name may be qualified in other ways. Holy Oak Close, in Donhead St Mary (Wilts), is near the parish boundary. Crouch Oak Field (*Crouch Hoke* 1469), in Great Warley (Ess), refers to a 'cross oak'. John Aubrey noted: "In . . . the great Wood call'd *Norwood* . . . was an ancient, remarkable Tree, call'd *Vicar's Oak*, where four parishes meet in a Point."[3] It had stood at the meeting place of the boundaries of Lambeth, Camberwell, Penge (then a detached part of Battersea), Croydon and Streatham (Sur).

What would be described today as the 'social side' of the Rogationtide ceremonies took the form of the taking of refreshments in the middle or at the end of the perambulation. "At Wilden [Beds] when the parish was perambulated there were two recognised places for refreshment; at one the townsfolk made dinner; at the other the vicar provided ale and plum cake; perhaps the cake was made from some of his tithe eggs (3 for a cock, 2 for a hen) . . ."[4] A local record referring to Vicar's Oak, in Norwood (mentioned above) relates that in 1704, "100 lbs of cheese were consumed at this spot by the Archbishop's men beating the bounds of Croydon."

ASSEMBLY PLACES

Evidence of the location of outdoor assemblies is occasionally provided by field-names. *Motlowefurlong* c.1245, in Hartshorne (Derbys), means 'furlong by or containing a meeting-place mound', from Old English (*ge*)*mōt* 'assembly' and *hlāw* 'a hill, a mound'. Old English (*ge*)*mōt* is probably also to be found in Mott Lands, in Kingsley (Hants), and Mot Close, in Thurlaston (Leics). Wymersley Bush, in Little Houghton (Northants), has been identified as *Motelowe* 13c., the moot site of Wymersley Hundred. The 'moot hill' of Thriplow Hundred (Cambs) was at Mutler Shot (*Mothlowe c.* 1250), in Newton. Mutlow Hill, in Great Wilbraham (Cambs), was at the junction of the boundaries of Staine, Radfield and Flendish Hundreds, and so was doubtless the place of assembly for each of them, or possibly for all three, meeting in a group. Mutlow Hill (*Motelowe* 1316), in Wendens Ambo (Ess), was the meeting place of Uttlesford Hundred. *Mot* is combined with *beorg* 'hill' in the well disguised Mulberry Hill (*Mudborowe* in the late sixteenth century) in Harlow (Ess), in Motborow (*Modberghefurlong* 1404) in Puddle-town (Dor), possibly the meeting place of Puddletown Hundred, and in *Modberge* 1219, in Stoke Holy Cross (Norf), which Sandred, following Arngart, identifies with *Henestede*, the meeting place of Henstead Hundred.[5]

Moot Hill, in Lighthorne (Warks), the meeting place of the Domesday Hundred of *Tremelau*, is just to the east of the parish church and in the centre of the hundred. Motslow Hill (*La Mustowe in bosc. de Dalle* 1260), in Stoneleigh (Warks), is commented on in the Leger Book of Stoneleigh Abbey: '. . . *montem de Motstowehull, ideo sic dictum quia ibi placitabant*' 'the hill of *Motstowehull*, so called because there they used to plead'. This may have been the meeting place of Knightlow Hundred. Murdishaw Wood (*Murder Shaw* 1746), in Sutton (Ches), is the junction of the boundaries of Aston, Norton, Sutton, Preston and Stockham. The name means 'spokesman's wood' (OE *mōtere* and *sceaga*). Mutler is the name of no less than sixteen modern closes in Brimstage (Ches), and is probably to be associated with Mutlow, a group of four fields in the adjoining township of Thornton Hough. The crossing of the township boundary is probably significant, but it is not known for what administrative area this was an assembly place.

In the south of England there are assembly places of the *Mustow* type from OE (*ge*)*mōt* and *stōw* 'a (sacred) place'. *La Mostowe*, in Henfield (Sus), now Moustows Manor, was the meeting place of Tipnoak Hundred. The memory of *Great Mustow* 1479, in Fulham (Middx, now Greater London), is preserved in Munster House, which gave its name to Munster Road. *Mustouwe c.* 1300, in Layer de la Haye (Ess), was almost certainly the assembly place of Winstree Hundred.

The Scandinavian *haugr* 'mound, hill' is probably the generic element in Mooter Hill Close, in West Leake (Notts), as it is in the earlier name for Hanger Hill, in Perlethorpe (Notts), *Thinghowe c.* 1300, becoming *Thingoe al. Thinko* by 1650. Hanger Hill lies at the junction of three parishes, a suitable spot for a local assembly or *Thing*. This name is found also in Rotherby (Leics), where it had earlier been *Thingou c.* 1300. *Hundredfelde* 1560, in Macclesfield (Ches), was probably the meeting place of the hundred centred on that place.

The early Hundred of Stoke, later part of Corby Hundred, met near Speller or Spellow Close, in Wilbarston (Nthants). This name (OE *spell* 'speech' and *hōh* 'a ridge, a hill') is also that of another Northamptonshire hundred, Spelhoe, which met in *Bush Field* otherwise *Spellhoe Field*, in Weston Favell. Spellow House, in Upper

Boddington (Nthants), is on a hill near the Three Shire Stones, the junction of the county boundaries of Northamptonshire, Warwickshire and Oxfordshire. The Speller, in Eaton under Heywood (Shrops), is on the Eaton/Munslow boundary, and was possibly the meeting place for Munslow Hundred.

Spellow and Over Spellow are recorded in the 1638 Glebe Terrier of Husbands Bosworth (Leics). Speller Hill lies by crossroads in Aslockton (Notts), at the highest point in a low-lying district. It was presumably the assembly place of a community, but not of Bingham Wapentake, in which it lies; that was at Moot-House Pit (*Motehowes* 1375 'assembly hills or mounds'), in Bingham (*Motehowes* is from (*ge*)*mōt* with Old Norse *haugr*.) The precise reason is not known for the naming of Spellow Field and Hill (*Spellow Hill* 1558), in Staveley, and of Ye Spellow Field, in South Stainley (YW). In the south of Ploughley Hundred (Oxon), *Spelburghe c.* 1139 'speech hill' appears among the field-names of Bletchingdon. In *Spelhonger Coppice* 1575, in Sevenhampton (Glos), the generic element is OE *hangra* 'a wooded hill'; this was probably the assembly place for this village 'of seven homesteads', which would entail special administration, below the authority of Bradley Hundred, itself a member, notably enough, of the Seven Hundreds of Cirencester. Old English *mæthel*, another term for 'speech', is found in Malsdon (*Maldon* 1287), a field in Westbury on Severn (Glos) and probably an early meeting place of Westbury Hundred.

Annual fairs were duly commemorated in the names of the fields on which they were held. Fairfield (*Fayrfelde* 1523), in Croydon, (Sur, now Greater London), was the site of a cattle market and fair held from 1314 to 1868. The Fairesteedes (*Le Fairestedes* 1360) 'the fair places', in Macclesfield (Ches), consisted of a fourteen-acre close on the west side of *The Backstreetes*. Cheap Side, in Tranmere (Ches), is near the site of the nineteenth-century wake fairs. Most of these events were originally annual gatherings of merchants for the sale of goods and stock of all kinds. In the course of time, entertainments developed and, in some instances, became the essential features of the fair.

TRIALS AND PENALTIES

The administrative and judicial functions of an assembly were often exercised on the same occasion. Directions would be given for the conduct of the public affairs of the community, and the trial of civil and criminal cases would be held in the open, with doubtless some alternative provision for inclement weather. Trial by battle, apparently belonging to the age of chivalry but not abolished until 1819, is probably alluded to in such names as Battle Flatt, in Frolesworth (Leics), Battle Croft, in Shrewsbury St Mary, Battle Field, in Alvechurch (Worcs), in Little Hallingbury (Ess), in Kemberton and in Madeley (Shrops), and Battle Mead, in Laindon (Ess).

Fields bearing names commemorating gallows and gibbets are usually to be found near parish and other boundaries and usually near crossroads (where the bodies of executed criminals were traditionally buried). Galleywood, in Wildboarclough (Ches), is near Three Shire Heads, the meeting-point of the boundaries of Cheshire, Derbyshire and Staffordshire. Gallows Corner, in Wroxton (Oxon) and in Ampney Crucis (Glos), suggests the crossroads location. A hillside site was preferred, perhaps because it offered the spectacle to a wider audience. *Galbergh Feld* 1354 'gallows-hill field', in Carlisle (Cumb), is paralleled by Galloper, in Tebay (Westm), which is from *galga* 'gallows' and *beorg* 'hill', and by Gallows Hill, in Steeple Morden (Cambs) and Appleby (Leics). Gallow Barrow (*Gallowbergh* 1431), in Kendal (Westm), alludes to 'the gallows of Kirkeby' (i.e. (Kirkby) Kendal) mentioned in a late twelfth-century document. Some names, such as Gallow Furze Leys, in Milcombe (Oxon), indicate a location in the wasteland of the parish, near the boundary. Gallow(s) Close is found in Hanborough (Oxon), Old Hutton (Westm) and Lubenham (Leics), Gallows Piece in Melbourne (Derbys), and Gallows Field in Essington (Staffs).

There are early records of many of the *Gallows* names, e.g. *Gallow Feld* 1493, in Mapledurham (Oxon). *Le Gallowbergh* 1567, in Appleby (Westm), was probably identical with Gallow Hill. *Galeweieshill* 1357, in Berkhamsted (Herts), later became Gallows Field. *Galeffeld* 1329, in Great Leighs, and *Galwefeld* 1370, in Gestingthorpe (Ess), became respectively Galleys Field and Galley Field. Variants of *Gallows* are *Gallas* and *Galley(s)*, found in Gallas Field, in Crigglestone (YW), Galleys Croft, in Meesden (Herts) (*Gallowcroft* 1511), and Galley Hill, in Stopsley (Beds). Galley Acre, in Yeardsley (Ches), however, was *The Garlicke Akers* in 1611, alluding not to the gallows but rather to the plant.

Gallow-Tree, in various guises, is found in names such as Gallows Tree Common, in Rotherfield Peppard (Oxon), Gallantry Bank, in Walton Superior (Ches), in Eyton and Alberbury (Shrops), Gallow Tree Close, in Lockington (Leics), Garrow Tree Hill, in Rotherham

(YW), Gallowtree Leasow, in Church Pulverbatch (Shrops), Galley Tree Meadow, in Alfreton (Derbys), and Gawtree Flat, in Wales (YW). Gallant Acres, in Chigwell, and Galley Field, in Waltham Holy Cross (Ess), are other possible examples. In Gawtree Thorn, in Castleton (Derbys) (*Le Galtrethorne* 1455), there is a reference to the thorn tree which was a frequent boundary mark. *Gallows* is occasionally a shape name, and if land so called is not near a parish boundary, it may be found that it has the shape of an inverted letter *L*. References to the hangman also occur, as in Hangmans Hill, in Sandford St Martin (Oxon) and in Ely, (Cambs), and the slight variant, Hangsmans Hill, in Thorne (YW). Hangmans Field on the common boundary of Birches, Hulse and Lostock Gralam (Ches). Hangman's Stone Corner, in High Melton (YW), is at a road junction and the junction of four townships. Hangman's Mound, in Fowlmere (Cambs) is said to be where sheep-stealers were hanged.

Some of these, especially such forms as *Hangman's Close* or *Hangman's Butts*, may be perquisites of the executioner rather than sites of hanging. In Preston (Glos) there are both Gallows Quar and Hangman Stone. The tenure of Hangman's Croft, in Ravenscroft (Ches), was by service of providing an executioner to the barony of Kinderton; the actual place of execution was Gallows Field, at the end of Lodge Lane, in Kinderton. A few other *Hang-* names may be connected with execution; Hangmoor, in Egham (Sur), is near *Hangmenehill* 1607. *Hanger* names, however, are not, but are normally derived from OE *hangra* 'a wooded slope'.

The gibbet was the framework from which the bodies of notorious criminals were suspended in chains after execution, though the term was often used synonymously with *gallows*; *Gibetclif* 1388 is *Gibbettcliffe als. Gallowhill* 1625, in Bilton (YW). *The Jebbet* or *Gallowes* occurs in Chester Corporation Records in 1580, perhaps alluding to the structures rather than the fields in which they were located. In Tarvin (Ches) there is a reference to *Gibbet Heath* in 1690, but only Gallows Hill, which may of course have been a different place, in the nineteenth century. References to this feature are not so frequent as *Gallows* names. *Gibetflat* is found at an unspecified place in the East Riding of Yorkshire in 1301. Gibbet Hill occurs in Tebay (Westm) and in Weston (Herts). The latter, *Gybethul* in the reign of Richard II, has a wide view to the north-west and became the site of a telegraph apparatus in the eighteenth century. Gibbet Knoll, in Market Lavington (Wilts), is also an elevated site. Gibbiting Field, in Walgherton (Ches), seems additionally unpleasant, by referring to the action of hanging on a gibbet rather than to the object itself.

There are field-name references to ducking-stools, e.g. Cuckstool Croft, in Norton in Hales (Shrops), Cook Stool Croft, in Weaverham (Ches), Cuckstool Meadow, in Little Marton (Lancs), and Gumstool Bank, in Cirencester (Glos). Another minor, but painful, punishment was performed at the whipping post, alluded to in *Stowperstocke* 1587, in Ecclesall (YW), which has a basic sense of 'a stock or stump at which one stoops', well describing the physical situation of the victim. The whipping post, the pillory and the stocks would normally have been in the centre of the village rather than in the fields, and so field-name references are not unexpectedly meagre. Two instances occur in Oxfordshire, each alluding to a barn. One is *Peloribarne* 1492–93, 'the barn by the pillory', in Great Haseley, and the other *Pellery Barne* 1552–53, in Watlington (Oxon).

REFERENCES AND DEDICATIONS TO SAINTS

Field-names associated with religious buildings, or indicating religious ownership, have been dealt with earlier. Those relating to dedications and rituals connected with certain saints have now to be discussed. Sometimes an entirely spurious saint has been called into existence by the working of popular etymology, as in the imaginary St Foin, found in numerous references to sainfoin, discussed in another chapter. St Anns Heath, in Egham (Sur), has been so called since the late eighteenth century but was earlier *Sunderne, Sinton, Sanden* and *Sundon Heath*. St Nicholas Field, in Shoreditch (Middx), was merely *Nicholes Feld* in 1258, from an early owner's name, *Saint* having been added only in the sixteenth century. Much the same thing happened to Queen Edith's name in St Edith's Marsh, in Bromham (Wilts). The Queen's holding there is mentioned in Domesday Book, and is referred to in names like *Edithelegh* 1374. The earliest reference to *Seyntydemershe* occurs in 1569, degenerating to Titty Marsh in 1862.

Occasionally a field bearing a saint's name may adjoin, or be the property of, a church or chapel of that dedication, as in some chantry names already mentioned. Other references to saints may allude to the celebration of a patronal feast-day, or to some other connection between the locality and the saint. Gillycroft, or St Giles Croft (*Croftum Sancti Egidii* 1407, *Seint Gilicroft* 1413), in Beverley (YE), belonged to the Hospital of St Giles in Beverley. Another reference to this saint occurs in St Giles's Field, in Shrewsbury Holy Cross.

Dedications to St Giles, the patron saint of cripples, are often in churches on the outskirts of towns. Georges Close (*St George Close* 1608), in Portland (Dor), was the land 'given to the guild of St George in Weymouth' in the reign of King Henry VI. Laurence Mead, in Great Wymondley (Herts), was *Seynt Laurence Medowe* in the reign of Henry VIII. The eighteenth-century name *St Martin's Field*, in Petsoe (Bucks), received its name from the dedication of a chapel in the deserted settlement of Ekering. A visitor of the time notes 'a toft of slightly elevated ground' in the field, marking the site of the chapel, materials from which had been used in the construction of a barn nearby. A dressed stone was found there even two centuries later.[6] *St Germaines Lands* 1569, in St Albans (Herts), was near a chapel dedicated to St Germanus of Auxerre. *St Elings Close* 1693, in Thorp Arch, and St Helens Field, in Wighill (YW), are instances of the frequent dedications in this area. St Helens (*St Elens c.* 1500), in Hodnell (Warks), is the land surrounding the ruined church of this decayed parish.

St John's Hill, a piece of land in Wareham (Dor) to which pigs were brought on market day, was the site of St John's chapel and was referred to in a deed of 1629 as "peece of ground where sometime stood the Church of St John". St John is in fact referred to fairly often, many allusions being to the midsummer bonfires lighted on 24 June, the feast of St John the Baptist. St John's Ground, in Shrewsbury St Chad (Shrops), St John Ground, in Burford (Oxon), St John's Acre, in Warter (YE), and St John's Green, in Salperton (Glos), may be instances of this. The cryptic St John and Half a St John, in Stanton St John (Oxon), has the earlier forms *Syngett* or *Singett* occurring in documents between 1522 and 1687, meaning 'burnt (place)'. Similarly St Johns Field, in Walkern (Herts), was *Sangetfeld* in 1381.

The easy familiarity of John o' Jerusalem's Patch, in Bowdon (Ches), is a reference to the Knights of St John, who held property here. The earlier form of Jones Field (*St Johns Lande* 1592), in Sible Hedingham (Ess), makes a more obvious allusion to the order, whose possessions included land in this parish. St John's Farm (*Saint Johnes Ground* 16c.), in Walthamstow (Ess, now Greater London), was earlier *Temple Fee* 1523, the succession of names recording the transfer of Templar property to the Knights of St John. *St Ions Asshes* 1577 was on the site of the former St John's Church, in Chedworth (Glos). *Seynte Johns Meade* 1538, in Cirencester (Glos), was part of the property of the Hospital of St John the Evangelist.

Lady references in field-names are not entirely unambiguous, but many are allusions to dedication to the Blessed Virgin. Relevant information is lacking with regard to Lady Field, in Rivenhall (Ess), Lady Furlong (*Leuedifurlong* 1247–48), in Moreton (Berks), or Lady Lands, in Layer Breton and in Willingale Spain (Ess). There was, however, some monastic property in Bilton (Nthumb), and *Lady Lands* 1624 may in fact have reference to a dedication. *Our Ladys Lande* 1588, in Burford (Oxon), leaves no doubt of the religious context. The sequence of aliases, *Lady Lande vel St Marie Land vel Lady Meade* 1575, in Painswick (Glos), clarifies the dedication of this piece of land, which was attached to a chapel of St Mary. *Seynte Marieclose* 1392–93, in Lambourn (Berks), *Seynt Marienge* 1410, in Leeds (YW), *St Marye Parrocke* 15c., in Mapledurham (Oxon), St Marys Croft, in Earls Colne (Ess), and Semmary Hill, in Beckbury (Shrops), avoid all difficulty of interpretation by eschewing the term *Lady*.

A holding located "In the West Field opposite St Trunnion's" (*St Trunian's Tree* 1681), in Barton upon Humber (Lincs), seems to be a reference to the Holy Trinity, for which the term *Trunnion* (a form of *Trinune*) was occasionally used. There is a Trinity Field, in Elloughton (YE), and Trinity Close, in Kirmington (Lincs); Trinity Dole (*Le Trinite Acre* 1414), in Macclelsfield (Ches), was an endowment to support the chantry of the Holy Trinity.

THE PLAYGROUNDS OF RURAL ENGLAND

Recreation of many kinds required the setting aside (at least temporarily) of land suitable for the games concerned, often generating appropriate field-names. Playstow, in Barley (Herts), is a piece of land assigned, under a deed of 1638, as a playground for children. The name is likely to have originated much earlier than the seventeenth century, and the *stōw* '(sacred) place' element in names of this type suggests that the purpose of the land may have been at one time much more serious. The fact that Plaistow, in West Ham (Ess, now Greater London), developed into a settlement possibly indicates its special nature. Plaistow, in Deerhurst (Glos), was the site of the manorial and the hundred court. Characteristic forms of this name include *Playstow t.* Hy 7, in Cheltenham (Glos), Plastows (*Plaister* 1609), in Cookham (Berks), Plaisters, in Stamford Rivers (Ess) and in St Michaels (Herts), Plaster Croft, in Burland (Ches), Plaster Field, in Wallerscote (Ches), and The Plasters, in Bromfield (Shrops).

Early names occur in Wiltshire, such as *Pleistude* 1278 'play-place', in Highworth, and *Playshott* 1598 'recreation *shot*', in Knoyle. Holliday Hill, in Marston and in Westwell (Oxon), dating from the early seventeenth century, may also refer to a place of recreation. Other general references occur in Play Close, in Rousham (Oxon), and Play Ground, in Pownall Fee (Ches). *Plangeyardhurst* 1518, in Bradfield (YW), was the hill by a recreation ground, or was perhaps part of the area on which festivities of some kind were held. Revels Field is found in Bobbingworth and several other Essex parishes; Revel(s) Mead occurs in Hampton Gay, Horspath and half a dozen other places in Oxfordshire, the earliest example being *The Revell Mead* 1614, in Cornwell. After enclosure, names such as Recreation Allotment, in Southorpe & Walcot (Nthants), usually designate land expressly set aside for public games. The references in Pleasure Grounds, in Finchampstead (Berks), in Tealby (Lincs) and elsewhere, is usually to the garden, grounds or park attached to a great house.

The best-known annual activities out of doors are those remembered in such names as May Day Field, in Preston (Lancs), Maypole Piece, in Ashford Carbonell (Shrops), Maypole Meadow, in Newham (Glos), Maypole Close, in Sevenhampton (Glos), May Pole Ground, in Whitchurch (Oxon), and Maypole Yard, in Worfield (Shrops). In Yartleton (Glos), May Hill was the scene of a folk custom of adjacent parishes contending for possession of the hill on May Day. Dancers Close, in Heydon (Ess), and Greensward Dancers, in Winstone (Glos), were places for country dancing, as was Morris Ground, in Clifford Chambers (Glos), possibly land on which morris dancers performed.

A little later in the year, midsummer festivities took place to celebrate the solstice. These were possibly a remnant of pagan rites and took the form of dancing and games around a bonfire on the night of 24 June, the feast of St John the Baptist. Field-names alluding to the feast have already been mentioned. Summer Gams (*Close of pasture comonly called Summergames* 1685), in Horkstow (Lincs), designates the land on which these celebrations took place. The date for this name suggests that it was then being placed on record soon after the resumption of the celebrations, following their temporary suppression under the Commonwealth.

Violent amusements in the Middle Ages included jousting, the records of which include a 1358 reference to *Les Justynglandes*, in Ardsley (YW). Two instances of *Justing Furlong*, one in a medieval rental of Shrewsbury Abbey and the other in a 1607 Wakefield (YW) document, no doubt had a history going back as far as the Ardsley example, and Justing Lands, in Ecclesfield (YW), survived (as a name) at least into the nineteenth century. There are two Cheshire examples: *Le Ioustyngheuedlond c.* 1290, in Newton by Chester, and The Justingcroft 1785, in Chester, which was *Le Justynge Haddelond* in 1450. *Le Lyste* 1499, in Bristol, seems to refer to a tilting enclosure, as do *Le Tyltefeld(e)* 1540, in Thornbury (Glos), and Tiltingfield Clough, in Long Drax (YW). There are references to tilting at a dummy target, in *Place Called La Quinteyne* 1261, in an unspecified parish in Warwickshire, and in *The Little Quintern Field* in Chetton (Shrops). Draw Swords, in Great Bentley (Ess), may allude either to jousting or to duelling.

Archery was practised over a wider social spectrum than jousting. The most frequent reference to this activity is in the *Butts* names when these are not remnants of land in the open fields. The land used for the purpose was often glebe or town land, such as Archery Mead, in Harlow (Ess). Archery Ground, in Trimingham (Norf), was a strip of glebe, seventeen perches in extent, east of the churchyard. The Butts, in Beeston-next-Mileham (Norf), was a long strip immediately adjoining the churchyard there.

More than one medieval document refers to *Le Schoterdicheheuet-lond*, in Newton by Chester. A ditch by a headland would be a suitable place for target practice by 'shooters' or 'archers'. Robin Hood Close, in Clipstone and in Newstead (Notts), may be a casual commemorative reference to the folk hero in his home county but may also allude to his particular skill as a bowman. Robin Hoods Butts, in Cuddington (Ches), seems to state such a connection by its generic, as does the earlier *Robin Hood Buttes* 1598, describing "ten days' work of medowe", in Farlam (Cumb). *The Play Close*, in Blandford Forum (Dor), is on record as being 'for the purpose of shooting at the butts'. *Popingeyfeld t.* Hy 8, in Barking (Ess), refers to the sport or custom of shooting at the figure of a popinjay. The Turks, in Chetwynd, and Turks Leasow, in Willey (Shrops), may allude to shooting at a *Turk* 'a dummy figure used for target practice'. Jackalints, in Swanage (Dor), alludes to Jack-a-Lent, a figure set up in Lent to be pelted, doubtless an expiatory symbol like the scapegoat.

Green Wrestling Field, in Sancreed (Corn), Wrestlers, in Thaxted (Ess), Wrestling Piece, in Brackenfield (Derbys), Wrestling Grounds, in Eynsham, and Wrestling Close, in Milcombe (Oxon), are among the few names relating to this sport. A local rough-and-tumble game is alluded to in Hare Crop (*Haire Craft Leas* 1678,

Hare Pie Bank 1707), in Hallaton (Leics), where scrambling for a hare-pie takes place annually on Easter Monday.

Ball-games probably account for the largest number of such names, though the designations of the sports themselves may not always be clear to modern eyes. Hurling Field, in St Buryan (Corn), for instance, alludes to the ancient Cornish ball-game, not to the Irish sport. Great & Little Camps, found in Stondon Massey, in Theydon Bois, in Roydon and in Takeley, and (The) Camping Close, in Langham, in Belchamp St Paul, in Belchamp Otten, in Bulmer and in Steeple Bumpstead (Ess), and in the Cambridgeshire parishes of Soham, Chesterton, Girton, Histon and Thriplow, are not tented sites but land on which was played the game of 'camp(ing)-ball'. Early references occur in *The Camping Pightel* 1469, in Hawstead (Suf), *le Camping Close* 1600, in Orwell, and *le Campingplace* 1540, in Fulbourn. This was a game which evidently called for great stamina. An *Oxford Dictionary* quotation, dated 1840, refers to "a celebrated Camping, Norfolk against Suffolk, on Diss Common, with 300 [*sic*] on each side". The game, won by the Suffolk men, ended after fourteen hours, and was the form known as a 'fighting camp', in which on this occasion the boxing and other violence resulted in nine fatalities.

Football Close, in Crich, and Football Field, in Bamford, are among the rare references to this game in Derbyshire. Essex examples are Football Field, in Bradwell-juxta-Mare, and Great & Little Football Field, in Nazeing. In Gloucestershire, one example, Football Butts, in Todenham, dates from 1715, and Football Close, in Bagendon, from 1792; but there is an earlier record, in Cheltenham, where *Footeball Close* was documented in 1605. Oxfordshire examples are Lower and Upper Football, in Churchill, and Football Ground, in Hailey and in North Newington. *Footeball Close* 1608–09 occurs in Wootton. Football Close is also found in Stanford in the Vale (Berks), in Crich (Derbys), in Barlow and in Yeadon (YW), where there are also Foot Ball Field, in Scammonden, and, to compare with Football Garth, in Calverley, the earlier *Footeball-garth* 1684, in Barwick in Elmet (YW). School Garth, in Aberford (YW), was previously *The Foot-ball Garth* 1675, then *The Vicars Close* or *Football now called the School Garth* 1764.

In addition to Cricket Close, in Heage (Derbys), there are examples of Cricket Ground, in Reighton (YE) and in Hunmanby (YE), the latter also possessing both a Golf Links and a Bowling Green Lane. Another township in the East Riding (Lund), and at least one, Thorner, in the West Riding, designated a close called

Cricket Field for the game. In Hillham (YW) a reference to *terr' in loco voc' Crickitt* is dated 1620, only a few decades after the earliest dictionary citations of the term. Cricketing Field occurs in West Hoathly (Sus), where there is also a Tennis Court Field. Bowling Alley occurs in each of the Berkshire parishes of Compton, Ufton Nervet, Shellingford and East Hendred; in the last named, it dates from 1628. There is a Bowling Alley Close in Yattendon. Bowling Alley Plantation, in Wytham, was *Bowling Alley Piece* in 1726. Another instance is Bowling Alley Furlong, in South Weston (Oxon), and there are others in Cheshire, Dorset, Gloucestershire and Shropshire. Bowling Green Ley and Bowling Hey are found in Brereton cum Smethwick (Ches). *Balgrene c.* 1260, in Rothwell (YW), uses the term later employed to mean 'bowling green'. It is likely that some of these names, e.g. Bowling Alley Head, in Weston Jones (Staffs), may allude not to playing sites but merely to land suitable for the game on account of its dimensions, shape and level surface.

Caution is required in the interpretation of such names as Ball Hill, in which the element *ball* 'boundary mark' is more likely to be present here than a reference to games. A slightly different skill will have been exercised in Skittle Croft, in Clee St Margaret (Shrops), Skittles, in Radley, and Skittle Ground, in Burghfield (Berks). A related activity is recorded in Nine Pins, in West Hagbourne (Berks), and Nine Pin Ground, in King's Stanley (Glos). The possibility of the allusion in the last names being to (say) nine standing stones, or trees, is rather remote but has to be mentioned. Other games and pastimes included quoits, referred to in Quoitings, in Montford (Shrops), Quoit Field, in Toppesfield, and Quoit Ley, in Bocking (Ess). *Hurlebat* 1376–77, in Newbury (Berks), probably refers to some sport in which a club was thrown.

A measure of certainty returns with names like Cockpitts or Cockpit Meadow, found respectively in Avening and in Moreton in Marsh, to which may be added The Cockpit, in Stanway (Glos). Cockpit is found also in Charlbury (Oxon), and Cockpitt in Northenden (Ches). Other examples in Cheshire are Cockpit Garden (Comberbach), Cockpit Field (Witton cum Twambrook), Cockpit Meadow (Crewe) and Cockpit Croft (Malpas). Cockpit Close occurs in Barnsley (where references to *Cockpitt Close* and *The Cockpitt House* occur in 1661) and in Oulton (YW). Burghfield (Berks) has a Cockpit Pasture. These fields were the scenes of cock fights, as is made particularly clear in one name. An explicit reference to the fight itself occurs in Cock Fight Field, in Acton Grange (Ches).

According to local informants, Cock Nook, in Burton Pidsea (YE), was once 'a cock-fighting field'. However, The Cockpit, in Barton (Westm), is a stone circle, and some names may refer to a similarity to cock-fighting locations rather than being a positive record of a scene of this activity. *Cocking*, meaning 'cock-fighting', is found in Cocking Close, in Armley (YW).

Few field-name references to bear-baiting seem to have survived. Three of these are in Shropshire: Bear Stake, in Edgmond, Bear Leys, in Meole Brace, and Bear Yard, in Acton Scott. In Witton (Ches) occur both Bear Park and Cock Pit Field. Some allusions may be found to bull-baiting, which lingered until the end of the eighteenth century. Bull Pit, in Peak Forest (Derbys), Bullpits, in Wimborne Minster (Dor), Bull Baiting Plot, in Wookey (Som), Bull Baiters, in Great Leighs (Ess), and Bull Ring, in Braithwell (YW), may have been fields in which bull-baiting took place. Bull Stake, in Hattersley (Ches), possibly refers to the post to which the bull was tethered, or it may have been the place where the cows were served.

Horse-racing is, not surprisingly, alluded to in the names of fields where it took place. In Oxfordshire there are The Race Course, in Curbridge, Racepost Piece, in East Hendred, and Race Ground Common, in Bicester. (The) Race Course is also found in Harleston (Nthants) and in Uppingham (Rut). In Shropshire there are two instances of Race Ground, in Morville and in Shrewsbury St Chad, as well as Race Field, in Richard's Castle, and Races Croft, in Ellesmere. In other counties there are Racing Field, in Folkton (YE), and Horse Race Piece, in Ivinghoe (Bucks). Race Course Hill, in Bingley, and Horse Race End, in Warmfield (YW), have been discussed by Mrs Atkin.[7]

Heskayth 1272, in Caldbeck (Cumb), Heskey Meadow, in Mobberley (Ches), and Hesketh (*Heskett c.* 1530), in Bracewell (YW), allude to a horse race-track, being derived from Old Norse *hesta-skeithi*, ultimately from *hestr* 'a horse' and *skeithi* 'a course, a track'. *Heskith Acres* 1666, in Bollington, and Hesketh Meadow, in Werneth (Ches), may have the same origin, but the first word may be the local surname. Even the equipment of a modern course is alluded to, e.g. in Grandstand, in Bridgnorth St Leonard (Shrops). *Hestlangs*, a thirteenth-century name in Kingerby (Lincs), may also allude to a race-course. The name is probably derived from Old Norse *hestr* and Old English *lang* 'a length of ground'. The Viking sport of horse-fighting (OE *fola-gefeoht*) is remembered in Foal Foot Close, in Eaton and Alsop (Derbys), as well as in Follifoot Carr & Ings, in

Wighill (YW). The fight was between two horses, urged on by men armed with goads.

Gost-End, in Hougham (Kent), is more likely to allude to gorse (OE *gorst*) than to a ghost. However, haunted places of various kinds are referred to in field-names, e.g. Fantom Hagg, in Matlock (Derbys), a 'clearing haunted by a phantom'. In Settle (YW), Skirsgill (*Skirskell* 1580) contains the Old Norse elements *skyrsi* 'a spectre' and *kelda* 'a spring'. Possibly less frightening features account for such names as Fairy Field, in Oakworth (YW), in Marton (Ches) and in Whitchurch (Shrops), Fairy Brow, in Bollington, Fairy Yard, in Sale (Ches), Fairy Croft, in Halstead Rural (Ess), Fairyland, in West Felton (Shrops), Powk Field, in Ditton Priors (Som), and Puckpit Meadow, in Aston Somerville (Glos). Goblins and elves are referred to in Hobs Croft (*Hobfield* 1598), in Bradwell (Ches), Goblin Meadow, in Shifnal (Shrops), Hobgoblins, in Great Beddow (Ess), The Hobgoblin, in Laughton (Leics), Elf Lands (*Elflandes* 13c.), in Eakring (Notts), and Boggard Close, in Netherthong (YW). Hob Croft appears six times in the Tithe Apportionment for Mobberley (Ches), and there is a tradition of a hobgoblin in the neighbourhood.

Beaugrove, in Radley (Berks), was earlier *Le Buggrove* 1547 'a grove haunted by a goblin'. Like the numerous *Cuckoo Pen* names, this might be a persistent memory of a pagan sacred grove, or a cautionary label applied to a place of danger. Marshy areas often produce uncanny lights, alluded to in Megaloffin Close, in Spondon (Derbys), from *Meg o' th' Lanthorn*, a dialect name for the phenomenon usually referred to as Will o' the Wisp.

Quindal Hole (*Congeoneshole* 1287), in Stebbing, Konjohns Hole (*Canyoneshole* 1401), in High Easter, Congons Grove, in Pleshey (Ess), Congon Park, in Gargrave (YW), and Congin Pits, in Linton (Derbys), allude to haunting by 'a dwarf, a changeling' (ME *kangun*). Some names referring to the devil have already been discussed. Apart from designating land of such poor quality that it was regarded as Satan's work, such names may also have referred to places of real or imagined physical danger. Devil's Den, in Thatcham (Berks), in Lingfield (Sur) and in Stanton upon Hine Heath (Shrops), is possibly one of this kind. The same name in Preshute (Wilts) alludes to an ancient burial chamber there. Devil's Pulpit, in Tidenham, is a deep declivity below Offa's Dyke and The Devil's Chapel, in Newland (Glos), refers to old (Roman) ironworkings in the Forest of Dean. Stories of the devil making his devotions in such inaccessible spots no doubt served as a warning of the dangerous nature of the places.

Names containing *Goodman* may also allude to the devil, as Bruce Dickins suggested for Good Mans Hey, in Northern Etchells (Ches); alternatively these may be merely conventional references to the landowner.

NOTES AND REFERENCES

1. Based on a private communication from Mr Roger Hadfield.
2. J. Evelyn, *Diary* (Everyman edn), ii., 280–1.
3. J. Aubrey, *The Natural History and Antiquities of the County of Surrey* (1718–19), ii, pp. 33–4.
4. J. Godber, *History of Bedfordshire* (1969), p. 345.
5. K.I. Sandred, *English Place-names in -stede* (Uppsala, 1963), p. 182.
6. A.C. Chibnall, *Beyond Sherington* (Chichester, 1979), p. 129.
7. M. Atkin, 'Viking race-courses? The distribution of *skeith* place-names in northern England'. *Journal of the EPNS* **10** (1977–78), pp. 26–39.

CHAPTER ELEVEN
Work in progress and prospect

FIELD-NAMES AND THE LOCAL RESEARCHER

Field-names, by their very numbers, offer great scope for further investigations, even when what appear to be definitive surveys have been published. Completeness can never be claimed for even the most extensive study, and persons living in the area concerned, with their special knowledge of local topography, flora and fauna, crafts, and so on, can often make important additions to the lists or amendments to the explanations. The study of the names in the course of a historical enquiry can be rewarding. New facts and connections may be revealed by the names, which will be all the better understood when they are seen to involve the daily lives of the human subjects of the documentation being reviewed.

References have been made earlier to field-name surveys under-taken by individual workers. Pioneers have been mentioned in Chapter One, including Waller and Wainwright, from whose works a number of examples have been used in this book. Contemporary writers, e.g. Charles Keene and R.W. Standing, have revealed much of what can be learned from the field-names of built-up or highly developed localities, respectively west London and the Sussex coast. Others have been prepared to collect names of areas considerably larger than single parishes. P.A.S. Pool has surveyed West Penwith in Cornwall (but is able to speak with authority on names well beyond the limits of his published study), and George Foxall made a lifetime study and record of the field-names of the entire county of Shropshire. Barbara Kerr brought to her studies of Dorset field-names a considerable knowledge of the agrarian and social history of her county as well as personal scientific experience of agriculture.[1]

250

This research is not necessarily a solitary activity. Groups of many kinds, both formal (e.g. WEA and university extension classes) and informal, have produced important results. Some groups, e.g. in Herefordshire, Shropshire, Norfolk and Suffolk, have aimed at the direct study and publication of the names they have collected.[2] Others, including many small local history societies, have assembled their lists of names as part of a more general survey of their locality.

A joint compilation was made in 1943, when members of the Rutland Home Guard, under the direction of their Intelligence Officer, R. Sterndale-Bennett, marked the field-names of their county on sheets of the 2½-inch Ordnance Survey map.[3] About twenty years later, Women's Institutes all over the country collected and recorded the field-names of their respective villages. The lists (many of which are now deposited in county record offices) were based on personal knowledge or the oral evidence of fellow villagers. Some were annotated in various ways; many include the names formerly used, at least within living memory, or refer back to the names entered in Tithe Apportionments. In many places, similar lists and field-maps were made in 1986, as part of the Domesday Book celebrations.

For those beginning such a project in their own locality, the guidance of an experienced tutor may be necessary in the finding of likely sources and to help unravel difficulties in extracting field-names from them. Most collecting will start from current or nine-teenth-century names, the Tithe Apportionment and Map usually forming a sound basis of research. Other principal sources have been mentioned in Chapter One. The title and date of the document, together with its location and reference number and the date of transcription, should be noted. Whether transcribed from printed texts (such as sales catalogues) or manuscript documents, the spellings should be copied as in the source, including apparent mistakes and inconsistencies, as well as the unconventional use or omission of initial capitals. The handwriting in recent manuscripts is often very carefully formed and easy to read, but the same name may be written in three or four different ways in a single document, or there may seem to be confusions of various kinds. It is not prudent to make decisions about 'right' or 'wrong' forms at the time of transcription, leading to selective copying. A clerk listing the names and other details of a Tithe Apportionment can be seen to have been capable of writing 'House Close' instead of 'Horse Close' (just as a twentieth-century local historian is), but the 'wrong' form should be collected, and what appear at the time to be unusual variants should be marked with the useful qualification '*sic*'. Lists obtained from printed works may well be subject to copyright, and clearance should be sought before publishing complete or partial transcripts from such sources.

Earlier documents present problems of decipherment, expansion of abbreviations, and occasionally translation from Latin. The practical sides of these matters are dealt with in specialist works, but a word or two may be appropriate here. Published calendars, and often the cards in record-office catalogues, summarize the contents of documents, usually noting the inclusion of field-names. A careful reading of a few documents in each class studied will acquaint the investigator with their general structure, the regular use of particular phrases, and the position within the document of references to field-names and essential descriptive material, such as the tenure and location of property, areas and land use.

The collecting of older names should proceed independently of the lists of modern forms already made. To search one set of documents in order to record only names corresponding to earlier or more recent forms obtained from other sources is wasteful of time and energy. Cross-references must come later, when collections (as nearly complete as possible) have been assembled from all available sources. Correspondences and possible identifications should then be noted, and other steps can be taken to establish the locations of the named fields, furlongs and closes.

Putting the names into geographical and historical context goes some way towards discovering their significance. The importance of plotting the field-names on a map must not be overlooked.[4] The relationship between similarly named fields becomes apparent when this is done, and the interpretation of ambiguous components in the names will sometimes be considerably aided by reference to the lie of the land. If there is an early charter with boundary clauses, the named points should be identified and marked on the map. A perambulation of the boundaries (preferably in fine weather) is both an instructive practical exercise and possibly an enjoyable outdoor entertainment for a local society. The value of field-names to archaeologists was described in Chapter Nine, as well as their use as clues to mineral extraction and industrial activities. Other examples have been seen of the ways in which field-names can be utilized in tracing the boundaries of medieval parks and the sites of deserted villages.

Dates of origin and of documentation are relevant to the interpretation of field-names. Nobody would seriously regard Top Twenty, in Shawell (Leics), as a reference to 'charts' of recorded popular music, but similar misjudgements are easily made in dealing with terms whose sense or spelling may have been altered in the passage of time. Willows Gate, in Great Bowden (Leics), is shown to have nothing to do with trees by its 1475 spelling, *Wilardesgate*, which indicates a derivation from a personal name, Wilheard. Examples in previous chapters have indicated how locations beside streams, or near to boundaries, readily confirmed on a map, are reflected in certain classes of names. Consultation of appropriate volumes of the *Victoria County History*, supplemented by earlier county histories and accounts of the locality, will place the study on a sound footing and provide much incidental information contributing to an understanding of the names. Elucidation can come both by analysing related lists of collected names and by being able to watch the emergence of later names against the legal and agricultural background of their use when Enclosure Awards or Tithe Apportionments were compiled.

Other local records will often provide important supplementary information, and parish registers, hearth tax, census, and similar returns need to be referred to in the identification of personal names, which also change in form across the centuries. *Maynerdesholm c.* 1300, in Great Bowden (Leics), became *Maynersholm* in the sixteenth century and *Mannersholme* by 1638, and alludes to the family of the fourteenth-century Hugh de Meyners. Local historians will enjoy an encounter with modern names like Leechy's Close, Sherrard's Meadow or White's Yard, and should find references to families mentioned in recent field-names just as valuable as those in names originating many centuries ago. In Chapter Eight the frequency of surnames as an element in field-names has been noted, indicating the place of the latter in family-name research and local social history.

Oral collection of field-names is a feasible option. A tape-recorder in conjunction with a notebook and a large-scale map will enable a collector to produce, from local information, an account of the current nomenclature of the area. Tapes should be preserved so that the transcripts can be checked by others. The collector may quite unwittingly 'correct' a spoken name in writing it down, only to be persuaded of his own fallibility when other evidence is forthcoming. Anecdotal descriptions of the genesis of particular names may also be given; these should be recorded for future reference and critical examination, and not immediately dismissed. Local traditions of events and family histories may sometimes be confused but are not necessarily entirely mistaken.

The results of these investigations should be published, in local journals or as separate booklets, not merely to avoid wasteful duplication of research by other workers, but mainly as an appropriate contribution to the written history of the locality. Many projects await publication, but this fact should not deter newcomers from beginning their research. There are now relatively easily operated means of producing well-presented reports or less formal accounts without putting them into the hands of professional publishers. The numbers of papers printed and published at home have been growing in recent years and will almost certainly increase still further in the future. The printed account may be embellished by a map showing the former layout of the fields. In a larger format such a map can make an impressive display at a society's annual exhibition, or a worthy permanent decoration for the village hall, and will generate a more fruitful discussion than any alphabetical list of names. In urban areas, the alignment of thoroughfares can be explained by the pattern of earlier field-boundaries,[5] perhaps confirmed by the street-names.

FIELD-NAMES AND STREET-NAMES

When an area is built over, some field-names are preserved by being transferred to streets. This occasionally gives rise to various problems. The position of thoroughfares may not correspond precisely to the location of the former fields bearing their names. Names resembling field-names are sometimes devised by developers to impart a spurious rural atmosphere to the new streets in order to attract residents to the area. Without necessarily commenting on the motivation, it is possible to have doubts about the regularity of the arrangement of such names in Colindale (London) as North Acre, Five Acre, Hundred Acre, Corner Mead and Long Mead.

East Acridge and West Acridge, in Barton upon Humber (Lincs), were originally "slipps of Common Ground", each of which doubtless offered a suitable shape for development into a street. The Conery, a footway in Leicester, perpetuates a frequent field-name. Long Acre, near Covent Garden in London, is an obvious (and genuine) transfer from field to street; it was *Pasture Called Longeacre* in 1547. Shortlands, in Hammersmith, has adopted the field-name *Shortelond*, dating from the reign of Henry V, and the commemorative *Bunkers Hill* is a street-name in Belvedere and other places. Littleworth, in Mansfield (Notts), perpetuates the derogatory name of *Littleworth Close*. When Welwyn Garden City (Herts) was brought into existence soon after the Great War, many of the street-names were transferred from the fields on which the thoroughfares were built, e.g. Shortlands, Knightsfield and Shepherd's Pightle. In the same county, Hemel Hempstead, developed as a new town thirty years later, also contained street-names, e.g. Great Close, Longlands and Malm Close, taken over from the fields, though not necessarily keeping to their precise location. Also in Hertfordshire, in Hatfield, "a triangle of built-up land north of a road called The Common is crossed by paths, called the Rights of Way, one of which still follows the curves of the open field strips".[6] The traditional terms for paths across the fields are also preserved in the streets into which they have grown, e.g. Occupation Road and Green Lane Road, in Leicester, many Green Lanes and several Warple (or Worple) Ways, Occupation Lanes and Occupation Roads, in Greater London, Occupation Lane, in Orston (Notts), and Occupation Street, in Peterborough (Nthants, now Cambs). The Baulk, in Wandsworth, is the only reference in Greater London to that feature of the open fields.

Other street-names are formed by the addition of *Avenue*, *Lane*, *Road* or *Street* to the field-name. Mention must also be made of the ambiguous *Close*, which means 'a cul-de-sac' when used in a street-name. Some of these roads may be located beside the named fields rather than built over them, but the fact of the transfer remains. The term *Lammas*, found in such field-names as Lammas Lands, in Melksham (Wilts), appears in Lammas Lane, in Esher (Sur), and Lammas Avenue, in Mitcham (Sur, now Greater London). Court-field Gardens, in Earl's Court (London), utilizes the name of a piece of land still in cultivation in the nineteenth century. Other examples are Linkfield Road (*Le Lynkefeld* 1431), in Isleworth (Middx), Cowleaze Road (*Pasture called Cowe Lease* 1574), in Kingston (Sur), Highfield Road (*Heghefeld c.* 1250), Houndsfield Road (*Houndesfeld* 1608) and Oakfield Road (*Okefeilde* 1608), in Edmonton (Middx), Bancroft Lane (*Bancroft* 1315), in Mansfield (Notts), Mudmead Lane (*Mudmede Furlong* 1491), in Steeple Ashton (Wilts), Horse-croft Road and Maylands Avenue (*Maylands* 1637), in Hemel Hempstead, Deadfield Lane (*Le Dedefeld* 1358), in Hertingfordbury, and Beanfield Road, in Sawbridgeworth (Herts), which preserves the alternative name of Bell Mead, mentioned in Chapter Nine.

Hungerdown, in Chingford, is the frequent Essex variant of *Hunger Hill*. Hungerhill Road and Peas Hill Road, in Sneinton (Notts), perpetuate the names *Hongerhill* and *Pesehill c.* 1300, respectively. In Wyke Regis (Dor), Broadmeadow Road is from *Brademede* 1322, Park Mead Road from *Parcmede* 1329, and Ryland's Lane from *Rilond* 1322. Conniger Lane, in Wareham (Dor), takes its name from *Cuniger Close c.* 1628, and street-names of similar origin are found elsewhere, e.g. Coniger Road, in Fulham (London), Conygre Lane, in Adlestrop, Conygre Road (*The Cuniger* 1678), in Filton (Glos), and Conery Lane, in Enderby (Leics).

The study of street-names is more limited than field-name research, but an extension of the enquiry back through the field-names will have the additional benefit of demonstrating the amicable continuity of rural and urban. This continuity is sympathetically detected by Gillian Tindall in her book *The Fields Beneath*, an account of the streets of Kentish Town (London), based on her conviction that "the town is simply disguised countryside".[7] The loss of green fields may be regrettable, but when it is recalled that the cultivated soil of many fields covers the carbonized remains of past settlements, the change may be viewed from a different perspective. For those with eyes to see, the tarmacadam, masonry, bricks and mortar constitute merely the temporary top layer of what Hoskins has called the 'cultural humus' that covers the historical landscape of England.

LOSS AND GAIN

However, it is not intended to argue that becoming a street is the highest perfection attainable by a humble arable close, or that a parish common is necessarily better for becoming a municipal park. There is a good case for naming new streets after the fields they are built on, but no real historical connection can be claimed unless there is identity of site.

Paradoxically, while some field-names are thus being kept in existence in urban areas, others are being irrevocably lost in the countryside consequent upon the removal of hedges and the conversion of numerous smaller closes into single enormous arable units, often identified by number rather than by name. Such changes are not entirely novel. In earlier centuries, thousands of acres of arable were lost by the creation of medieval deer-parks, Tudor sheep-ranges, or the great *Grounds* and *Pastures* in the Midlands, but these, it should be added, did not necessarily add the destruction of wild-life habitat to the extinction of furlong-names.

To find field-names interesting in themselves is a taste that may come from frequent transcription sessions in record offices followed by a systematic consideration of the names in their geographical, agricultural and historical contexts. Careful study will show that the apparently commonplace names are often not what they seem. There will be indications of ownership, land use, agricultural techniques, internal boundaries and building sites, with a valuable extension of the historical range when earlier forms can be found and compared, and further insights when locations can be traced, on maps if not actually on the ground. References, by name or profession, to the owners or occupiers of the land are likely to provide important information about the forerunners of the current population. The creation of the names, whether casual or deliberate, bears witness to intelligence, observation, imagination, wit, frustration and even anger. In some places, there will be a monotonous repetition of certain types of name; other lists will be enlivened by what has rather patronizingly been described as "rustic humour".[8] The names reflect and are affected by human actions, but only occasionally influence further activity. Hollis's extensive renaming in Halstock and Corscombe might, however, be regarded as subliminal republican propaganda.

Relevance to environmental issues such as are involved in building developments or motorway construction, or a change of agricultural land to recreational use, will often, if only briefly, bring the names to public attention. A full and accurate record, and an account of the significance of the field-names, will be of the greatest benefit to every local historian and not without use to those wishing to understand their environment or (for whatever reason) to preserve an existing landscape. Above all, such a record of the names will provide an intelligible link between the modern population and their known or unknown predecessors.

NOTES AND REFERENCES

1. C.H. Keene, *Field-Names of the London Borough of Ealing* (Nottingham, EPNS, 1976); R.W. Standing, *Field-Names of Angmering, Ferring, Rustington, East Preston, and Kingston* (West Sussex) (Nottingham, EPNS, 1984); P.A.S. Pool, *Field-Names of West Penwith* (Hayle, priv. pub., 1990); H.G. Foxall, *Shropshire Field-Names* (Shrewsbury, Shropshire Arch. Soc., 1980); B. Kerr,

'Dorset field-names and the agricultural revolution', *Proc. Dorset Nat. Hist. & Arch. Soc.* **82** (1960), pp. 133–42; 'Dorset fields and their names', *ibid.* **89** (1967), pp. 233–56.

2. Herefordshire field-names have been published by the Archaeological Research Section of the Woolhope Naturalists' Field Club. Shropshire names (to be published in the EPNS county volumes) were collected by a group, led by Dr M. Gelling, originally under the auspices of the University of Birmingham Extra-Mural Department. The Norfolk Archaeological & Historical Research Group collects the field-names of that county (also for publication by the EPNS). In Suffolk, the Upper Deben Valley Place-Name Survey has now been completed. Among others, an informal Nottingham group has a survey awaiting publication.

3. The project is summarized in an article, 'Rutland field-names: interesting results of an interesting inquiry', by Sterndale-Bennett in *The Stamford Mercury*, 27 June 1943. The master copy of the map is now in Leicestershire County Record Office.

4. An example to be imitated is the procedure followed by A.C. Chibnall and modestly described in the Introduction to his *Sherington: Fields and Fiefs of a Buckinghamshire Village* (Cambridge University Press 1965), pp. xxi–xxii.

5. Some examples are given in C.C. Taylor, *Fields in the English Landscape* (Dent, 1975), pp. 160–1 and Plate XII, which illustrates a housing estate in Swaffham Bulbeck (Cambs), "fitted into a field formed . . . in 1801". Gillian Bebbington observes that the "jealously guarded boundaries of [former monastic] properties have left ineradicable traces in the shape of London's streets" (*Street-names of London* (Batsford, 1972), p. 3). She notes later the "countless examples of non-communication between minor streets, caused by long forgotten field boundaries that the builders could not cross" (p. 4). This can be readily confirmed from the maps annexed to her work, on which the estate boundaries are marked.

6. L.M. Mumby, *The Hertfordshire Landscape* (Hodder & Stoughton, 1977), p. 29. The information on Welwyn Garden City was kindly provided by Mr Maurice de Soissons in a private communication.

7. G. Tindall, *The Fields Beneath* (Maurice Smith Temple, 1977; repr. Paladin Books, 1980), p. 13.

8. "Many of the names are commonplace and uninteresting, relieved from sheer monotony only by sporadic examples of rustic humour" (P.H. Reaney, *The Origin of English Place-Names*,

Routledge & Kegan Paul, 1960, p. 207). Note, however, an earlier remark by Wainwright: "Apparently humorous names sometimes turn out to be sober descriptions in dialect or corruptions of earlier forms" ('Field-names of Amounderness Hundred', p. 184).

Appendix

LARGE ACREAGE NAMES IRONICALLY APPLIED TO VERY SMALL FIELDS

Any list of field-names of a particular type is bound to be incomplete, but the following notes are offered by way of evidence that the name *Hundred Acres* is usually an ironic one, and not a reference to an ancient Hundred, or a corruption of some other term. *Thousand Acre(s)* names are added by way of reinforcement. Earlier forms, if any, are in parentheses after the current names. Areas are given, wherever known, in acres, roods and perches, and it will be seen that most examples do not exceed one acre. Unless otherwise noted, the name used is *(The) Hundred Acres* or, in the second section *(The, One) Thousand Acres*.

HUNDRED ACRES

Berkshire: Bray, Wargrave.

Cambridgeshire: Comberton (1r 36p), Steeple Morden (*le Hundaker* 13c.) (1r 3p). In other Cambridgeshire examples of the name, such as The Hundreds, in Littleport (*croft voc' hundreth ac'* 1549), Hundred Acre Drove, in Swaffham Bulbeck, and Hundred Acres, in Soham, there appears to be no evidence of irony.

Dorset: Bere Hackett ('a very small field'), Bishop's Caundle (36p), Cann, Castleton (1r 13p), Cheselbourne ('an ironical name for a tiny field'), More Crichel, Hamworthy (One

260

Hundred Acres 'a small field'), Kinson (now Hants; described as 'a small field'), Milton Abbas (*Hundred Acres Field* 1659), Stalbridge (a very small field'), Hampreston ('a small field'), Stoke Wake ('a small field of about one acre'), Upwey ('ironically applied to a very small field'). On the other hand, 100 Acres, in Lytchett Minster, is said to be 'a medium-sized field', Lower and Upper Hundred Acres, in Winterborne Tomson, are described as 'two quite large fields', and for Winterborne Came is the note 'these fields are neither very small nor very large'.

Essex: Upwards of thirty examples have been found; in at least one parish there are two instances of the name. Hundred Acre Field, in Boxtead, is anomalous, in having an area of just over six acres. There are two instances of Hundred Acre Piece – in Shenfield (1a 1r) and in Little Maplestead (1a 1r 32p). Examples of Little Hundred Acres occur in Stanstead Mountfitchet (2r 22p) and in Wimbish-cum-Thunderley (2r 10p).

Hampshire: Basing (27p), Binstead & Neatham (3r 7p), Weyhill (2r 23p), Worldham (39p).

Hertfordshire: Ashwell (One Hundred Acres, 1r 2p); Aston ('a very small field'), Flamstead (1a 38p), St Peter's (3r 3p).

Lancashire: Hardhorn with Newton (2r).

Lincolnshire: Cadney (2r 23p).

Middlesex: Hendon (16p).

Norfolk: Shropham (*Hundred Acres Close* 1714, 2r 10p).*

Nottinghamshire: Carlton in Lindrick (Hundred Acre Wood).

Oxfordshire: Cowley, Forest Hill with Shotover.

Rutland: Leighfield Forest (2a 1r 14p) (OS No. 47).

Wiltshire: All Cannings (2r 1p), Boulshot (3r 38p), Broad Town (1r 33p), Coulston (3r), Fittleton (28p), Heddington (20p), Hilmarton (2r 11p), Idmiston (31p), Seend (2r 14p), Sopworth (1a 2r 0p), Stert and Urchfont ('very small'), Whiteparish.

THOUSAND ACRES

Cornwall: Sennen (21p), St Agnes.

Dorset: Corfe Mullen, Hampreston (Cowleaze Thousand Acres, 'a small field'), Whitchurch Canonicorum.

---

* Gray, Map on p. 312.

Essex: Forty or more examples. In Barking there are two instances of the name (2r and 35p), as also in Sandon (1a 1r 20p and 2r 20p); there are three instances in Tolleshunt D'Arcy (1a 2r 34p, 1a 0r 32p and 2r 3p). The smallest examples seem to be in Belchamp Otten (17p) and Inworth (30p), and the largest in Messing (3a).

Hampshire: Ringwood.

Hertfordshire: Rickmansworth.

Middlesex: Ickenham.

Surrey: Horley (1r 4p).

General Index

This index lists selected topics and the names of persons and of places mentioned in the text (other than those in which field-names are located) not readily found by means of the Index of Field-Names.

Index of Field-Names

Some headwords cover related names bearing different generics or with only slight spelling differences (sometimes indicated by '&c.'). Numerical acreage names and early forms of modern names have not normally been included. *Close, Field, Furlong, Ground, Land, Leasow, Mead(ow), Park, Piece, Plantation, Wood* and *Yard* are abbreviated to *Cl, Fd, Flg, Grd, Ld, Lsw, Md(w), Pk, Pce, Plantn, Wd* and *Yd*, respectively.

Index

Index

Index

Index